GREEN LANTERN CORPS

REVOLT OF THE ALPHA-LANTERNS

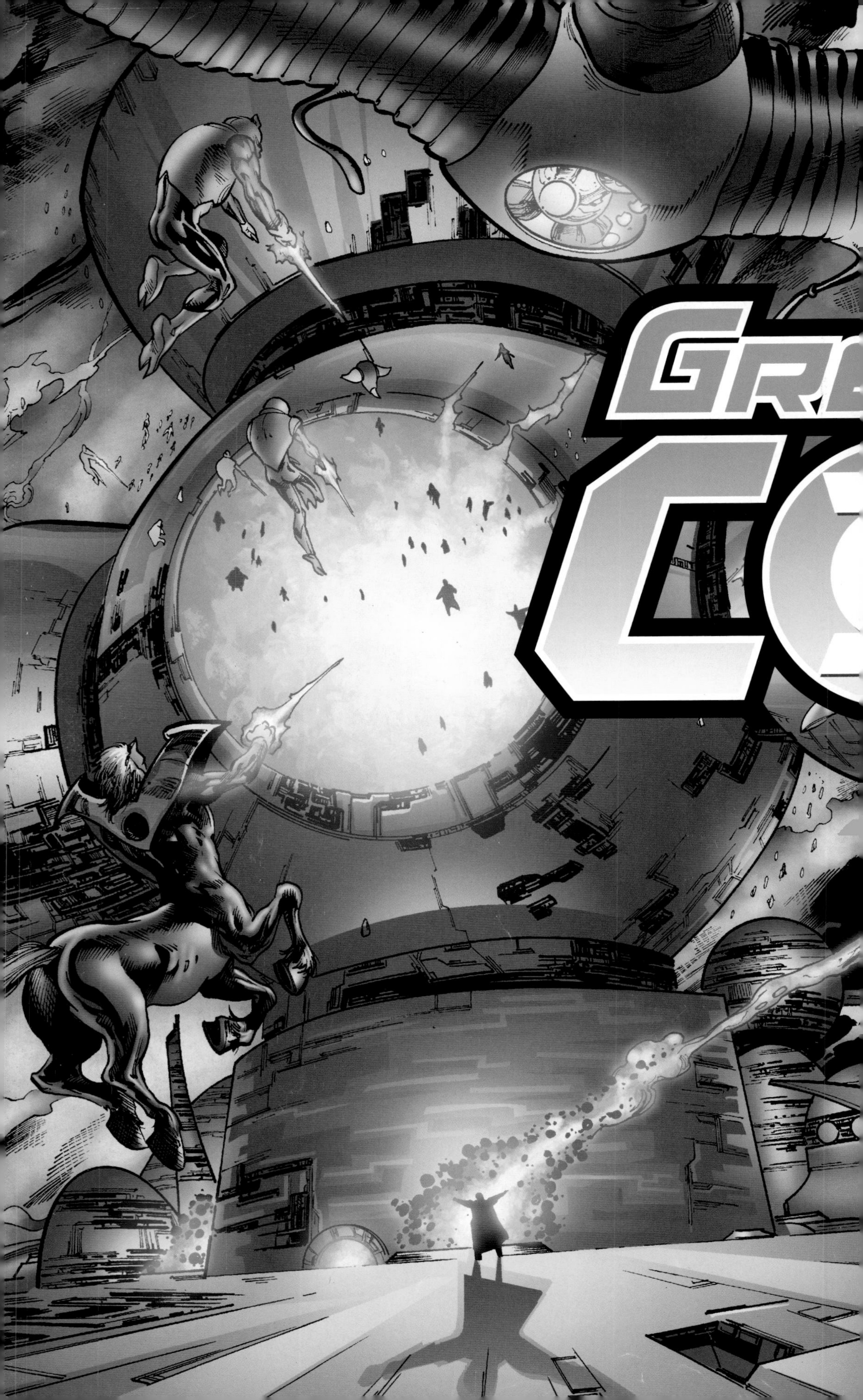

EN LANTERN
ORPS

REVOLT OF THE ALPHA-LANTERNS

TONY BEDARD Writer   **ARDIAN SYAF** Penciller   **VICENTE CIFUENTES** Inker

RANDY MAYOR WITH **GABE ELTAEB & CARRIE STRACHAN** Colorists

THE CURSE OF THE ALPHA-LANTERN

STERLING GATES Writer   **NELSON** Artist

DEREK FRIDOLFS AND **ROB HUNTER** Additional Inks   **GUY MAJOR** Colorist

STEVE WANDS Letterer

ARDIAN SYAF, VICENTE CIFUENTES & ULISES ARREOLA Collection cover artists

Eddie Berganza Adam Schlagman Editors-original series
Bob Harras Group Editor-Collected Editions
Robbin Brosterman Design Director-Books

DC COMICS
Diane Nelson President
Dan DiDio and **Jim Lee** Co-Publishers
Geoff Johns Chief Creative Officer
Patrick Caldon EVP-Finance and Administration
John Rood EVP-Sales, Marketing and Business Development
Amy Genkins SVP-Business and Legal Affairs
Steve Rotterdam SVP-Sales and Marketing
John Cunningham VP-Marketing
Terri Cunningham VP-Managing Editor
Alison Gill VP-Manufacturing
David Hyde VP-Publicity
Sue Pohja VP-Book Trade Sales
Alysse Soll VP-Advertising and Custom Publishing
Bob Wayne VP-Sales
Mark Chiarello Art Director

Library of Congress Cataloging-in-Publication Data

Bedard, Tony.
  Green Lantern Corps : revolt of the alpha-lanterns / writer, Tony
Bedard ; pencils, Ardian Syaf.
      p. cm.
  "Originally published in single magazine form in Green Lantern Corps
#21, 22, 48-52."
  ISBN 978-1-4012-3139-2 (hardcover)
  1. Graphic novels. I. Syaf, Ardian. II. Title. III. Title: Revolt of
the alpha-lanterns.
  PN6728.G742B43 2011
  741.5'973--dc22
                                          2011008932

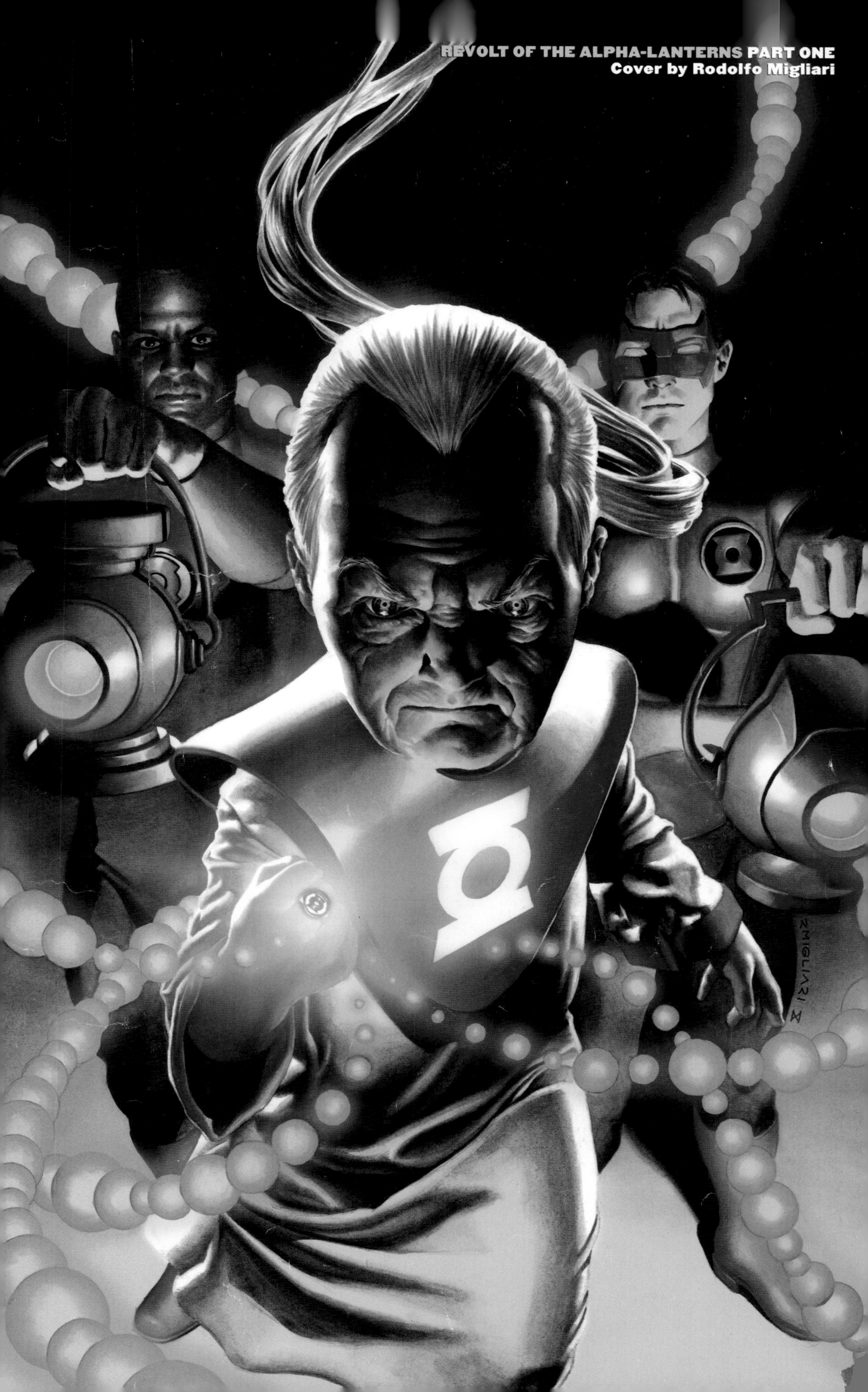

REVOLT OF THE ALPHA-LANTERNS PART ONE
Cover by Rodolfo Migliari

Variant by Patrick Gleason, Mark Irwin & Randy Mayor

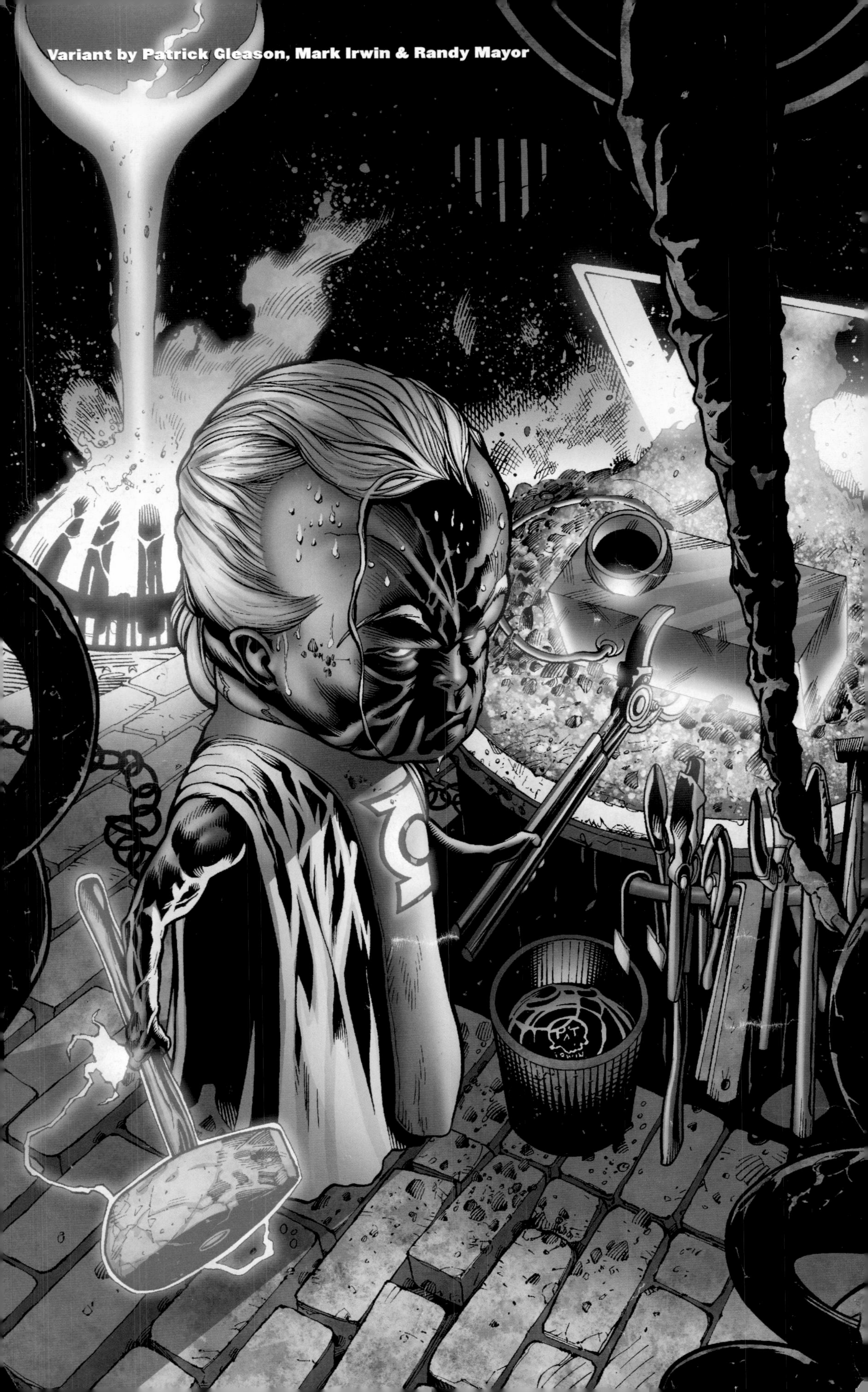

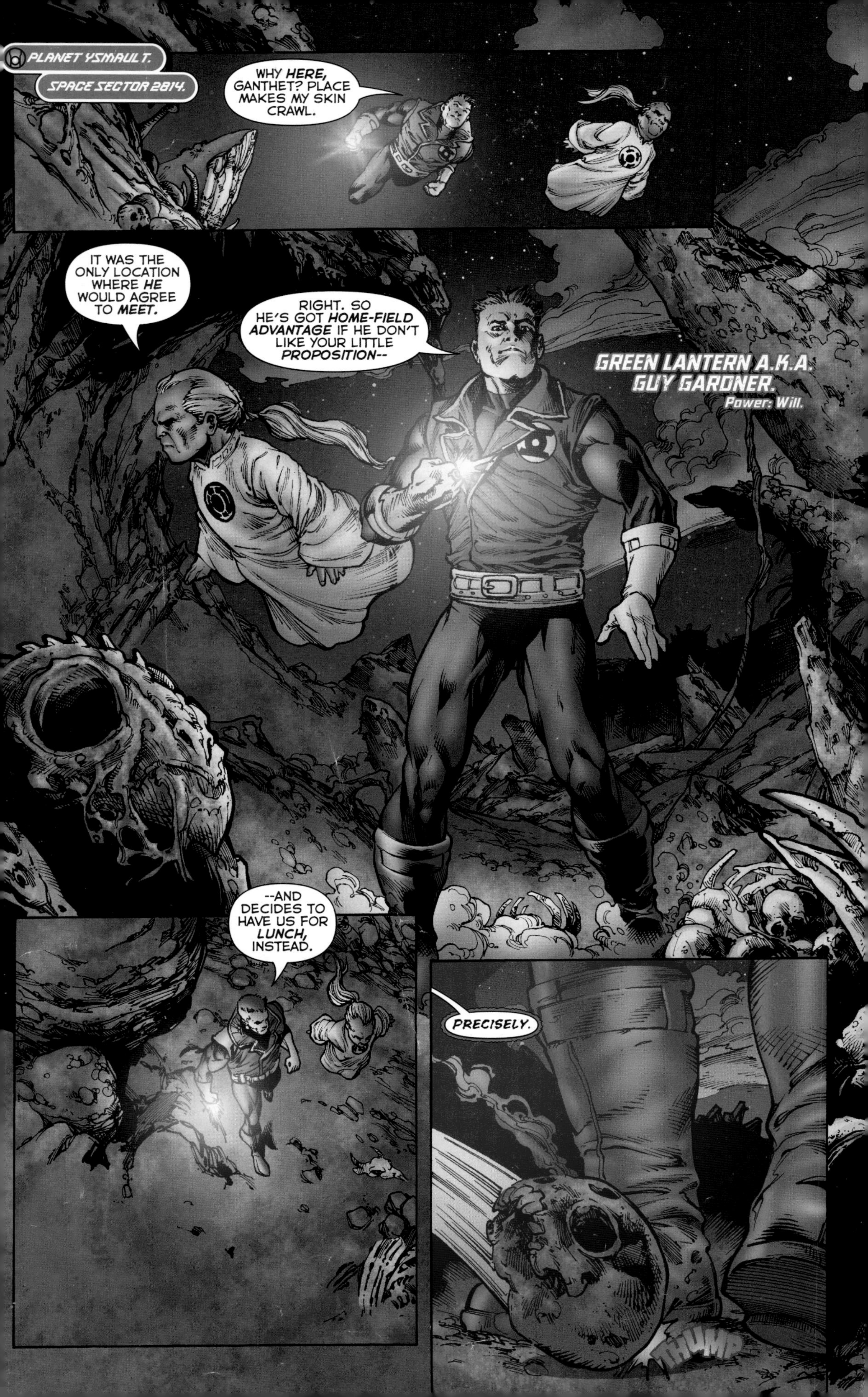
PLANET YSMAULT.
SPACE SECTOR 2814.
WHY HERE, GANTHET? PLACE MAKES MY SKIN CRAWL.
IT WAS THE ONLY LOCATION WHERE HE WOULD AGREE TO MEET.
RIGHT. SO HE'S GOT HOME-FIELD ADVANTAGE IF HE DON'T LIKE YOUR LITTLE PROPOSITION--
GREEN LANTERN A.K.A. GUY GARDNER.
Power: Will.
--AND DECIDES TO HAVE US FOR LUNCH, INSTEAD.
PRECISELY.
THUMP

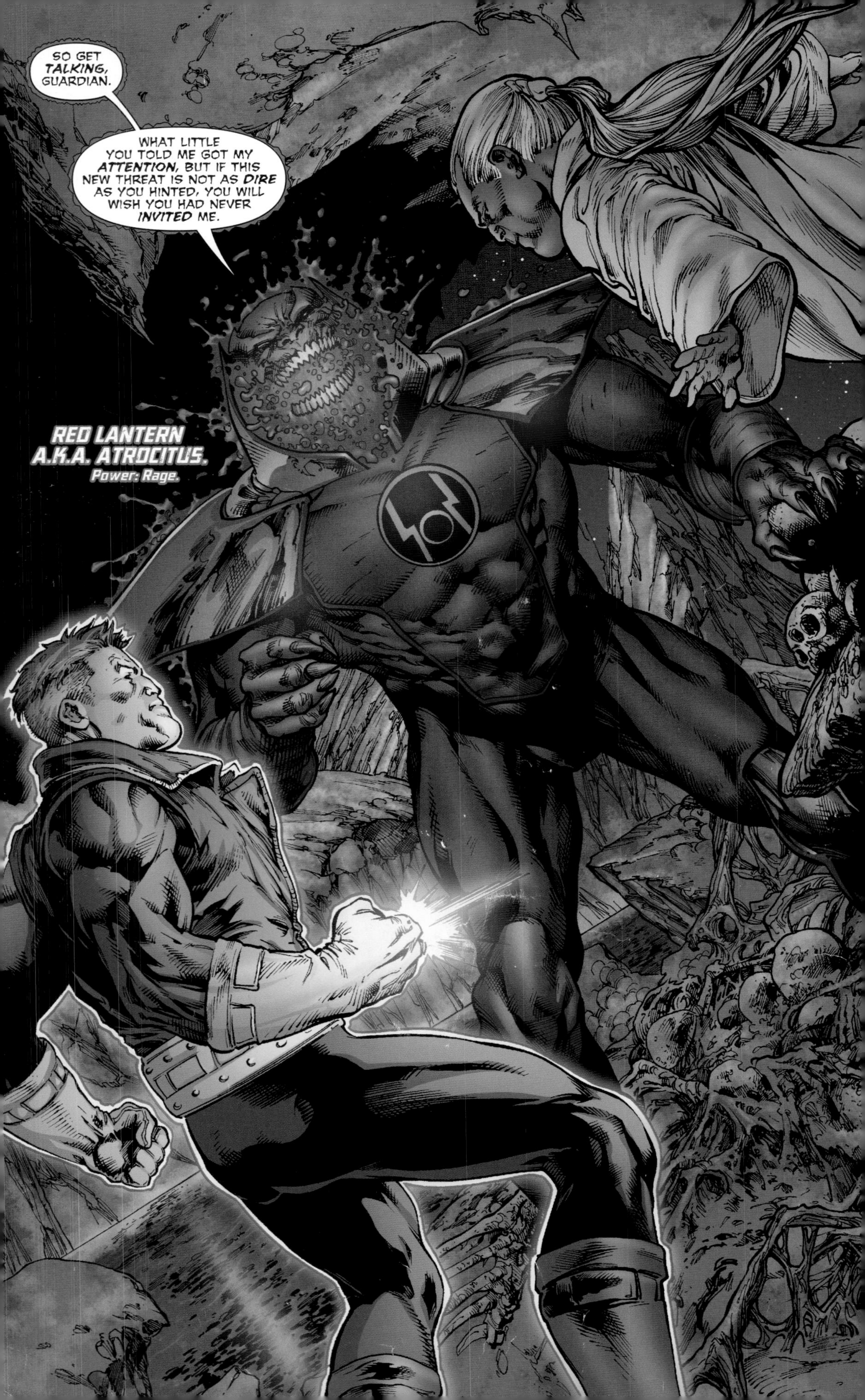
SO GET TALKING, GUARDIAN.
WHAT LITTLE YOU TOLD ME GOT MY ATTENTION, BUT IF THIS NEW THREAT IS NOT AS DIRE AS YOU HINTED, YOU WILL WISH YOU HAD NEVER INVITED ME.
RED LANTERN A.K.A. ATROCITUS.
Power: Rage.

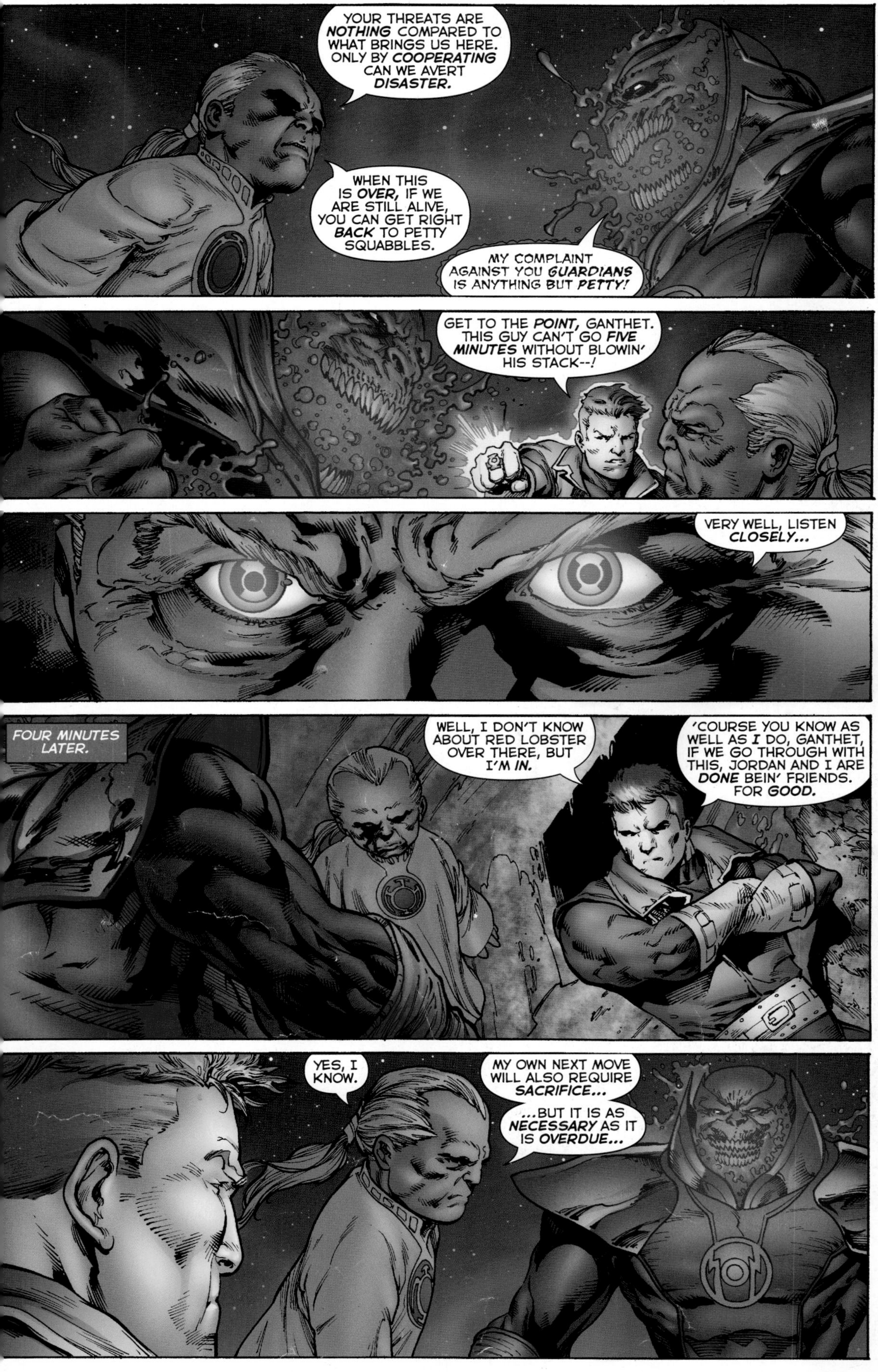

YOUR THREATS ARE NOTHING COMPARED TO WHAT BRINGS US HERE. ONLY BY COOPERATING CAN WE AVERT DISASTER.
WHEN THIS IS OVER, IF WE ARE STILL ALIVE, YOU CAN GET RIGHT BACK TO PETTY SQUABBLES.
MY COMPLAINT AGAINST YOU GUARDIANS IS ANYTHING BUT PETTY!
GET TO THE POINT, GANTHET. THIS GUY CAN'T GO FIVE MINUTES WITHOUT BLOWIN' HIS STACK--!
VERY WELL, LISTEN CLOSELY...
FOUR MINUTES LATER.
WELL, I DON'T KNOW ABOUT RED LOBSTER OVER THERE, BUT I'M IN.
'COURSE YOU KNOW AS WELL AS I DO, GANTHET, IF WE GO THROUGH WITH THIS, JORDAN AND I ARE DONE BEIN' FRIENDS. FOR GOOD.
YES, I KNOW.
MY OWN NEXT MOVE WILL ALSO REQUIRE SACRIFICE...
...BUT IT IS AS NECESSARY AS IT IS OVERDUE...

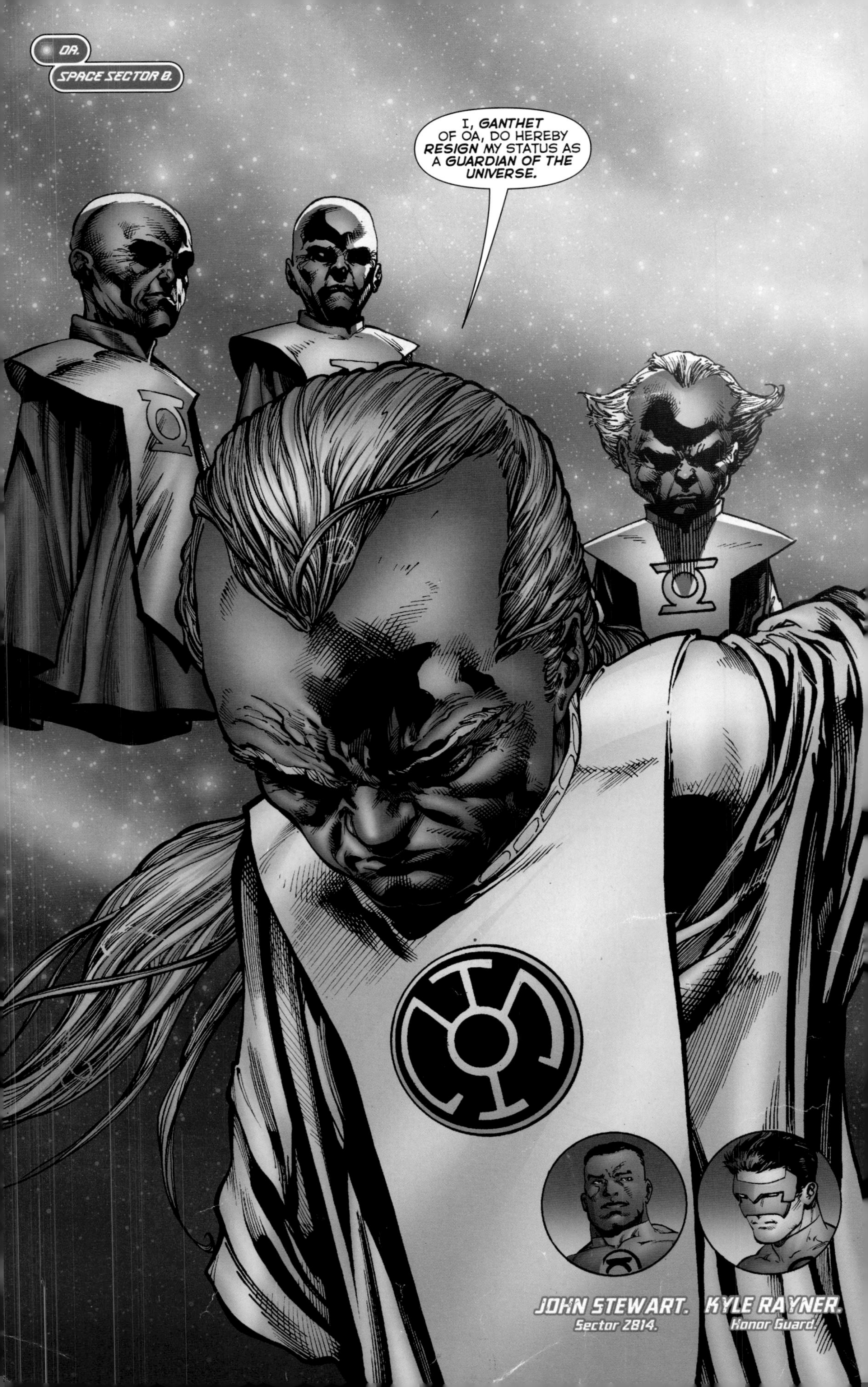
OA.
SPACE SECTOR 0.
I, GANTHET OF OA, DO HEREBY RESIGN MY STATUS AS A GUARDIAN OF THE UNIVERSE.
JOHN STEWART.
Sector 2814.
KYLE RAYNER.
Honor Guard.

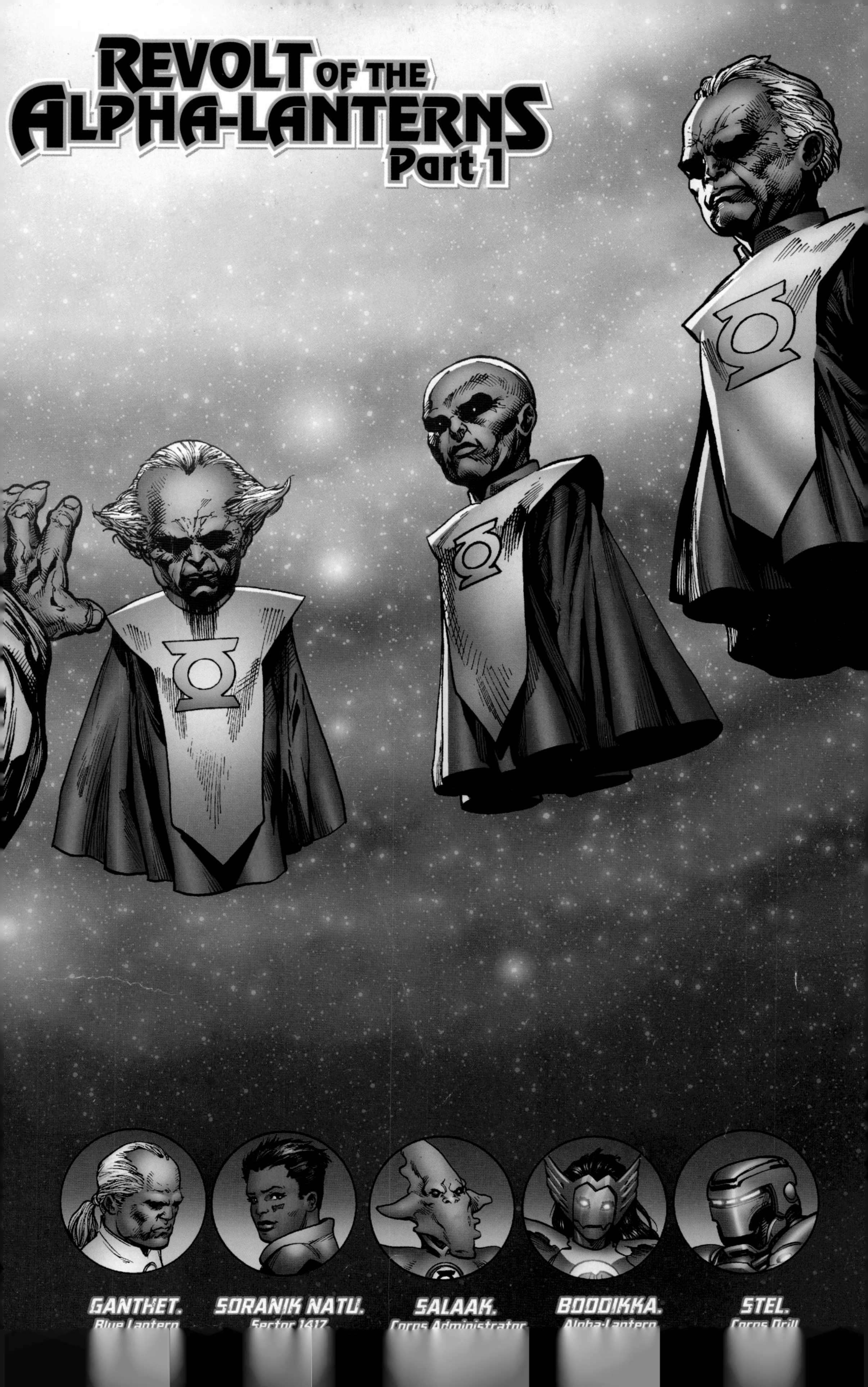
REVOLT OF THE ALPHA-LANTERNS
Part 1
GANTHET.
Blue Lantern
SORANIK NATU.
Sector 1417
SALAAK.
Corps Administrator
BOODIKKA.
Alpha-Lantern
STEL.
Corps Drill

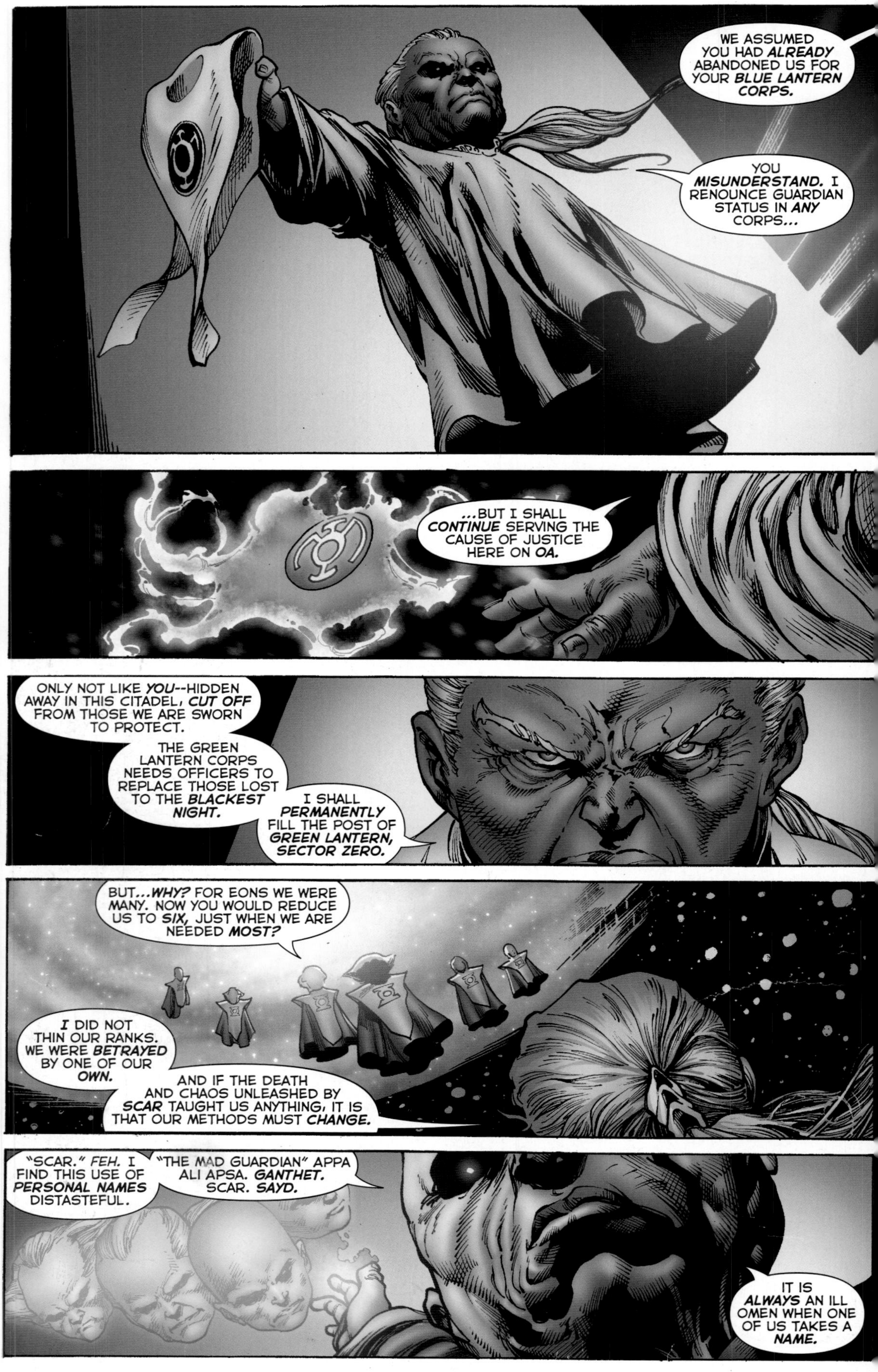
WE ASSUMED YOU HAD ALREADY ABANDONED US FOR YOUR BLUE LANTERN CORPS.
YOU MISUNDERSTAND. I RENOUNCE GUARDIAN STATUS IN ANY CORPS...
...BUT I SHALL CONTINUE SERVING THE CAUSE OF JUSTICE HERE ON OA.
ONLY NOT LIKE YOU--HIDDEN AWAY IN THIS CITADEL, CUT OFF FROM THOSE WE ARE SWORN TO PROTECT.
THE GREEN LANTERN CORPS NEEDS OFFICERS TO REPLACE THOSE LOST TO THE BLACKEST NIGHT.
I SHALL PERMANENTLY FILL THE POST OF GREEN LANTERN, SECTOR ZERO.
BUT...WHY? FOR EONS WE WERE MANY. NOW YOU WOULD REDUCE US TO SIX, JUST WHEN WE ARE NEEDED MOST?
I DID NOT THIN OUR RANKS. WE WERE BETRAYED BY ONE OF OUR OWN.
AND IF THE DEATH AND CHAOS UNLEASHED BY SCAR TAUGHT US ANYTHING, IT IS THAT OUR METHODS MUST CHANGE.
"SCAR." FEH. I FIND THIS USE OF PERSONAL NAMES DISTASTEFUL.
"THE MAD GUARDIAN" APPA ALI APSA. GANTHET. SCAR. SAYD.
IT IS ALWAYS AN ILL OMEN WHEN ONE OF US TAKES A NAME.

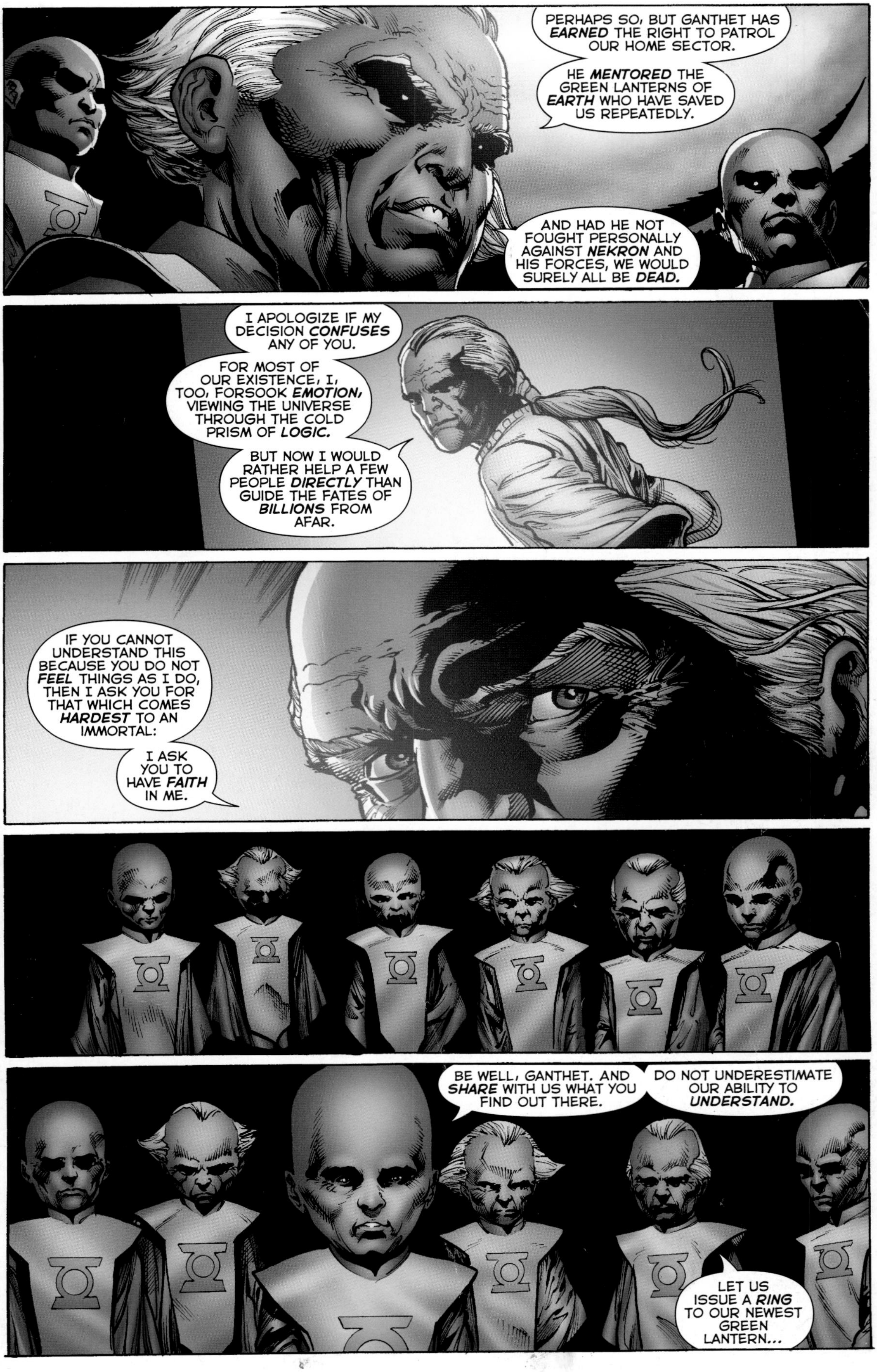
PERHAPS SO, BUT GANTHET HAS EARNED THE RIGHT TO PATROL OUR HOME SECTOR.
HE MENTORED THE GREEN LANTERNS OF EARTH WHO HAVE SAVED US REPEATEDLY.
AND HAD HE NOT FOUGHT PERSONALLY AGAINST NEKRON AND HIS FORCES, WE WOULD SURELY ALL BE DEAD.
I APOLOGIZE IF MY DECISION CONFUSES ANY OF YOU.
FOR MOST OF OUR EXISTENCE, I, TOO, FORSOOK EMOTION, VIEWING THE UNIVERSE THROUGH THE COLD PRISM OF LOGIC.
BUT NOW I WOULD RATHER HELP A FEW PEOPLE DIRECTLY THAN GUIDE THE FATES OF BILLIONS FROM AFAR.
IF YOU CANNOT UNDERSTAND THIS BECAUSE YOU DO NOT FEEL THINGS AS I DO, THEN I ASK YOU FOR THAT WHICH COMES HARDEST TO AN IMMORTAL:
I ASK YOU TO HAVE FAITH IN ME.
BE WELL, GANTHET. AND SHARE WITH US WHAT YOU FIND OUT THERE.
DO NOT UNDERESTIMATE OUR ABILITY TO UNDERSTAND.
LET US ISSUE A RING TO OUR NEWEST GREEN LANTERN...

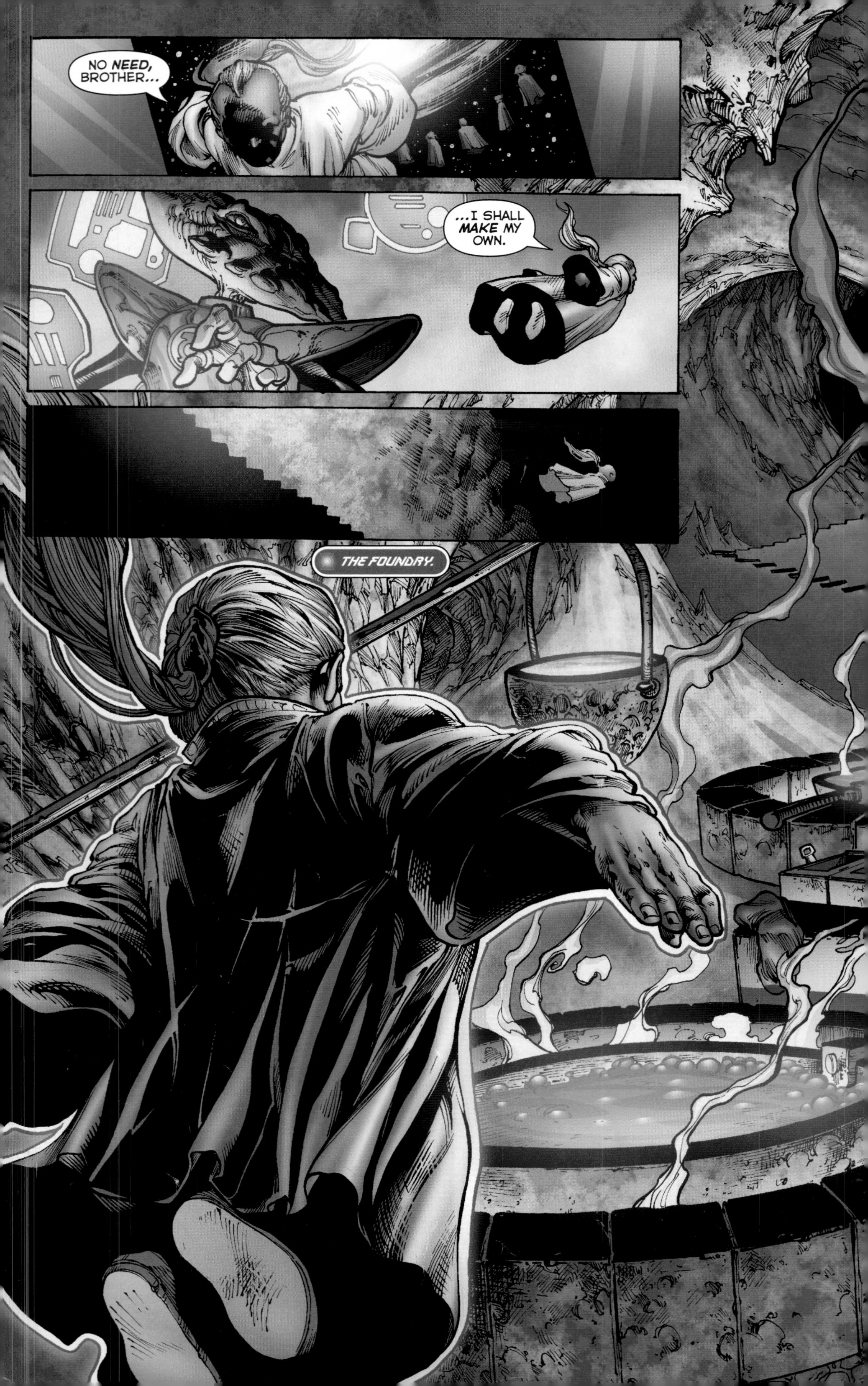
NO NEED, BROTHER...
...I SHALL MAKE MY OWN.
THE FOUNDRY.

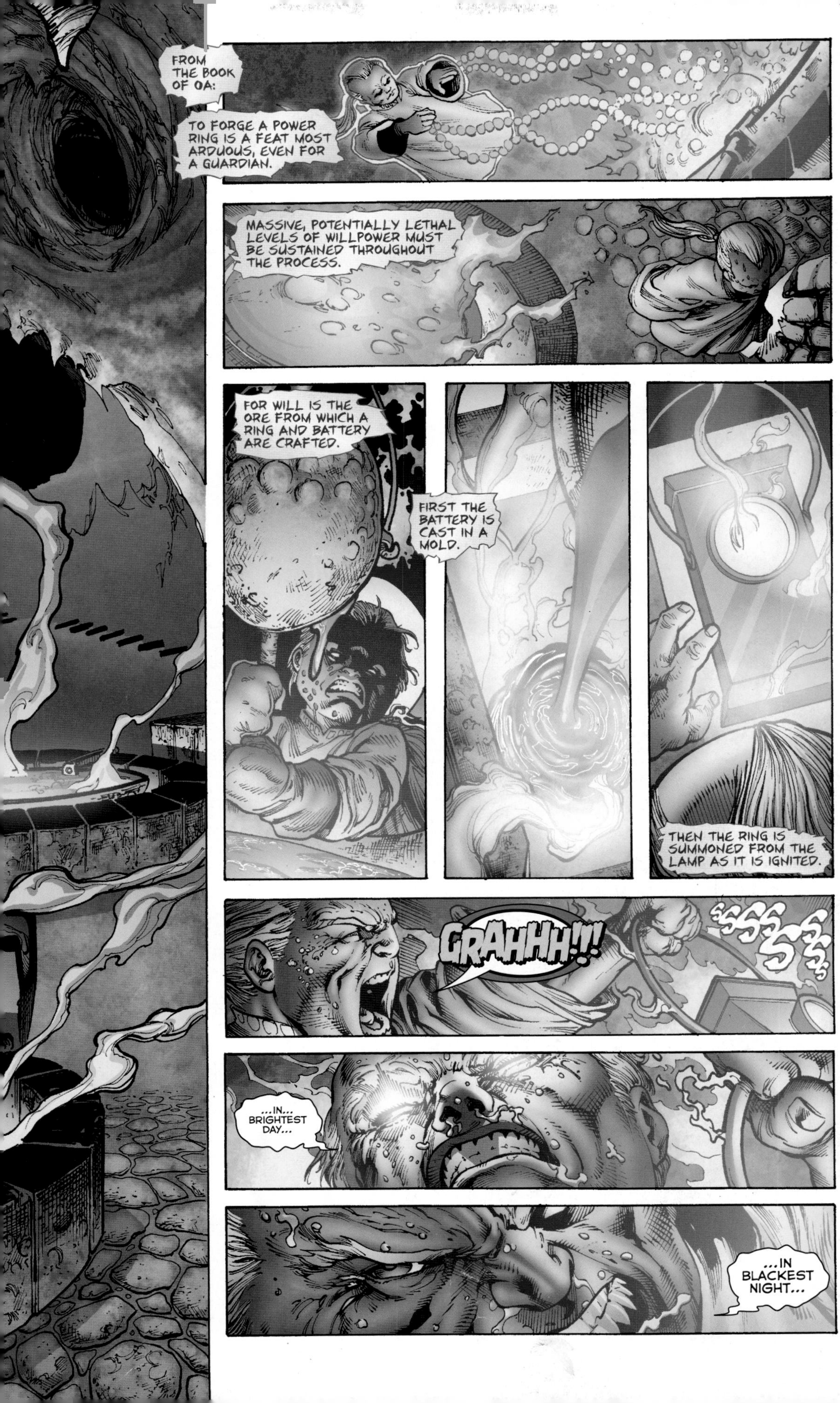
FROM THE BOOK OF OA:
TO FORGE A POWER RING IS A FEAT MOST ARDUOUS, EVEN FOR A GUARDIAN.
MASSIVE, POTENTIALLY LETHAL LEVELS OF WILLPOWER MUST BE SUSTAINED THROUGHOUT THE PROCESS.
FOR WILL IS THE ORE FROM WHICH A RING AND BATTERY ARE CRAFTED.
FIRST THE BATTERY IS CAST IN A MOLD.
THEN THE RING IS SUMMONED FROM THE LAMP AS IT IS IGNITED.
GRAHHH!!!
SSSSS
...IN... BRIGHTEST DAY...
...IN BLACKEST NIGHT...

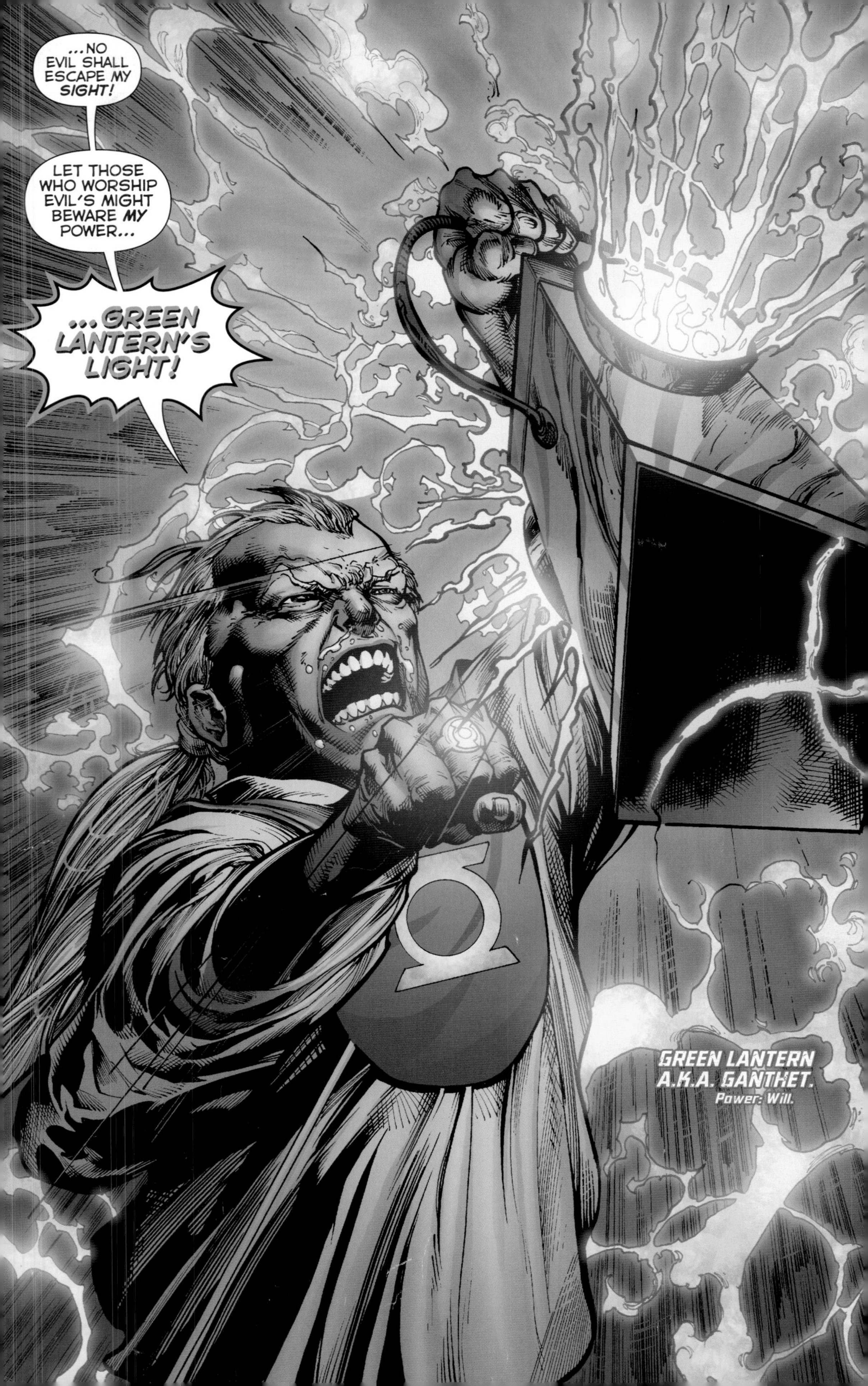
...NO EVIL SHALL ESCAPE MY SIGHT!
LET THOSE WHO WORSHIP EVIL'S MIGHT BEWARE MY POWER...
...GREEN LANTERN'S LIGHT!
GREEN LANTERN A.K.A. GANTHET.
Power: Will.

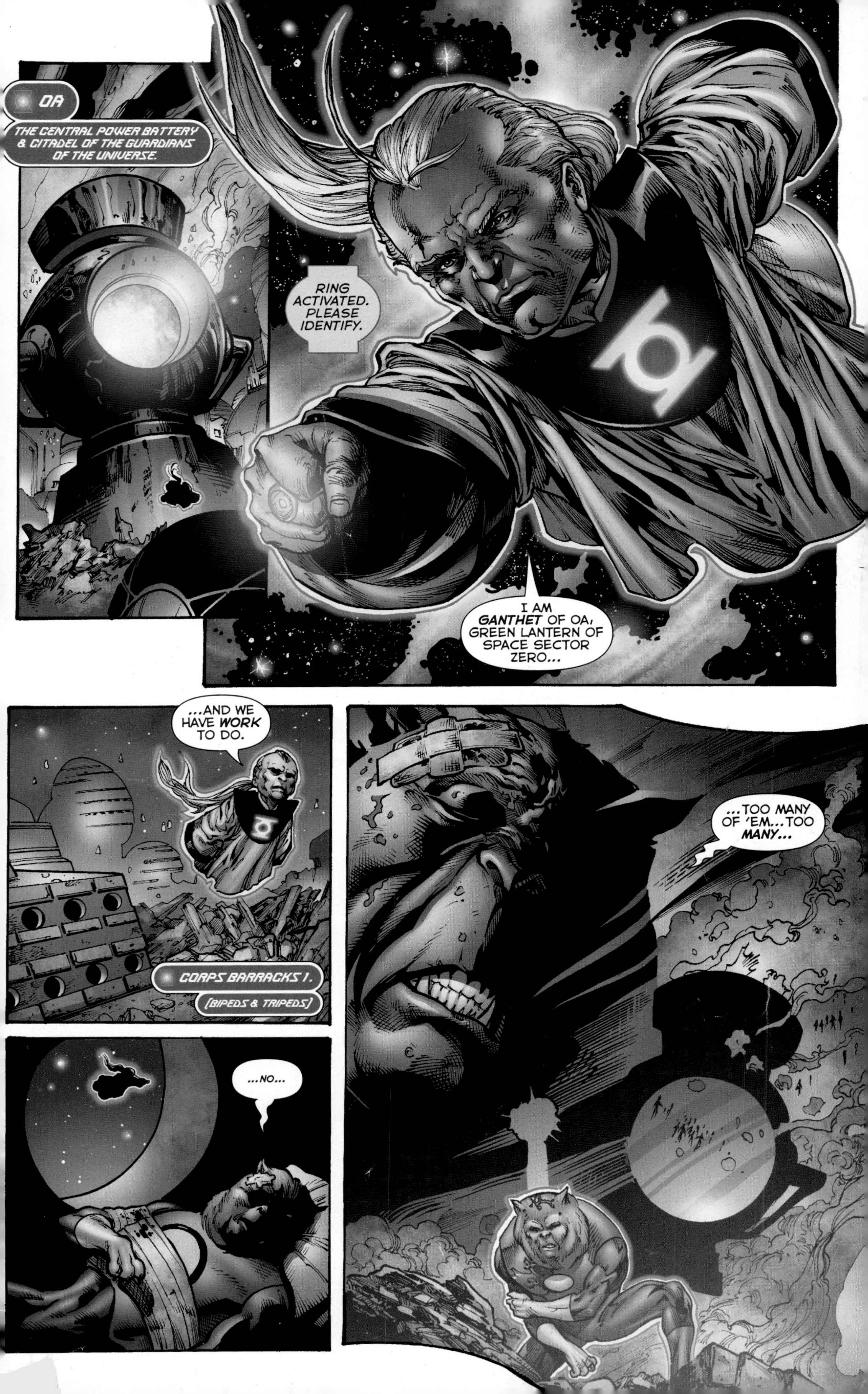
OA
THE CENTRAL POWER BATTERY & CITADEL OF THE GUARDIANS OF THE UNIVERSE.
RING ACTIVATED. PLEASE IDENTIFY.
I AM GANTHET OF OA, GREEN LANTERN OF SPACE SECTOR ZERO...
...AND WE HAVE WORK TO DO.
CORPS BARRACKS 1.
[BIPEDS & TRIPEDS]
...NO...
...TOO MANY OF 'EM...TOO MANY...

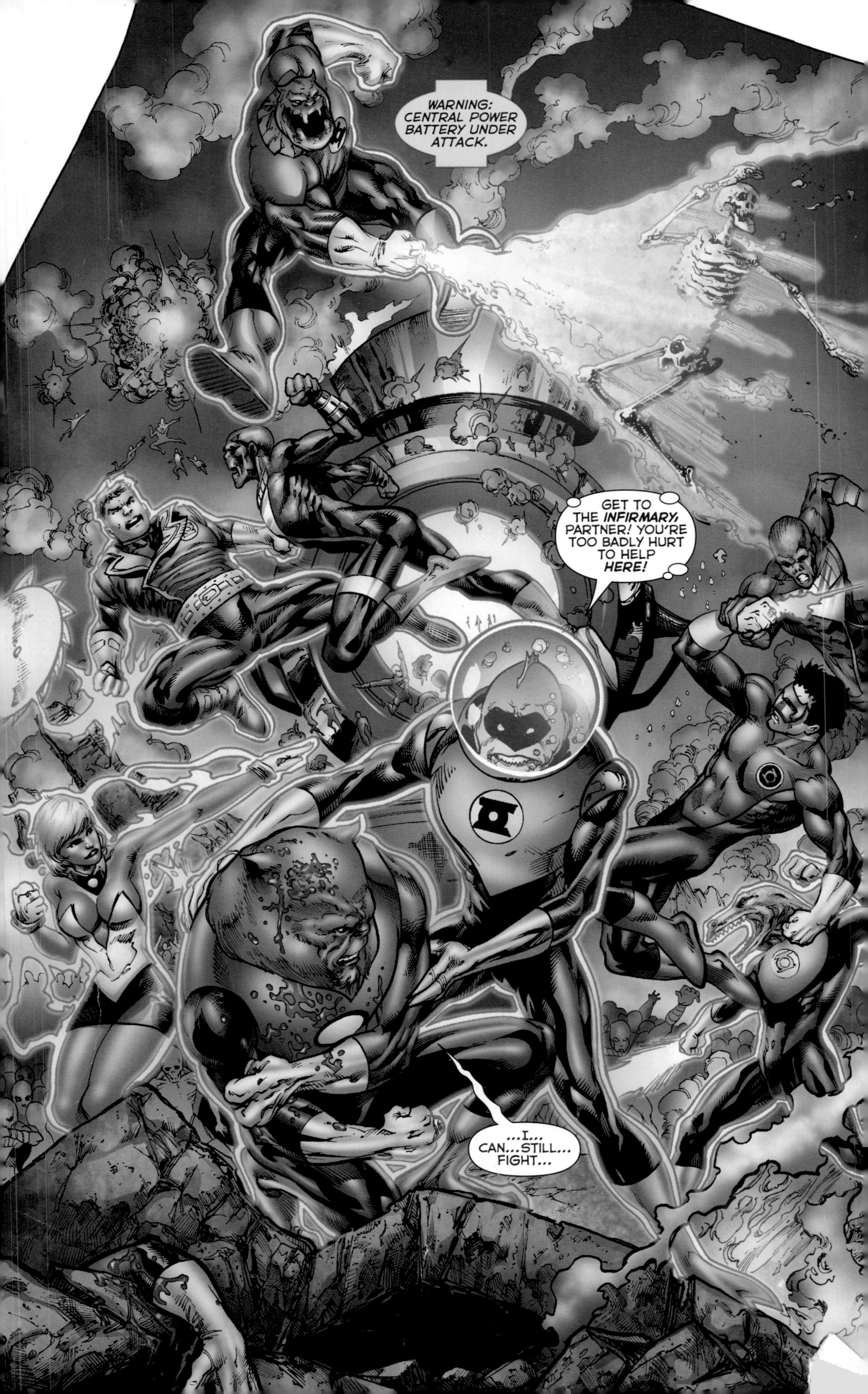
WARNING: CENTRAL POWER BATTERY UNDER ATTACK.
GET TO THE *INFIRMARY,* PARTNER! YOU'RE TOO BADLY HURT TO HELP *HERE!*
...I... CAN...STILL... FIGHT...

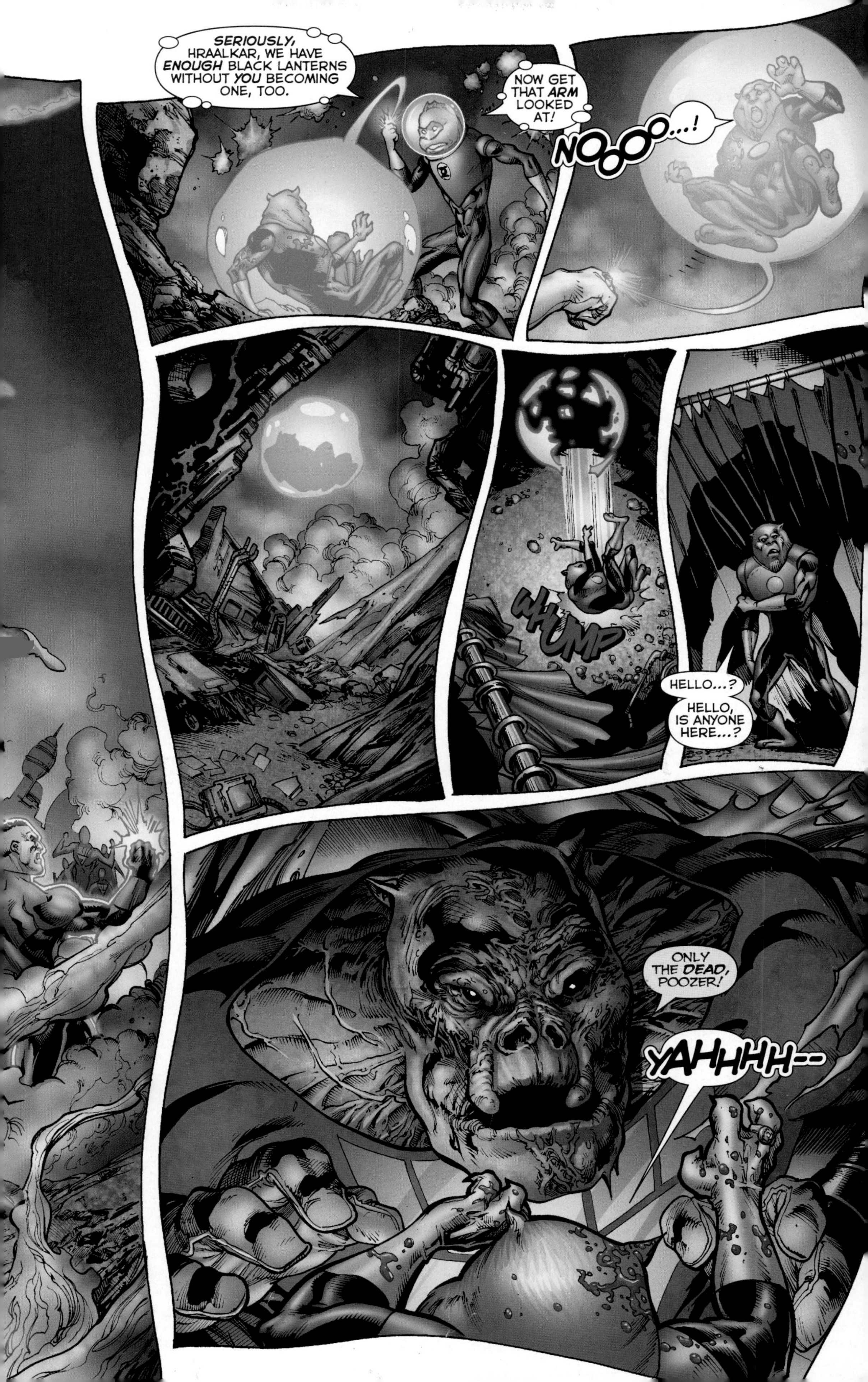
SERIOUSLY, HRAALKAR, WE HAVE ENOUGH BLACK LANTERNS WITHOUT YOU BECOMING ONE, TOO.
NOW GET THAT ARM LOOKED AT!
NOOOO...!
WHUMP
HELLO...?
HELLO, IS ANYONE HERE...?
ONLY THE DEAD, POOZER!
YAHHHH--

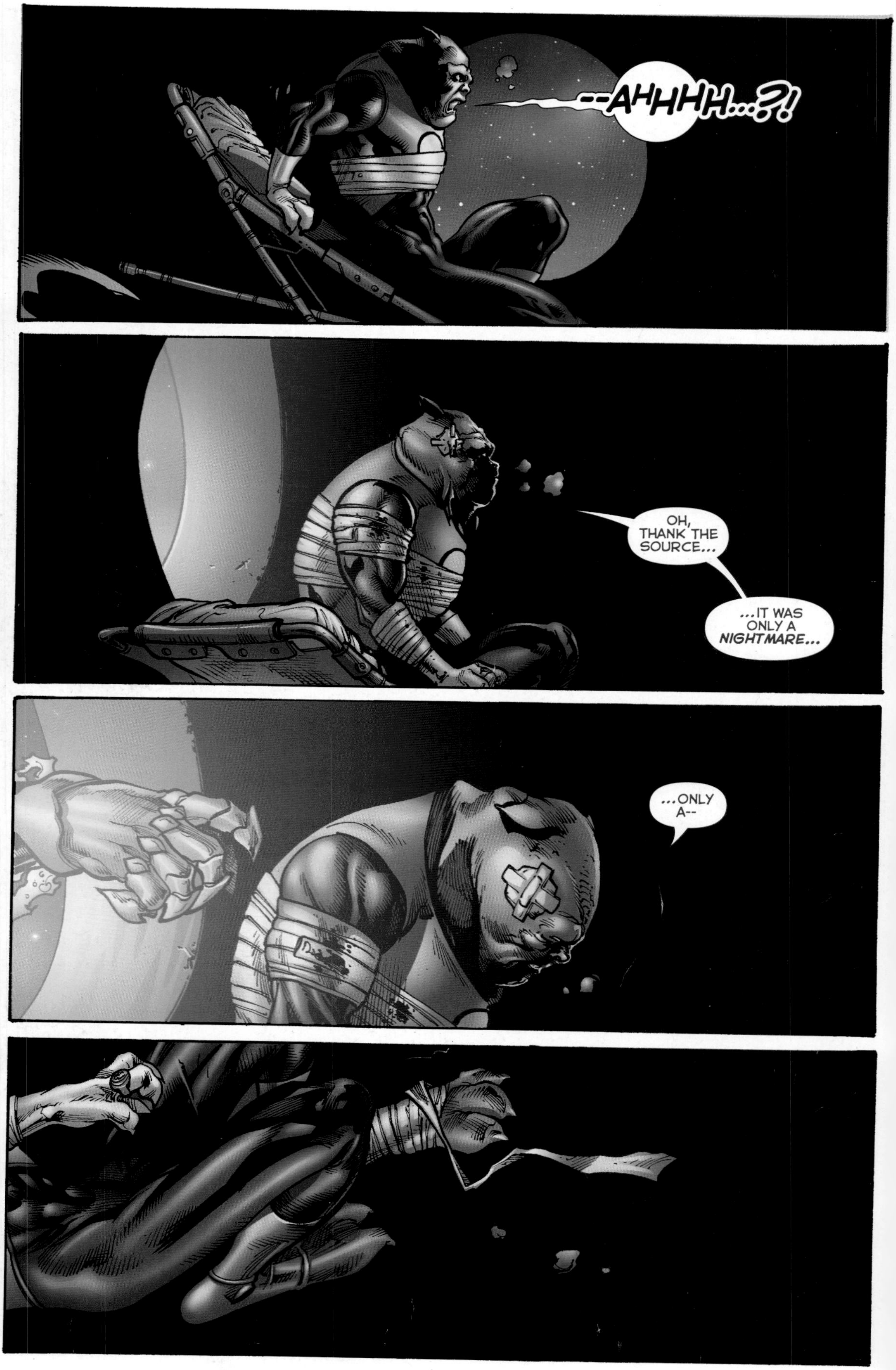
--AHHHH...?!
OH, THANK THE SOURCE...
...IT WAS ONLY A NIGHTMARE...
...ONLY A--

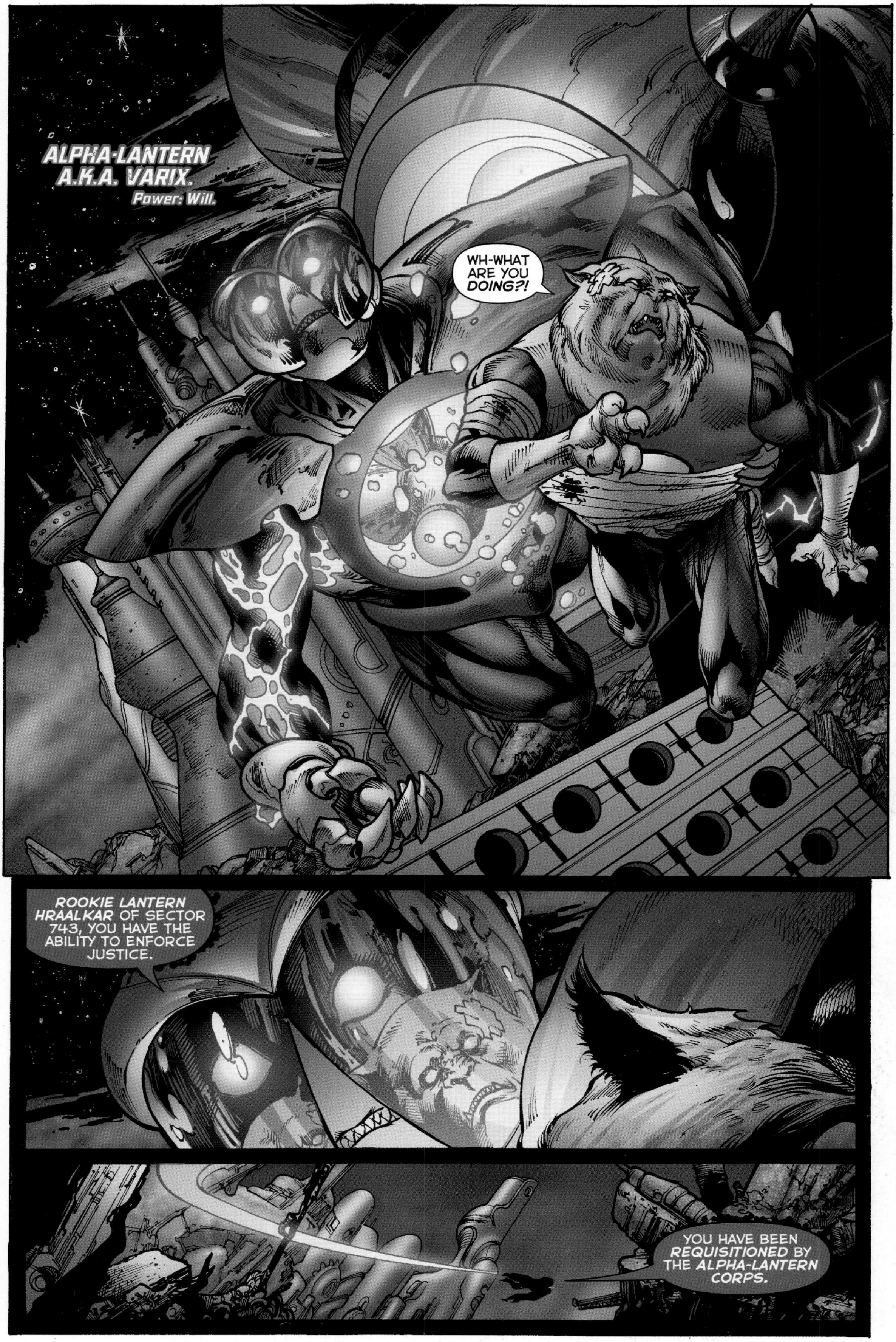
ALPHA-LANTERN A.K.A. VARIX.
Power: Will.
WH-WHAT ARE YOU DOING?!
ROOKIE LANTERN HRAALKAR OF SECTOR 743, YOU HAVE THE ABILITY TO ENFORCE JUSTICE.
YOU HAVE BEEN REQUISITIONED BY THE ALPHA-LANTERN CORPS.

OKAY, GET THIS BLOCK CORDONED OFF! THE WHOLE THING'S CONDEMNED.

HEY, *JOHN!* GUESS WHO GOT HIMSELF *DEMOTED* TO BEAT COP?

I *HEARD,* KYLE.

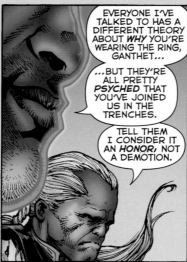

EVERYONE I'VE TALKED TO HAS A DIFFERENT THEORY ABOUT *WHY* YOU'RE WEARING THE RING, GANTHET...

...BUT THEY'RE ALL PRETTY *PSYCHED* THAT YOU'VE JOINED US IN THE TRENCHES.

TELL THEM I CONSIDER IT AN *HONOR,* NOT A DEMOTION.

MAN, THE BLACK LANTERNS REALLY DID A NUMBER ON THIS PLACE. HOW'S THE *RECONSTRUCTION* COMING?

WORSE THAN I HOPED. ABOUT EIGHTY PERCENT OF THE CITY IS *IRREPARABLE.*

WHOEVER WROTE THE *BUILDING CODES* ON ANCIENT OA DIDN'T RECKON ON THE "BLACKEST NIGHT."

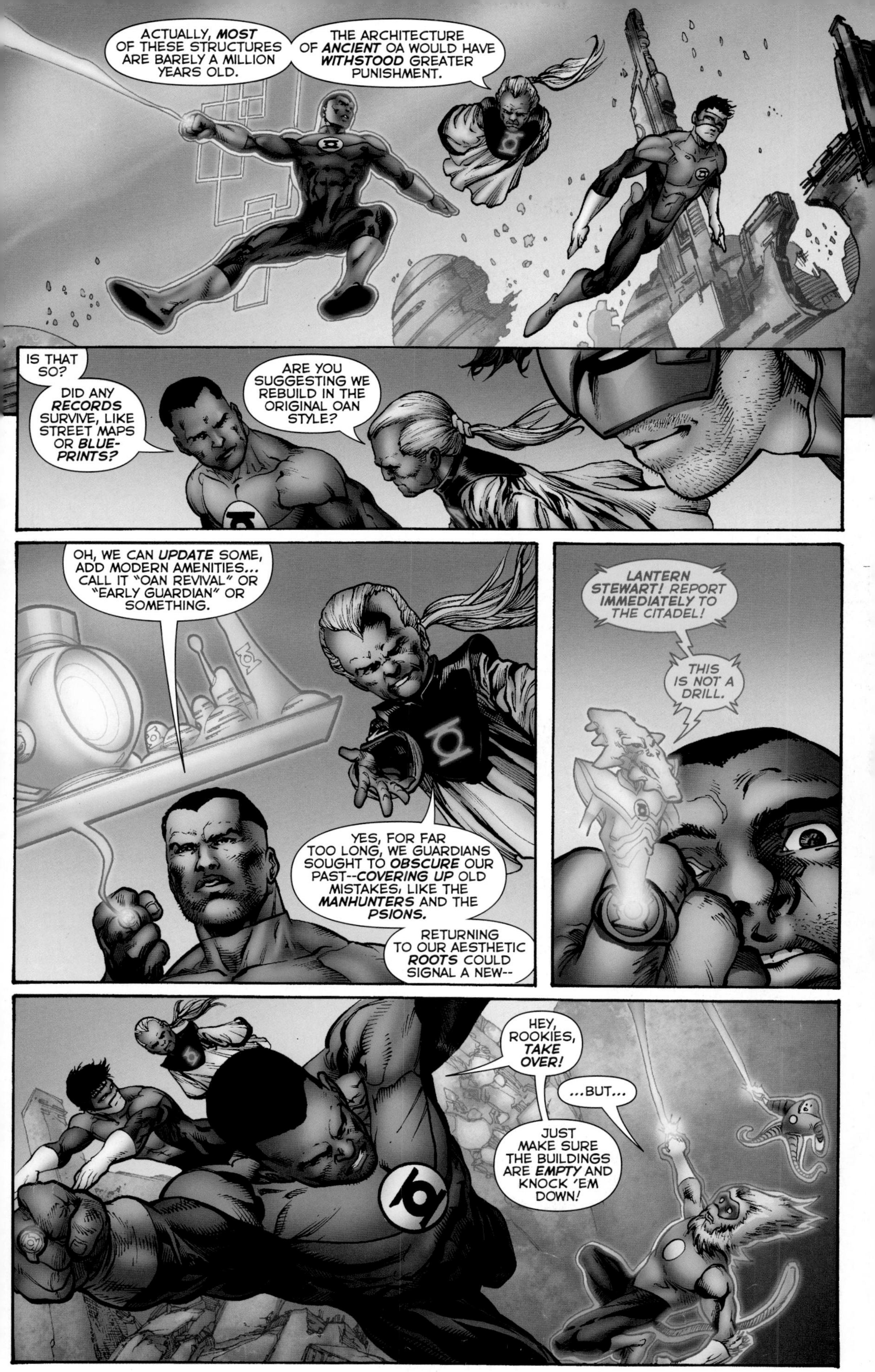

ACTUALLY, MOST OF THESE STRUCTURES ARE BARELY A MILLION YEARS OLD.
THE ARCHITECTURE OF ANCIENT OA WOULD HAVE WITHSTOOD GREATER PUNISHMENT.
IS THAT SO?
DID ANY RECORDS SURVIVE, LIKE STREET MAPS OR BLUE-PRINTS?
ARE YOU SUGGESTING WE REBUILD IN THE ORIGINAL OAN STYLE?
OH, WE CAN UPDATE SOME, ADD MODERN AMENITIES... CALL IT "OAN REVIVAL" OR "EARLY GUARDIAN" OR SOMETHING.
YES, FOR FAR TOO LONG, WE GUARDIANS SOUGHT TO OBSCURE OUR PAST--COVERING UP OLD MISTAKES, LIKE THE MANHUNTERS AND THE PSIONS.
RETURNING TO OUR AESTHETIC ROOTS COULD SIGNAL A NEW--
LANTERN STEWART! REPORT IMMEDIATELY TO THE CITADEL!
THIS IS NOT A DRILL.
HEY, ROOKIES, TAKE OVER!
...BUT...
JUST MAKE SURE THE BUILDINGS ARE EMPTY AND KNOCK 'EM DOWN!

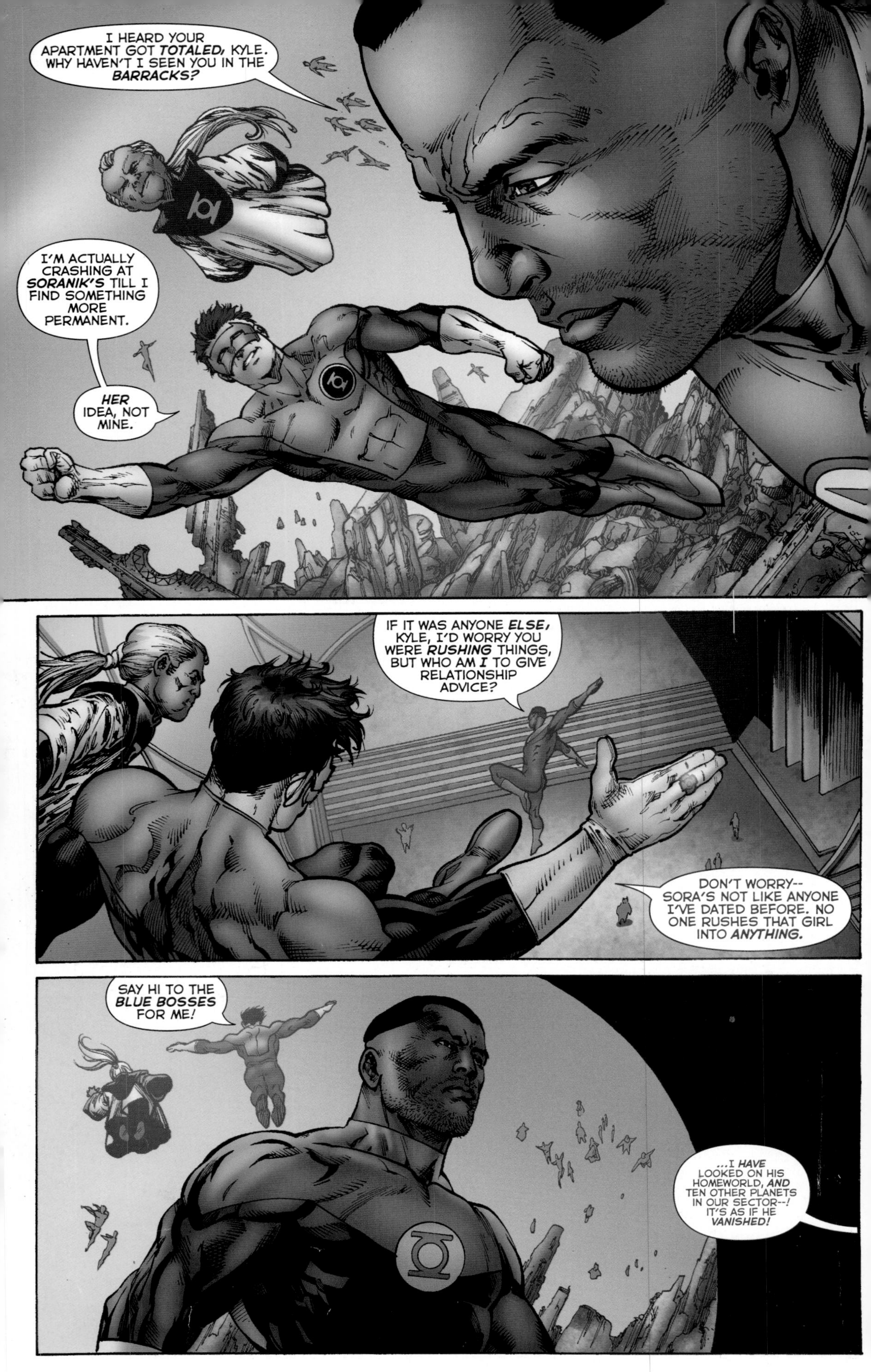
I HEARD YOUR APARTMENT GOT *TOTALED,* KYLE. WHY HAVEN'T I SEEN YOU IN THE *BARRACKS?*
I'M ACTUALLY CRASHING AT *SORANIK'S* TILL I FIND SOMETHING MORE PERMANENT.
HER IDEA, NOT MINE.
IF IT WAS ANYONE *ELSE,* KYLE, I'D WORRY YOU WERE *RUSHING* THINGS, BUT WHO AM *I* TO GIVE RELATIONSHIP ADVICE?
DON'T WORRY-- SORA'S NOT LIKE ANYONE I'VE DATED BEFORE. NO ONE RUSHES THAT GIRL INTO *ANYTHING.*
SAY HI TO THE *BLUE BOSSES* FOR ME!
...I *HAVE* LOOKED ON HIS HOMEWORLD, *AND* TEN OTHER PLANETS IN OUR SECTOR--! IT'S AS IF HE *VANISHED!*

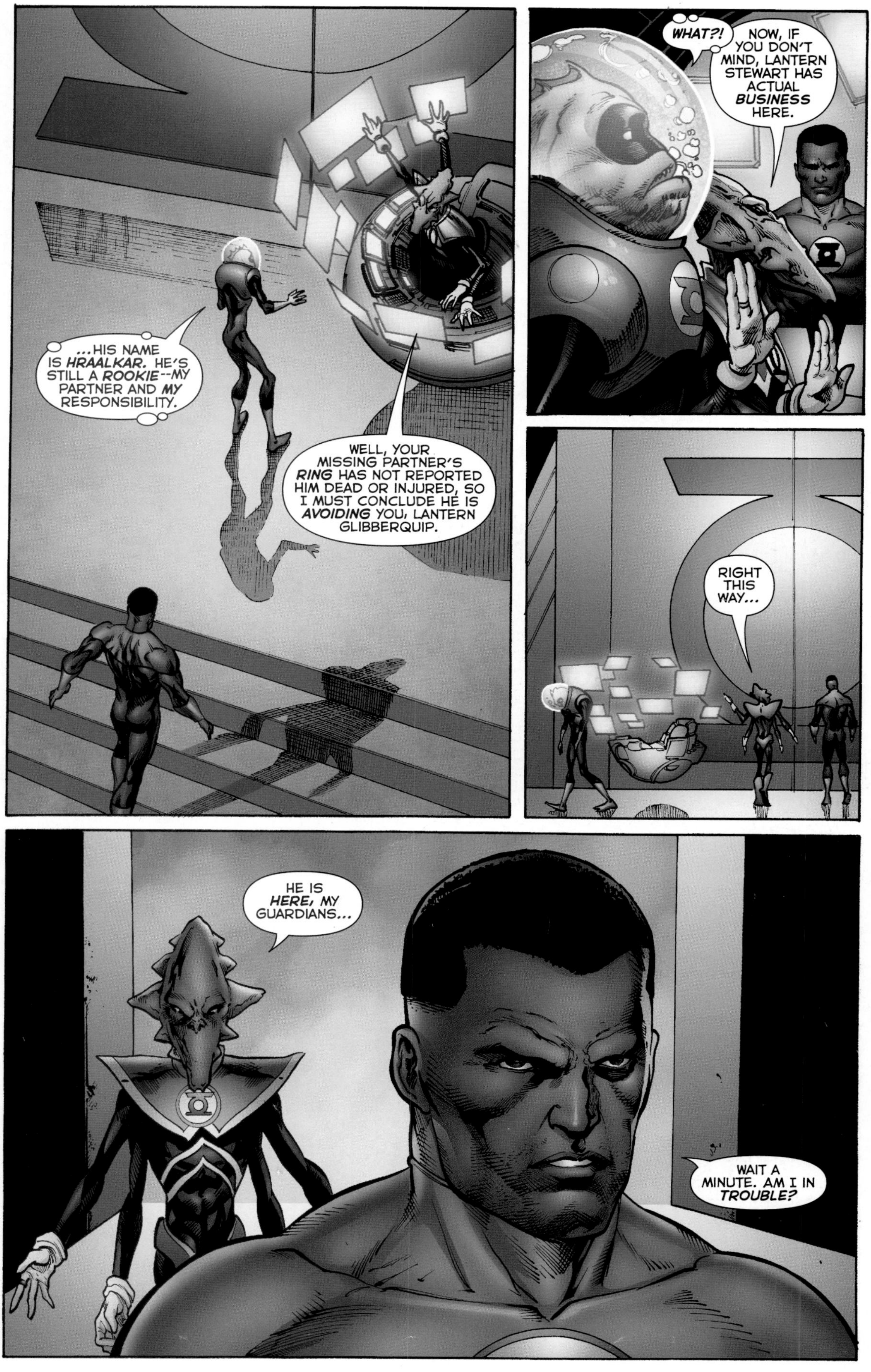
...HIS NAME IS HRAALKAR. HE'S STILL A ROOKIE--MY PARTNER AND MY RESPONSIBILITY.
WELL, YOUR MISSING PARTNER'S RING HAS NOT REPORTED HIM DEAD OR INJURED, SO I MUST CONCLUDE HE IS AVOIDING YOU, LANTERN GLIBBERQUIP.
NOW, IF YOU DON'T MIND, LANTERN STEWART HAS ACTUAL BUSINESS HERE.
WHAT?!
RIGHT THIS WAY...
HE IS HERE, MY GUARDIANS...
WAIT A MINUTE. AM I IN TROUBLE?

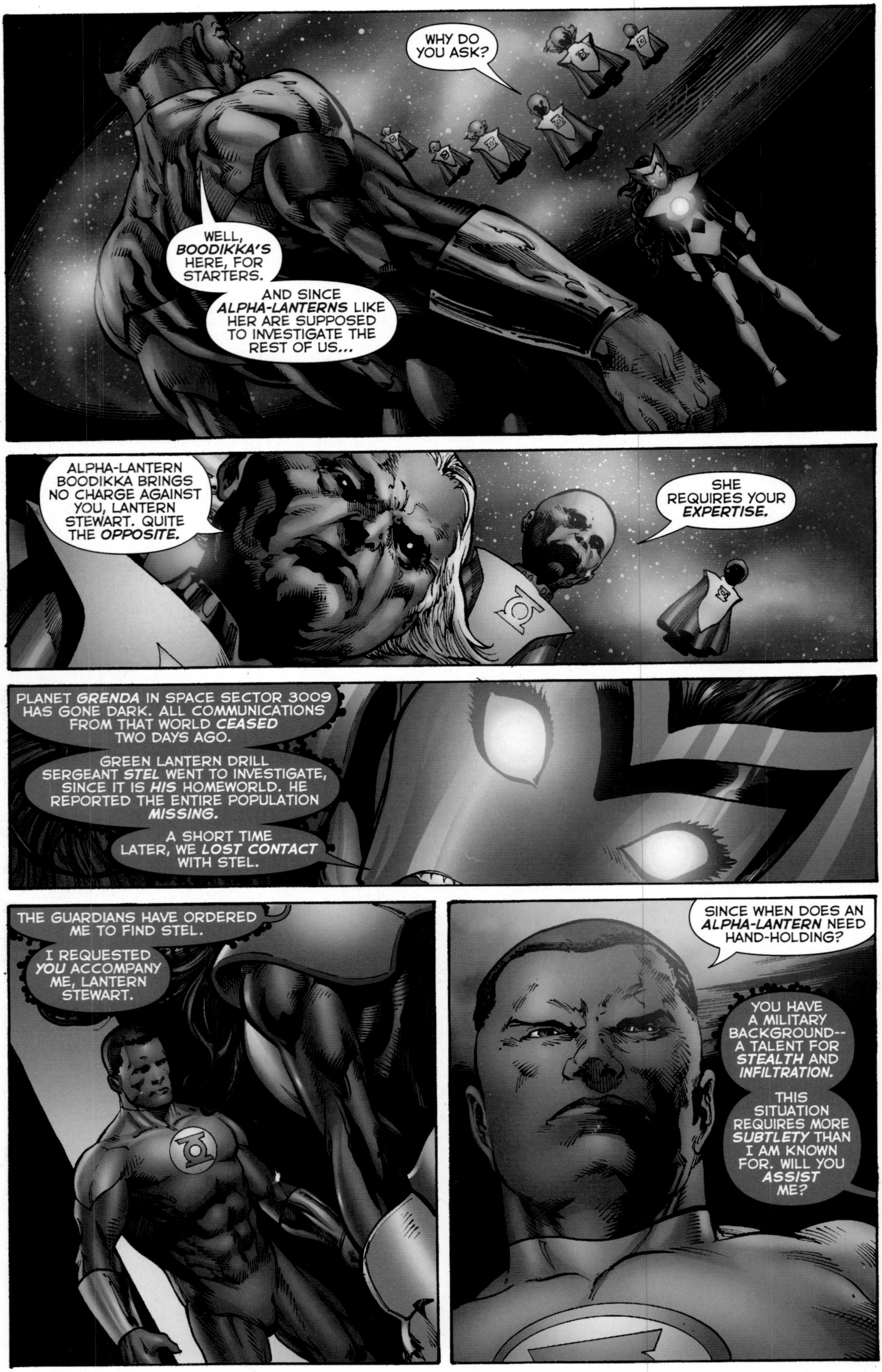
WHY DO YOU ASK?
WELL, BOODIKKA'S HERE, FOR STARTERS.
AND SINCE ALPHA-LANTERNS LIKE HER ARE SUPPOSED TO INVESTIGATE THE REST OF US...
ALPHA-LANTERN BOODIKKA BRINGS NO CHARGE AGAINST YOU, LANTERN STEWART. QUITE THE OPPOSITE.
SHE REQUIRES YOUR EXPERTISE.
PLANET GRENDA IN SPACE SECTOR 3009 HAS GONE DARK. ALL COMMUNICATIONS FROM THAT WORLD CEASED TWO DAYS AGO.
GREEN LANTERN DRILL SERGEANT STEL WENT TO INVESTIGATE, SINCE IT IS HIS HOMEWORLD. HE REPORTED THE ENTIRE POPULATION MISSING.
A SHORT TIME LATER, WE LOST CONTACT WITH STEL.
THE GUARDIANS HAVE ORDERED ME TO FIND STEL.
I REQUESTED YOU ACCOMPANY ME, LANTERN STEWART.
SINCE WHEN DOES AN ALPHA-LANTERN NEED HAND-HOLDING?
YOU HAVE A MILITARY BACKGROUND-- A TALENT FOR STEALTH AND INFILTRATION.
THIS SITUATION REQUIRES MORE SUBTLETY THAN I AM KNOWN FOR. WILL YOU ASSIST ME?

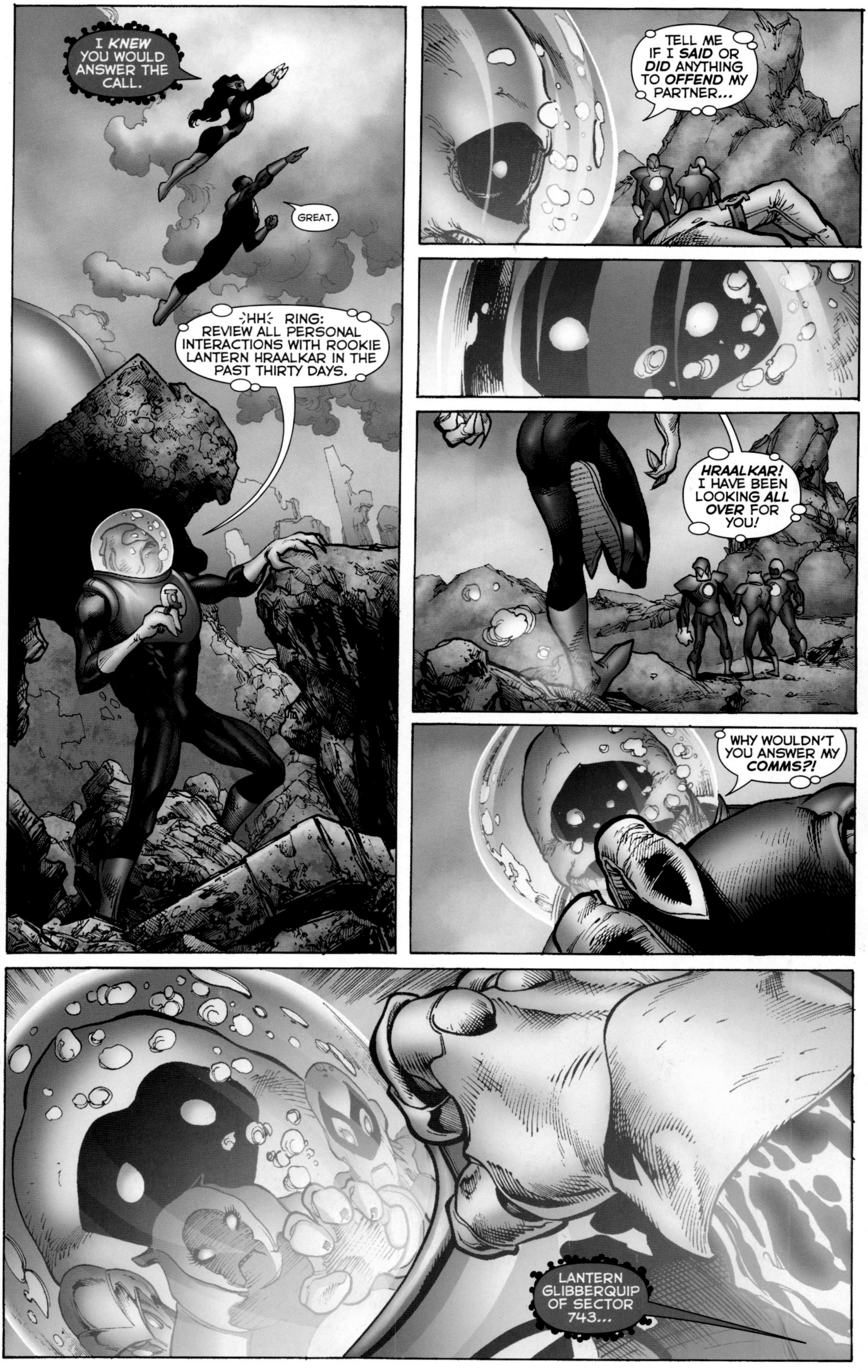
I KNEW YOU WOULD ANSWER THE CALL.
GREAT.
HH RING: REVIEW ALL PERSONAL INTERACTIONS WITH ROOKIE LANTERN HRAALKAR IN THE PAST THIRTY DAYS.
TELL ME IF I SAID OR DID ANYTHING TO OFFEND MY PARTNER...
HRAALKAR! I HAVE BEEN LOOKING ALL OVER FOR YOU!
WHY WOULDN'T YOU ANSWER MY COMMS?!
LANTERN GLIBBERQUIP OF SECTOR 743...

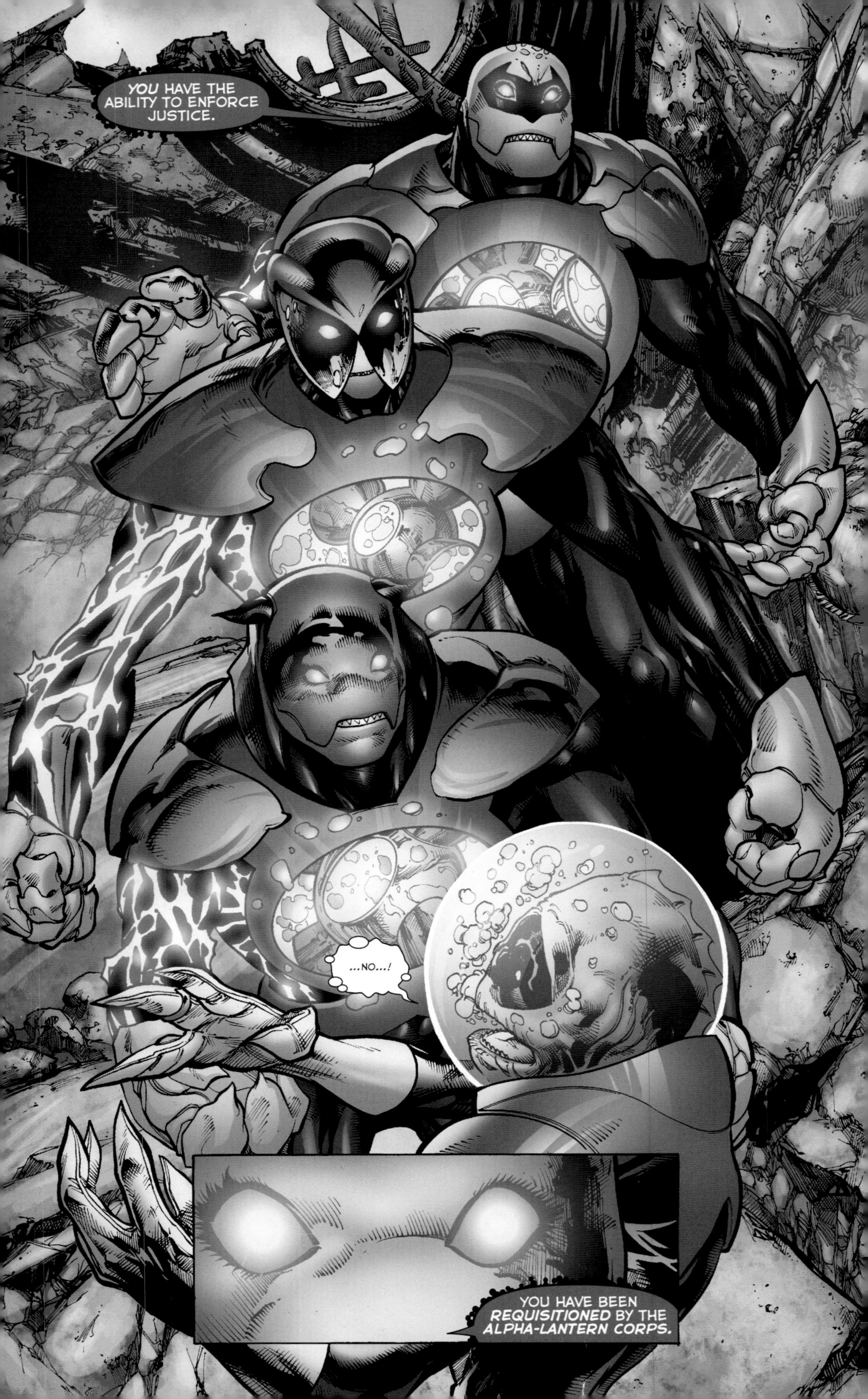
YOU HAVE THE ABILITY TO ENFORCE JUSTICE.
...NO...!
YOU HAVE BEEN REQUISITIONED BY THE ALPHA-LANTERN CORPS.

REVOLT OF THE ALPHA-LANTERNS PART TWO
Cover by Ardian Syaf, Vicente Cifuentes & Ulises Arreola

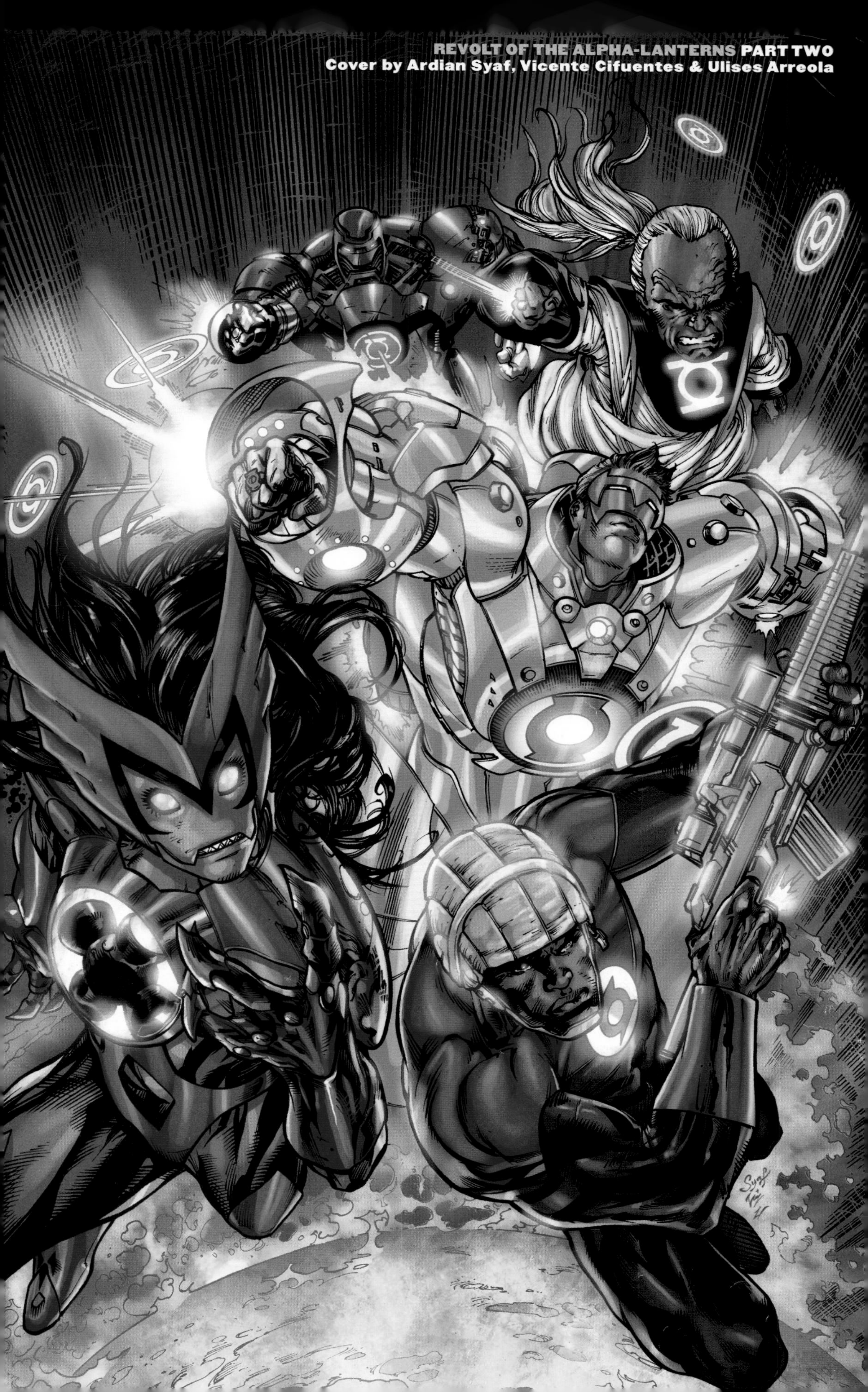

Variant by Patrick Gleason, John Dell & Randy Mayor

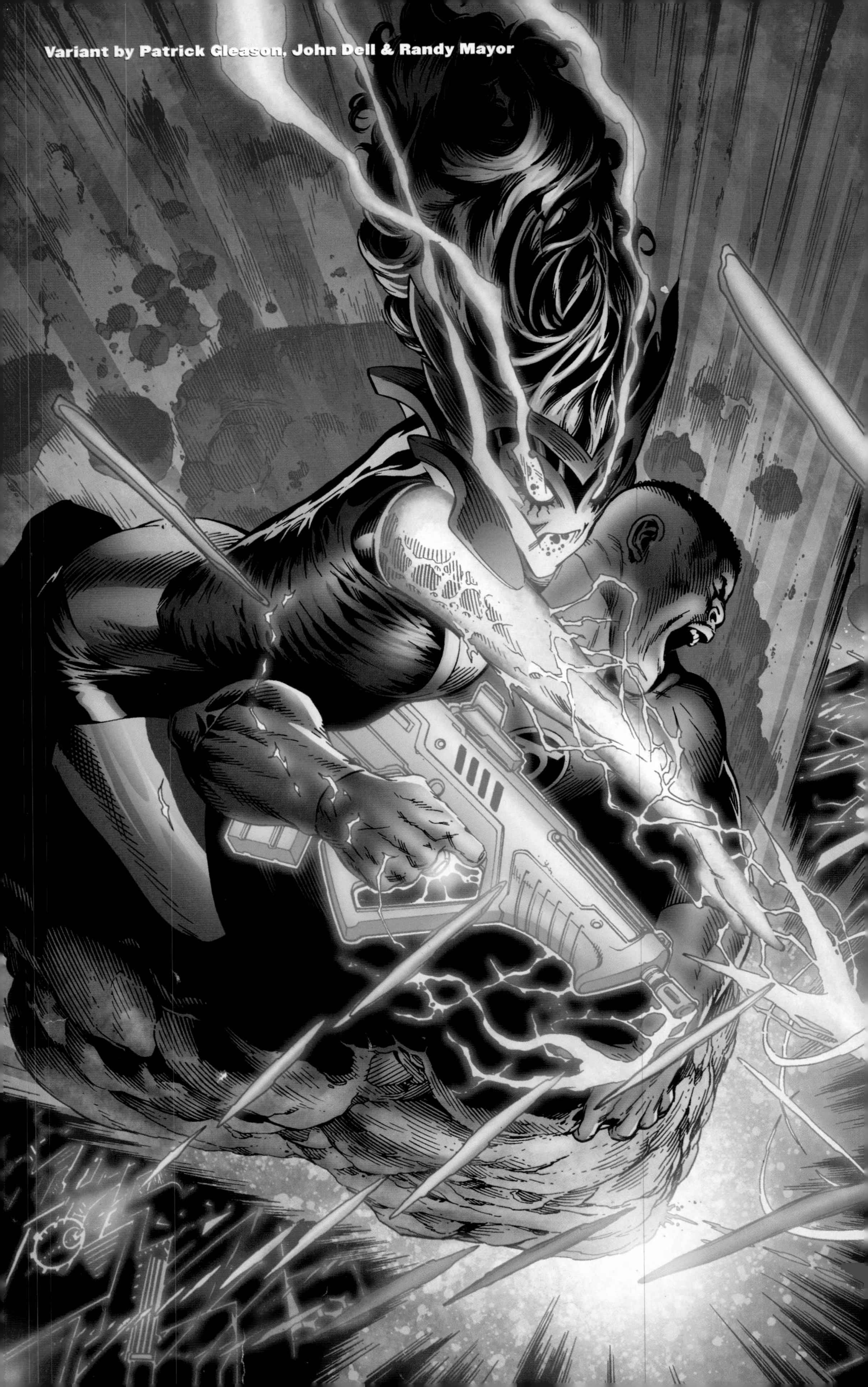

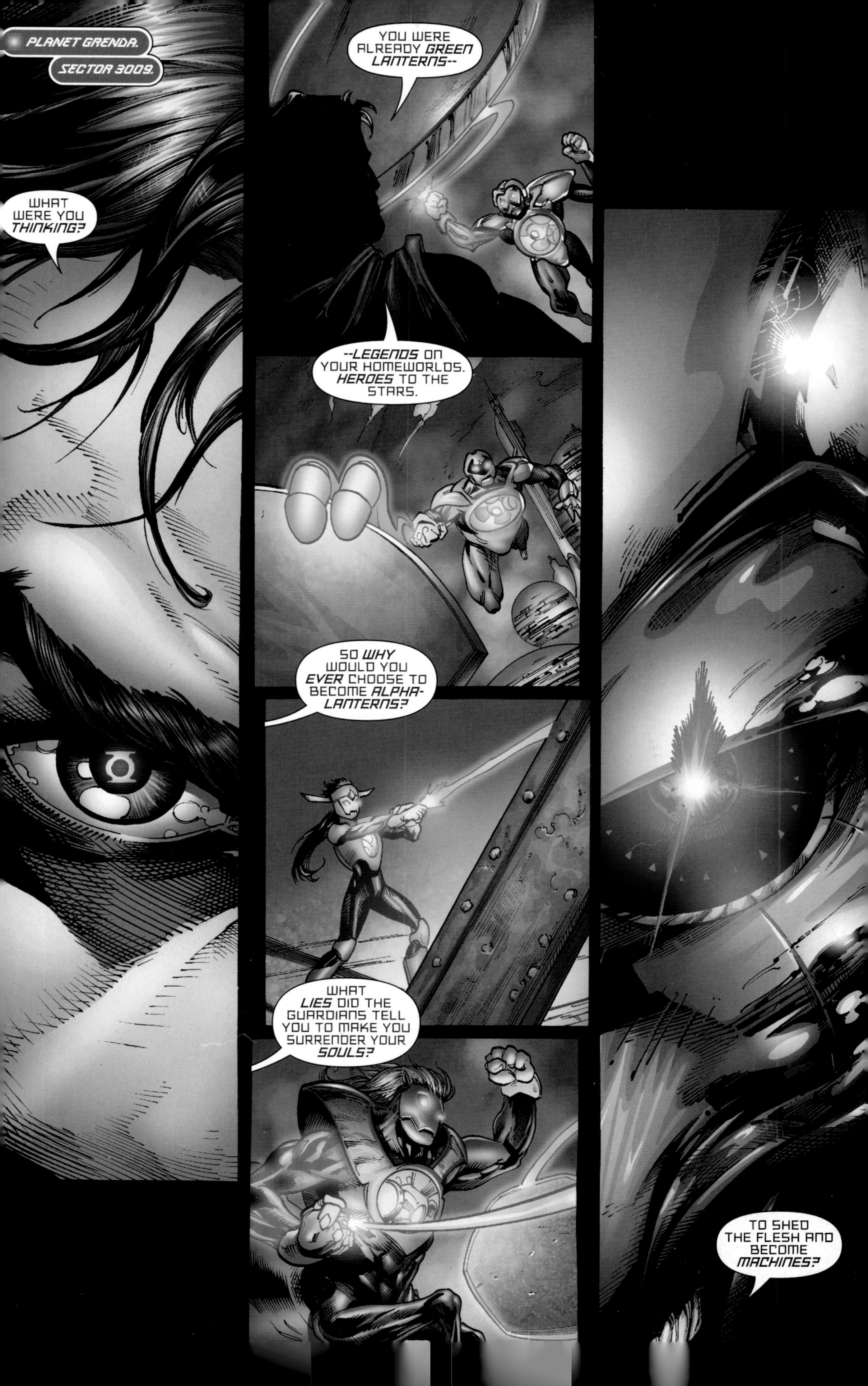
PLANET GRENDA.
SECTOR 3009.
WHAT WERE YOU THINKING?
YOU WERE ALREADY GREEN LANTERNS--
--LEGENDS ON YOUR HOMEWORLDS. HEROES TO THE STARS.
SO WHY WOULD YOU EVER CHOOSE TO BECOME ALPHA-LANTERNS?
WHAT LIES DID THE GUARDIANS TELL YOU TO MAKE YOU SURRENDER YOUR SOULS?
TO SHED THE FLESH AND BECOME MACHINES?

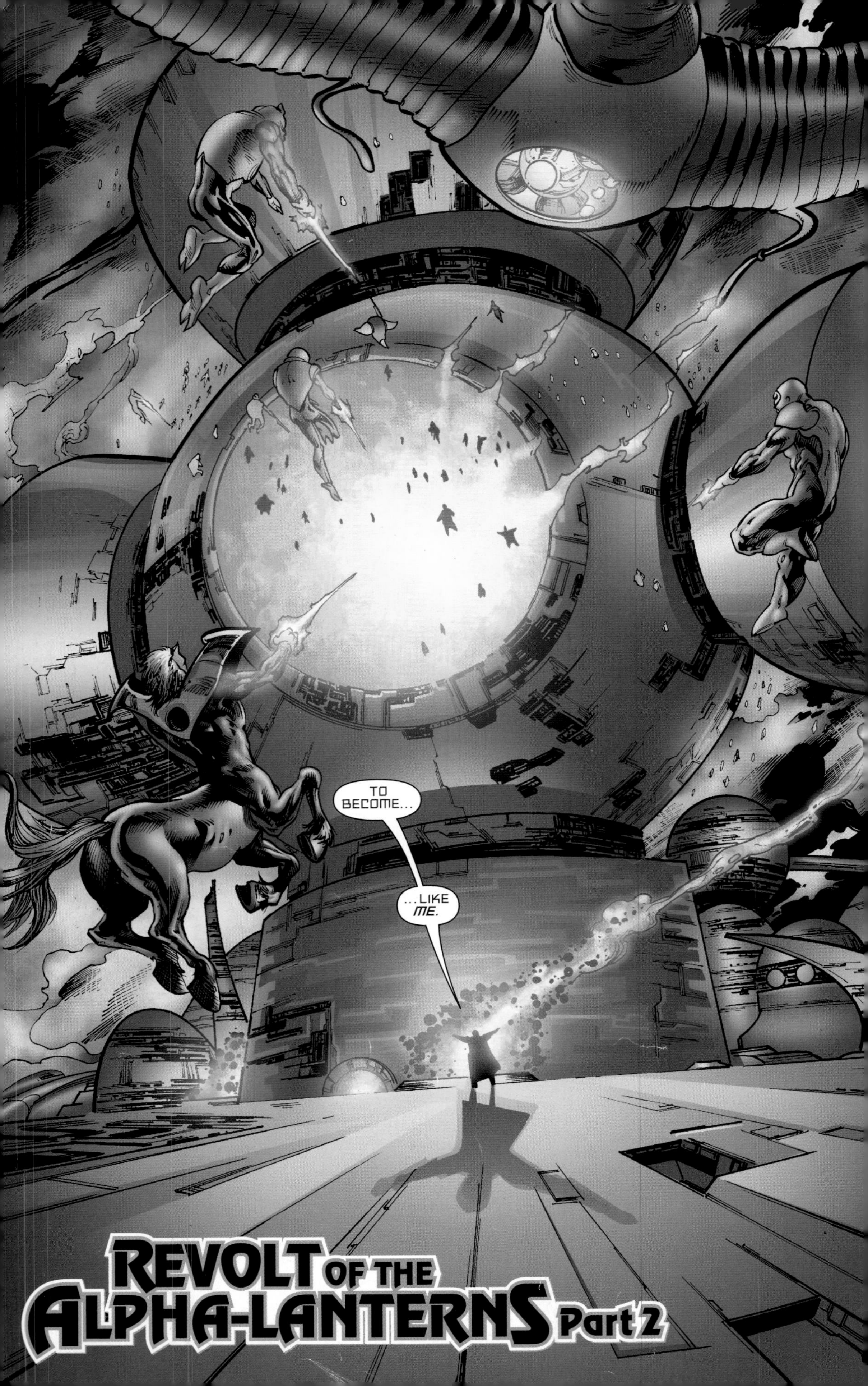
TO BECOME...
...LIKE ME.
REVOLT OF THE ALPHA-LANTERNS Part 2

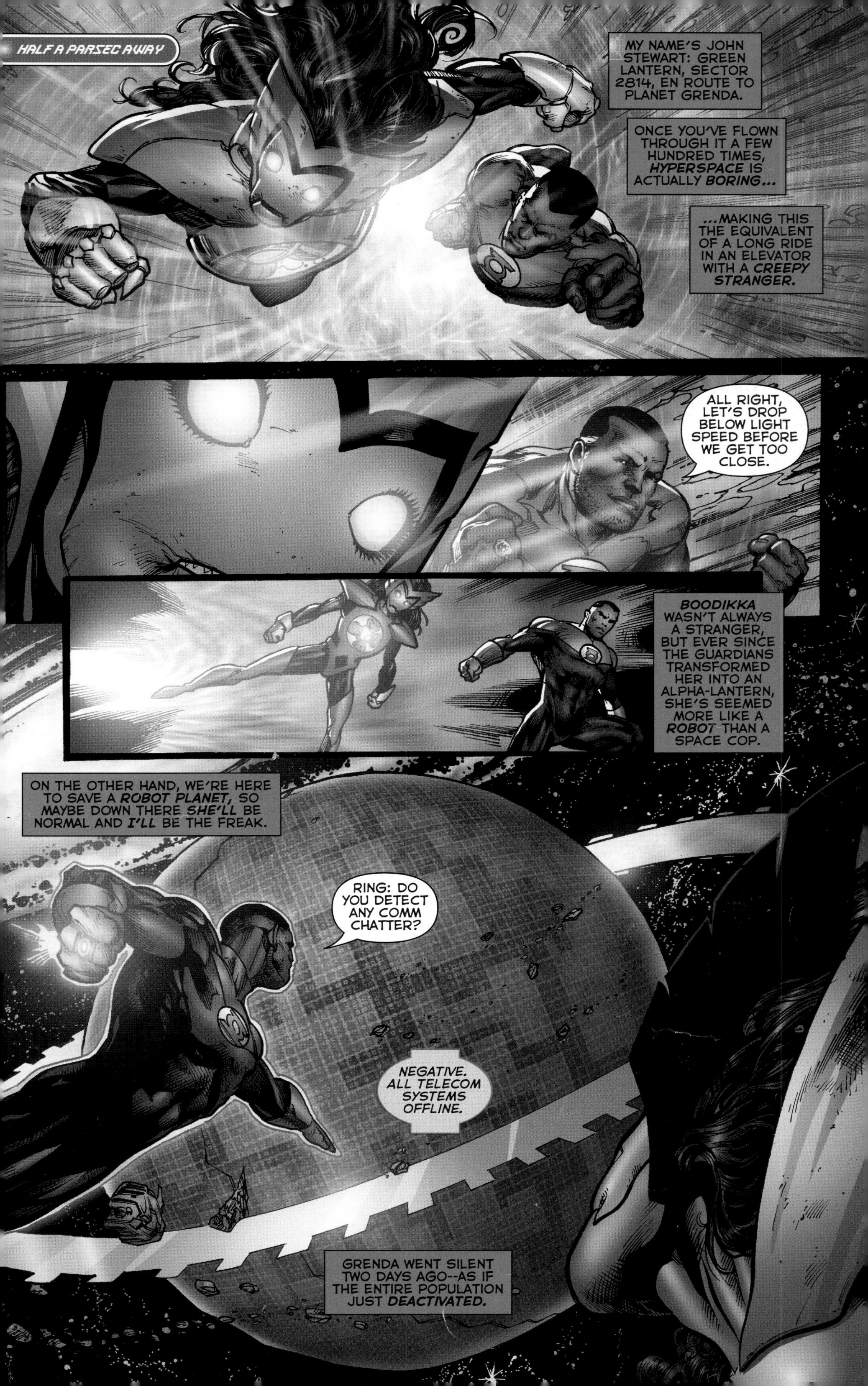
HALF A PARSEC AWAY
MY NAME'S JOHN STEWART: GREEN LANTERN, SECTOR 2814, EN ROUTE TO PLANET GRENDA.
ONCE YOU'VE FLOWN THROUGH IT A FEW HUNDRED TIMES, HYPERSPACE IS ACTUALLY BORING...
...MAKING THIS THE EQUIVALENT OF A LONG RIDE IN AN ELEVATOR WITH A CREEPY STRANGER.
ALL RIGHT, LET'S DROP BELOW LIGHT SPEED BEFORE WE GET TOO CLOSE.
BOODIKKA WASN'T ALWAYS A STRANGER, BUT EVER SINCE THE GUARDIANS TRANSFORMED HER INTO AN ALPHA-LANTERN, SHE'S SEEMED MORE LIKE A ROBOT THAN A SPACE COP.
ON THE OTHER HAND, WE'RE HERE TO SAVE A ROBOT PLANET, SO MAYBE DOWN THERE SHE'LL BE NORMAL AND I'LL BE THE FREAK.
RING: DO YOU DETECT ANY COMM CHATTER?
NEGATIVE. ALL TELECOM SYSTEMS OFFLINE.
GRENDA WENT SILENT TWO DAYS AGO--AS IF THE ENTIRE POPULATION JUST DEACTIVATED.

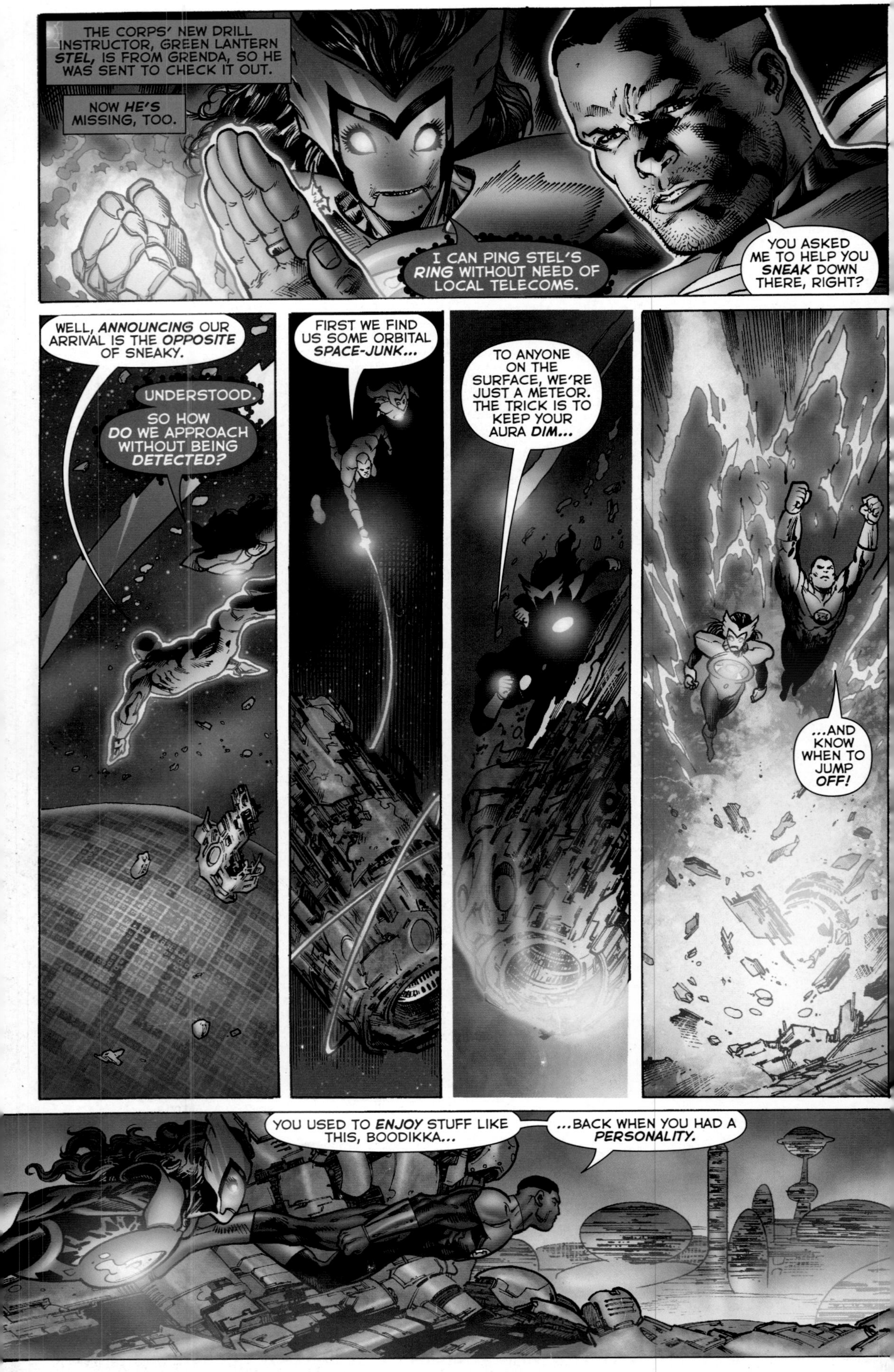
THE CORPS' NEW DRILL INSTRUCTOR, GREEN LANTERN STEL, IS FROM GRENDA, SO HE WAS SENT TO CHECK IT OUT.
NOW HE'S MISSING, TOO.
I CAN PING STEL'S RING WITHOUT NEED OF LOCAL TELECOMS.
YOU ASKED ME TO HELP YOU SNEAK DOWN THERE, RIGHT?
WELL, ANNOUNCING OUR ARRIVAL IS THE OPPOSITE OF SNEAKY.
UNDERSTOOD.
SO HOW DO WE APPROACH WITHOUT BEING DETECTED?
FIRST WE FIND US SOME ORBITAL SPACE-JUNK...
TO ANYONE ON THE SURFACE, WE'RE JUST A METEOR. THE TRICK IS TO KEEP YOUR AURA DIM...
...AND KNOW WHEN TO JUMP OFF!
YOU USED TO ENJOY STUFF LIKE THIS, BOODIKKA...
...BACK WHEN YOU HAD A PERSONALITY.

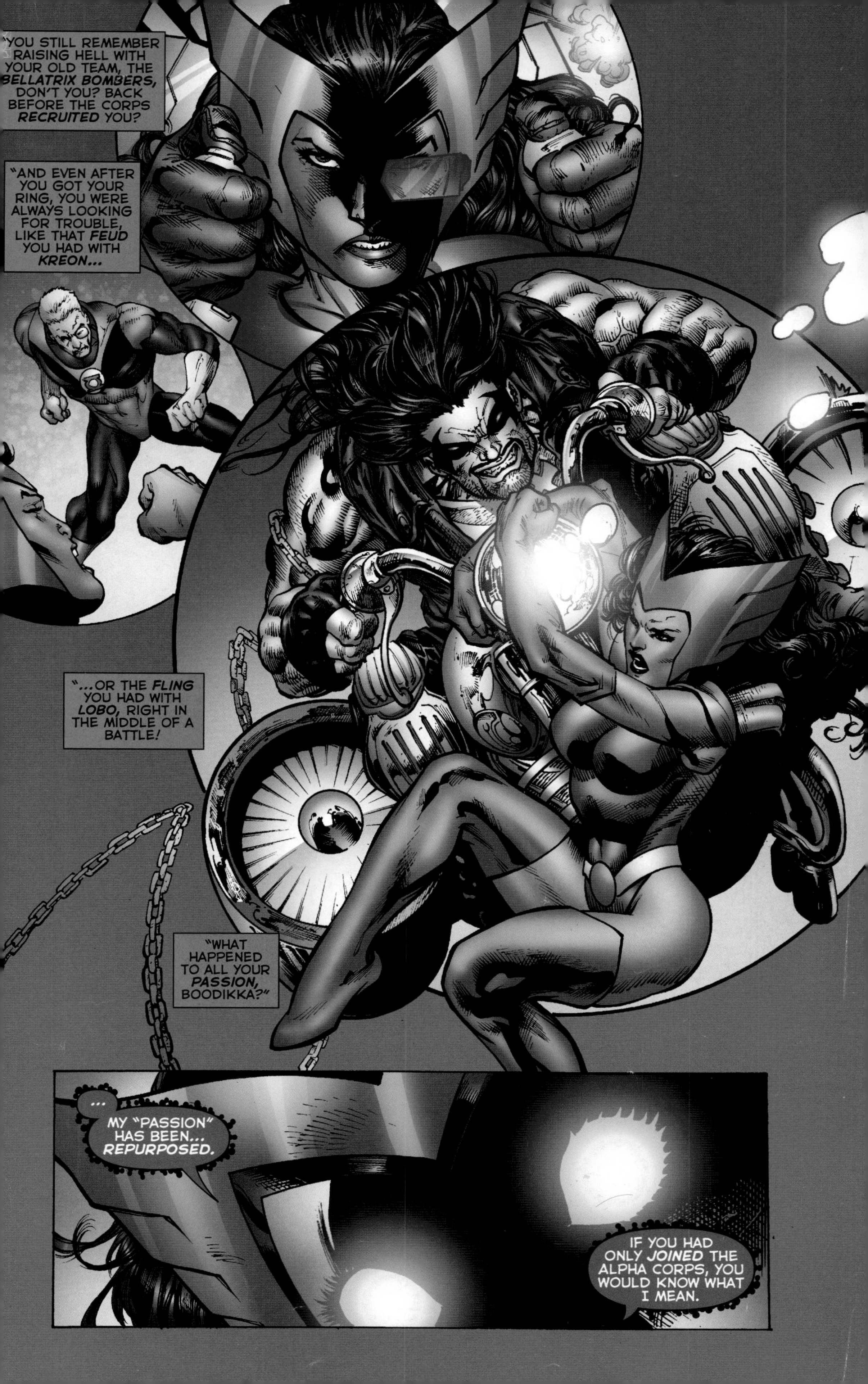

YOU STILL REMEMBER RAISING HELL WITH YOUR OLD TEAM, THE *BELLATRIX BOMBERS,* DON'T YOU? BACK BEFORE THE CORPS *RECRUITED* YOU?
"AND EVEN AFTER YOU GOT YOUR RING, YOU WERE ALWAYS LOOKING FOR TROUBLE, LIKE THAT *FEUD* YOU HAD WITH *KREON*...
"...OR THE *FLING* YOU HAD WITH *LOBO,* RIGHT IN THE MIDDLE OF A BATTLE!
"WHAT HAPPENED TO ALL YOUR *PASSION,* BOODIKKA?"
... MY "PASSION" HAS BEEN... *REPURPOSED.*
IF YOU HAD ONLY *JOINED* THE ALPHA CORPS, YOU WOULD KNOW WHAT I MEAN.

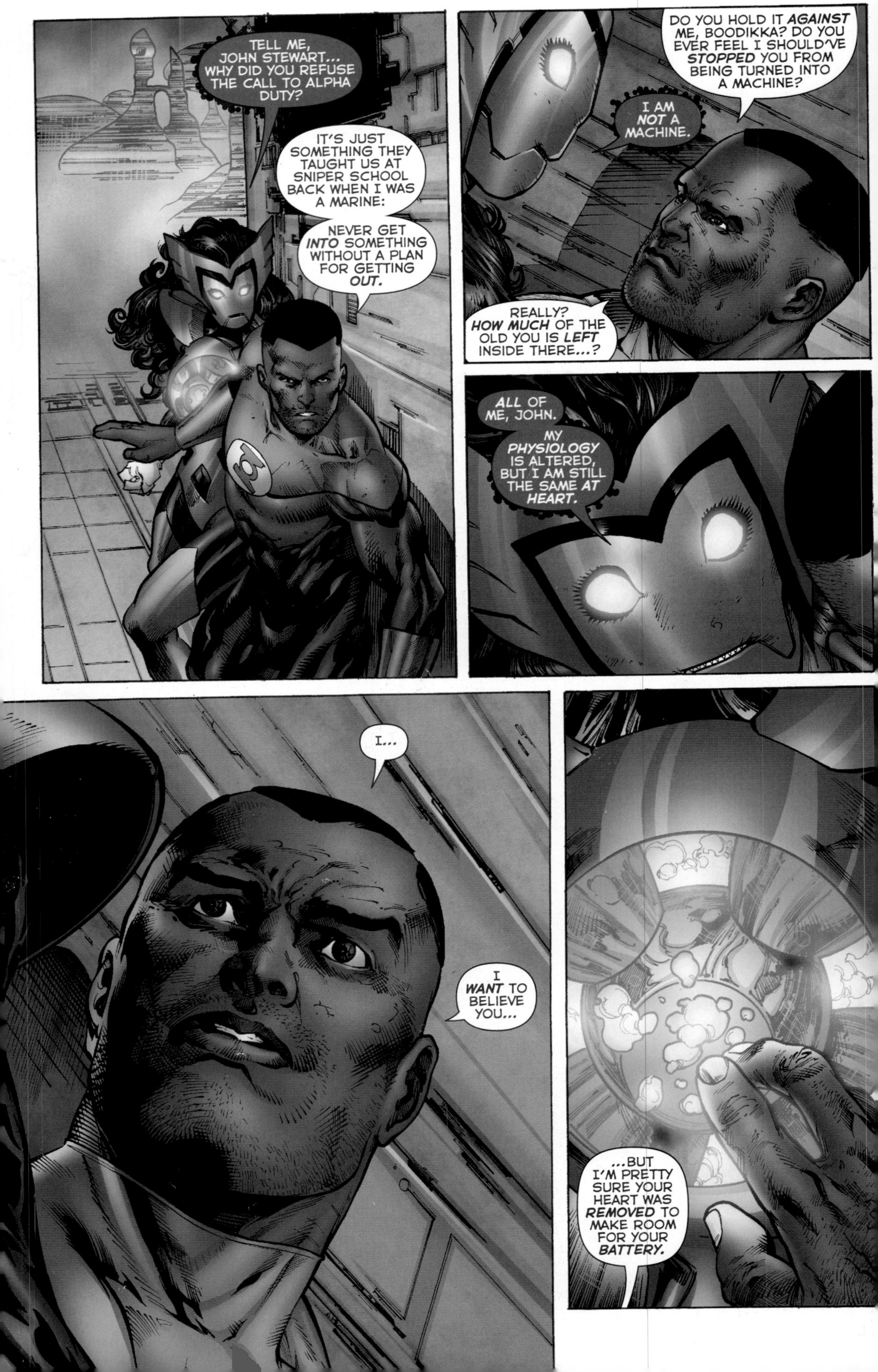
TELL ME, JOHN STEWART... WHY DID YOU REFUSE THE CALL TO ALPHA DUTY?
IT'S JUST SOMETHING THEY TAUGHT US AT SNIPER SCHOOL BACK WHEN I WAS A MARINE:
NEVER GET INTO SOMETHING WITHOUT A PLAN FOR GETTING OUT.
DO YOU HOLD IT AGAINST ME, BOODIKKA? DO YOU EVER FEEL I SHOULD'VE STOPPED YOU FROM BEING TURNED INTO A MACHINE?
I AM NOT A MACHINE.
REALLY? HOW MUCH OF THE OLD YOU IS LEFT INSIDE THERE...?
ALL OF ME, JOHN.
MY PHYSIOLOGY IS ALTERED, BUT I AM STILL THE SAME AT HEART.
I...
I WANT TO BELIEVE YOU...
...BUT I'M PRETTY SURE YOUR HEART WAS REMOVED TO MAKE ROOM FOR YOUR BATTERY.

O-KAY, *THAT* LOOKS NEW. IS IT A *SECTOR HOUSE?*

IF SO, IT IS *NOT SANCTIONED* BY THE GUARDIANS.

WE'LL GO IN THROUGH THE SEWERS. *NO TALKING* FROM HERE ON IN...

HOW CAN SHE INSIST SHE'S STILL *HERSELF?*

AND HER PASSION'S BEEN *REPURPOSED?* WHAT THE HELL DID SHE *MEAN* BY THAT?!

THE MINUTE WE RESCUE THE GRENDANS, I'M GONNA HAVE A WORD WITH OUR BLUE BOSSES ABOUT THEIR WHOLE ALPHA-LANTERN *PLAN.*

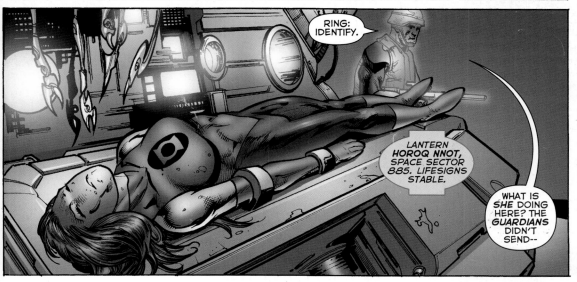

RING: IDENTIFY.

LANTERN *HOROQ NNOT,* SPACE SECTOR 885. LIFESIGNS STABLE.

WHAT IS *SHE* DOING HERE? THE *GUARDIANS* DIDN'T SEND--

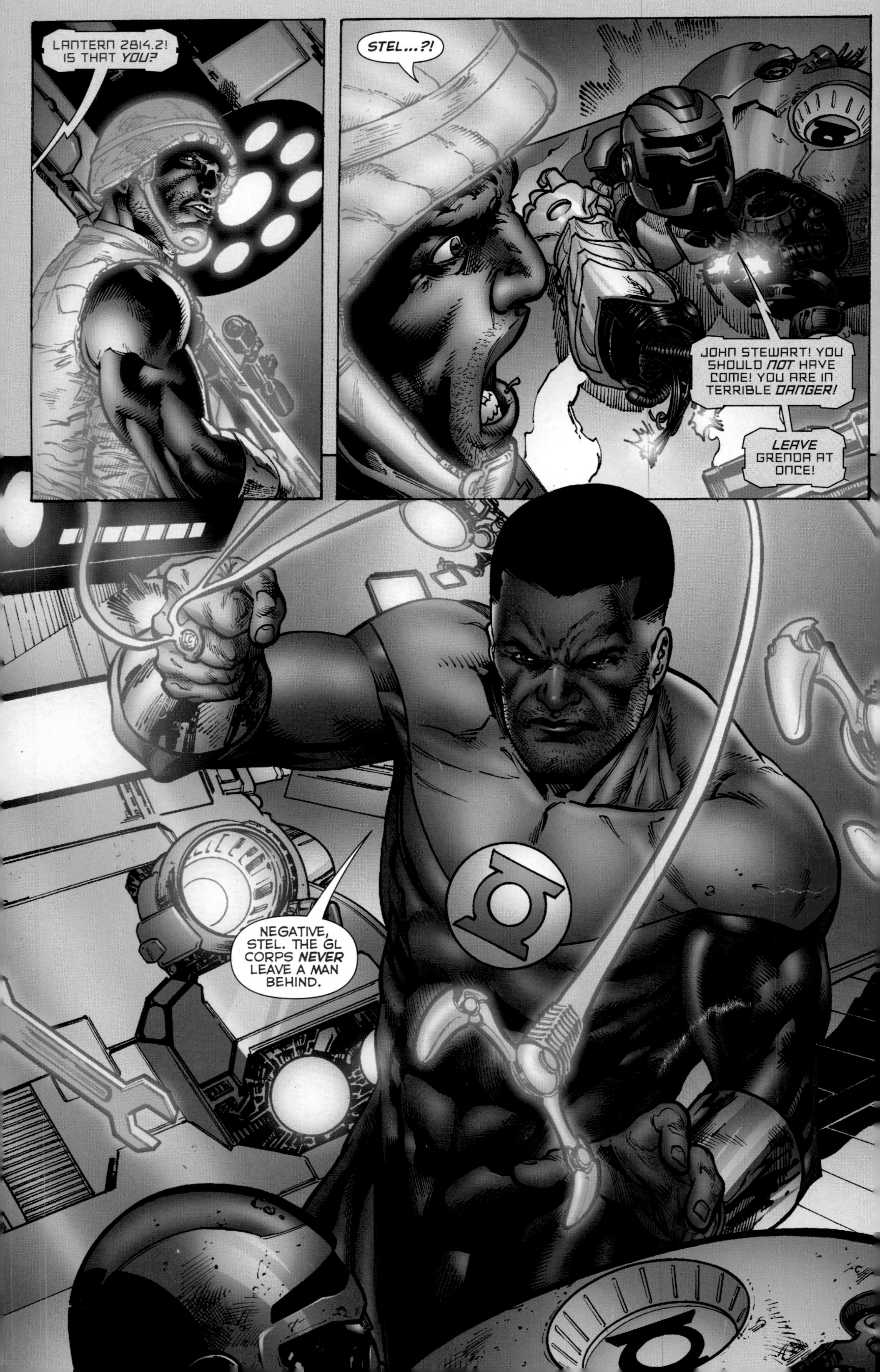
LANTERN 2814.2! IS THAT *YOU?*
STEL...?!
JOHN STEWART! YOU SHOULD *NOT* HAVE COME! YOU ARE IN TERRIBLE *DANGER!*
LEAVE GRENDA AT ONCE!
NEGATIVE, STEL. THE GL CORPS *NEVER* LEAVE A MAN BEHIND.

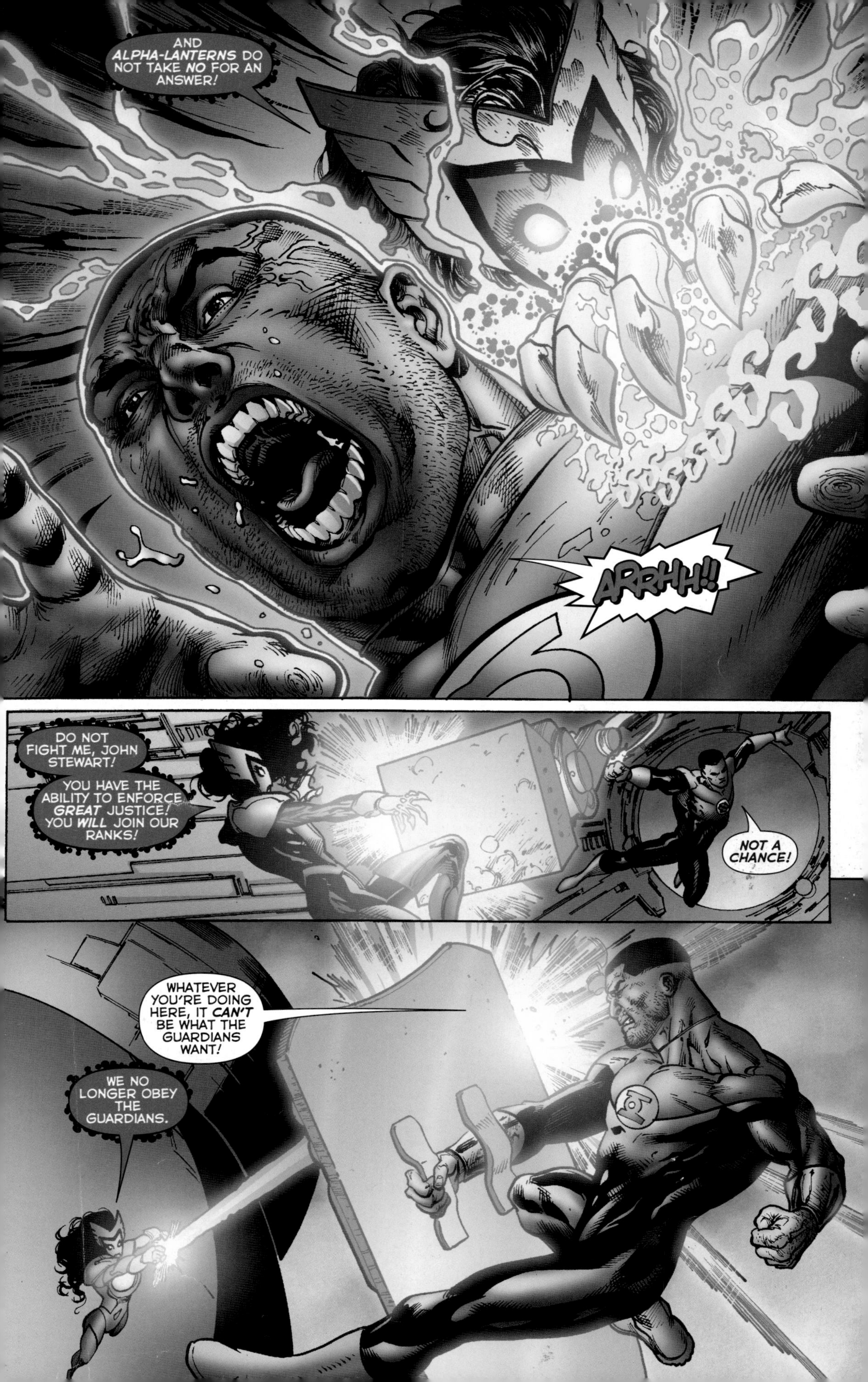
AND *ALPHA-LANTERNS* DO NOT TAKE *NO* FOR AN ANSWER!
ARRHH!!
DO NOT FIGHT ME, JOHN STEWART!
YOU HAVE THE ABILITY TO ENFORCE *GREAT* JUSTICE! YOU *WILL* JOIN OUR RANKS!
NOT A CHANCE!
WHATEVER YOU'RE DOING HERE, IT *CAN'T* BE WHAT THE GUARDIANS WANT!
WE NO LONGER OBEY THE GUARDIANS.

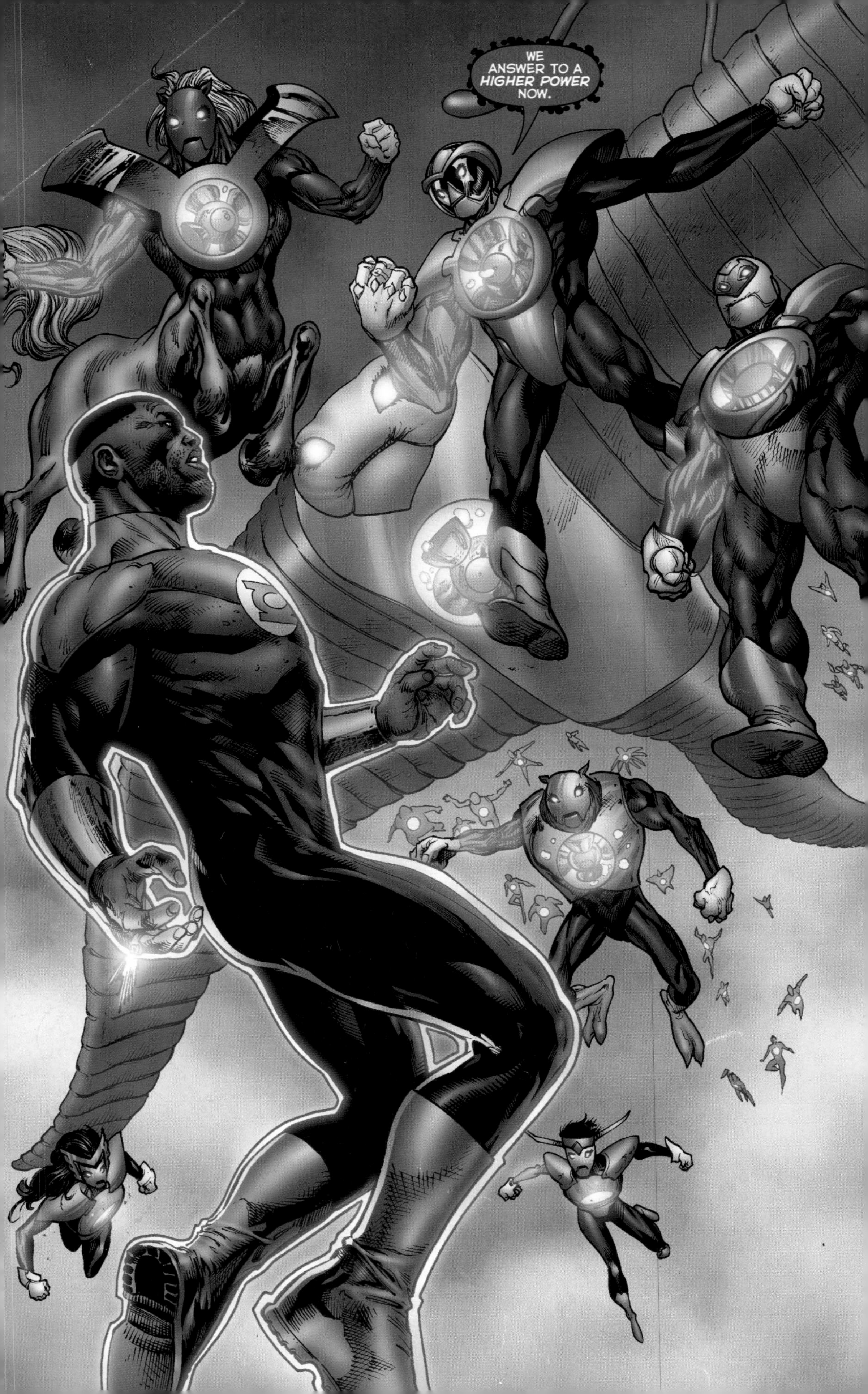
WE ANSWER TO A *HIGHER POWER* NOW.

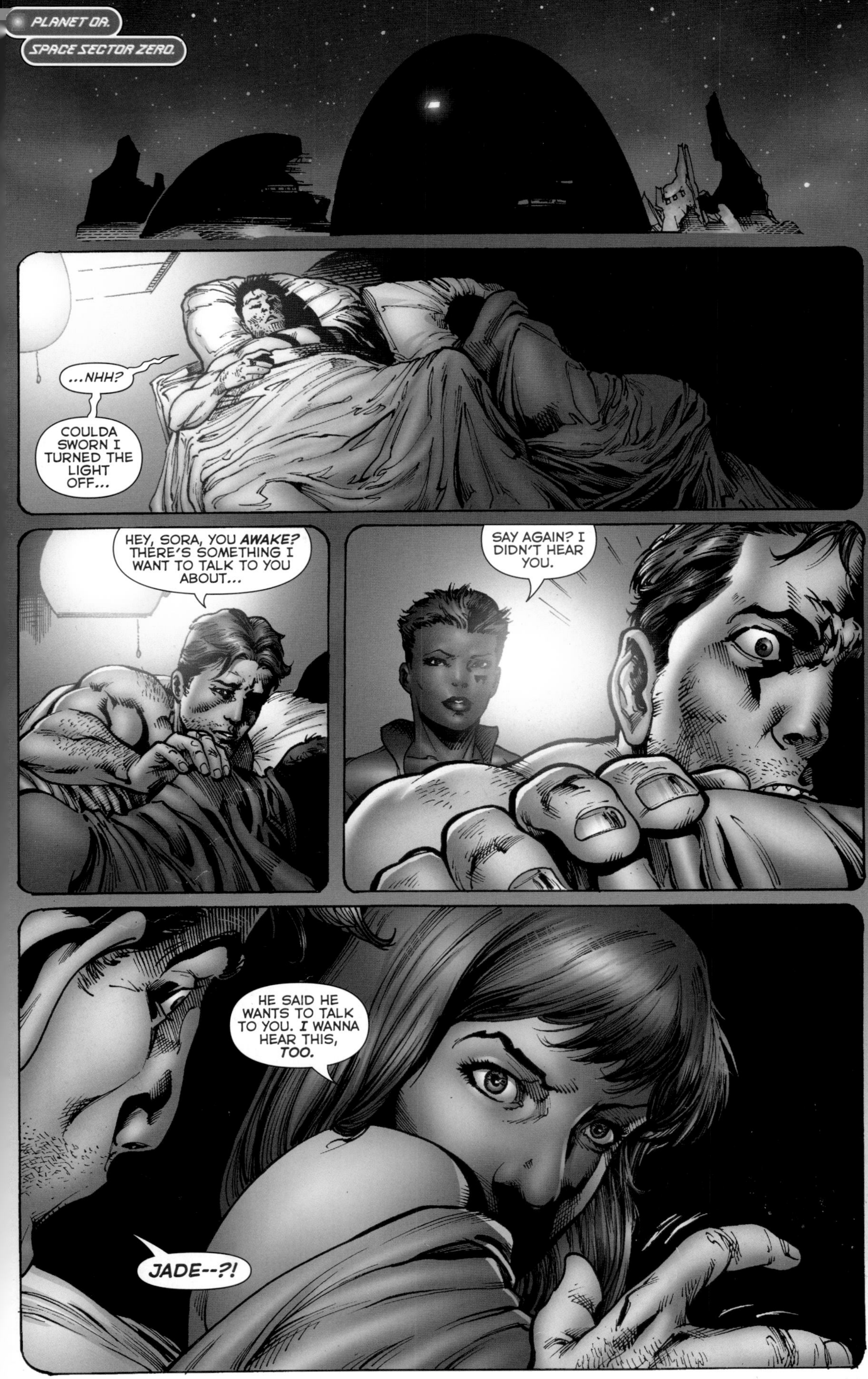
PLANET OA.
SPACE SECTOR ZERO.
...NHH?
COULDA SWORN I TURNED THE LIGHT OFF...
HEY, SORA, YOU AWAKE? THERE'S SOMETHING I WANT TO TALK TO YOU ABOUT...
SAY AGAIN? I DIDN'T HEAR YOU.
HE SAID HE WANTS TO TALK TO YOU. I WANNA HEAR THIS, TOO.
JADE--?!

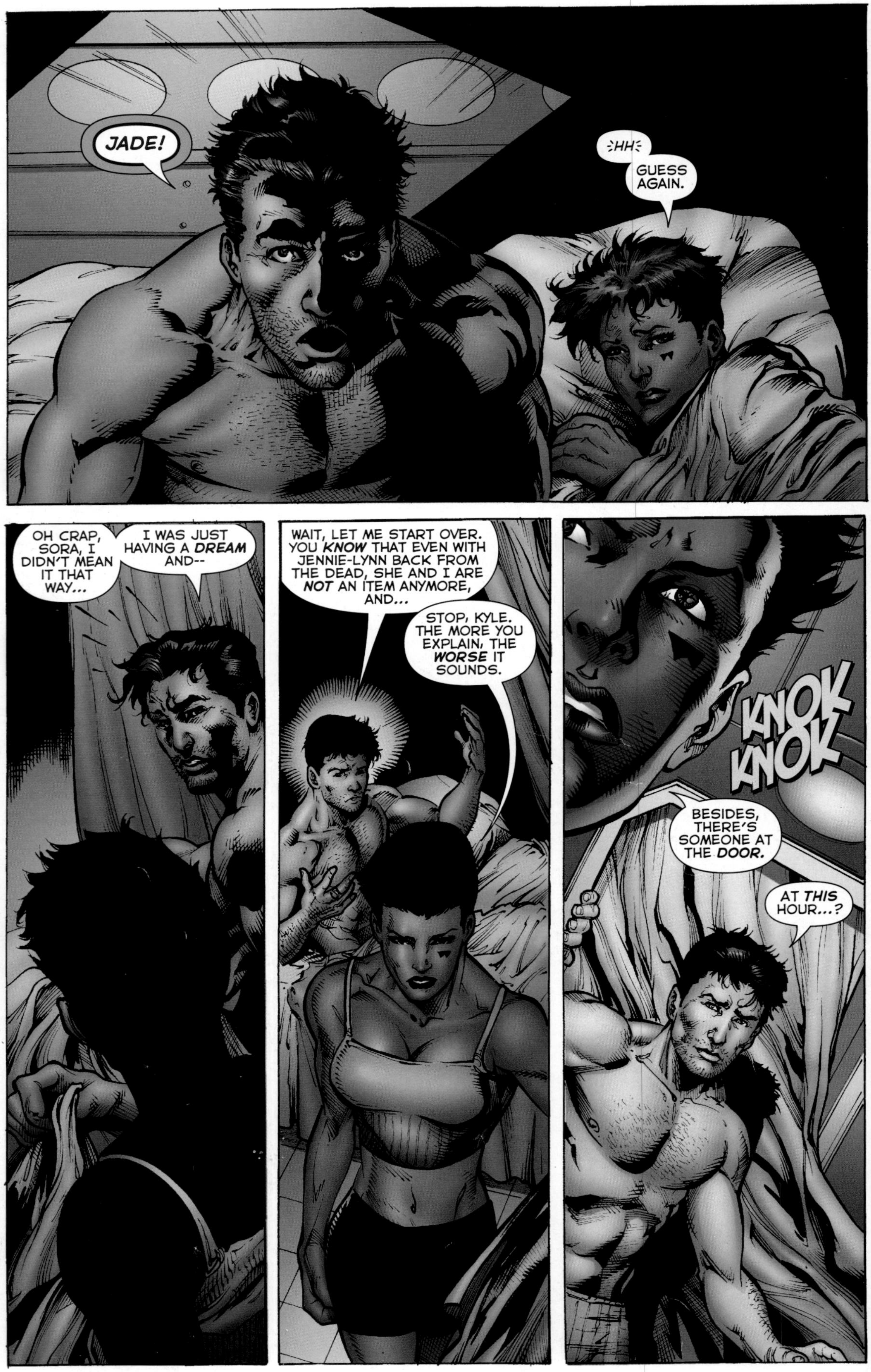
JADE!
HH
GUESS AGAIN.
OH CRAP, SORA, I DIDN'T MEAN IT THAT WAY...
I WAS JUST HAVING A DREAM AND--
WAIT, LET ME START OVER. YOU KNOW THAT EVEN WITH JENNIE-LYNN BACK FROM THE DEAD, SHE AND I ARE NOT AN ITEM ANYMORE, AND...
STOP, KYLE. THE MORE YOU EXPLAIN, THE WORSE IT SOUNDS.
KNOK KNOK
BESIDES, THERE'S SOMEONE AT THE DOOR.
AT THIS HOUR...?

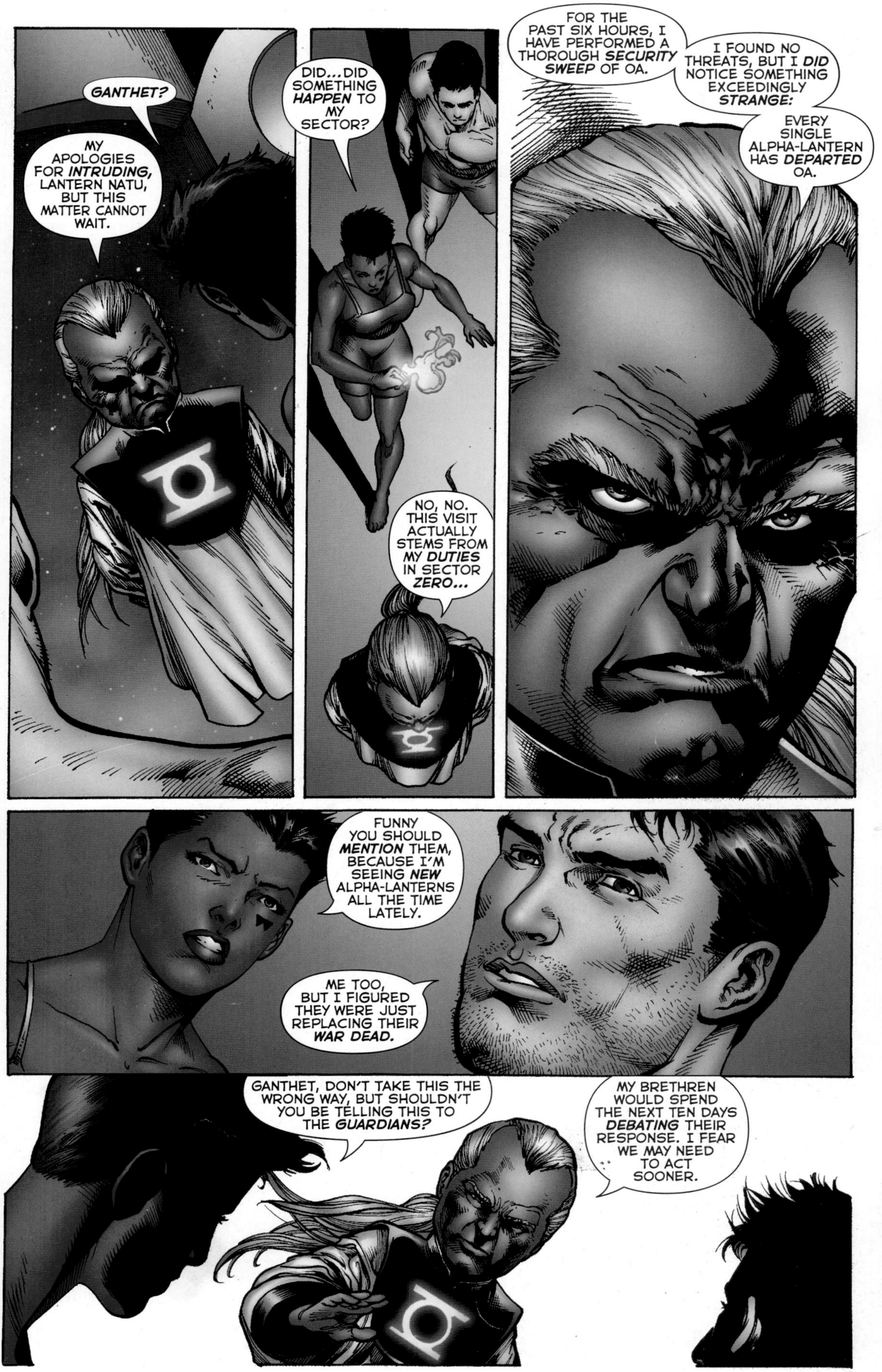
GANTHET?
MY APOLOGIES FOR INTRUDING, LANTERN NATU, BUT THIS MATTER CANNOT WAIT.
DID...DID SOMETHING HAPPEN TO MY SECTOR?
NO, NO. THIS VISIT ACTUALLY STEMS FROM MY DUTIES IN SECTOR ZERO...
FOR THE PAST SIX HOURS, I HAVE PERFORMED A THOROUGH SECURITY SWEEP OF OA.
I FOUND NO THREATS, BUT I DID NOTICE SOMETHING EXCEEDINGLY STRANGE:
EVERY SINGLE ALPHA-LANTERN HAS DEPARTED OA.
FUNNY YOU SHOULD MENTION THEM, BECAUSE I'M SEEING NEW ALPHA-LANTERNS ALL THE TIME LATELY.
ME TOO, BUT I FIGURED THEY WERE JUST REPLACING THEIR WAR DEAD.
GANTHET, DON'T TAKE THIS THE WRONG WAY, BUT SHOULDN'T YOU BE TELLING THIS TO THE GUARDIANS?
MY BRETHREN WOULD SPEND THE NEXT TEN DAYS DEBATING THEIR RESPONSE. I FEAR WE MAY NEED TO ACT SOONER.

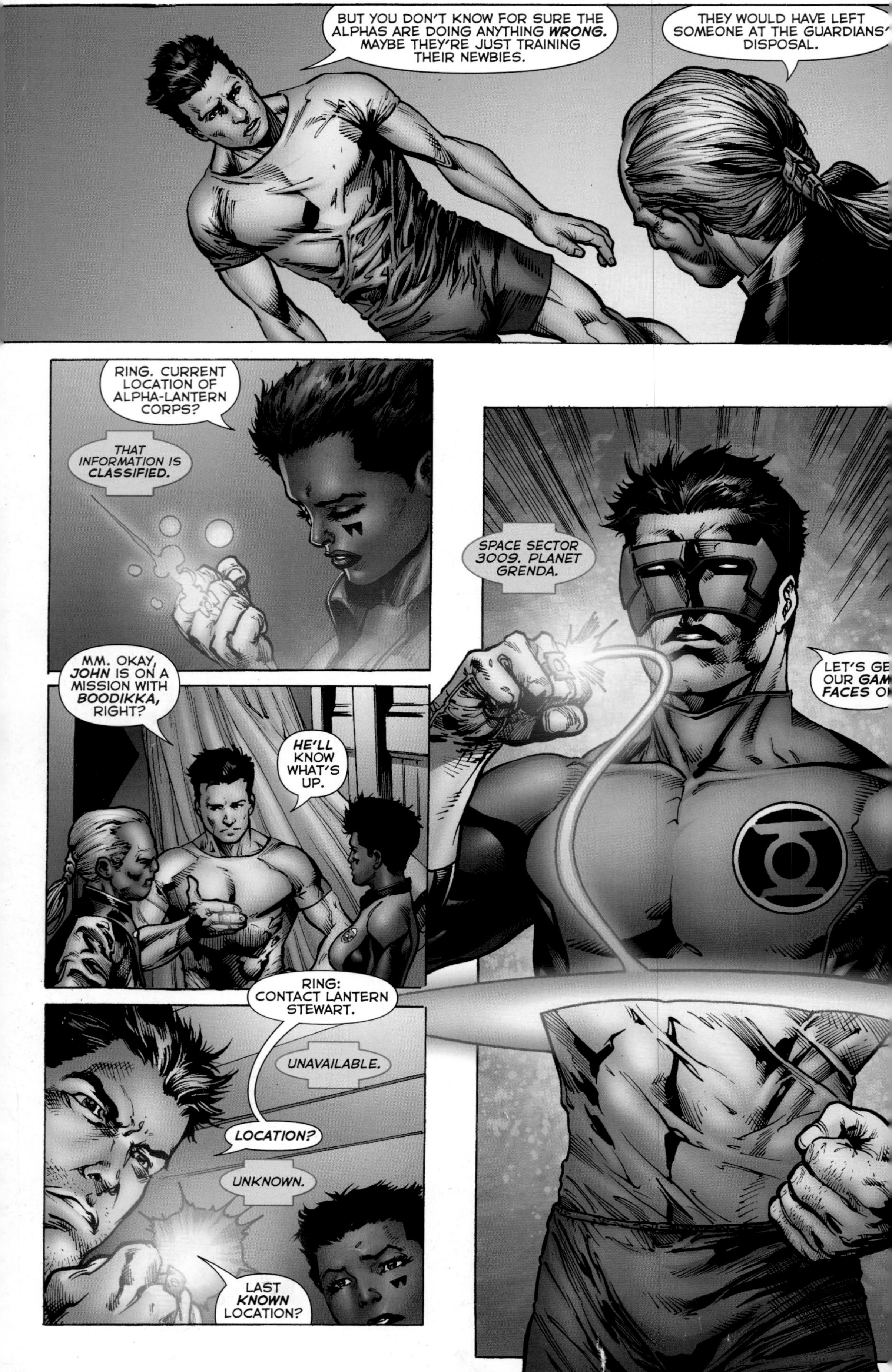
BUT YOU DON'T KNOW FOR SURE THE ALPHAS ARE DOING ANYTHING ***WRONG.*** MAYBE THEY'RE JUST TRAINING THEIR NEWBIES.
THEY WOULD HAVE LEFT SOMEONE AT THE GUARDIANS' DISPOSAL.
RING. CURRENT LOCATION OF ALPHA-LANTERN CORPS?
THAT INFORMATION IS ***CLASSIFIED.***
SPACE SECTOR 3009. PLANET GRENDA.
MM. OKAY, ***JOHN*** IS ON A MISSION WITH ***BOODIKKA,*** RIGHT?
HE'LL KNOW WHAT'S UP.
RING: CONTACT LANTERN STEWART.
UNAVAILABLE.
LOCATION?
UNKNOWN.
LAST ***KNOWN*** LOCATION?
LET'S GE
OUR ***GAM***
FACES O

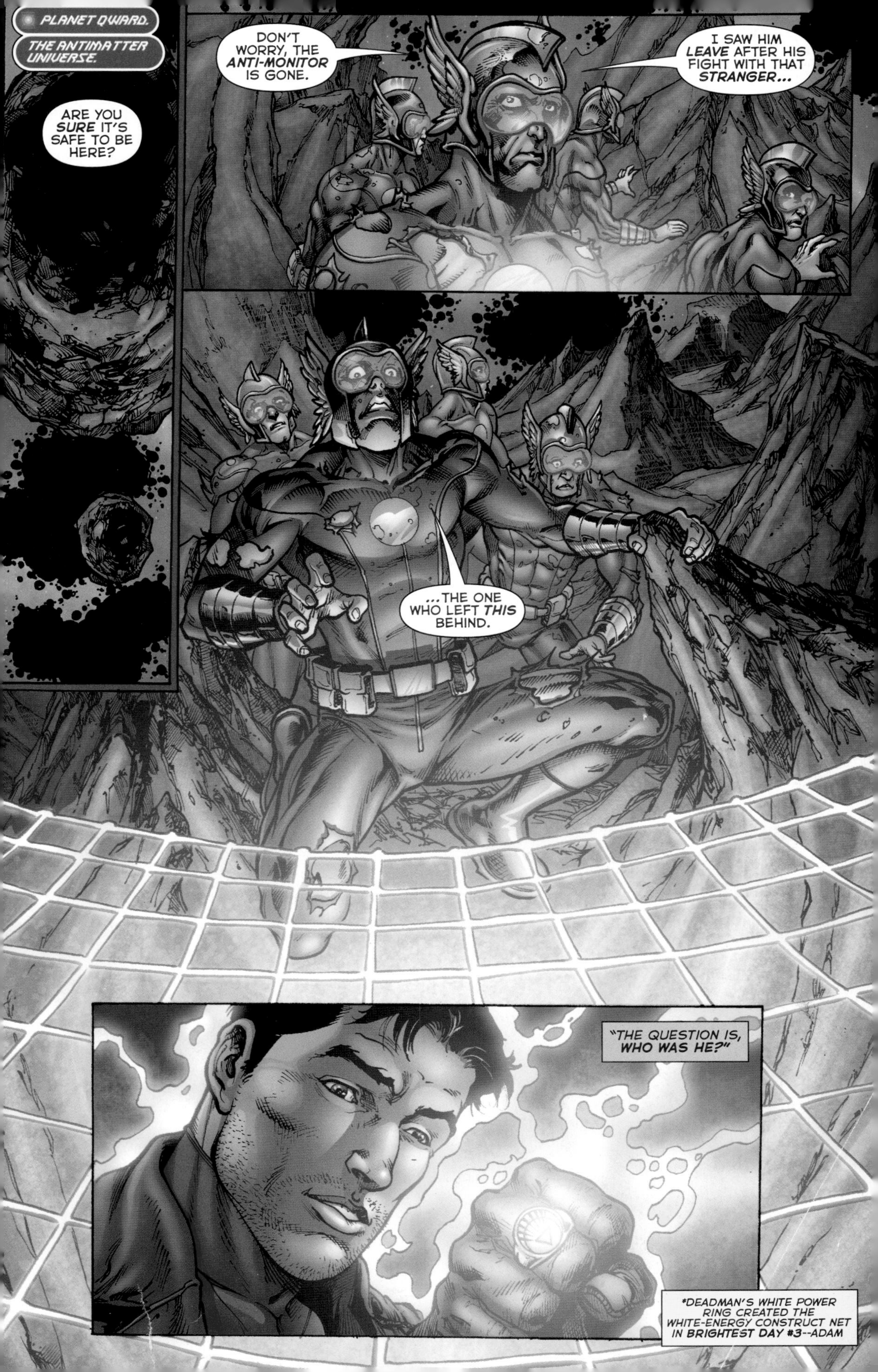
PLANET QWARD.
THE ANTIMATTER UNIVERSE.
ARE YOU SURE IT'S SAFE TO BE HERE?
DON'T WORRY, THE ANTI-MONITOR IS GONE.
I SAW HIM LEAVE AFTER HIS FIGHT WITH THAT STRANGER...
...THE ONE WHO LEFT THIS BEHIND.
"THE QUESTION IS, WHO WAS HE?"
*DEADMAN'S WHITE POWER RING CREATED THE WHITE-ENERGY CONSTRUCT NET IN BRIGHTEST DAY #3--ADAM

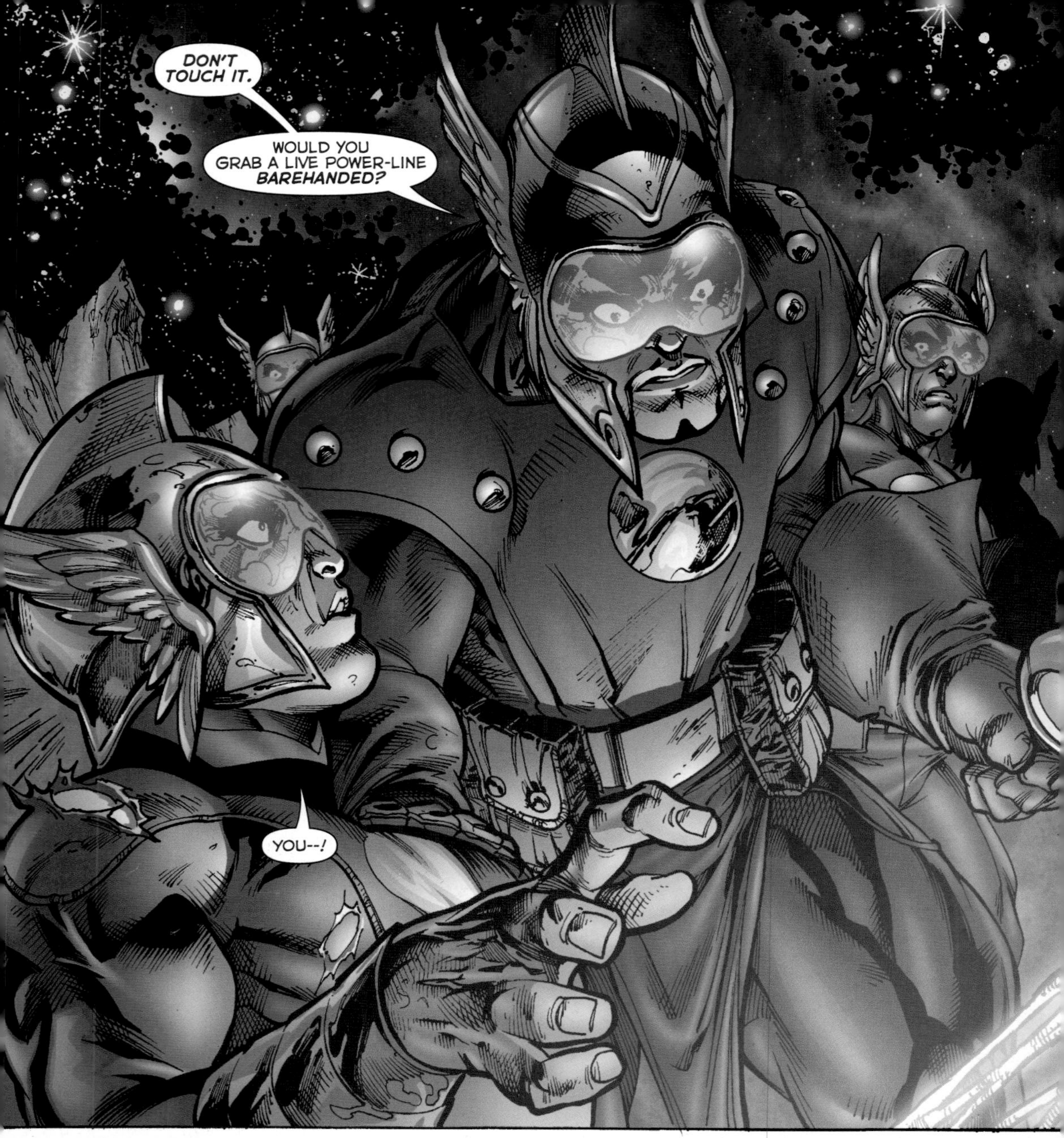
DON'T TOUCH IT.
WOULD YOU GRAB A LIVE POWER-LINE BAREHANDED?
YOU--!

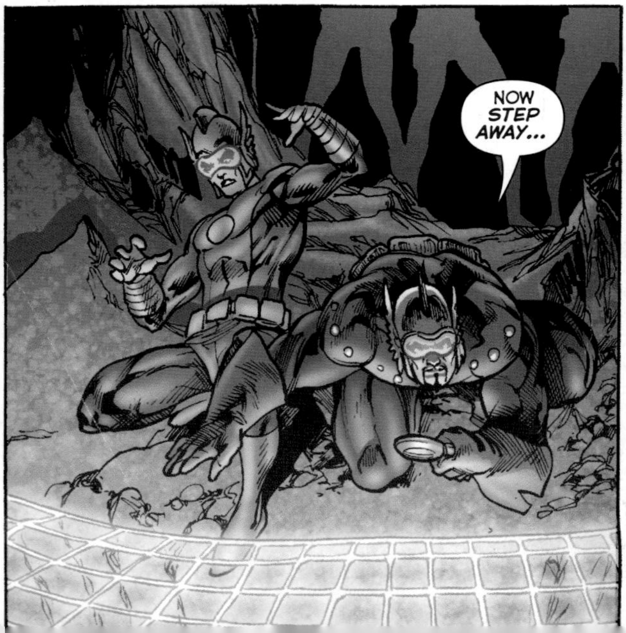
NOW STEP AWAY...

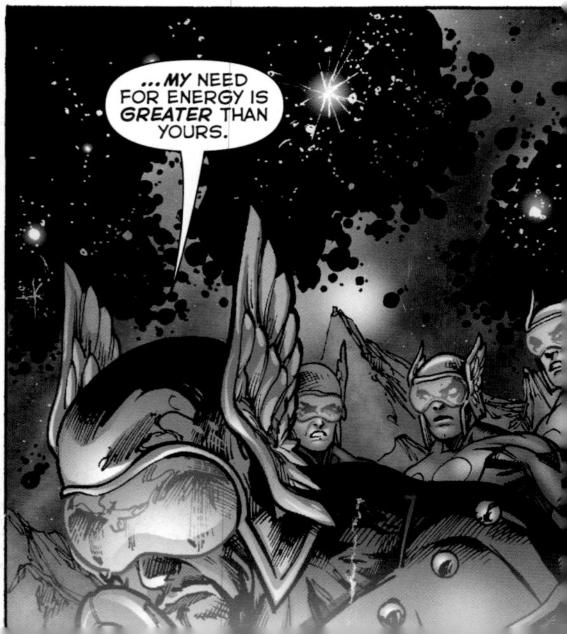
...MY NEED FOR ENERGY IS GREATER THAN YOURS.

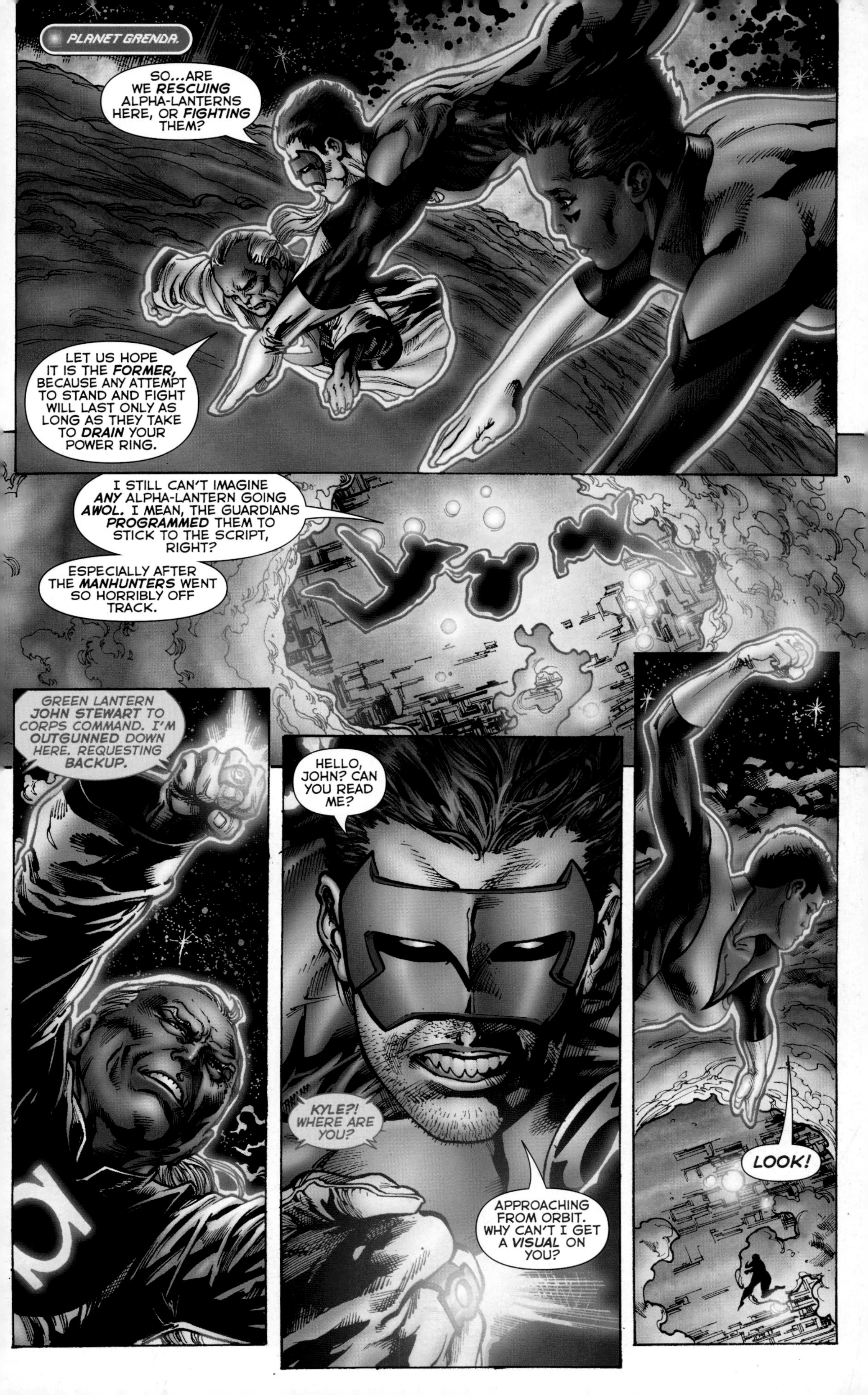
PLANET GRENDA.
SO...ARE WE RESCUING ALPHA-LANTERNS HERE, OR FIGHTING THEM?
LET US HOPE IT IS THE FORMER, BECAUSE ANY ATTEMPT TO STAND AND FIGHT WILL LAST ONLY AS LONG AS THEY TAKE TO DRAIN YOUR POWER RING.
I STILL CAN'T IMAGINE ANY ALPHA-LANTERN GOING AWOL. I MEAN, THE GUARDIANS PROGRAMMED THEM TO STICK TO THE SCRIPT, RIGHT?
ESPECIALLY AFTER THE MANHUNTERS WENT SO HORRIBLY OFF TRACK.
GREEN LANTERN JOHN STEWART TO CORPS COMMAND. I'M OUTGUNNED DOWN HERE. REQUESTING BACKUP.
HELLO, JOHN? CAN YOU READ ME?
KYLE?! WHERE ARE YOU?
APPROACHING FROM ORBIT. WHY CAN'T I GET A VISUAL ON YOU?
LOOK!

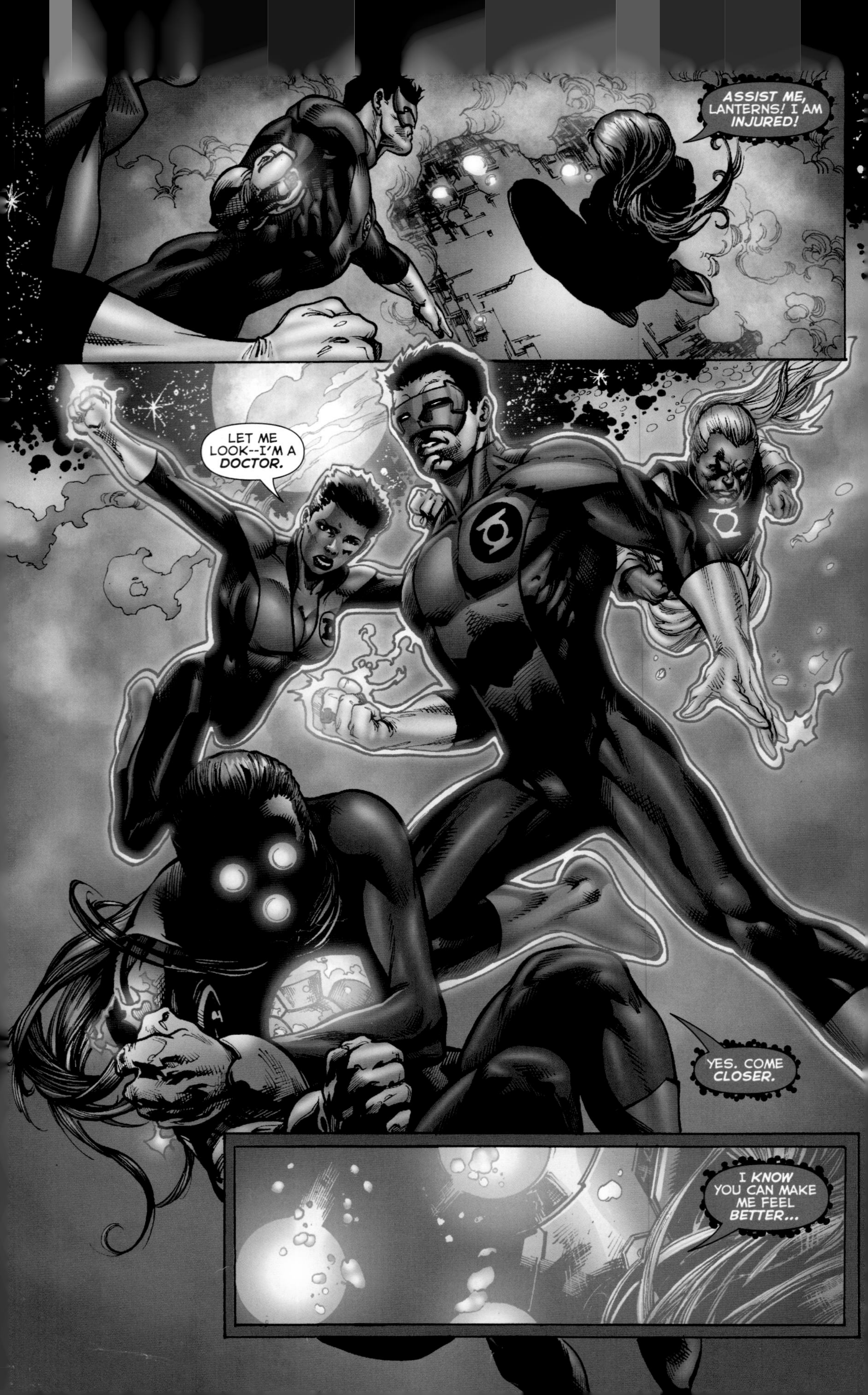
ASSIST ME, LANTERNS! I AM INJURED!
LET ME LOOK--I'M A DOCTOR.
YES. COME CLOSER.
I KNOW YOU CAN MAKE ME FEEL BETTER...

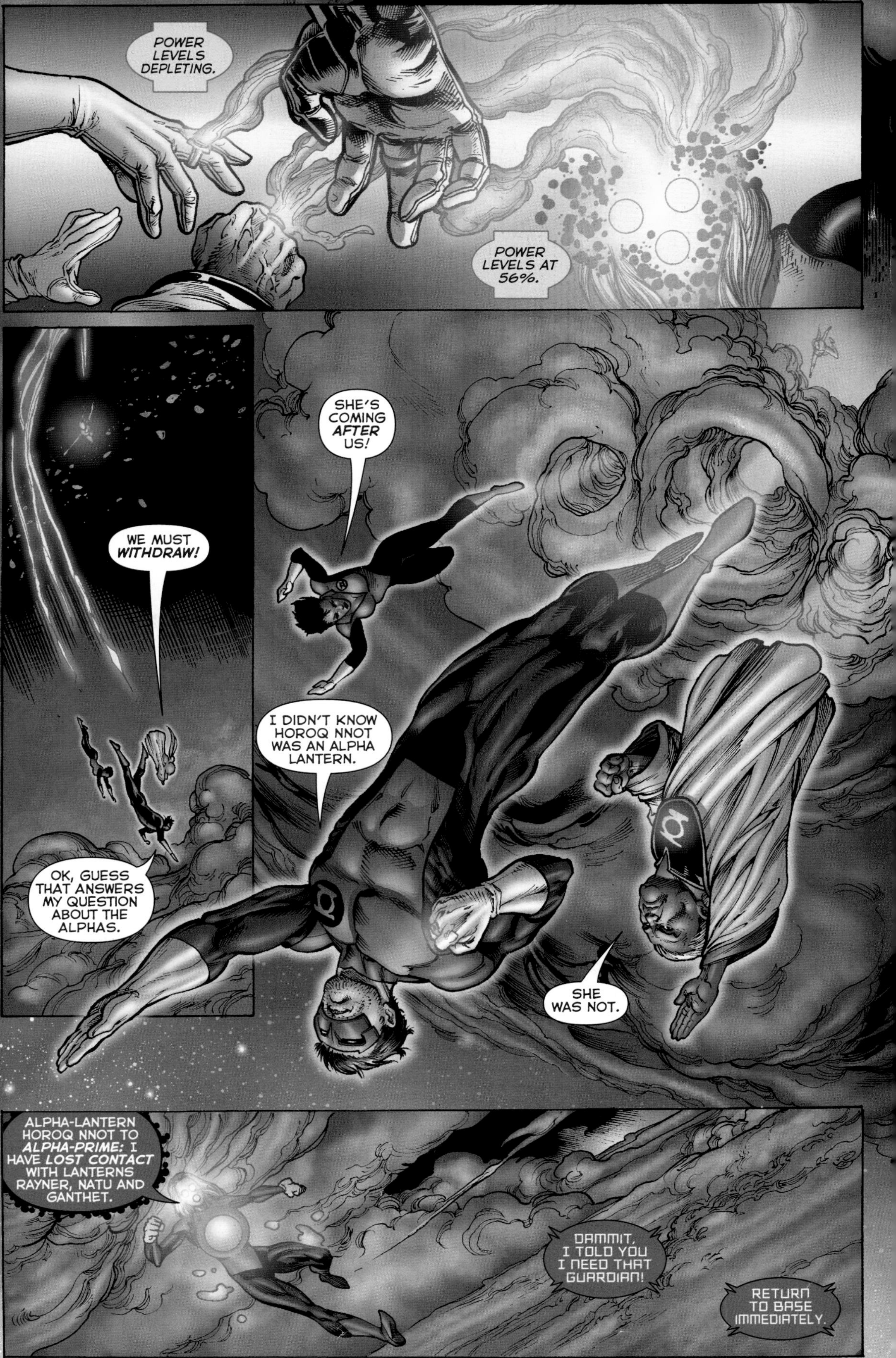
POWER LEVELS DEPLETING.
POWER LEVELS AT 56%.
WE MUST WITHDRAW!
SHE'S COMING AFTER US!
I DIDN'T KNOW HOROQ NNOT WAS AN ALPHA LANTERN.
OK, GUESS THAT ANSWERS MY QUESTION ABOUT THE ALPHAS.
SHE WAS NOT.
ALPHA-LANTERN HOROQ NNOT TO ALPHA-PRIME: I HAVE LOST CONTACT WITH LANTERNS RAYNER, NATU AND GANTHET.
DAMMIT, I TOLD YOU I NEED THAT GUARDIAN!
RETURN TO BASE IMMEDIATELY.

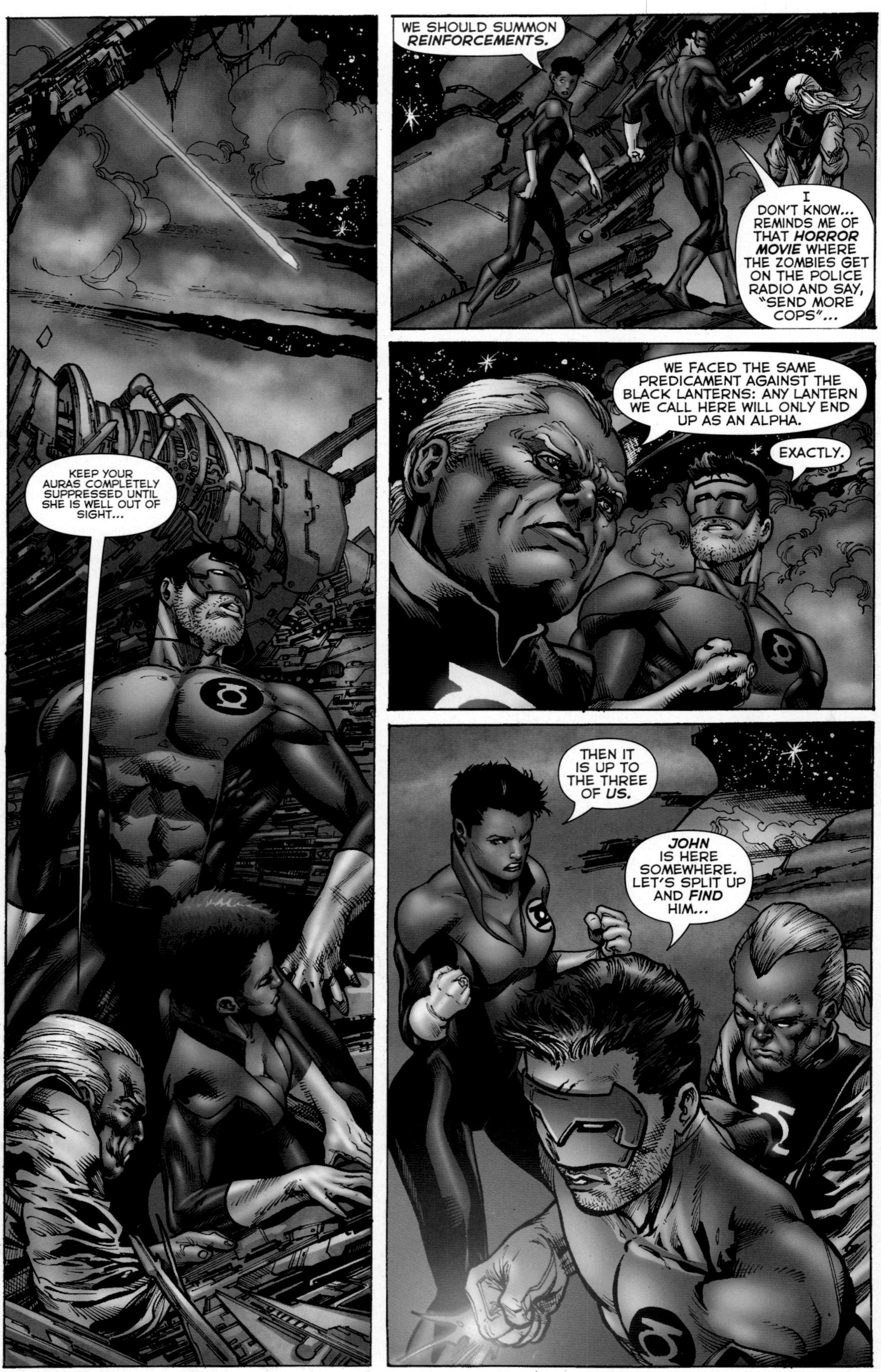
KEEP YOUR AURAS COMPLETELY SUPPRESSED UNTIL SHE IS WELL OUT OF SIGHT...
WE SHOULD SUMMON REINFORCEMENTS.
I DON'T KNOW... REMINDS ME OF THAT HORROR MOVIE WHERE THE ZOMBIES GET ON THE POLICE RADIO AND SAY, "SEND MORE COPS"...
WE FACED THE SAME PREDICAMENT AGAINST THE BLACK LANTERNS: ANY LANTERN WE CALL HERE WILL ONLY END UP AS AN ALPHA.
EXACTLY.
THEN IT IS UP TO THE THREE OF US.
JOHN IS HERE SOMEWHERE. LET'S SPLIT UP AND FIND HIM...

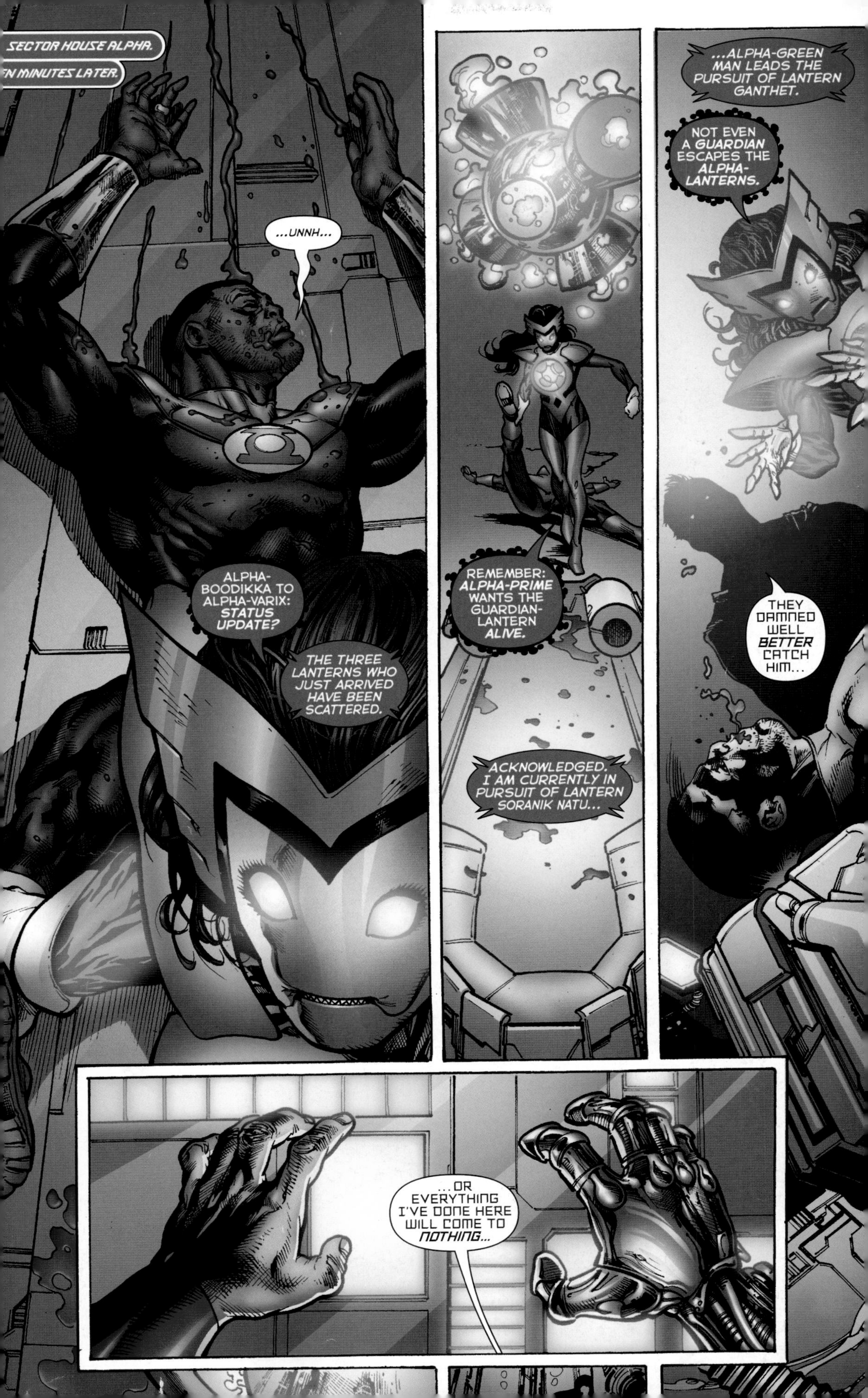

SECTOR HOUSE ALPHA.
EN MINUTES LATER.
...UNNH...
ALPHA-BOODIKKA TO ALPHA-VARIX: STATUS UPDATE?
THE THREE LANTERNS WHO JUST ARRIVED HAVE BEEN SCATTERED.
REMEMBER: ALPHA-PRIME WANTS THE GUARDIAN-LANTERN ALIVE.
ACKNOWLEDGED. I AM CURRENTLY IN PURSUIT OF LANTERN SORANIK NATU...
...ALPHA-GREEN MAN LEADS THE PURSUIT OF LANTERN GANTHET.
NOT EVEN A GUARDIAN ESCAPES THE ALPHA-LANTERNS.
THEY DAMNED WELL BETTER CATCH HIM...
...OR EVERYTHING I'VE DONE HERE WILL COME TO NOTHING...

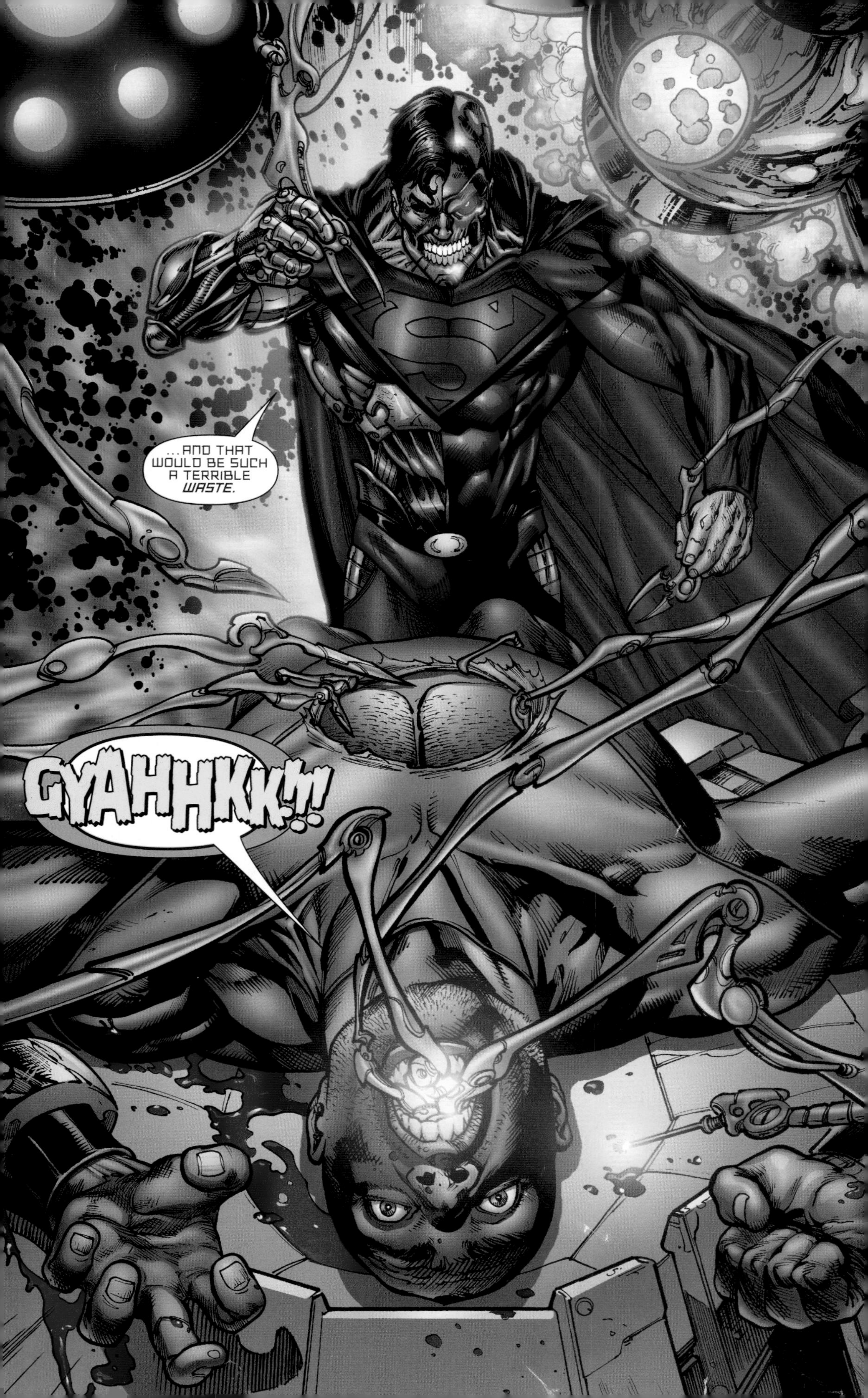
...AND THAT WOULD BE SUCH A TERRIBLE *WASTE.*
GYAHHKK!!!

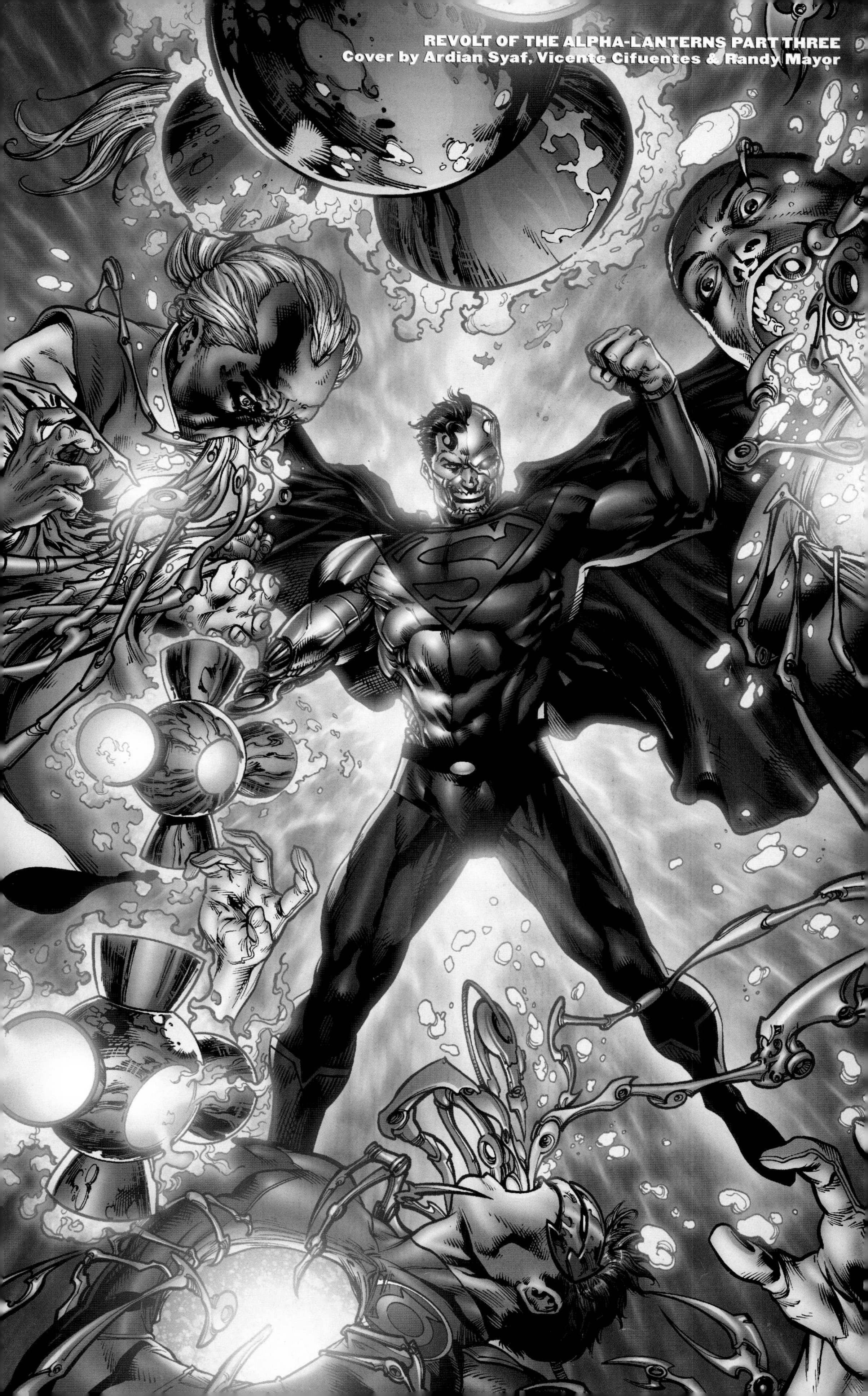
REVOLT OF THE ALPHA-LANTERNS PART THREE
Cover by Ardian Syaf, Vicente Cifuentes & Randy Mayor

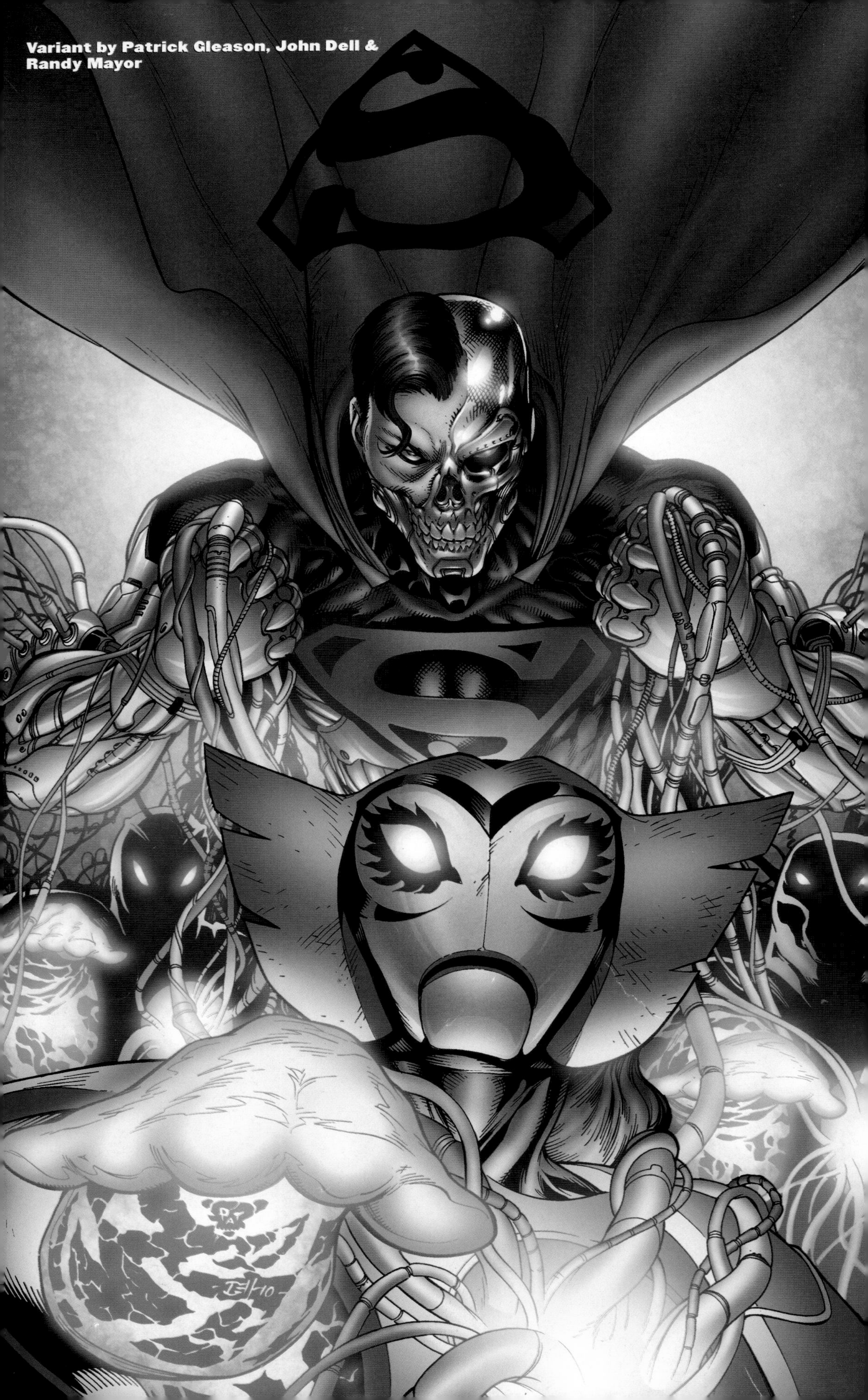

Variant by Patrick Gleason, John Dell & Randy Mayor

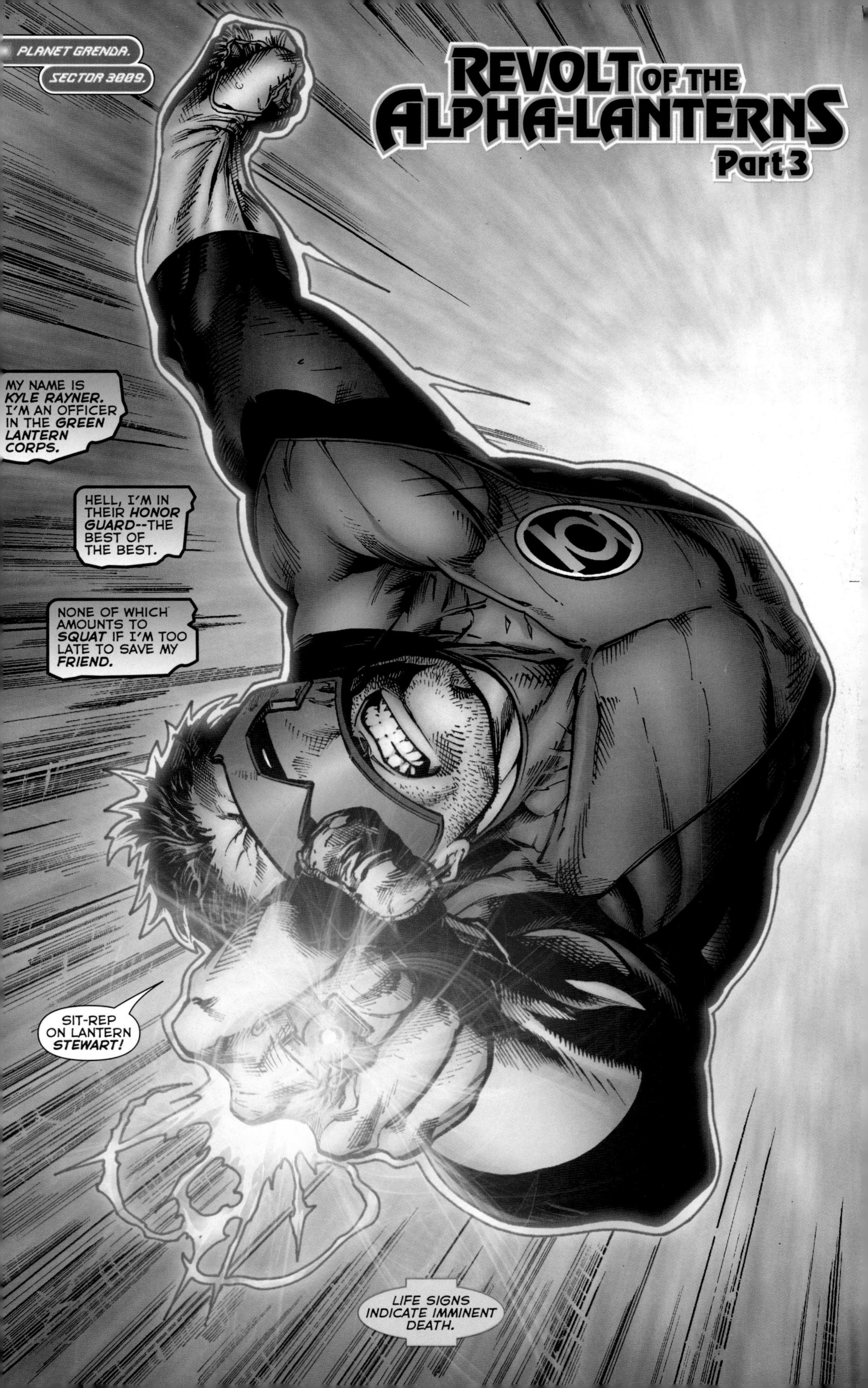

PLANET GRENDA.
SECTOR 3009.
REVOLT OF THE ALPHA-LANTERNS Part 3
MY NAME IS KYLE RAYNER. I'M AN OFFICER IN THE GREEN LANTERN CORPS.
HELL, I'M IN THEIR HONOR GUARD--THE BEST OF THE BEST.
NONE OF WHICH AMOUNTS TO SQUAT IF I'M TOO LATE TO SAVE MY FRIEND.
SIT-REP ON LANTERN STEWART!
LIFE SIGNS INDICATE IMMINENT DEATH.

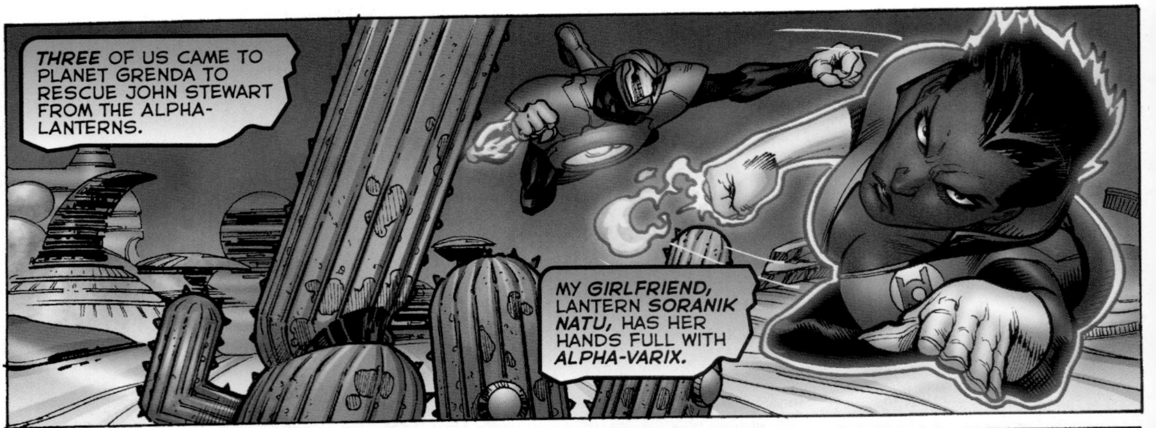
THREE OF US CAME TO PLANET GRENDA TO RESCUE JOHN STEWART FROM THE ALPHA-LANTERNS.
MY GIRLFRIEND, LANTERN SORANIK NATU, HAS HER HANDS FULL WITH ALPHA-VARIX.

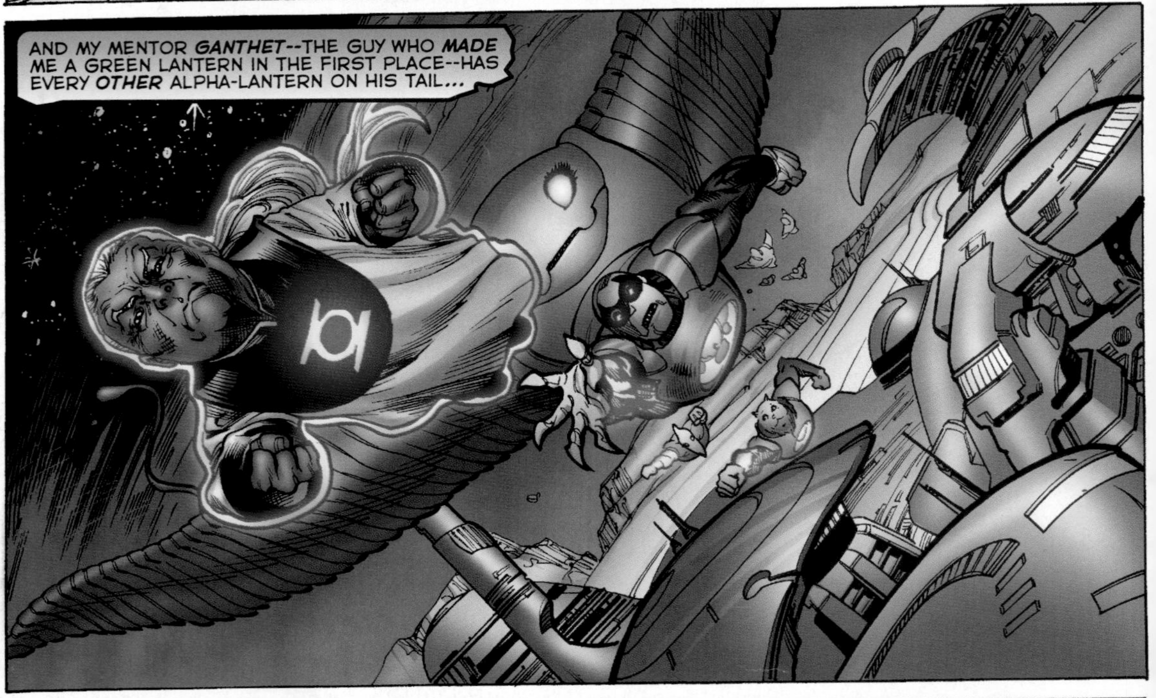
AND MY MENTOR GANTHET--THE GUY WHO MADE ME A GREEN LANTERN IN THE FIRST PLACE--HAS EVERY OTHER ALPHA-LANTERN ON HIS TAIL...

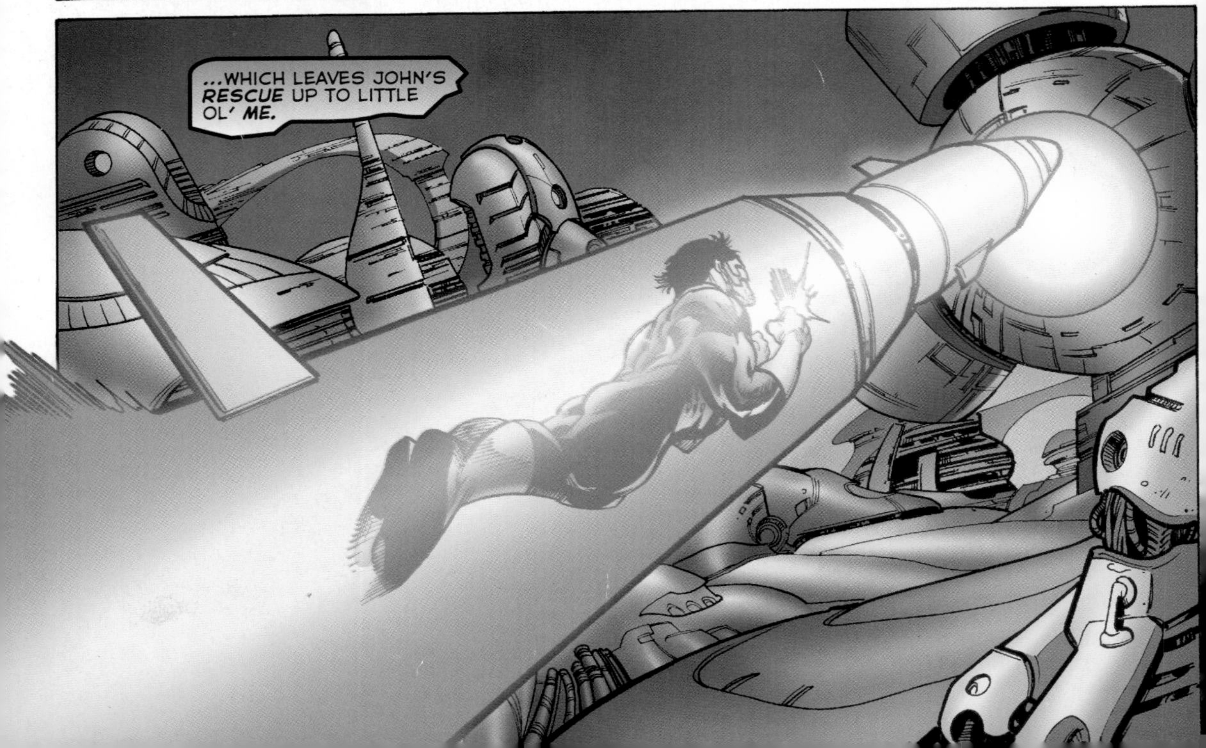
...WHICH LEAVES JOHN'S RESCUE UP TO LITTLE OL' ME.

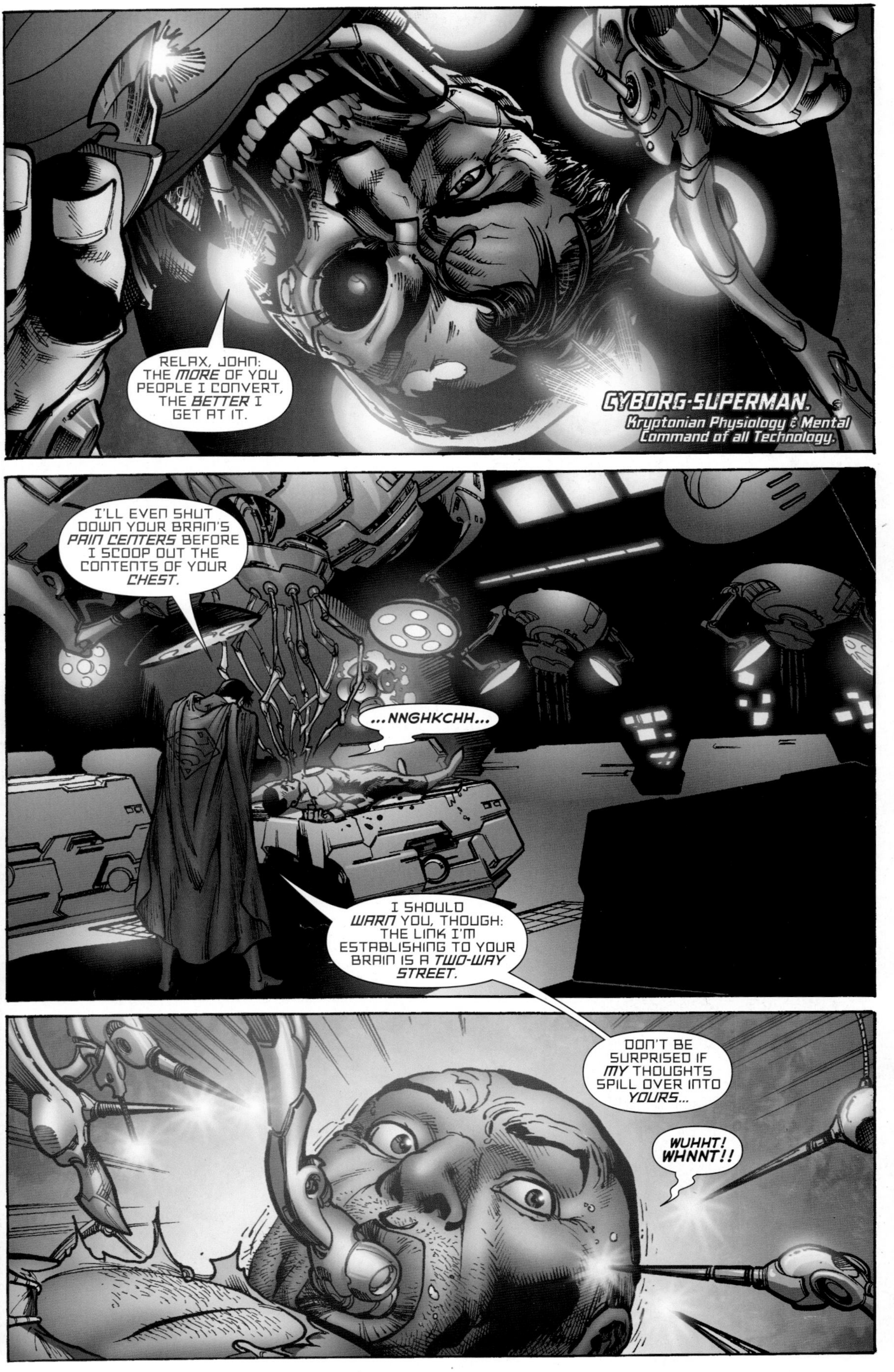
RELAX, JOHN: THE MORE OF YOU PEOPLE I CONVERT, THE BETTER I GET AT IT.
CYBORG-SUPERMAN.
Kryptonian Physiology & Mental Command of all Technology.
I'LL EVEN SHUT DOWN YOUR BRAIN'S PAIN CENTERS BEFORE I SCOOP OUT THE CONTENTS OF YOUR CHEST.
...NNGHKCHH...
I SHOULD WARN YOU, THOUGH: THE LINK I'M ESTABLISHING TO YOUR BRAIN IS A TWO-WAY STREET.
DON'T BE SURPRISED IF MY THOUGHTS SPILL OVER INTO YOURS...
WUHHT! WHNNT!!

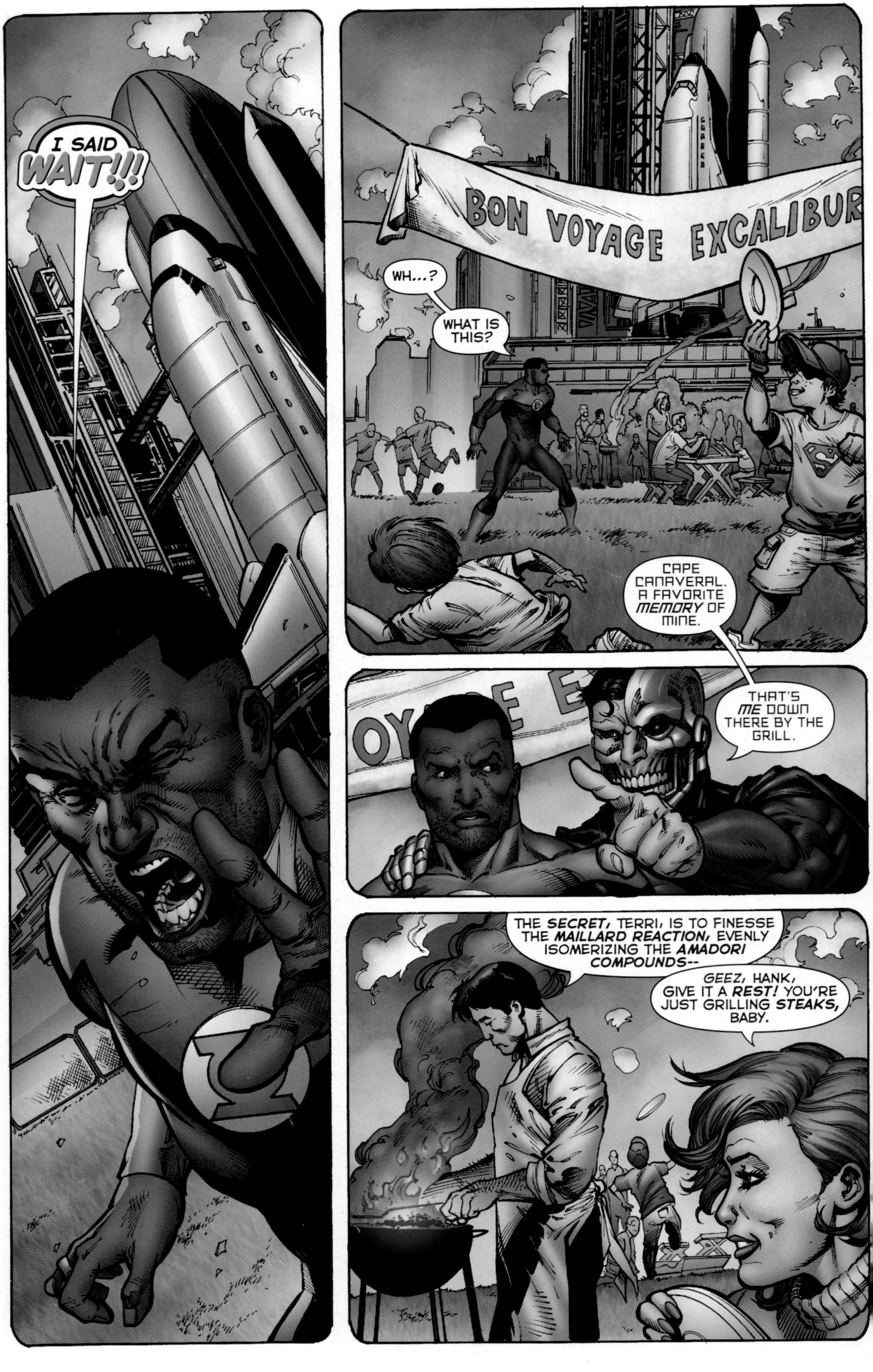
I SAID WAIT!!!
BON VOYAGE EXCALIBUR
WH...?
WHAT IS THIS?
CAPE CANAVERAL. A FAVORITE MEMORY OF MINE.
THAT'S ME DOWN THERE BY THE GRILL.
THE SECRET, TERRI, IS TO FINESSE THE MAILLARD REACTION, EVENLY ISOMERIZING THE AMADORI COMPOUNDS--
GEEZ, HANK, GIVE IT A REST! YOU'RE JUST GRILLING STEAKS, BABY.

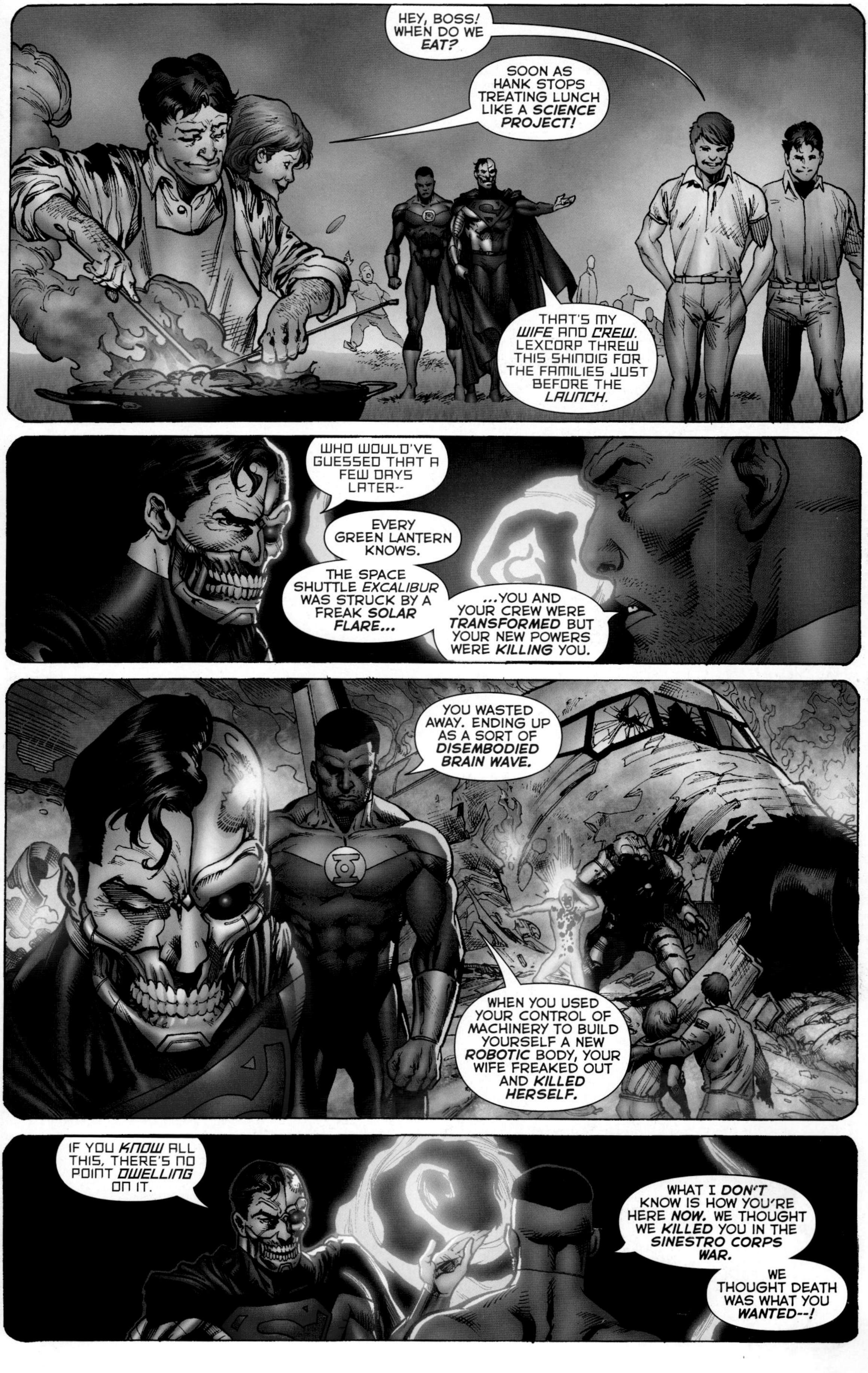
HEY, BOSS! WHEN DO WE EAT?
SOON AS HANK STOPS TREATING LUNCH LIKE A SCIENCE PROJECT!
THAT'S MY WIFE AND CREW. LEXCORP THREW THIS SHINDIG FOR THE FAMILIES JUST BEFORE THE LAUNCH.
WHO WOULD'VE GUESSED THAT A FEW DAYS LATER--
EVERY GREEN LANTERN KNOWS.
THE SPACE SHUTTLE EXCALIBUR WAS STRUCK BY A FREAK SOLAR FLARE...
...YOU AND YOUR CREW WERE TRANSFORMED BUT YOUR NEW POWERS WERE KILLING YOU.
YOU WASTED AWAY. ENDING UP AS A SORT OF DISEMBODIED BRAIN WAVE.
WHEN YOU USED YOUR CONTROL OF MACHINERY TO BUILD YOURSELF A NEW ROBOTIC BODY, YOUR WIFE FREAKED OUT AND KILLED HERSELF.
IF YOU KNOW ALL THIS, THERE'S NO POINT DWELLING ON IT.
WHAT I DON'T KNOW IS HOW YOU'RE HERE NOW. WE THOUGHT WE KILLED YOU IN THE SINESTRO CORPS WAR.
WE THOUGHT DEATH WAS WHAT YOU WANTED--!

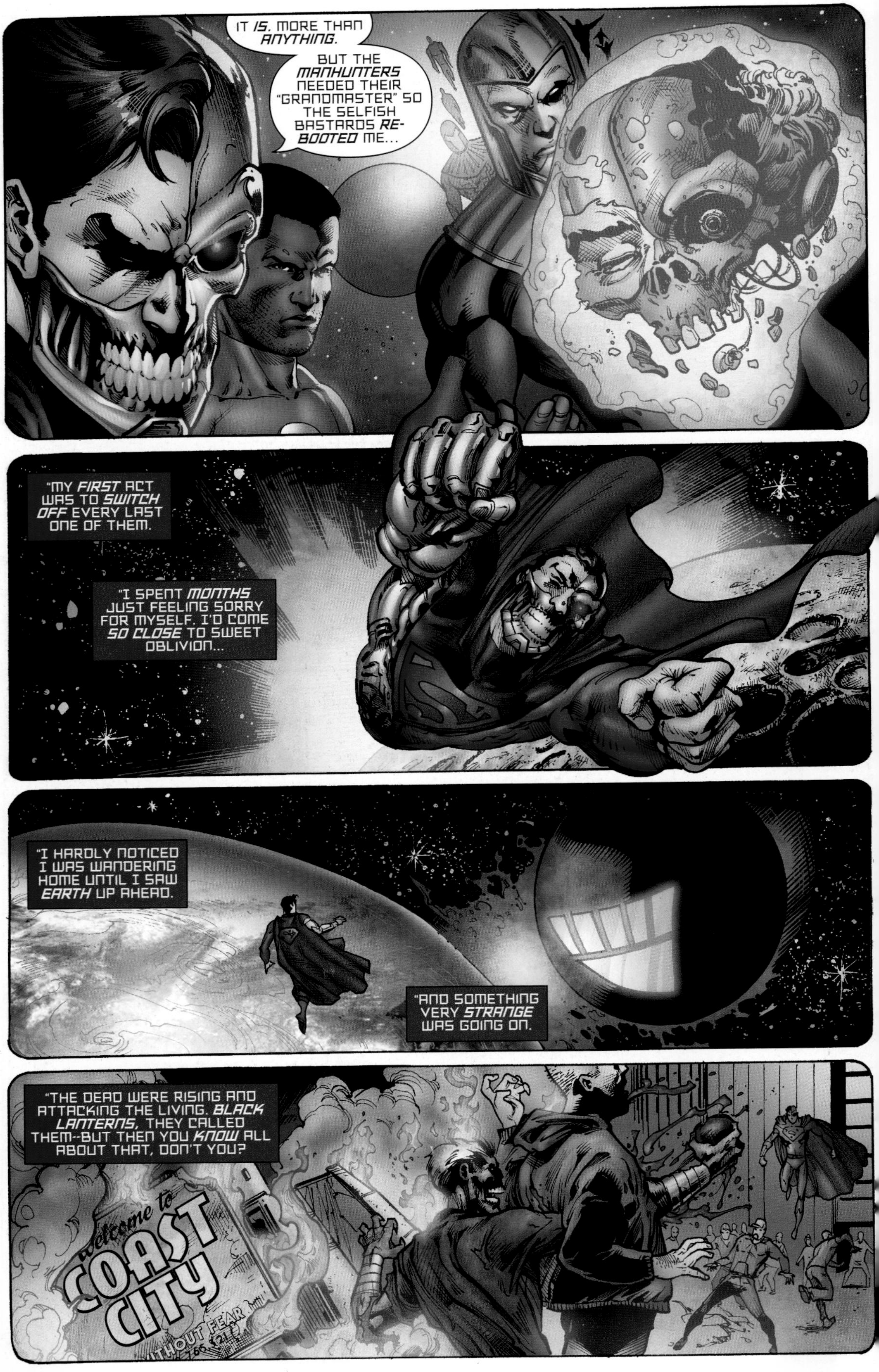
IT IS, MORE THAN ANYTHING.
BUT THE MANHUNTERS NEEDED THEIR "GRANDMASTER" SO THE SELFISH BASTARDS RE-BOOTED ME...
"MY FIRST ACT WAS TO SWITCH OFF EVERY LAST ONE OF THEM.
"I SPENT MONTHS JUST FEELING SORRY FOR MYSELF. I'D COME SO CLOSE TO SWEET OBLIVION...
"I HARDLY NOTICED I WAS WANDERING HOME UNTIL I SAW EARTH UP AHEAD.
"AND SOMETHING VERY STRANGE WAS GOING ON.
"THE DEAD WERE RISING AND ATTACKING THE LIVING. BLACK LANTERNS, THEY CALLED THEM--BUT THEN YOU KNOW ALL ABOUT THAT, DON'T YOU?
welcome to COAST CITY

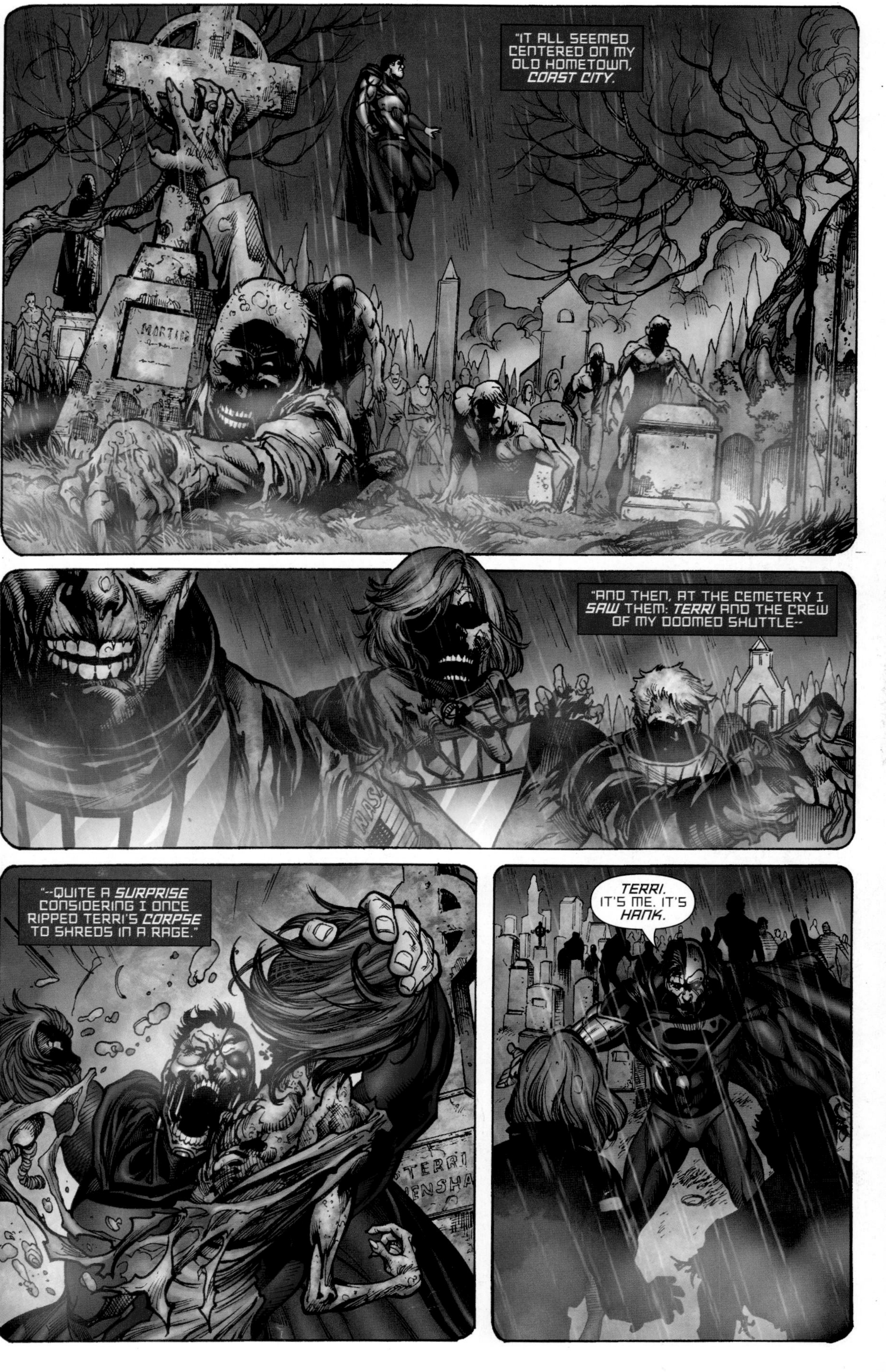
"IT ALL SEEMED CENTERED ON MY OLD HOMETOWN, COAST CITY.
MARTIN
"AND THEN, AT THE CEMETERY I SAW THEM: TERRI AND THE CREW OF MY DOOMED SHUTTLE--
"--QUITE A SURPRISE CONSIDERING I ONCE RIPPED TERRI'S CORPSE TO SHREDS IN A RAGE."
TERRI. IT'S ME. IT'S HANK.

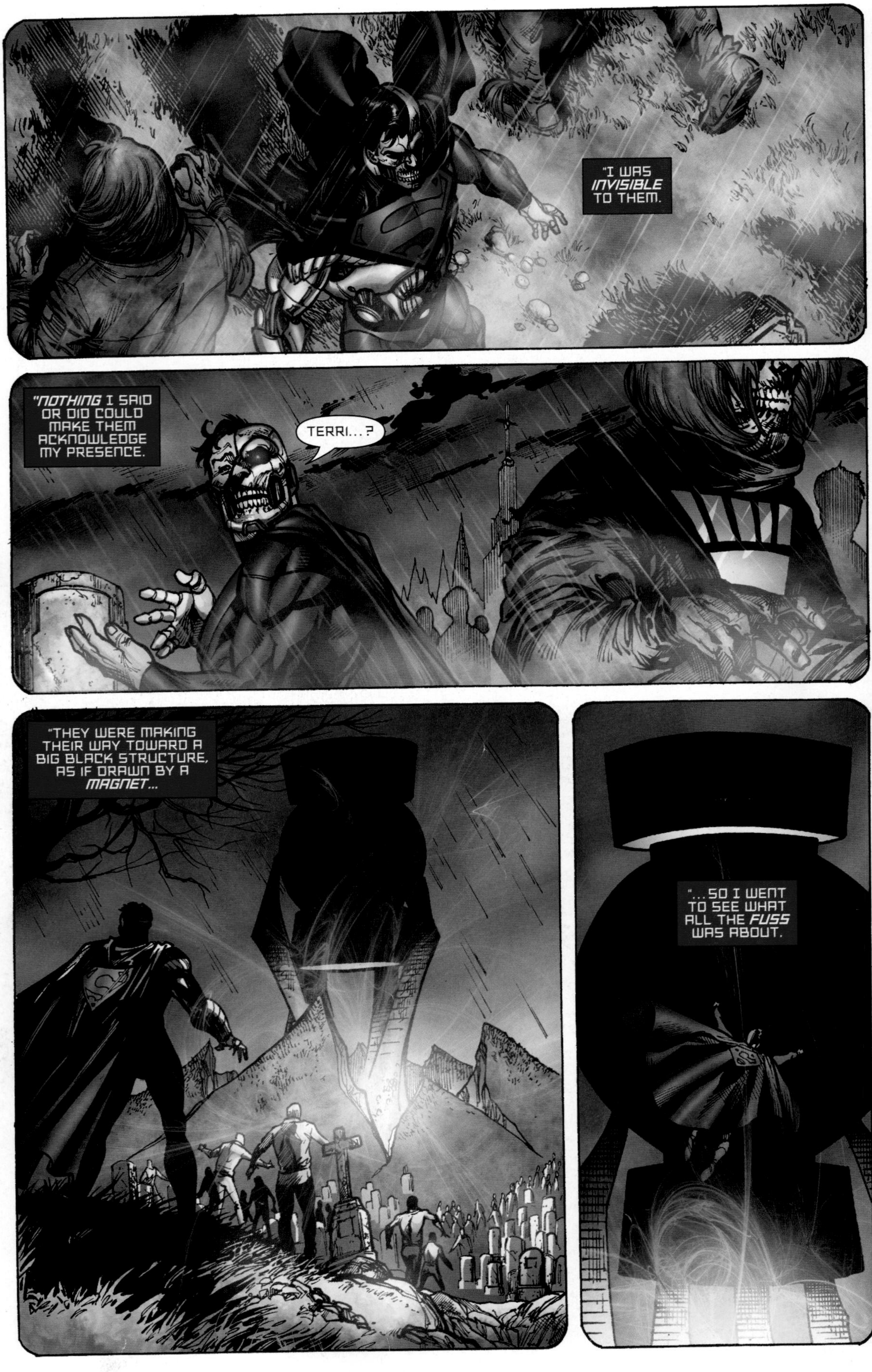
"I WAS INVISIBLE TO THEM.
"NOTHING I SAID OR DID COULD MAKE THEM ACKNOWLEDGE MY PRESENCE.
TERRI...?
"THEY WERE MAKING THEIR WAY TOWARD A BIG BLACK STRUCTURE, AS IF DRAWN BY A MAGNET...
"...SO I WENT TO SEE WHAT ALL THE FUSS WAS ABOUT.

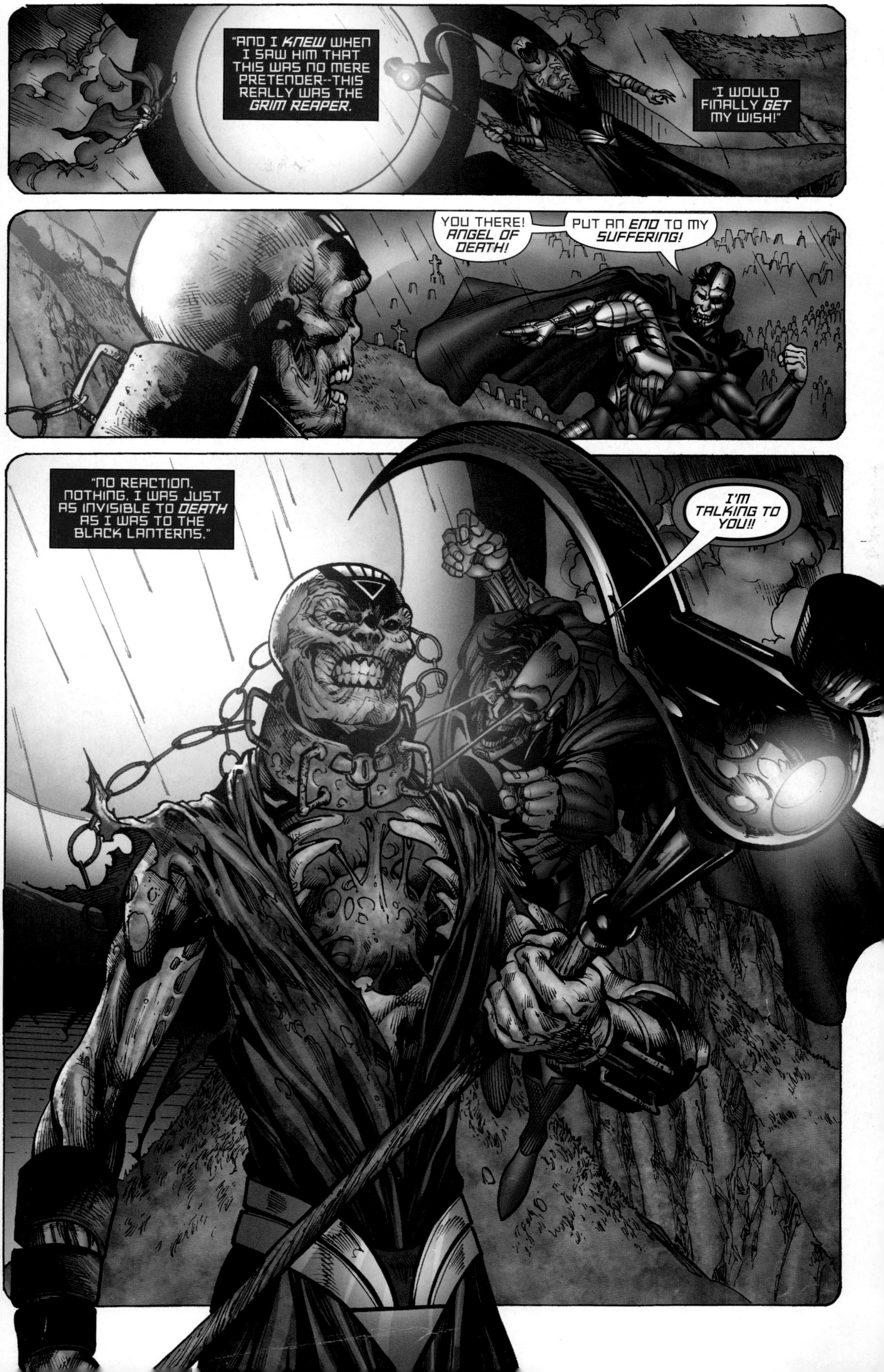
"AND I KNEW WHEN I SAW HIM THAT THIS WAS NO MERE PRETENDER--THIS REALLY WAS THE GRIM REAPER.
"I WOULD FINALLY GET MY WISH!"
YOU THERE! ANGEL OF DEATH!
PUT AN END TO MY SUFFERING!
"NO REACTION. NOTHING. I WAS JUST AS INVISIBLE TO DEATH AS I WAS TO THE BLACK LANTERNS."
I'M TALKING TO YOU!!

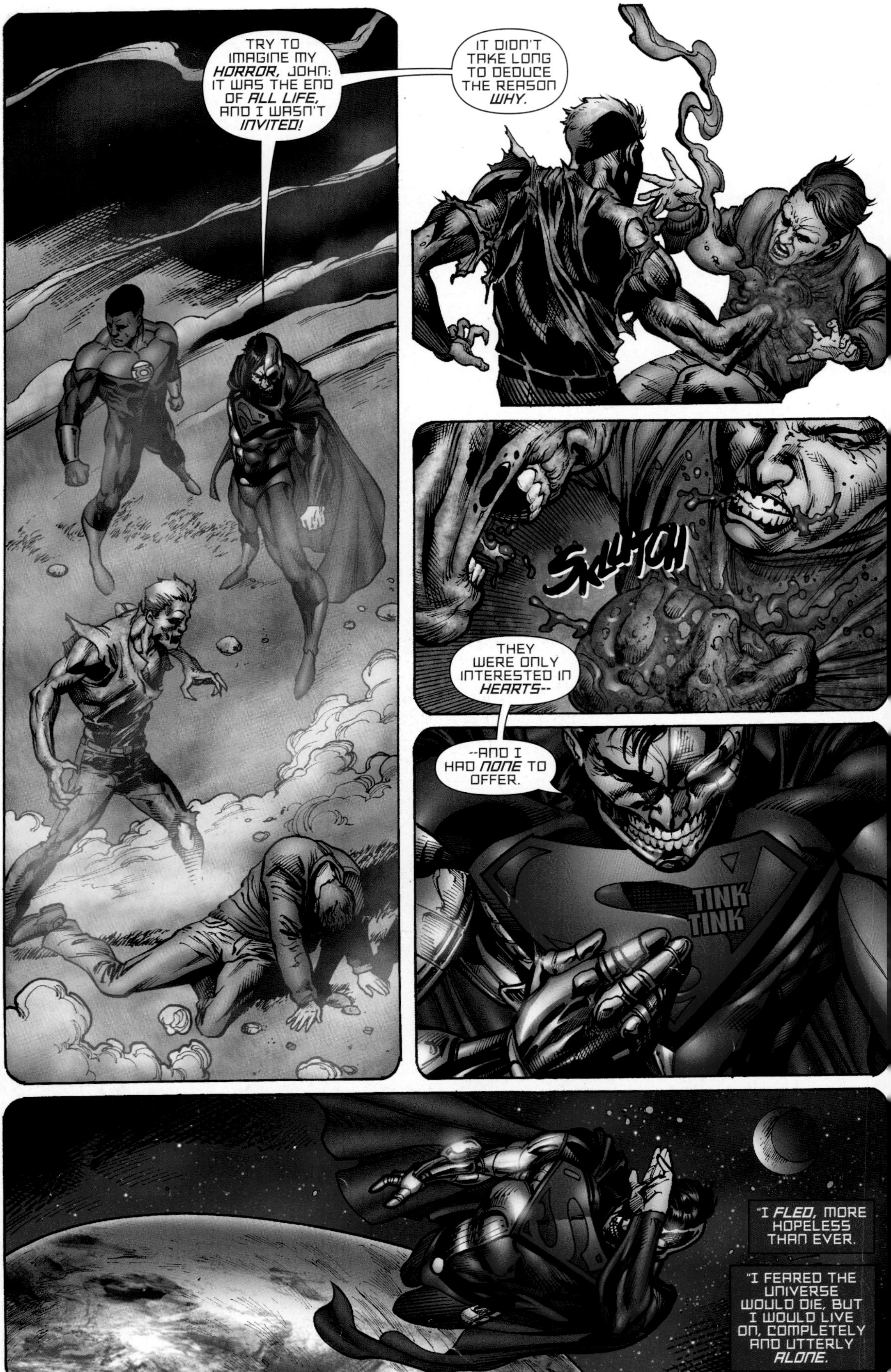
TRY TO IMAGINE MY HORROR, JOHN: IT WAS THE END OF ALL LIFE, AND I WASN'T INVITED!
IT DIDN'T TAKE LONG TO DEDUCE THE REASON WHY.
SKLLUTCH
THEY WERE ONLY INTERESTED IN HEARTS--
--AND I HAD NONE TO OFFER.
TINK TINK
"I FLED, MORE HOPELESS THAN EVER.
"I FEARED THE UNIVERSE WOULD DIE, BUT I WOULD LIVE ON, COMPLETELY AND UTTERLY ALONE.

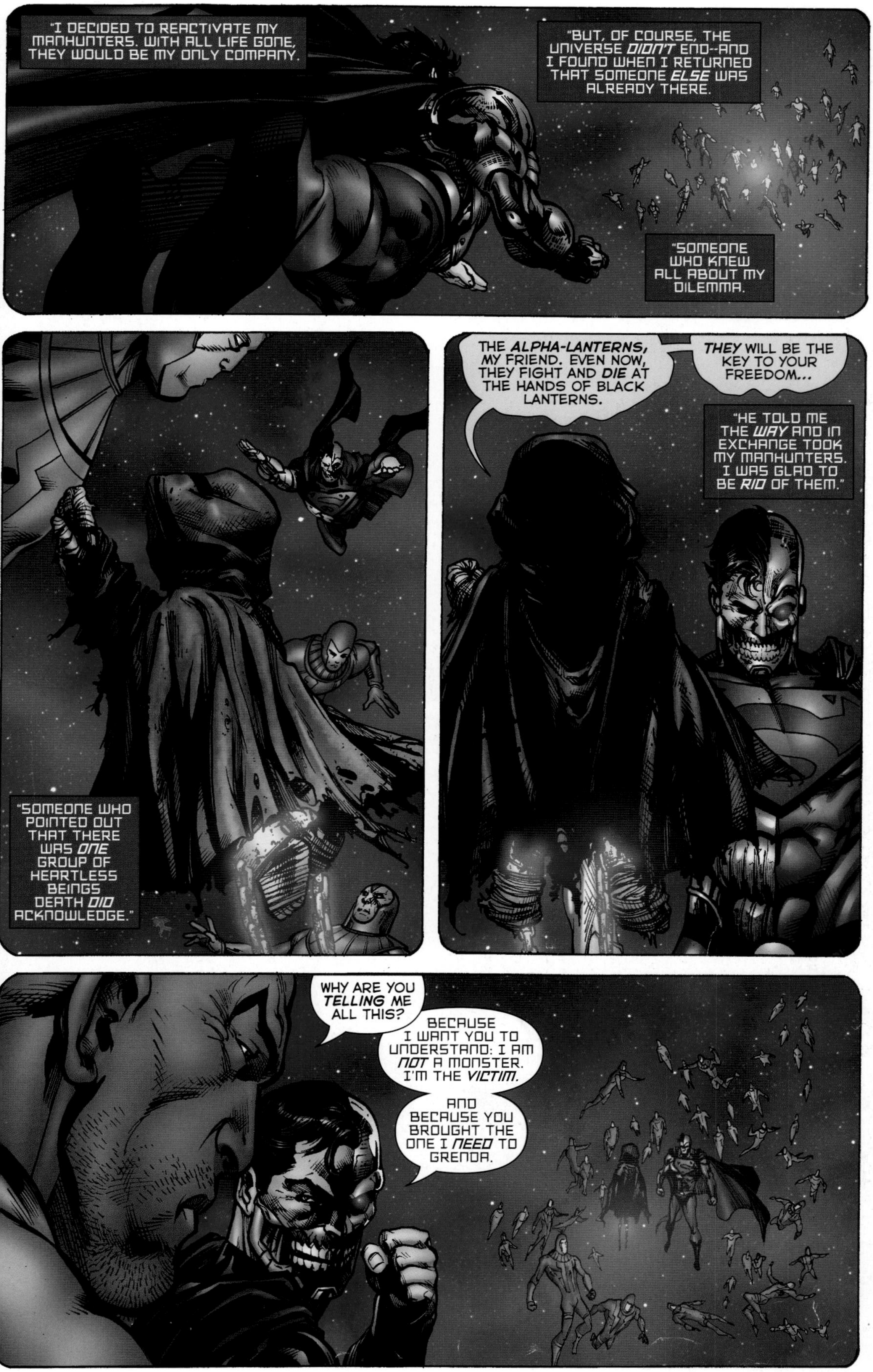
"I DECIDED TO REACTIVATE MY MANHUNTERS. WITH ALL LIFE GONE, THEY WOULD BE MY ONLY COMPANY.
"BUT, OF COURSE, THE UNIVERSE DIDN'T END--AND I FOUND WHEN I RETURNED THAT SOMEONE ELSE WAS ALREADY THERE.
"SOMEONE WHO KNEW ALL ABOUT MY DILEMMA.
"SOMEONE WHO POINTED OUT THAT THERE WAS ONE GROUP OF HEARTLESS BEINGS DEATH DID ACKNOWLEDGE."
THE ALPHA-LANTERNS, MY FRIEND. EVEN NOW, THEY FIGHT AND DIE AT THE HANDS OF BLACK LANTERNS.
THEY WILL BE THE KEY TO YOUR FREEDOM...
"HE TOLD ME THE WAY AND IN EXCHANGE TOOK MY MANHUNTERS. I WAS GLAD TO BE RID OF THEM."
WHY ARE YOU TELLING ME ALL THIS?
BECAUSE I WANT YOU TO UNDERSTAND: I AM NOT A MONSTER. I'M THE VICTIM.
AND BECAUSE YOU BROUGHT THE ONE I NEED TO GRENDA.

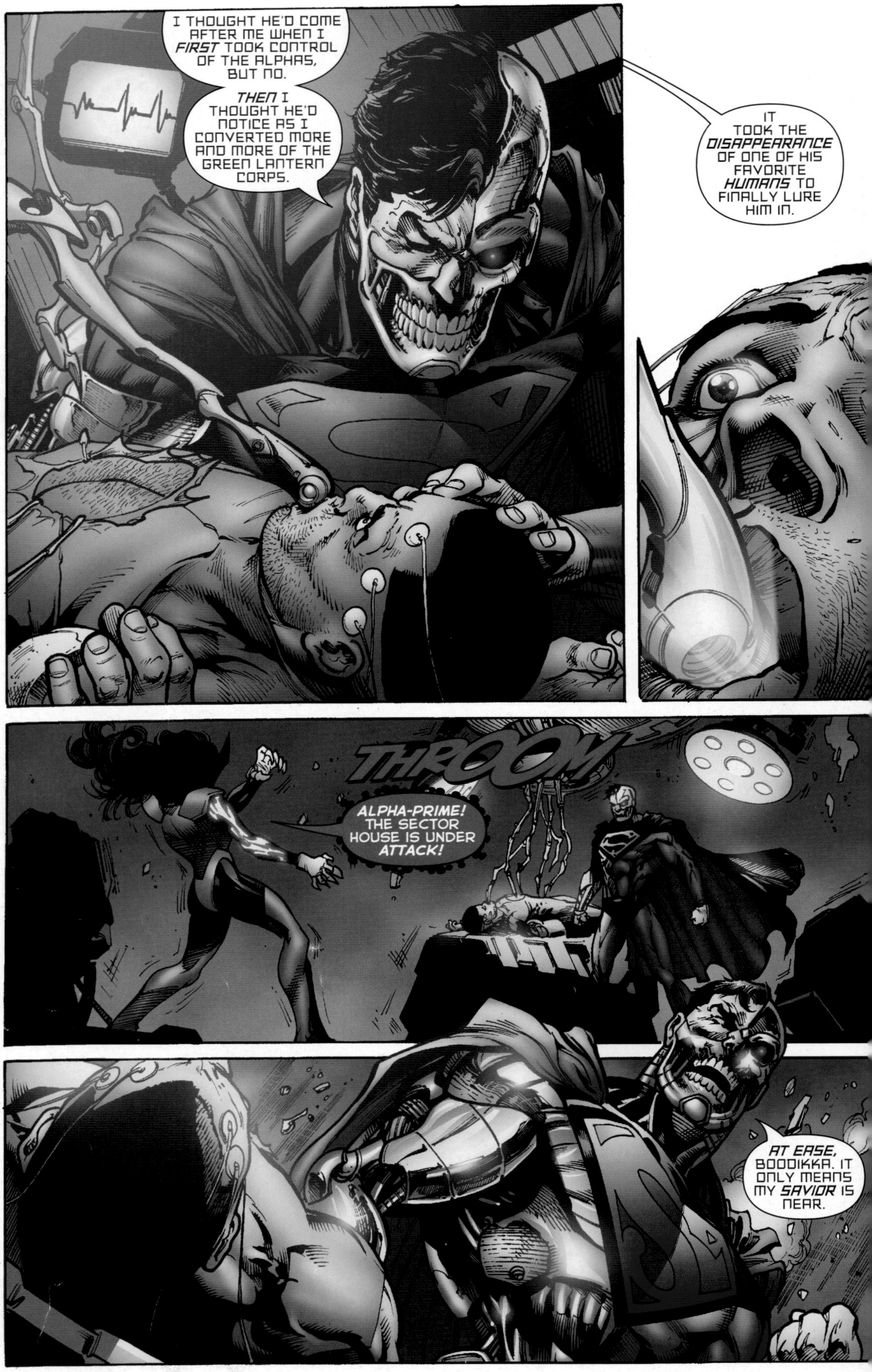
I THOUGHT HE'D COME AFTER ME WHEN I FIRST TOOK CONTROL OF THE ALPHAS, BUT NO.
THEN I THOUGHT HE'D NOTICE AS I CONVERTED MORE AND MORE OF THE GREEN LANTERN CORPS.
IT TOOK THE DISAPPEARANCE OF ONE OF HIS FAVORITE HUMANS TO FINALLY LURE HIM IN.
THROOOM
ALPHA-PRIME! THE SECTOR HOUSE IS UNDER ATTACK!
AT EASE, BOODIKKA. IT ONLY MEANS MY SAVIOR IS NEAR.

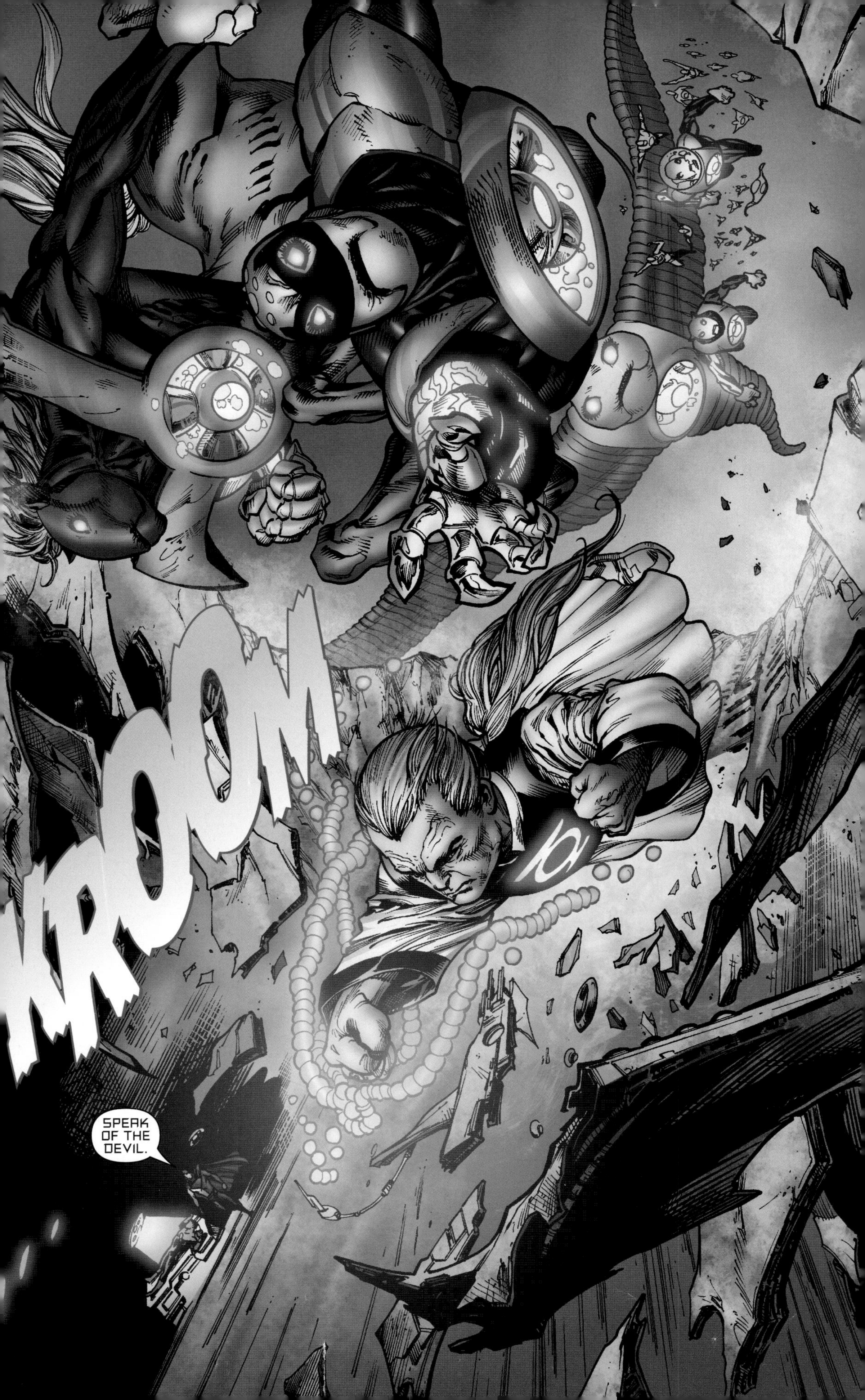
SPEAK OF THE DEVIL.

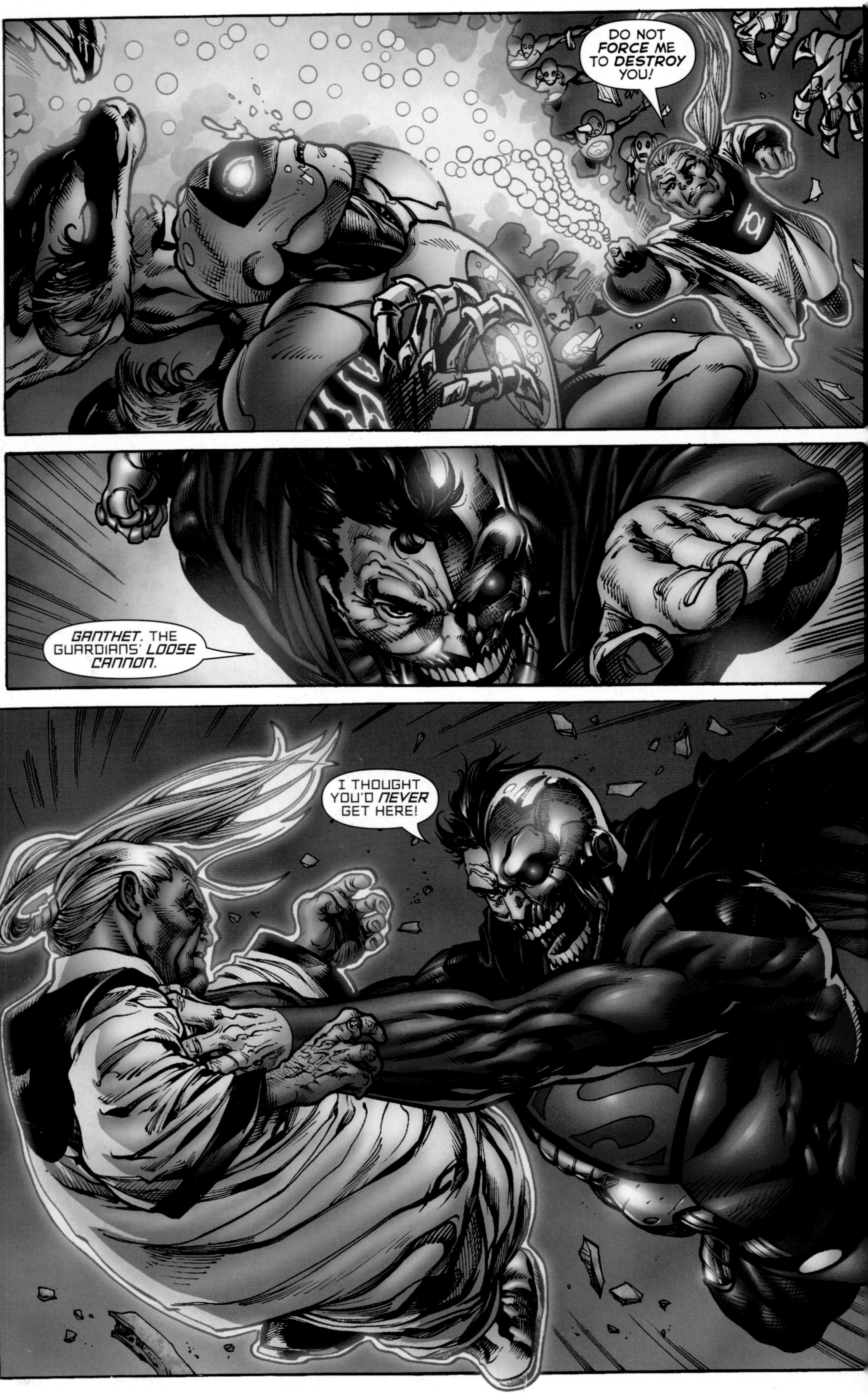
DO NOT FORCE ME TO DESTROY YOU!
GANTHET. THE GUARDIANS' LOOSE CANNON.
I THOUGHT YOU'D NEVER GET HERE!

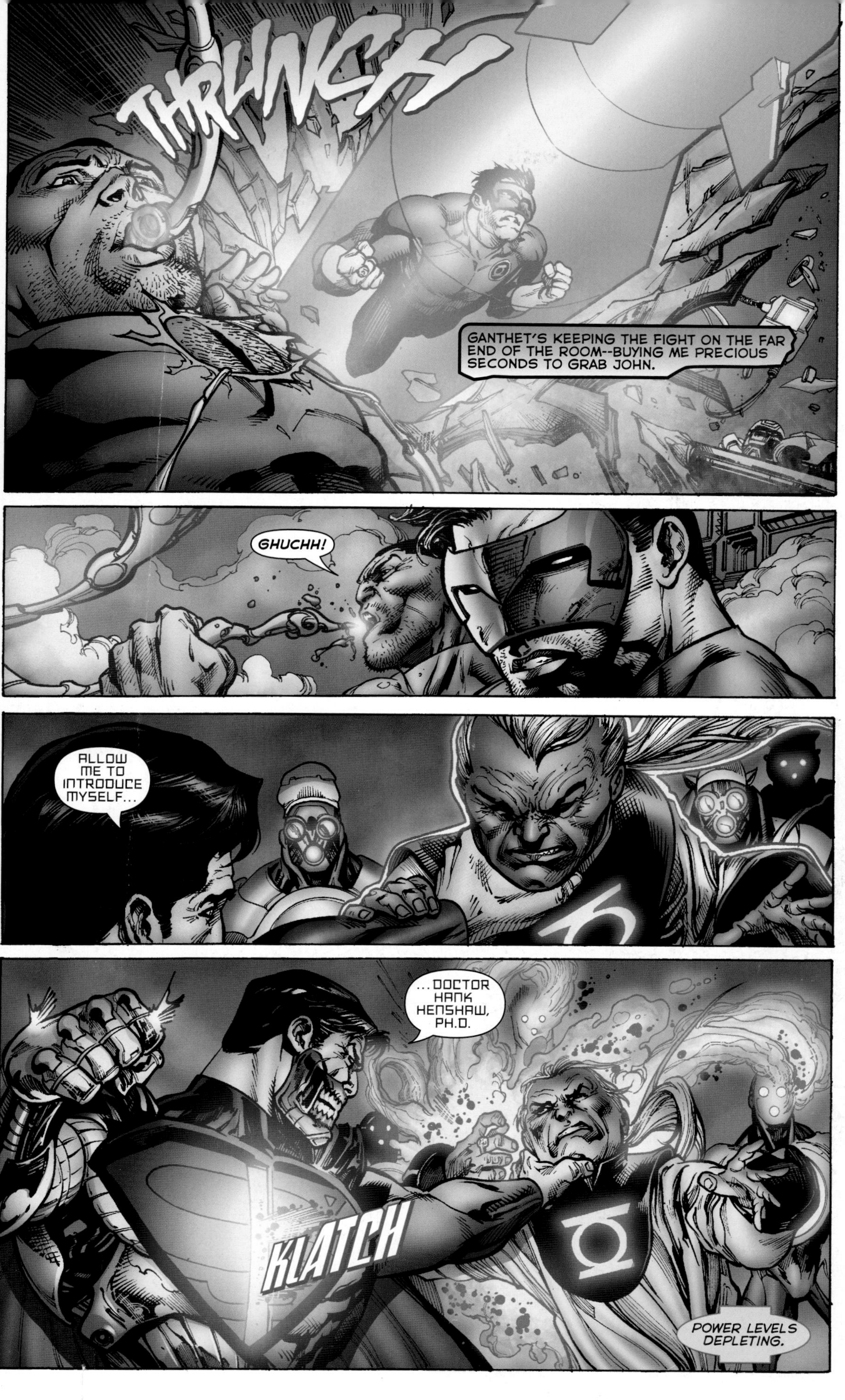
THRUNCH
GANTHET'S KEEPING THE FIGHT ON THE FAR END OF THE ROOM--BUYING ME PRECIOUS SECONDS TO GRAB JOHN.
GHUCHH!
ALLOW ME TO INTRODUCE MYSELF...
...DOCTOR HANK HENSHAW, PH.D.
KLATCH
POWER LEVELS DEPLETING.

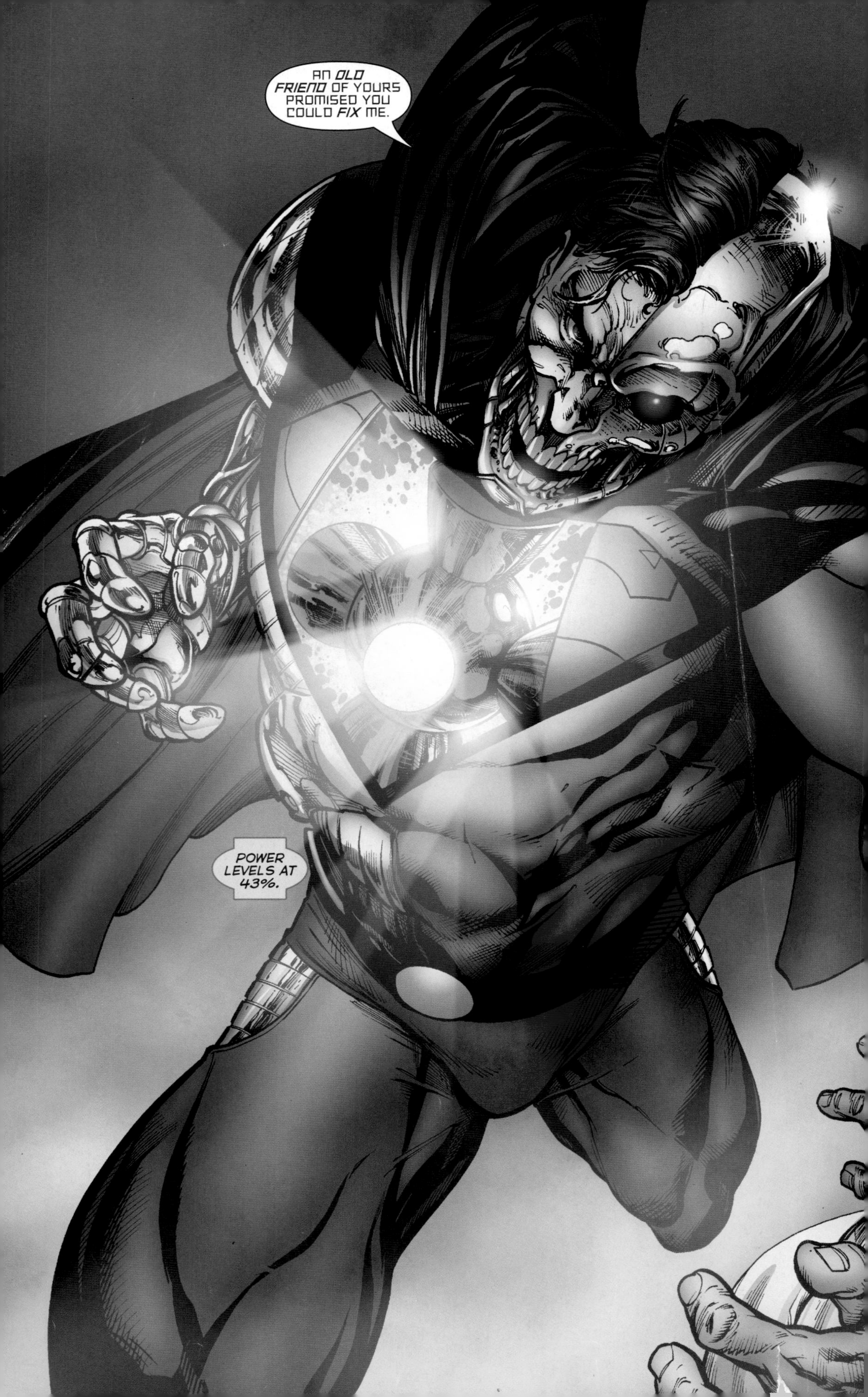
AN *OLD FRIEND* OF YOURS PROMISED YOU COULD *FIX* ME.
POWER LEVELS AT 43%.

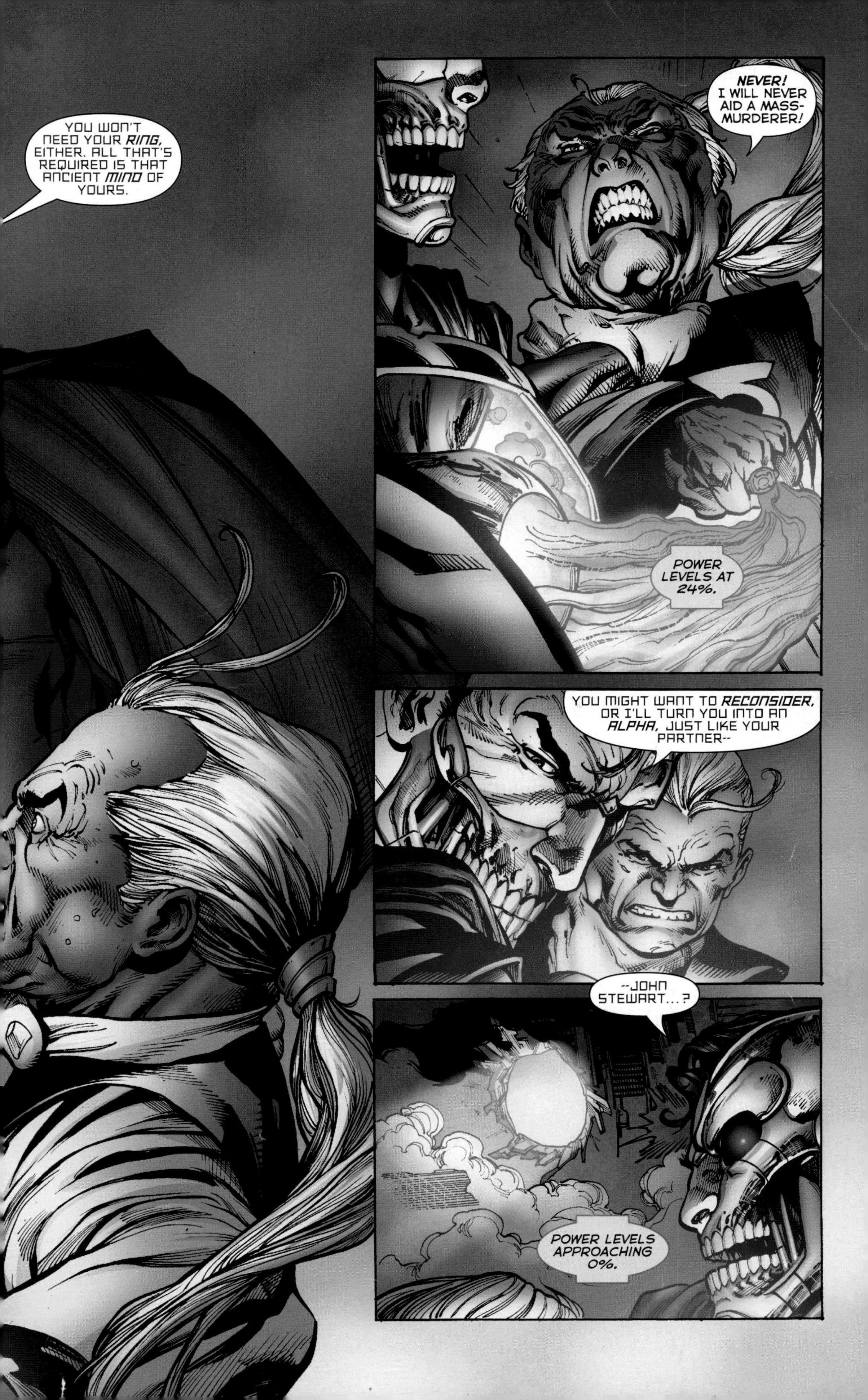
YOU WON'T NEED YOUR RING, EITHER. ALL THAT'S REQUIRED IS THAT ANCIENT MIND OF YOURS.
NEVER! I WILL NEVER AID A MASS-MURDERER!
POWER LEVELS AT 24%.
YOU MIGHT WANT TO RECONSIDER, OR I'LL TURN YOU INTO AN ALPHA, JUST LIKE YOUR PARTNER--
--JOHN STEWART...?
POWER LEVELS APPROACHING 0%.

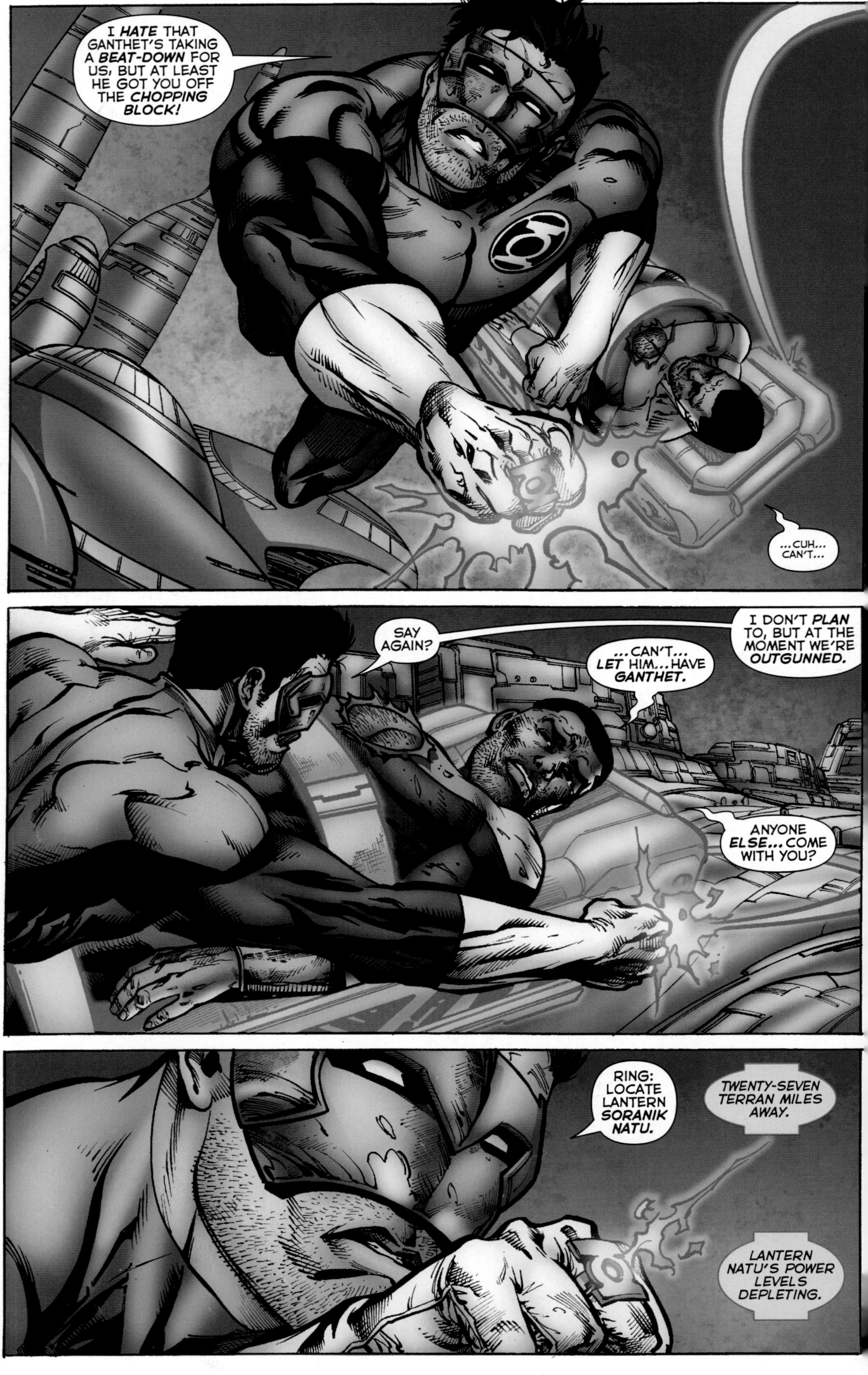
I HATE THAT GANTHET'S TAKING A BEAT-DOWN FOR US, BUT AT LEAST HE GOT YOU OFF THE CHOPPING BLOCK!
...CUH... CAN'T...
SAY AGAIN?
...CAN'T... LET HIM...HAVE GANTHET.
I DON'T PLAN TO, BUT AT THE MOMENT WE'RE OUTGUNNED.
ANYONE ELSE...COME WITH YOU?
RING: LOCATE LANTERN SORANIK NATU.
TWENTY-SEVEN TERRAN MILES AWAY.
LANTERN NATU'S POWER LEVELS DEPLETING.

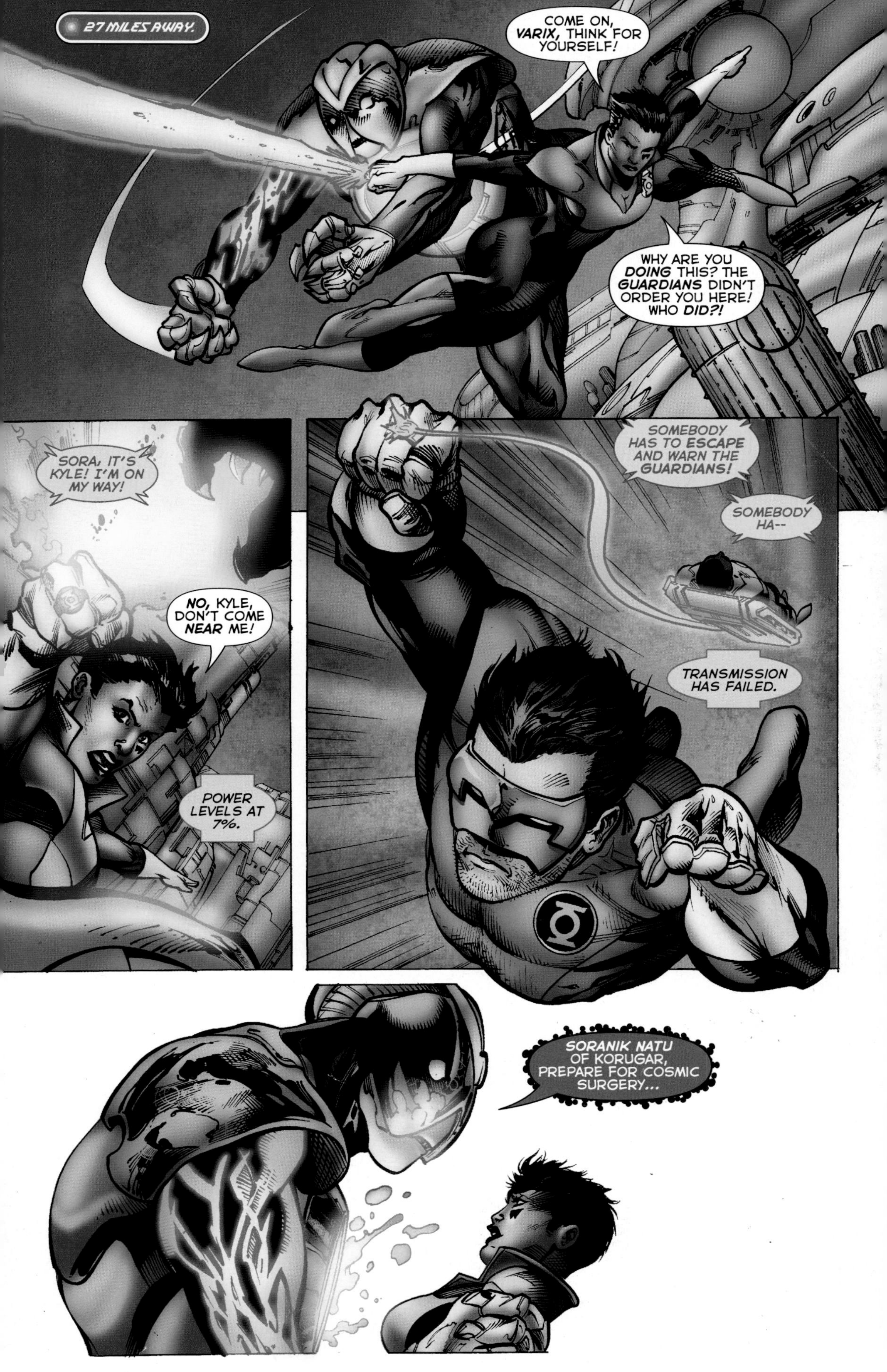
27 MILES AWAY.
COME ON, VARIX, THINK FOR YOURSELF!
WHY ARE YOU DOING THIS? THE GUARDIANS DIDN'T ORDER YOU HERE! WHO DID?!
SORA, IT'S KYLE! I'M ON MY WAY!
NO, KYLE, DON'T COME NEAR ME!
POWER LEVELS AT 7%.
SOMEBODY HAS TO ESCAPE AND WARN THE GUARDIANS!
SOMEBODY HA--
TRANSMISSION HAS FAILED.
SORANIK NATU OF KORUGAR, PREPARE FOR COSMIC SURGERY...

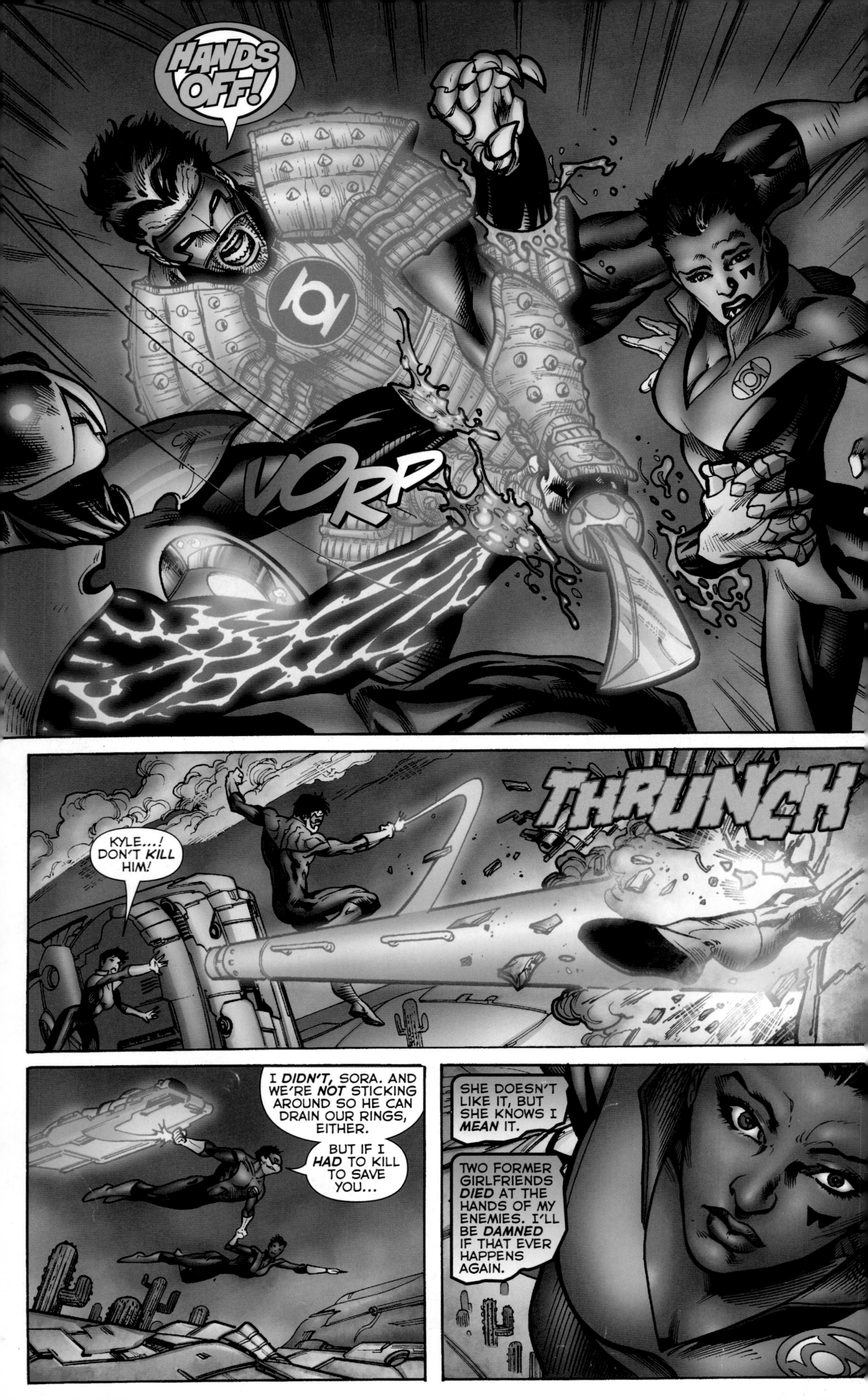
HANDS OFF!
VORP
THRUNCH
KYLE...! DON'T KILL HIM!
I DIDN'T, SORA. AND WE'RE NOT STICKING AROUND SO HE CAN DRAIN OUR RINGS, EITHER.
BUT IF I HAD TO KILL TO SAVE YOU...
SHE DOESN'T LIKE IT, BUT SHE KNOWS I MEAN IT.
TWO FORMER GIRLFRIENDS DIED AT THE HANDS OF MY ENEMIES. I'LL BE DAMNED IF THAT EVER HAPPENS AGAIN.

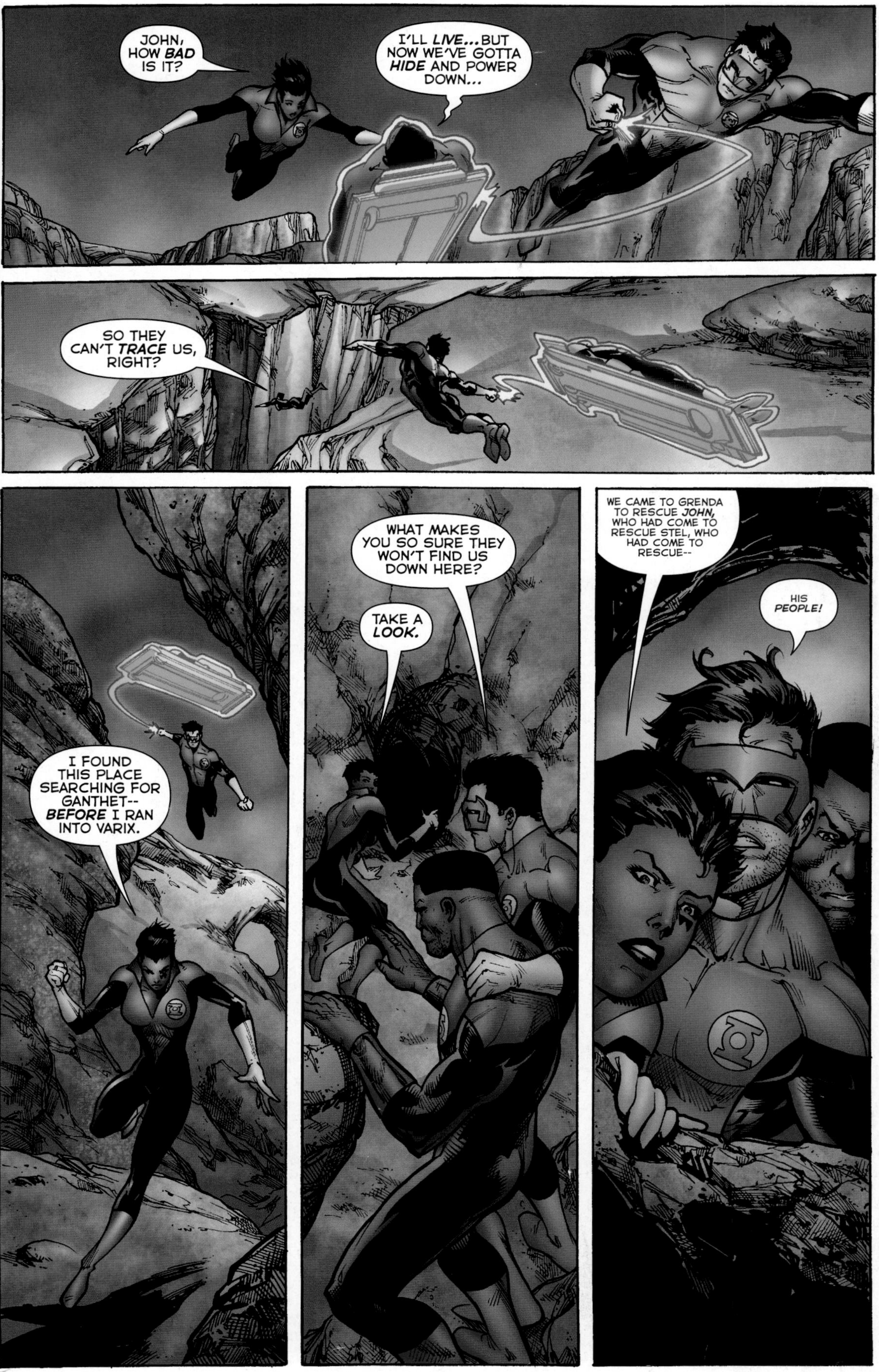
JOHN, HOW BAD IS IT?
I'LL LIVE... BUT NOW WE'VE GOTTA HIDE AND POWER DOWN...
SO THEY CAN'T TRACE US, RIGHT?
I FOUND THIS PLACE SEARCHING FOR GANTHET-- BEFORE I RAN INTO VARIX.
WHAT MAKES YOU SO SURE THEY WON'T FIND US DOWN HERE?
TAKE A LOOK.
WE CAME TO GRENDA TO RESCUE JOHN, WHO HAD COME TO RESCUE STEL, WHO HAD COME TO RESCUE--
HIS PEOPLE!

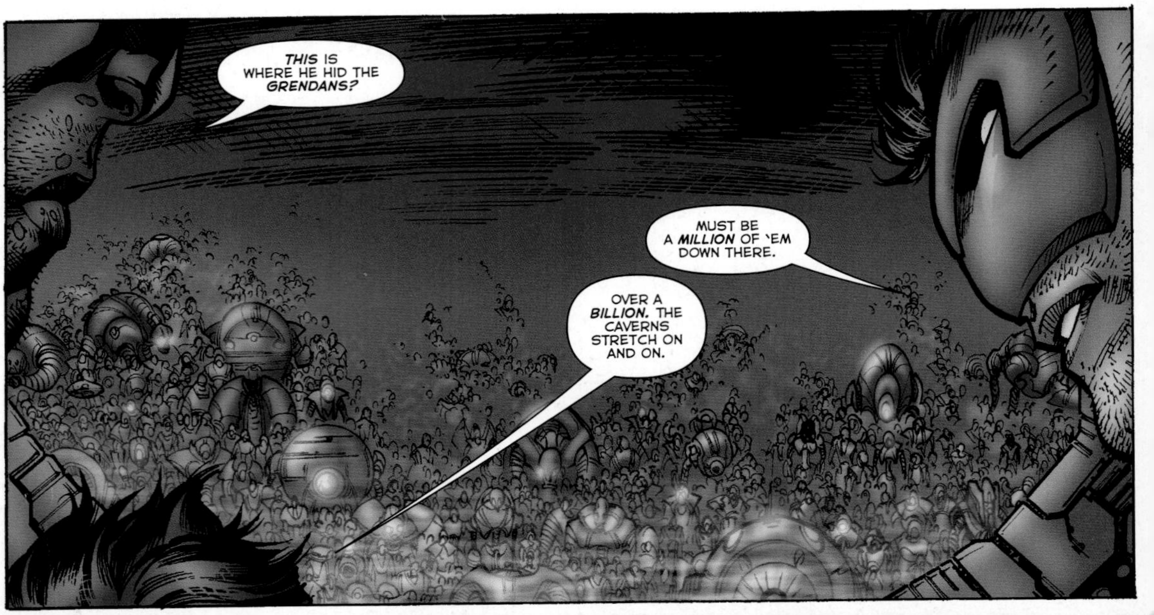
THIS IS WHERE HE HID THE GRENDANS?
MUST BE A MILLION OF 'EM DOWN THERE.
OVER A BILLION. THE CAVERNS STRETCH ON AND ON.

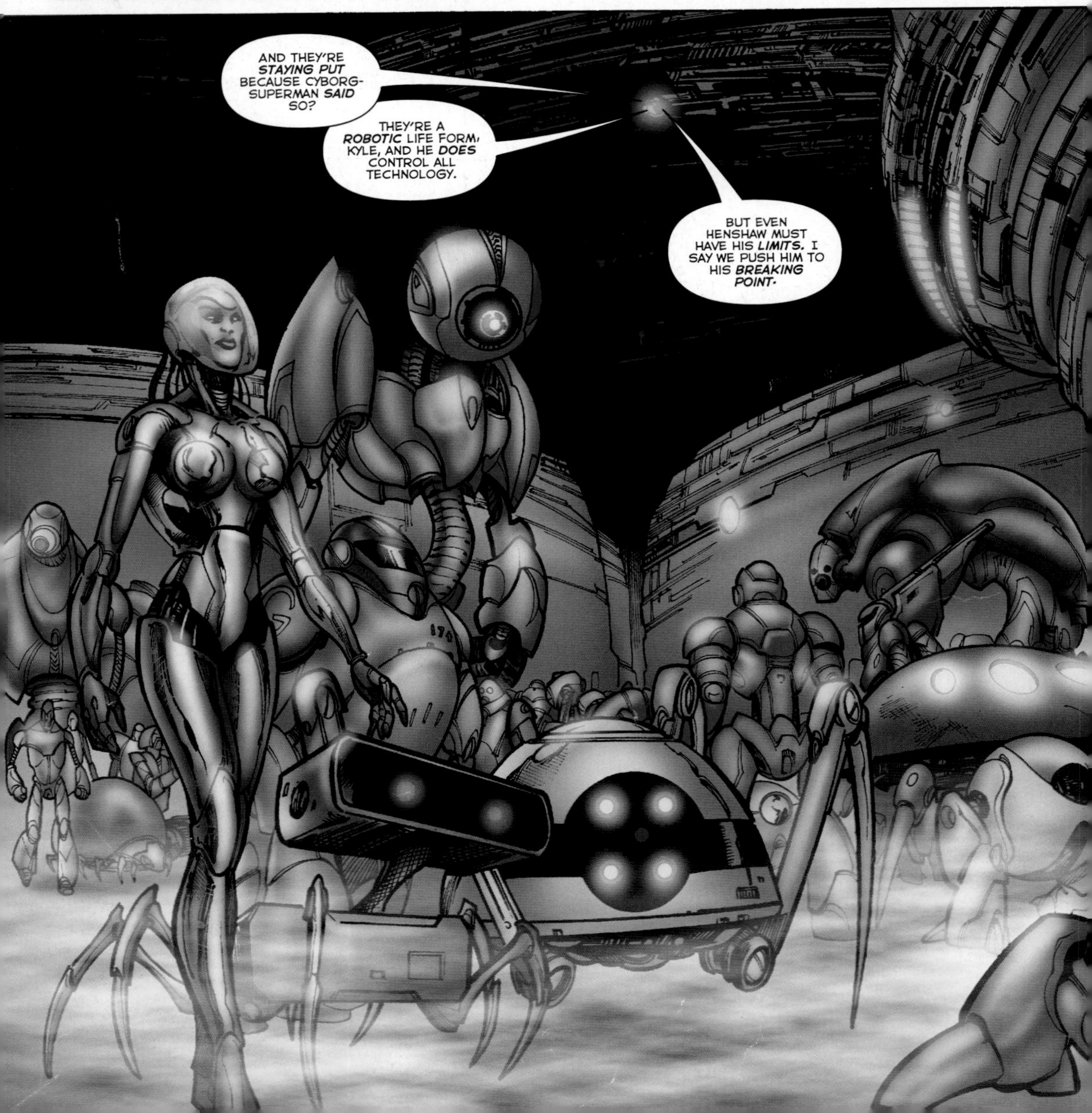
AND THEY'RE STAYING PUT BECAUSE CYBORG-SUPERMAN SAID SO?
THEY'RE A ROBOTIC LIFE FORM, KYLE, AND HE DOES CONTROL ALL TECHNOLOGY.
BUT EVEN HENSHAW MUST HAVE HIS LIMITS. I SAY WE PUSH HIM TO HIS BREAKING POINT.

REVOLT OF THE ALPHA-LANTERNS **PART FOUR**
Cover by Ardian Syaf, Vicente Cifuentes & Randy Mayor

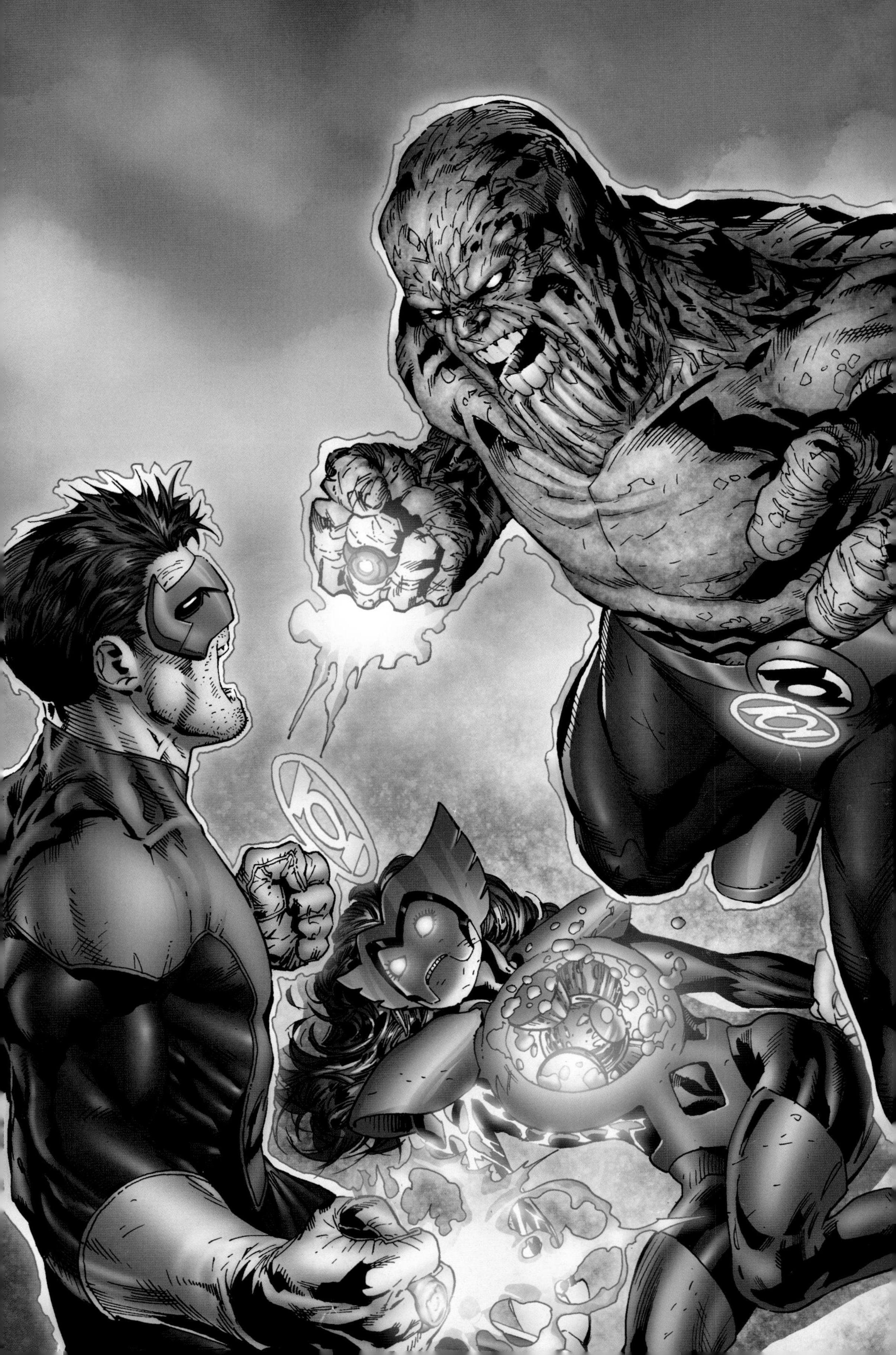

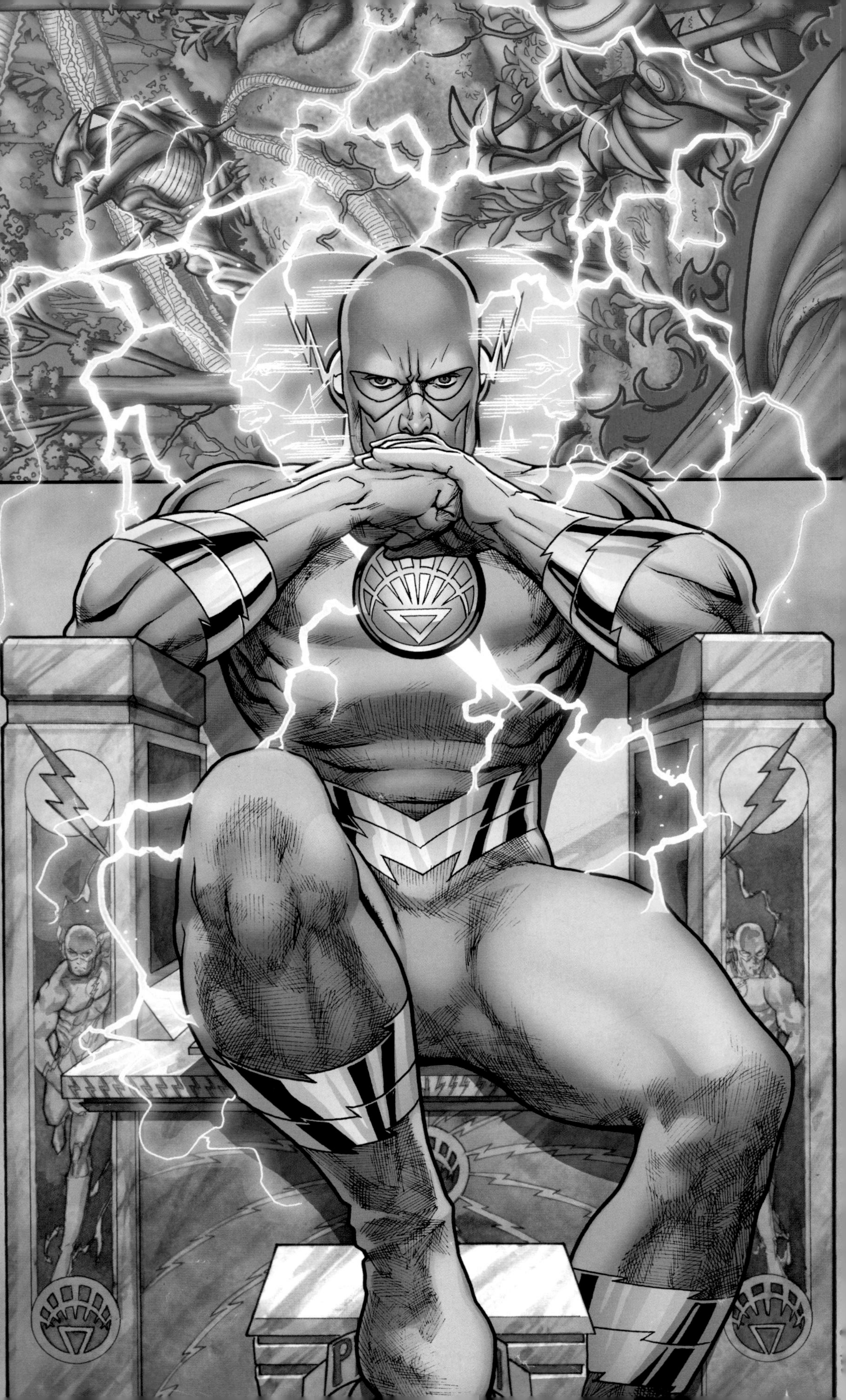

Variant by Ryan Sook, Joel Gomez, Fernando Pasarin, Randy Mayor & Carrie Strachan

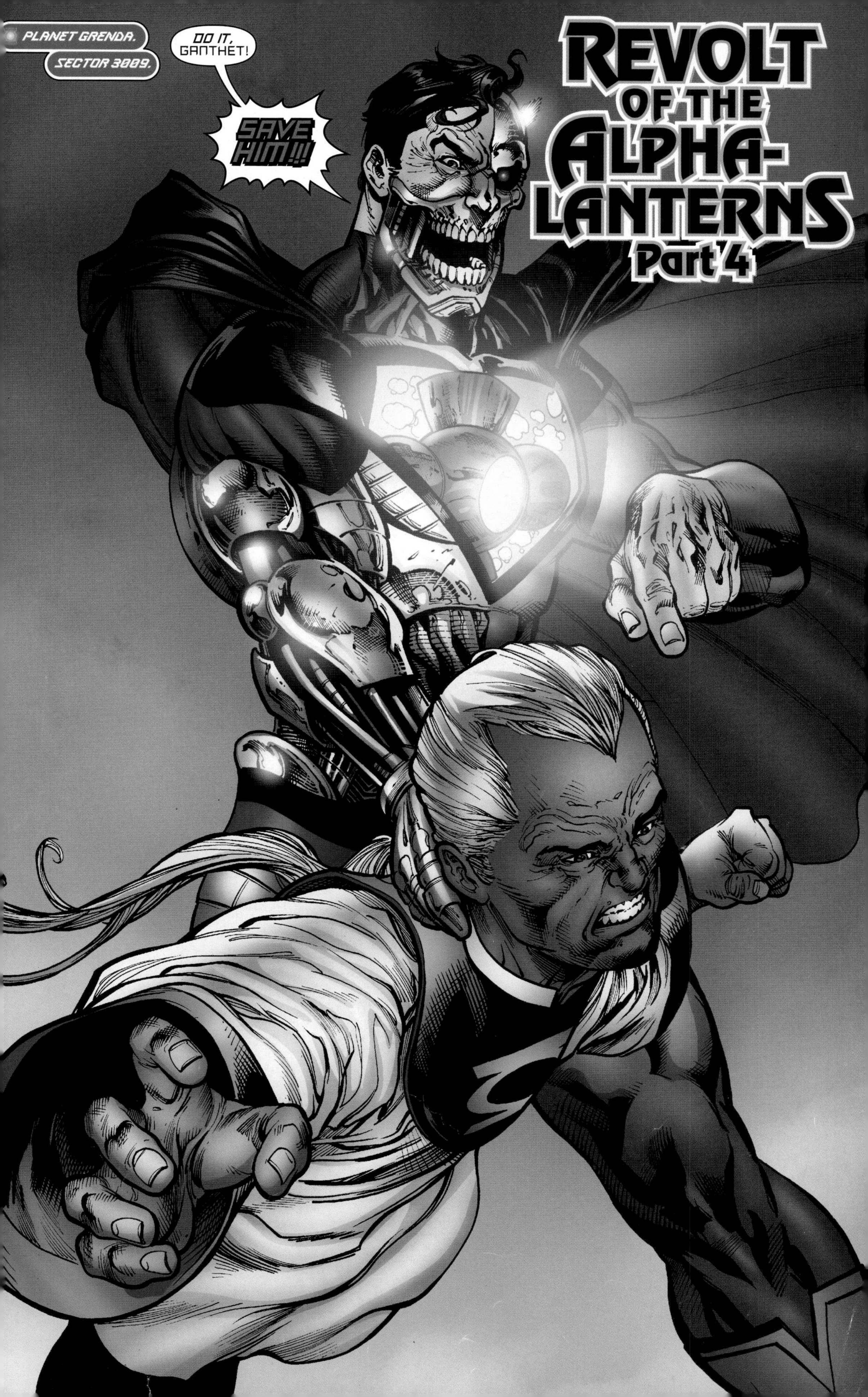
PLANET GRENDA.
SECTOR 3009.
DO IT, GANTHET!
SAVE HIM!!!
REVOLT OF THE ALPHA-LANTERNS
Part 4

I **TOLD** YOU, HENSHAW--I **CANNOT** "SAVE" THIS ALPHA-LANTERN. I CANNOT SAVE **ANY** OF THEM!

YOU'RE **STALLING**.

I **LEFT** THE GUARDIANS OF THE UNIVERSE **BEFORE** THEY CREATED THE **ALPHA-LANTERN CORPS**. I DO NOT KNOW **HOW** THEY WERE ASSEMBLED.

YOU WANT ME TO **REVERSE** THE PROCESS, BUT I WILL ONLY END UP **KILLING** THEM--!

HONESTLY, I DOUBT **ANY** GUARDIAN CAN CHANGE AN ALPHA-LANTERN BACK TO NORMAL.

EVERY ASPECT OF THEIR DESIGN AND FUNCTION SUGGESTS THEIR TRANSFORMATION IS **PERMANENT** AND **IRREVOCABLE**.

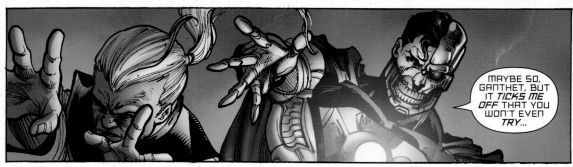

MAYBE SO, GANTHET, BUT IT **TICKS ME OFF** THAT YOU WON'T EVEN **TRY**...

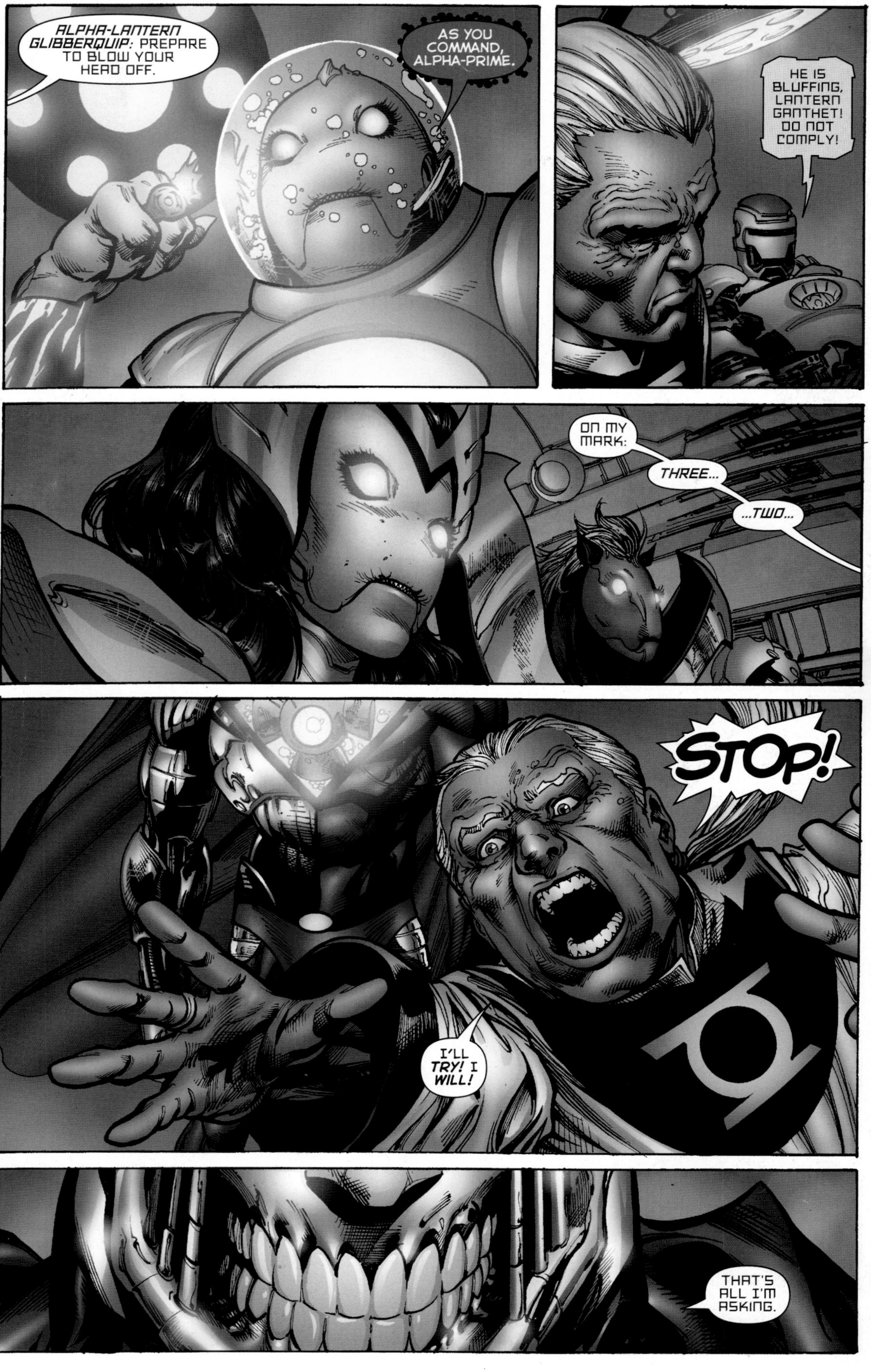
ALPHA-LANTERN GLIBBERQUIP: PREPARE TO BLOW YOUR HEAD OFF.
AS YOU COMMAND, ALPHA-PRIME.
HE IS BLUFFING, LANTERN GANTHET! DO NOT COMPLY!
ON MY MARK:
THREE...
...TWO...
STOP!
I'LL TRY! I WILL!
THAT'S ALL I'M ASKING.

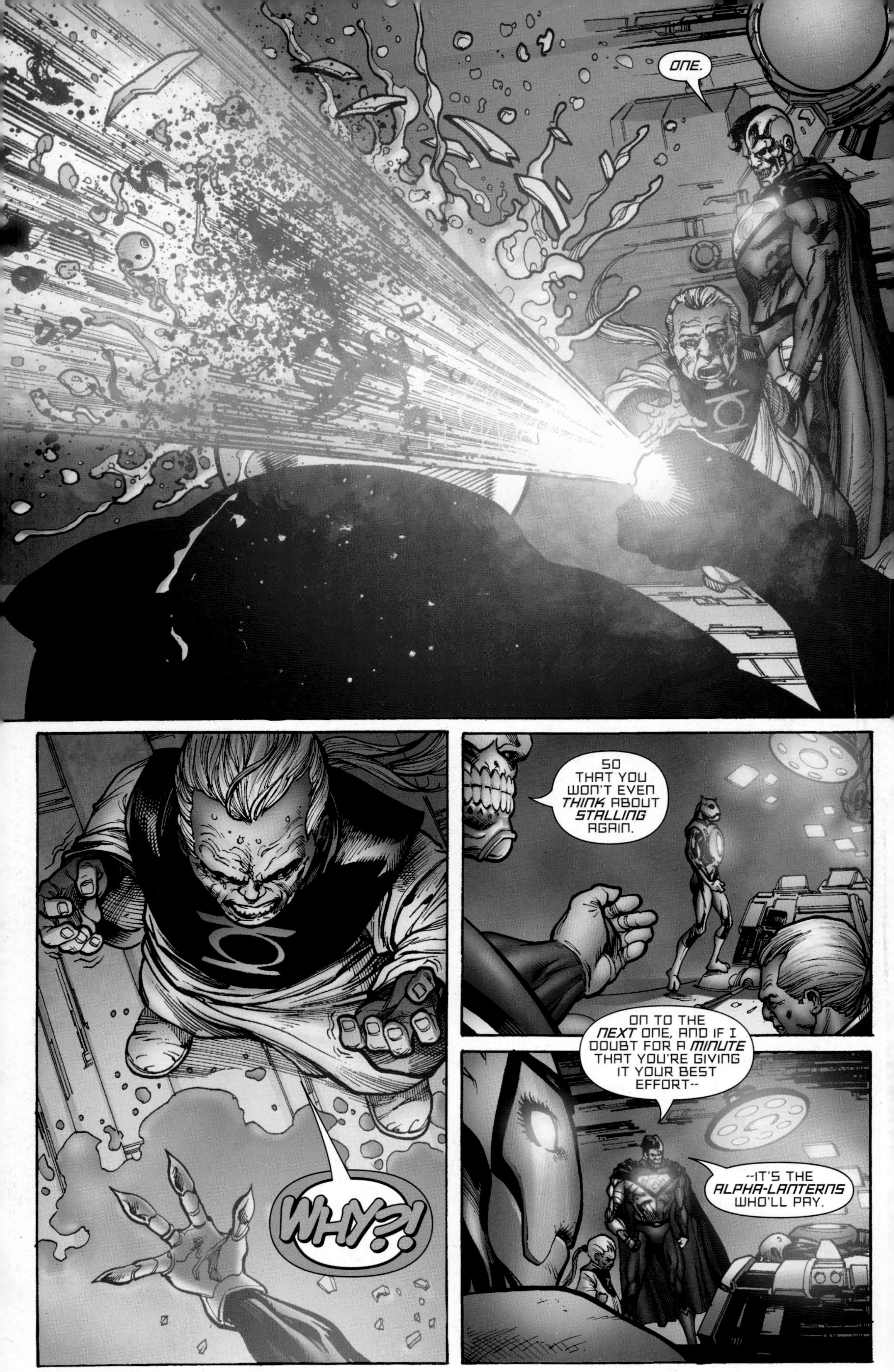
ONE.
WHY?!
SO THAT YOU WON'T EVEN THINK ABOUT STALLING AGAIN.
ON TO THE NEXT ONE, AND IF I DOUBT FOR A MINUTE THAT YOU'RE GIVING IT YOUR BEST EFFORT--
--IT'S THE ALPHA-LANTERNS WHO'LL PAY.

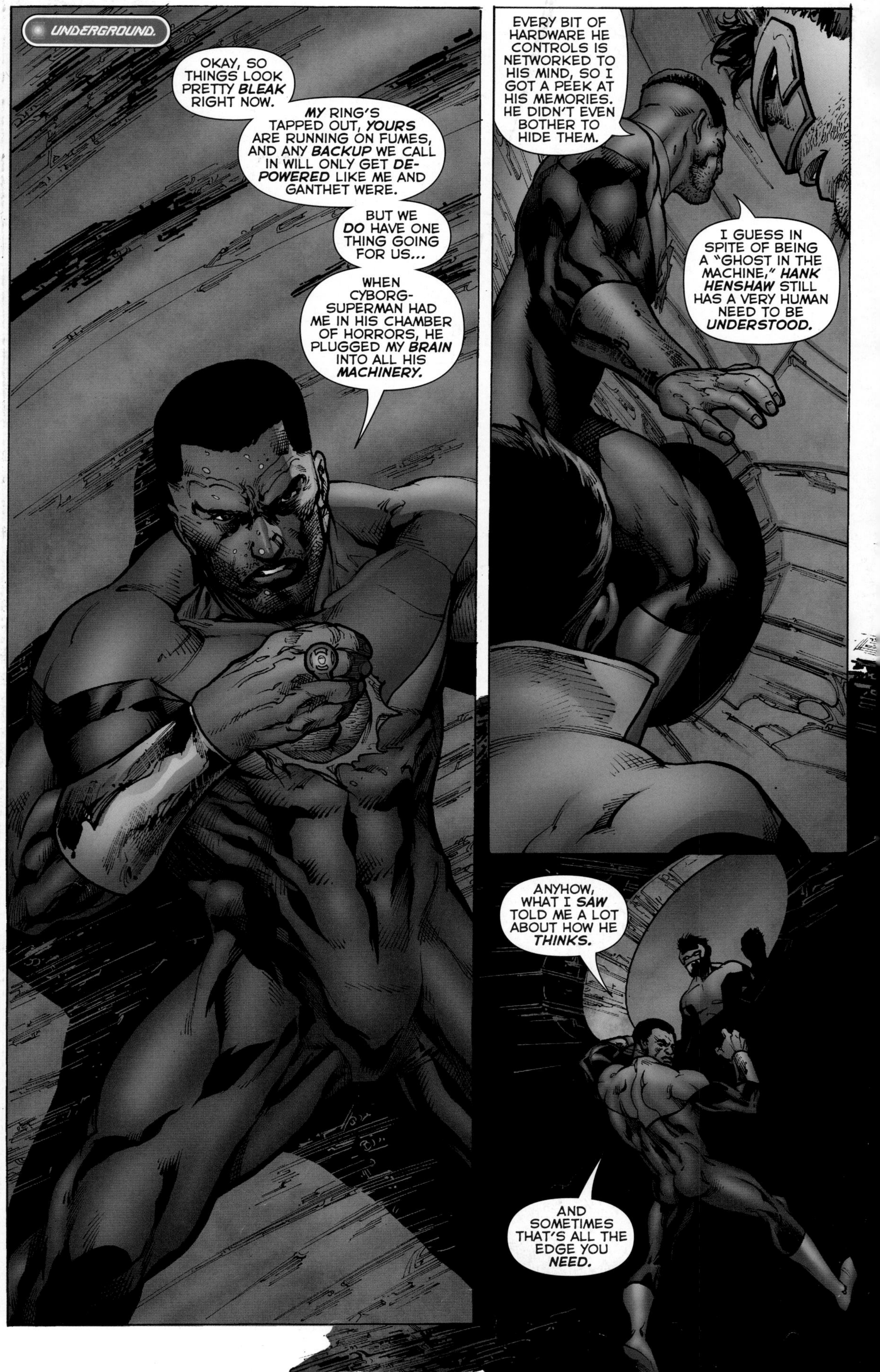
UNDERGROUND.
OKAY, SO THINGS LOOK PRETTY BLEAK RIGHT NOW.
MY RING'S TAPPED OUT, YOURS ARE RUNNING ON FUMES, AND ANY BACKUP WE CALL IN WILL ONLY GET DE-POWERED LIKE ME AND GANTHET WERE.
BUT WE DO HAVE ONE THING GOING FOR US...
WHEN CYBORG-SUPERMAN HAD ME IN HIS CHAMBER OF HORRORS, HE PLUGGED MY BRAIN INTO ALL HIS MACHINERY.
EVERY BIT OF HARDWARE HE CONTROLS IS NETWORKED TO HIS MIND, SO I GOT A PEEK AT HIS MEMORIES. HE DIDN'T EVEN BOTHER TO HIDE THEM.
I GUESS IN SPITE OF BEING A "GHOST IN THE MACHINE," HANK HENSHAW STILL HAS A VERY HUMAN NEED TO BE UNDERSTOOD.
ANYHOW, WHAT I SAW TOLD ME A LOT ABOUT HOW HE THINKS.
AND SOMETIMES THAT'S ALL THE EDGE YOU NEED.

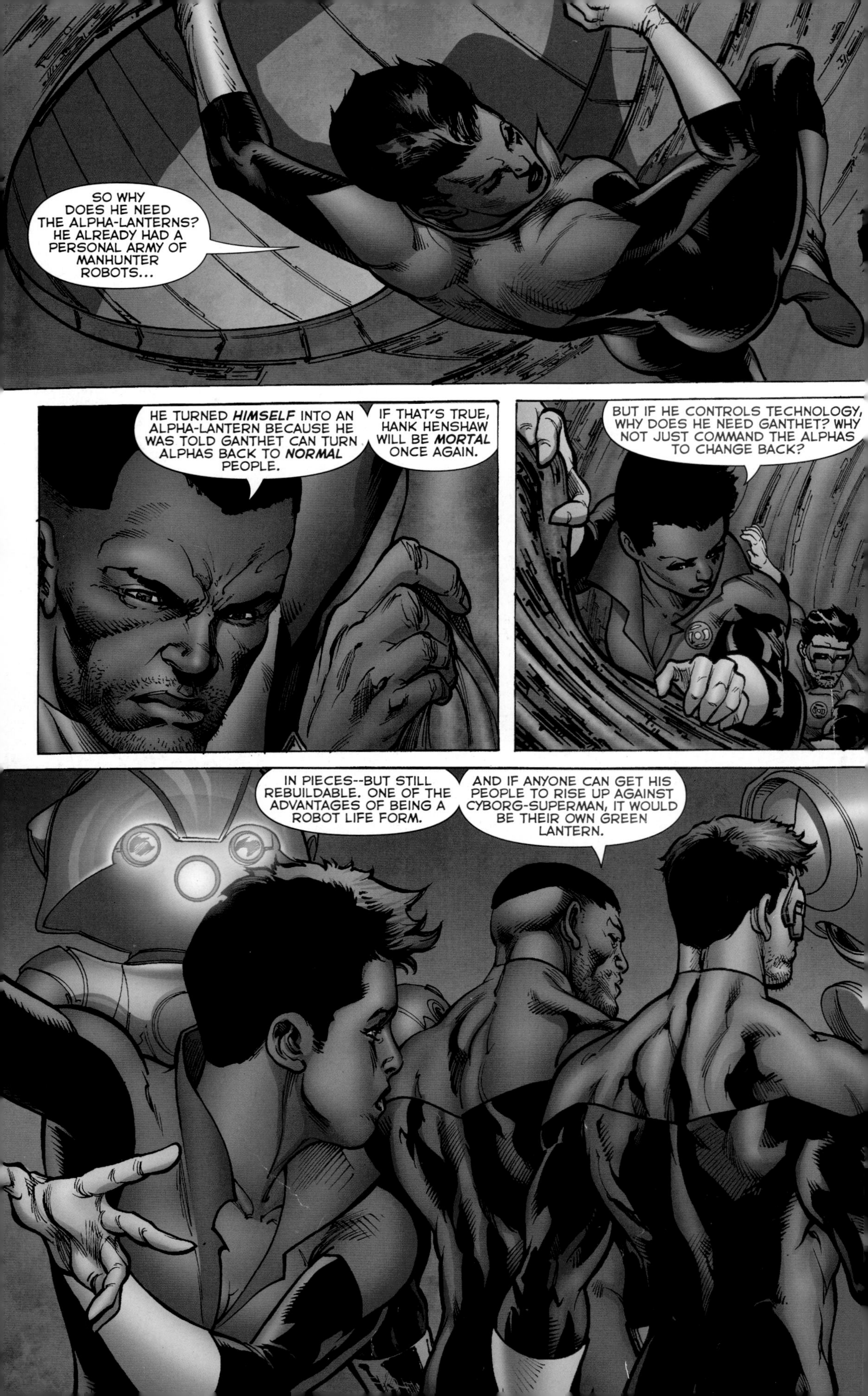
SO WHY DOES HE NEED THE ALPHA-LANTERNS? HE ALREADY HAD A PERSONAL ARMY OF MANHUNTER ROBOTS...
HE TURNED *HIMSELF* INTO AN ALPHA-LANTERN BECAUSE HE WAS TOLD GANTHET CAN TURN ALPHAS BACK TO *NORMAL* PEOPLE.
IF THAT'S TRUE, HANK HENSHAW WILL BE *MORTAL* ONCE AGAIN.
BUT IF HE CONTROLS TECHNOLOGY, WHY DOES HE NEED GANTHET? WHY NOT JUST COMMAND THE ALPHAS TO CHANGE BACK?
IN PIECES--BUT STILL REBUILDABLE. ONE OF THE ADVANTAGES OF BEING A ROBOT LIFE FORM.
AND IF ANYONE CAN GET HIS PEOPLE TO RISE UP AGAINST CYBORG-SUPERMAN, IT WOULD BE THEIR OWN GREEN LANTERN.

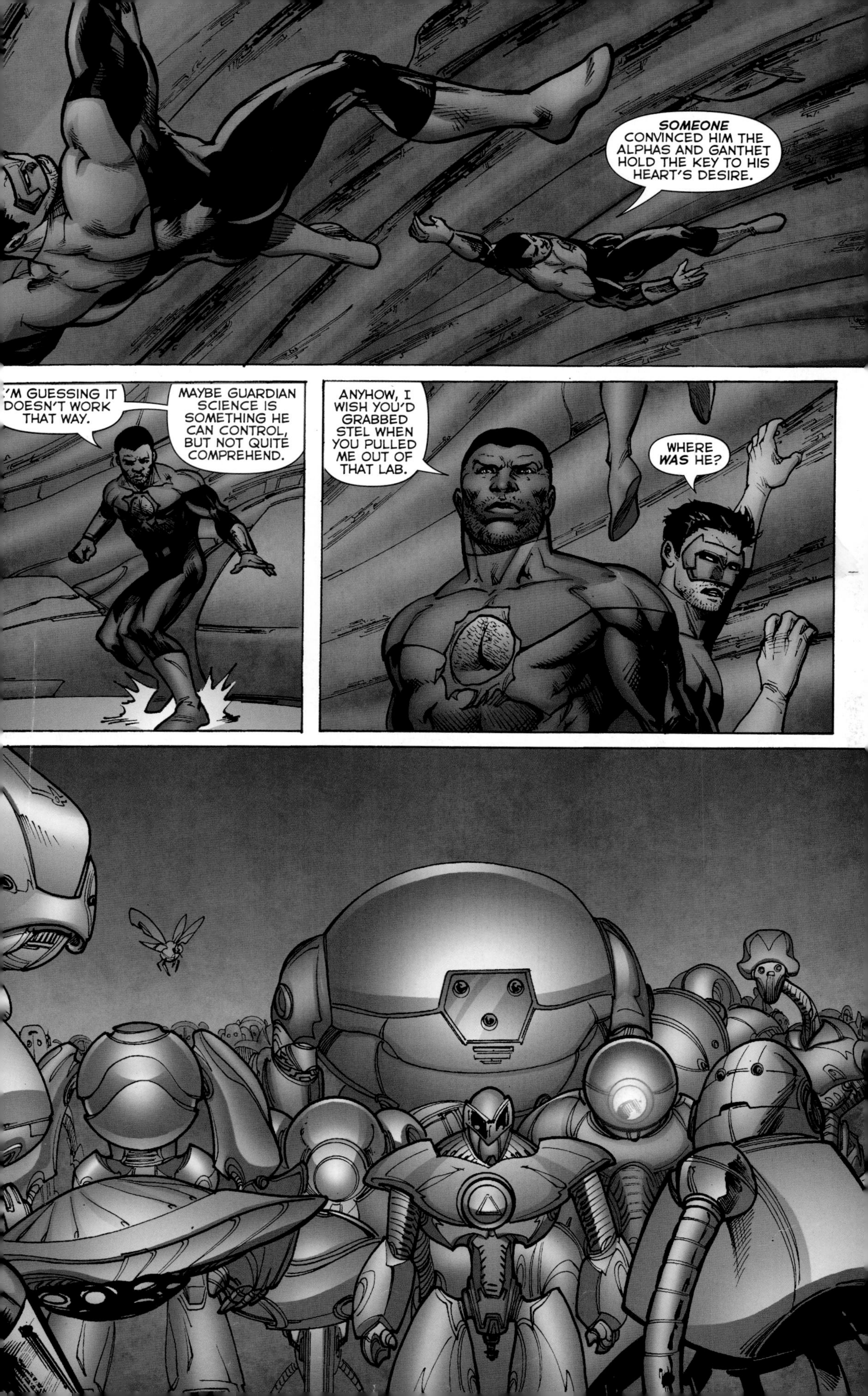
SOMEONE CONVINCED HIM THE ALPHAS AND GANTHET HOLD THE KEY TO HIS HEART'S DESIRE.
I'M GUESSING IT DOESN'T WORK THAT WAY.
MAYBE GUARDIAN SCIENCE IS SOMETHING HE CAN CONTROL, BUT NOT QUITE COMPREHEND.
ANYHOW, I WISH YOU'D GRABBED STEL WHEN YOU PULLED ME OUT OF THAT LAB.
WHERE WAS HE?

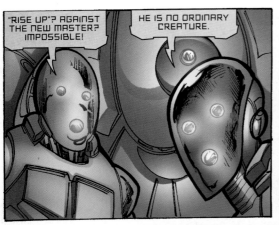
"RISE UP"? AGAINST THE NEW MASTER? IMPOSSIBLE!

HE IS NO ORDINARY CREATURE.

HIS COMMAND IS TOTAL. HE TOLD US TO STAY HERE. WE HAVE TO OBEY.

I CAN FEEL HIS AUTHORITY DOWN TO MY *MICROCIRCUITS*--!

WE'VE FOUGHT HIM BEFORE, AND HE *CAN* BE BEATEN!

BUT WE NEED YOUR *HELP!* OUR RINGS ARE NO GOOD AGAINST HIS *ALPHA-LANTERNS!*

WAIT A MINUTE...

SORA, I KNOW WHO WE *CAN* CALL IN!

YOUR *JUSTICE LEAGUE* FRIENDS?

THEY'RE ON THE OTHER SIDE OF THE GALAXY. THE GUY I'M THINKING OF IS *CLOSER*...

...BUT IF I MAKE THE CALL, THE ALPHAS WILL DETECT MY *SIGNAL* AND ZERO IN ON US.

WELL, WE CAN'T HIDE FOREVER. NOT WITH *GANTHET* AND *STEL* IN ENEMY HANDS.

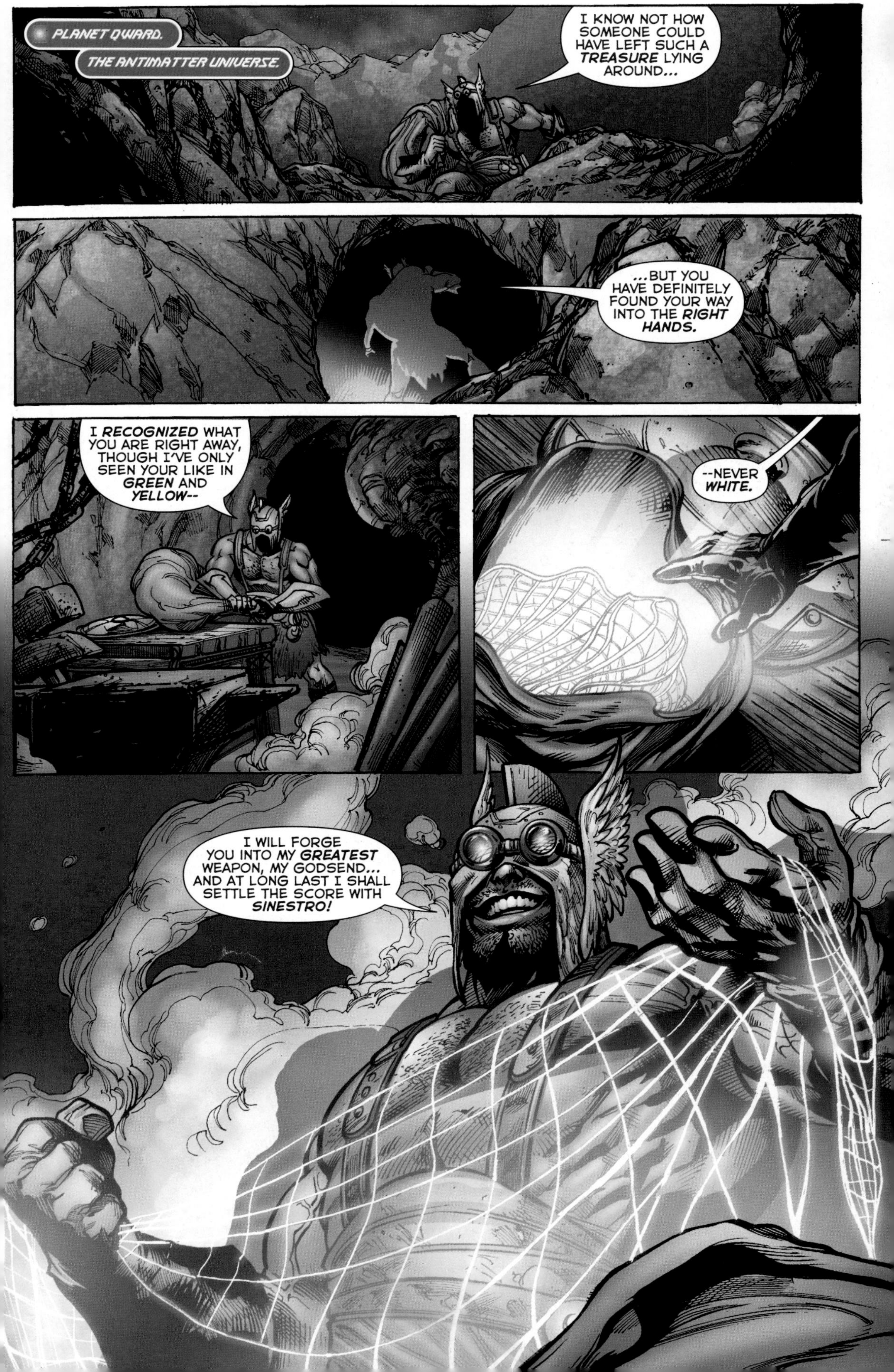
PLANET QWARD.
THE ANTIMATTER UNIVERSE.
I KNOW NOT HOW SOMEONE COULD HAVE LEFT SUCH A TREASURE LYING AROUND...
...BUT YOU HAVE DEFINITELY FOUND YOUR WAY INTO THE RIGHT HANDS.
I RECOGNIZED WHAT YOU ARE RIGHT AWAY, THOUGH I'VE ONLY SEEN YOUR LIKE IN GREEN AND YELLOW--
--NEVER WHITE.
I WILL FORGE YOU INTO MY GREATEST WEAPON, MY GODSEND... AND AT LONG LAST I SHALL SETTLE THE SCORE WITH SINESTRO!

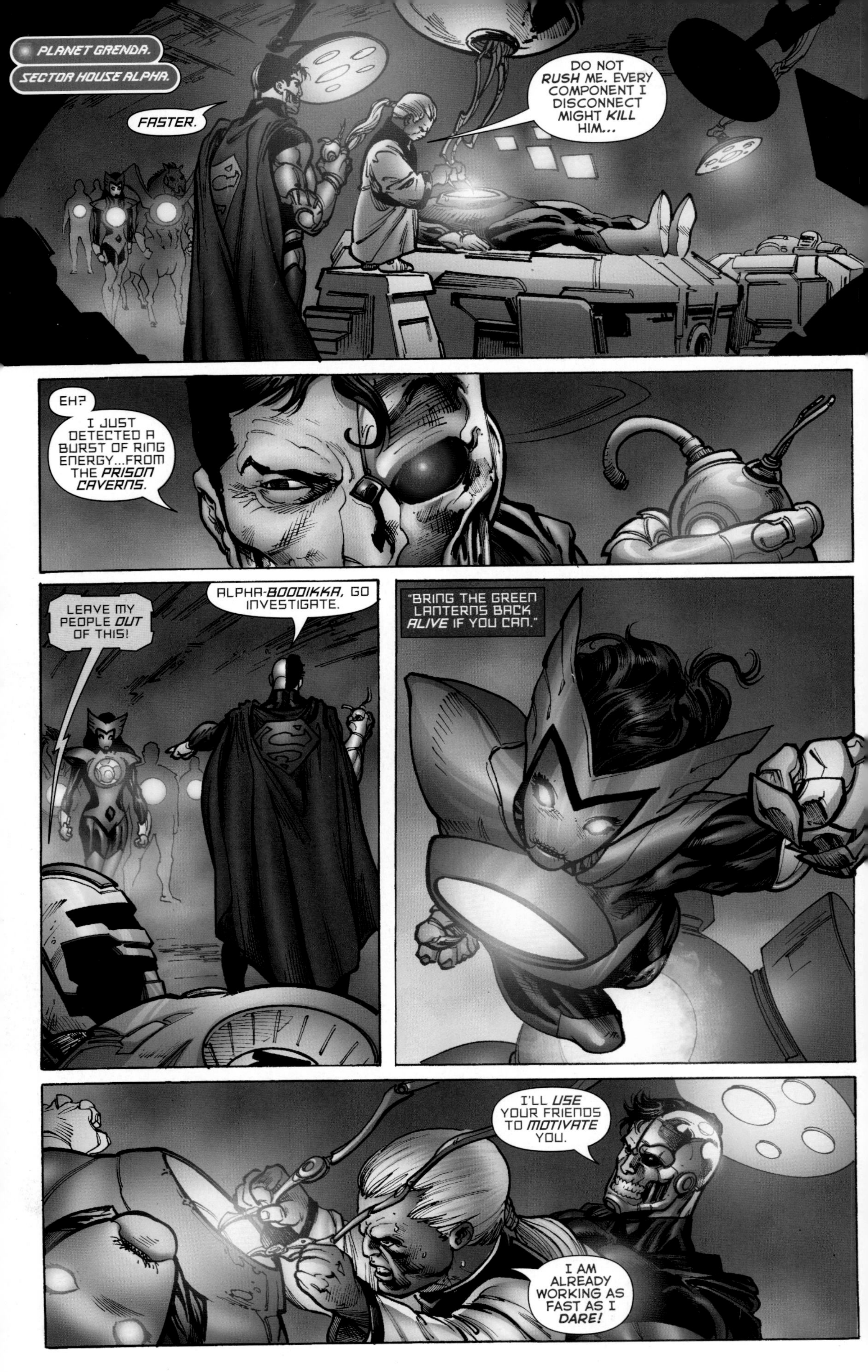
PLANET GRENDA.
SECTOR HOUSE ALPHA.
FASTER.
DO NOT RUSH ME. EVERY COMPONENT I DISCONNECT MIGHT KILL HIM...
EH?
I JUST DETECTED A BURST OF RING ENERGY...FROM THE PRISON CAVERNS.
ALPHA-BOODIKKA, GO INVESTIGATE.
LEAVE MY PEOPLE OUT OF THIS!
"BRING THE GREEN LANTERNS BACK ALIVE IF YOU CAN."
I'LL USE YOUR FRIENDS TO MOTIVATE YOU.
I AM ALREADY WORKING AS FAST AS I DARE!

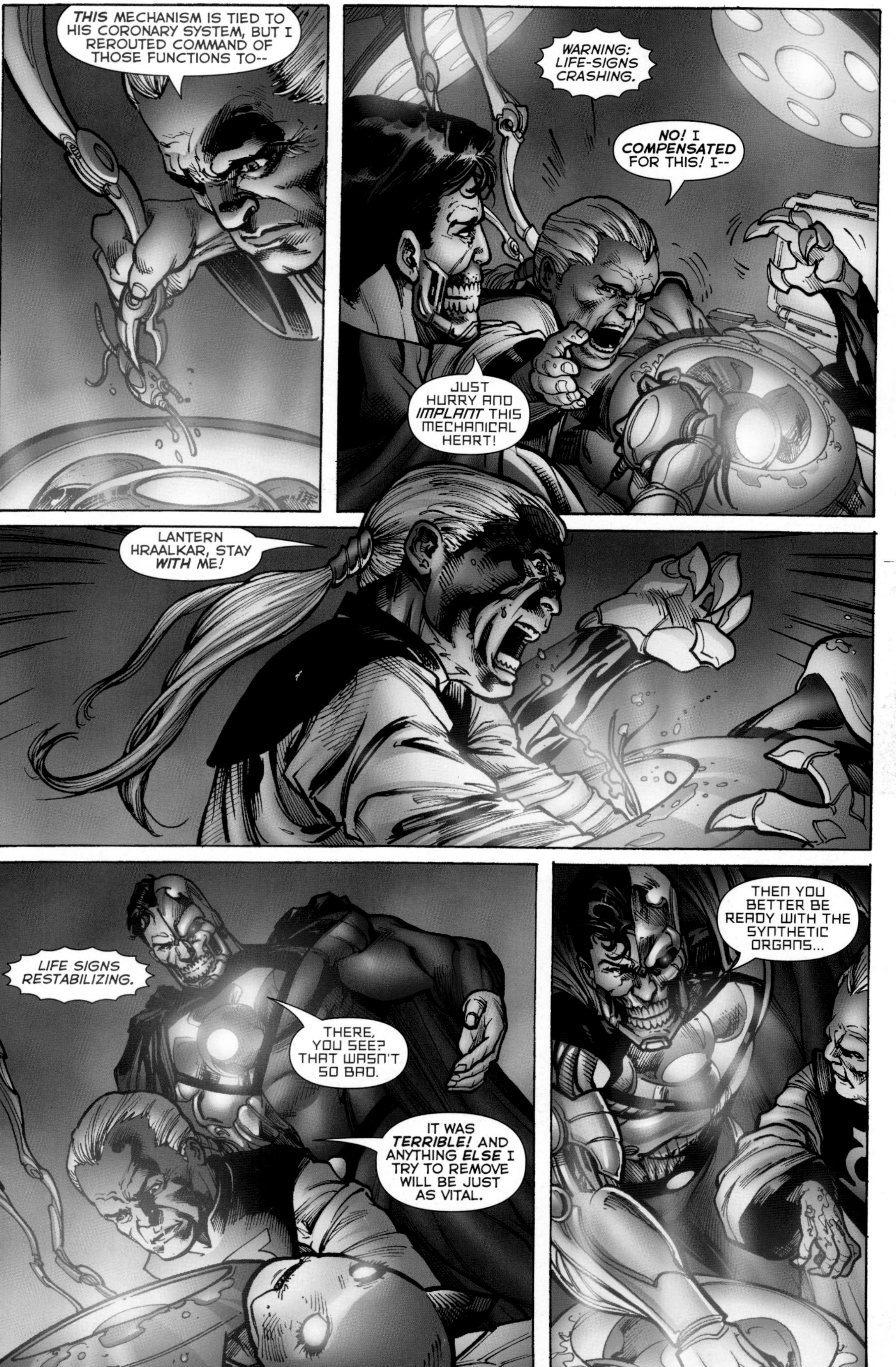
THIS MECHANISM IS TIED TO HIS CORONARY SYSTEM, BUT I REROUTED COMMAND OF THOSE FUNCTIONS TO--
WARNING: LIFE-SIGNS CRASHING.
NO! I COMPENSATED FOR THIS! I--
JUST HURRY AND IMPLANT THIS MECHANICAL HEART!
LANTERN HRAALKAR, STAY WITH ME!
LIFE SIGNS RESTABILIZING.
THERE, YOU SEE? THAT WASN'T SO BAD.
IT WAS TERRIBLE! AND ANYTHING ELSE I TRY TO REMOVE WILL BE JUST AS VITAL.
THEN YOU BETTER BE READY WITH THE SYNTHETIC ORGANS...

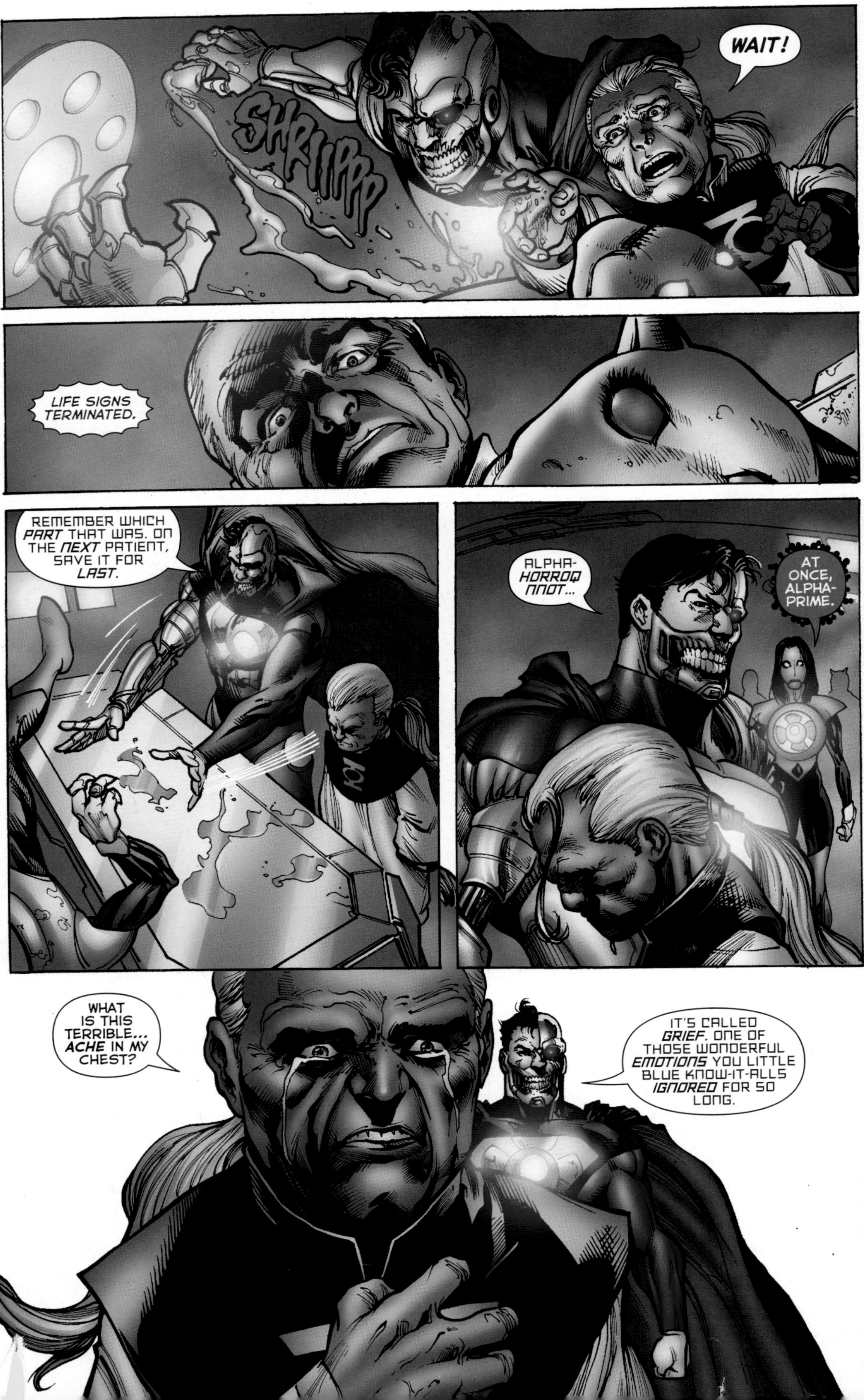

SHRUPP
WAIT!
LIFE SIGNS TERMINATED.
REMEMBER WHICH PART THAT WAS. ON THE NEXT PATIENT, SAVE IT FOR LAST.
ALPHA-HORROQ NNOT...
AT ONCE, ALPHA-PRIME.
WHAT IS THIS TERRIBLE... ACHE IN MY CHEST?
IT'S CALLED GRIEF. ONE OF THOSE WONDERFUL EMOTIONS YOU LITTLE BLUE KNOW-IT-ALLS IGNORED FOR SO LONG.

...SO HOW *QUICK* CAN YOU GET HERE?

I AM ONE HYPERSPACE JUMP AWAY. STAY ALIVE UNTIL THEN.

WE'LL DO OUR *BEST.* RAYNER OUT.

WE'D BETTER GET *OUT* OF HERE BEFORE THE ALPHAS CONVERGE.

HOW MUCH MORE *JUICE* YOU GOT IN THAT RING? IF THEY'RE COMING ANYWAY, I HAVE A PERFECT *USE* FOR WHAT'S LEFT.

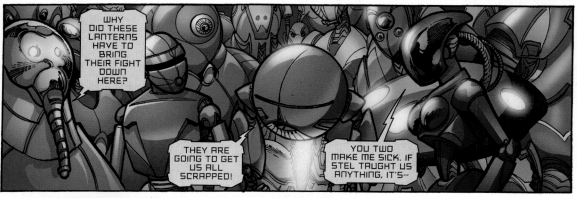

WHY DID THESE LANTERNS HAVE TO BRING THEIR FIGHT DOWN HERE?

THEY ARE GOING TO GET US ALL SCRAPPED!

YOU TWO MAKE ME SICK. IF STEL TAUGHT US ANYTHING, IT'S--

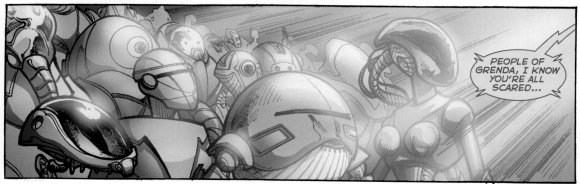

PEOPLE OF GRENDA, I KNOW YOU'RE ALL SCARED...

...BUT IF YOU CAN'T FIND THE COURAGE TO FIGHT FOR YOUR OWN FREEDOM, THEN DO IT FOR HIM! DO IT FOR GREEN LANTERN STEL!

FOR YEARS HE'S PROTECTED EVERY ONE OF YOU, AND HE'S NEVER ASKED FOR MUCH IN RETURN...

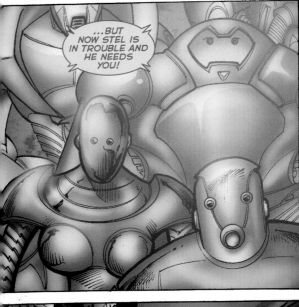

...BUT NOW STEL IS IN TROUBLE AND HE NEEDS YOU!

HE TAUGHT YOU THE MEANING OF COURAGE! WILL YOU JUST HIDE DOWN HERE AND LET THESE INVADERS DESTROY EVERYTHING YOU'VE BUILT?

WE WILL!

WE WILL!

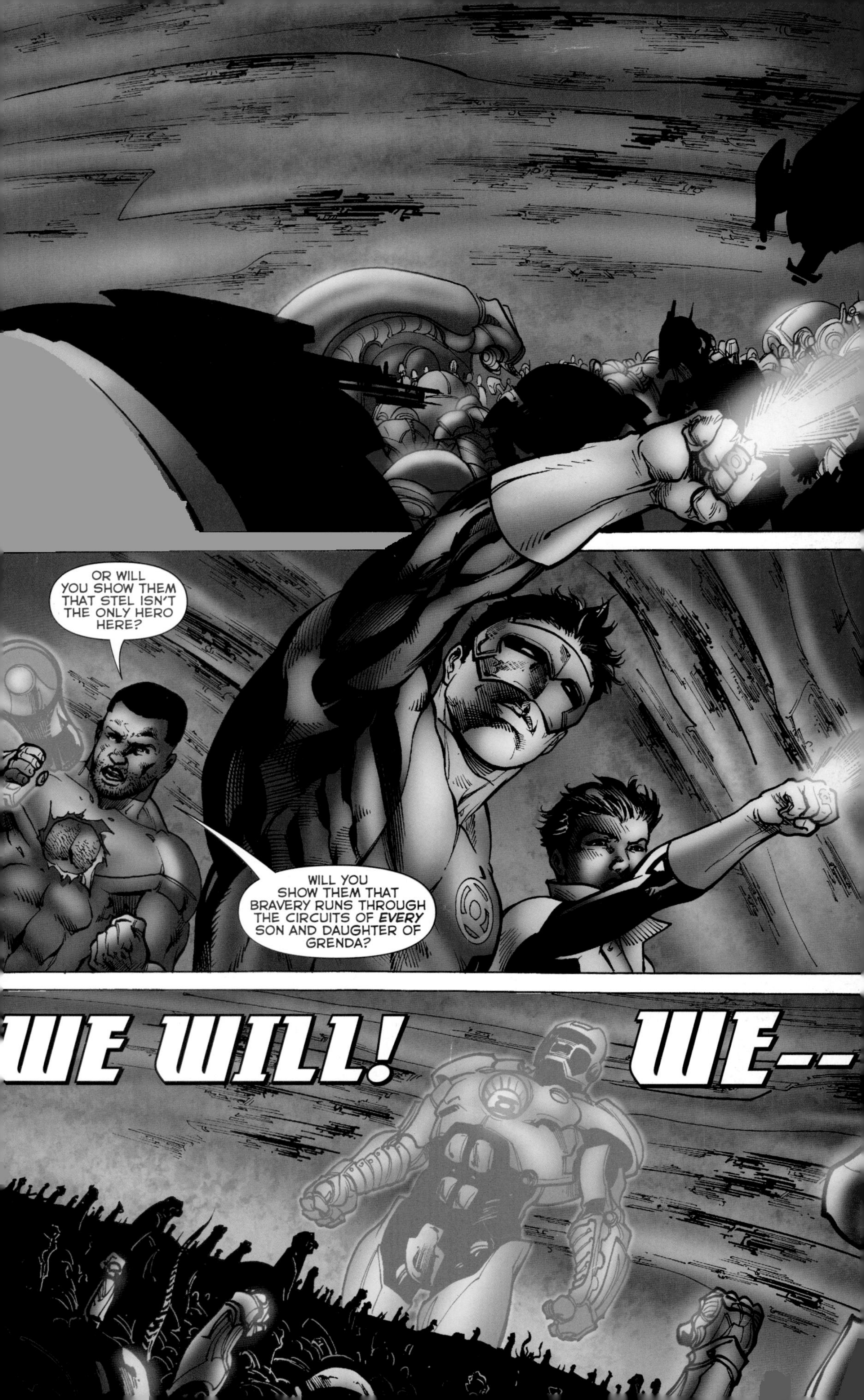
OR WILL YOU SHOW THEM THAT STEL ISN'T THE ONLY HERO HERE?
WILL YOU SHOW THEM THAT BRAVERY RUNS THROUGH THE CIRCUITS OF *EVERY* SON AND DAUGHTER OF GRENDA?
WE WILL!
WE--

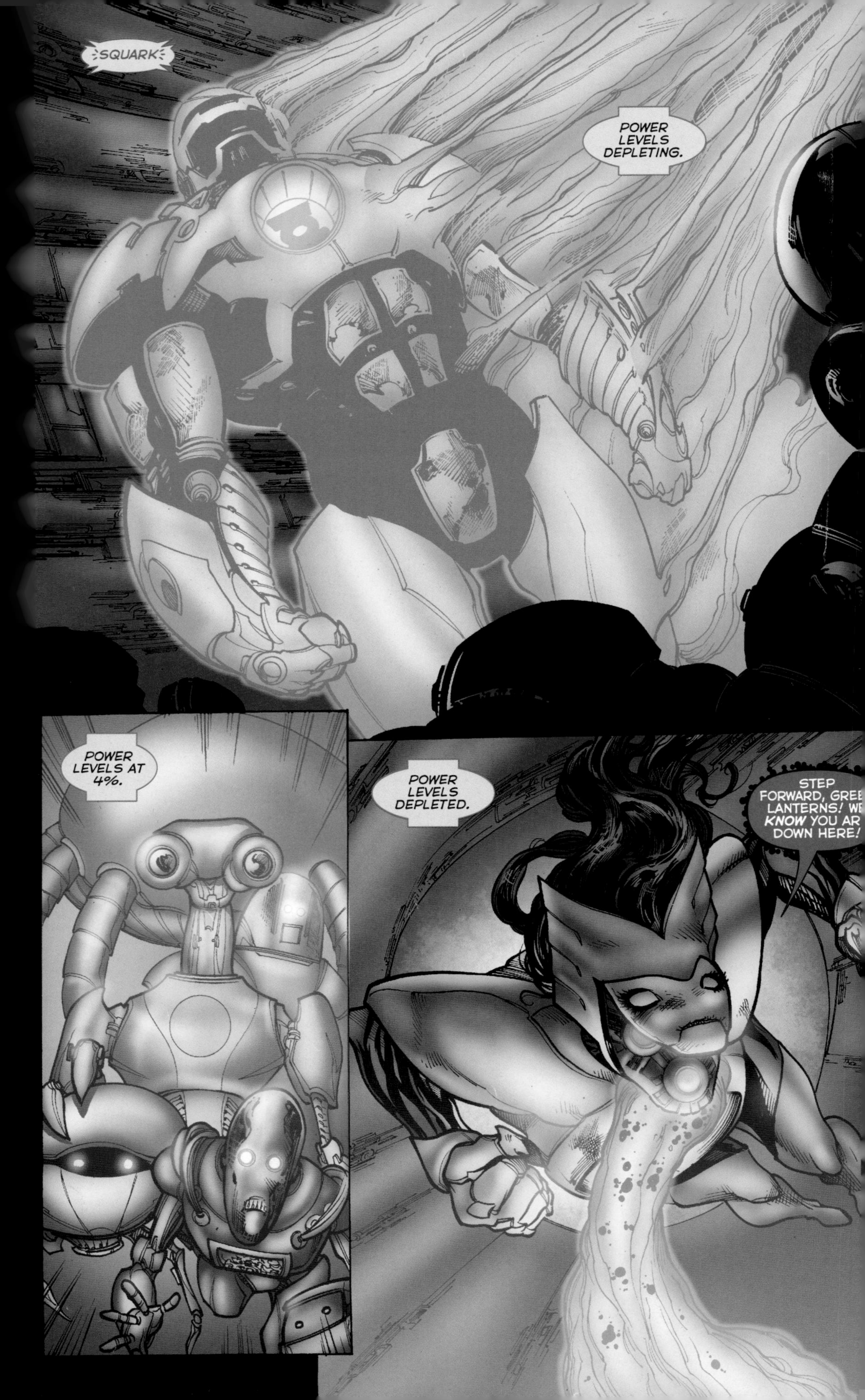
SQUARK
POWER LEVELS DEPLETING.
POWER LEVELS AT 4%.
POWER LEVELS DEPLETED.
STEP FORWARD, GREE LANTERNS! WE KNOW YOU AR DOWN HERE!

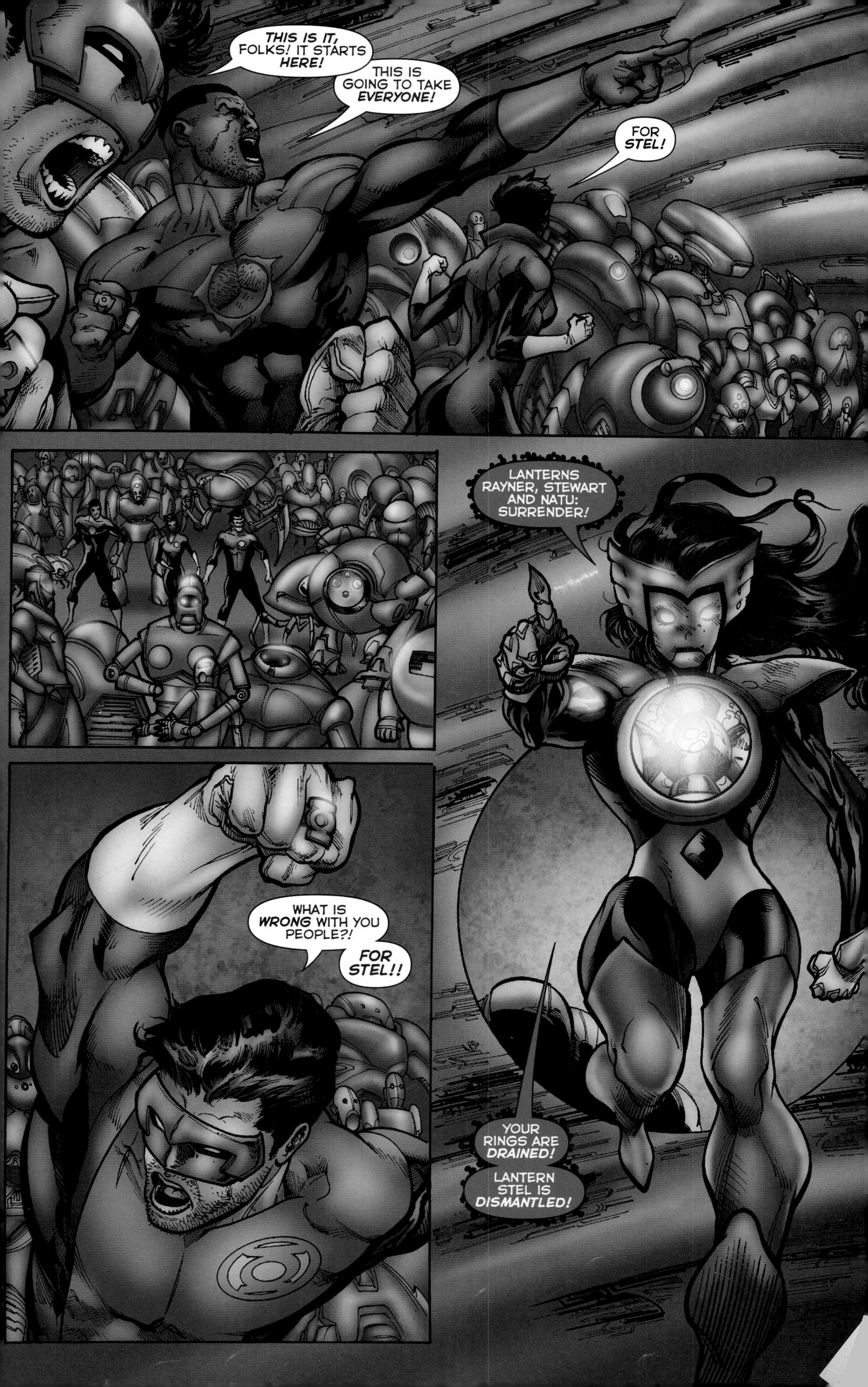
THIS IS IT, FOLKS! IT STARTS HERE!
THIS IS GOING TO TAKE EVERYONE!
FOR STEL!
LANTERNS RAYNER, STEWART AND NATU: SURRENDER!
WHAT IS WRONG WITH YOU PEOPLE?!
FOR STEL!!
YOUR RINGS ARE DRAINED!
LANTERN STEL IS DISMANTLED!

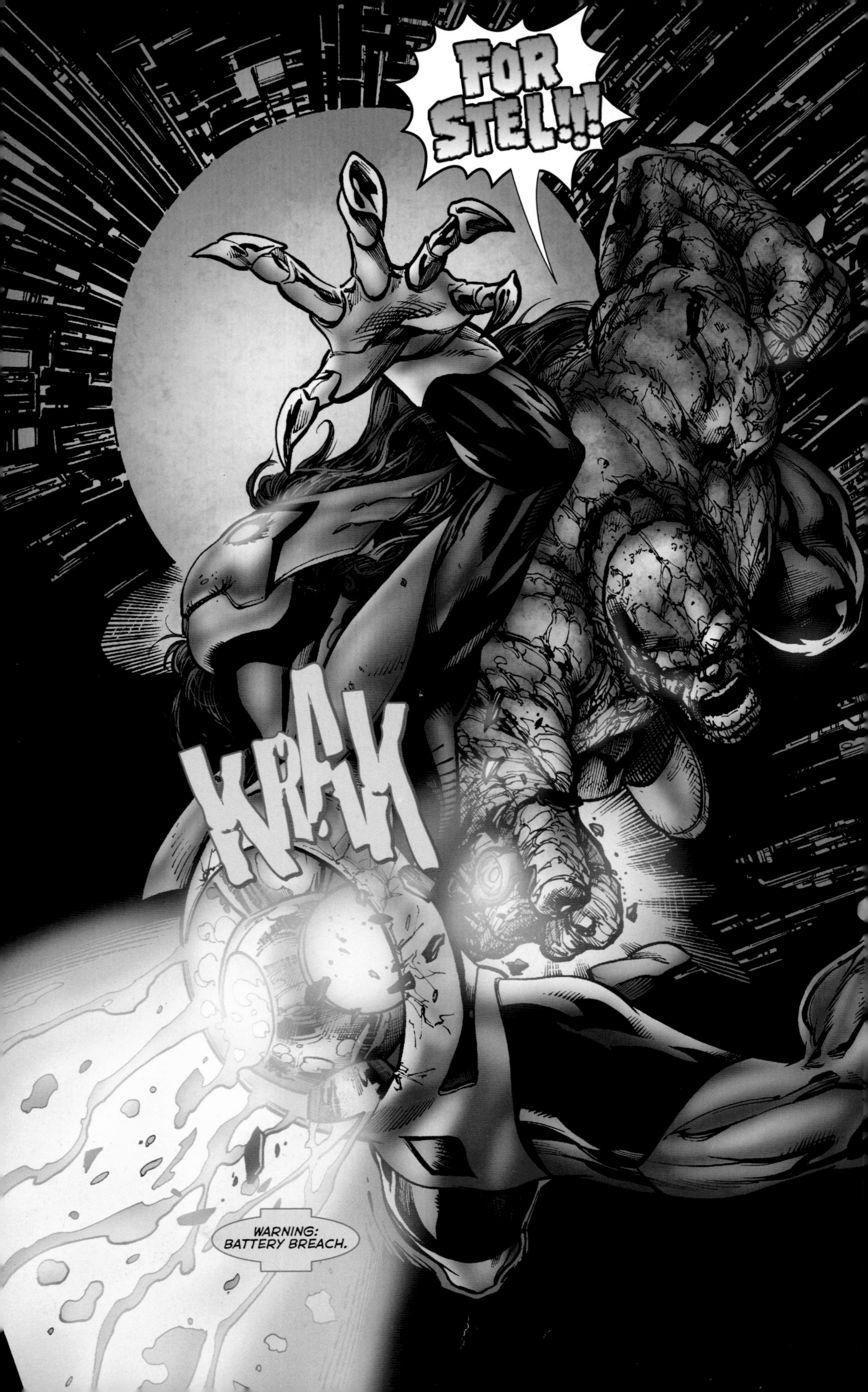
FOR STEL!!!
KRAK
WARNING: BATTERY BREACH.

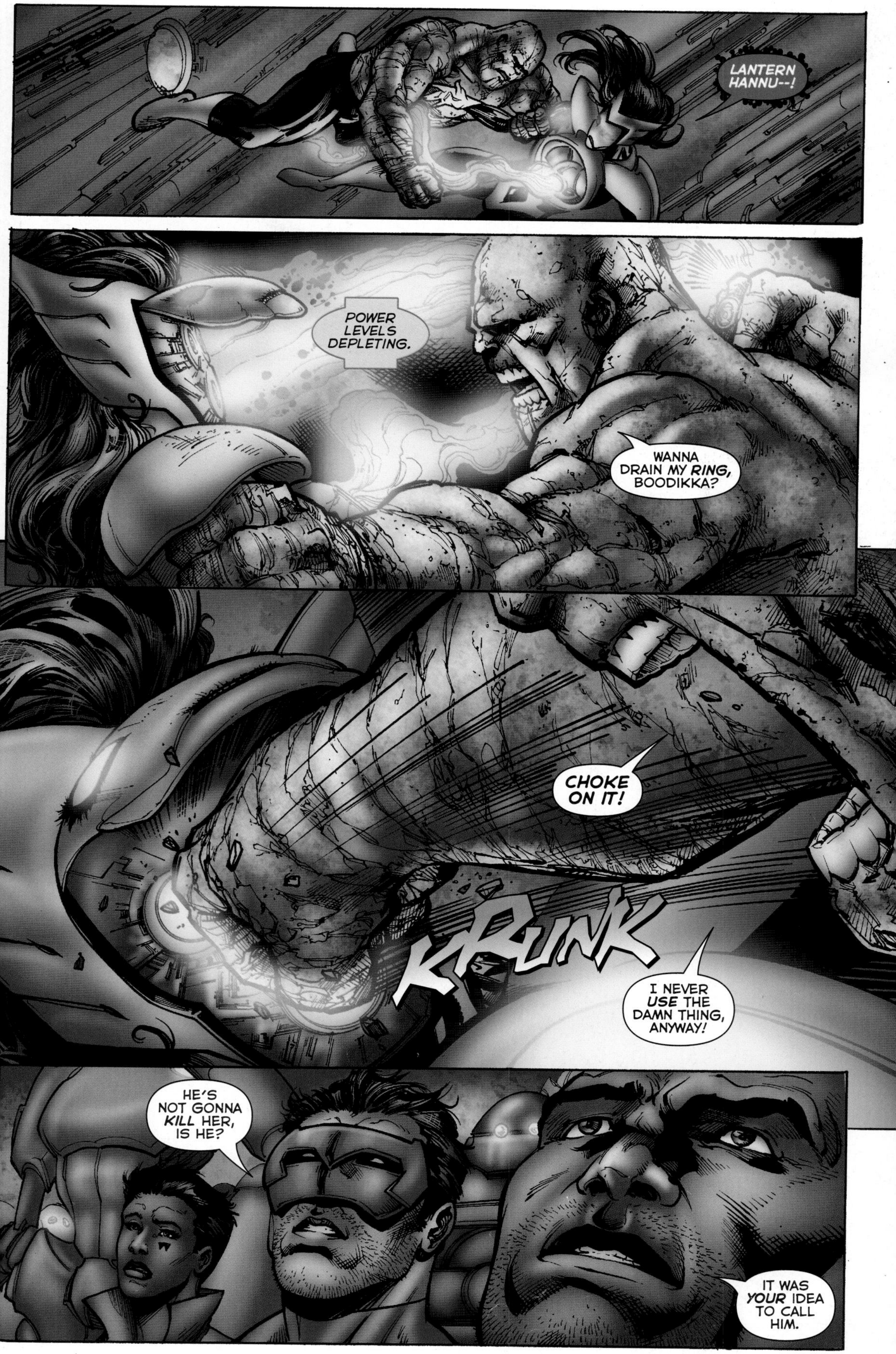
LANTERN HANNU--!
POWER LEVELS DEPLETING.
WANNA DRAIN MY RING, BOODIKKA?
CHOKE ON IT!
KRUNK
I NEVER USE THE DAMN THING, ANYWAY!
HE'S NOT GONNA KILL HER, IS HE?
IT WAS YOUR IDEA TO CALL HIM.

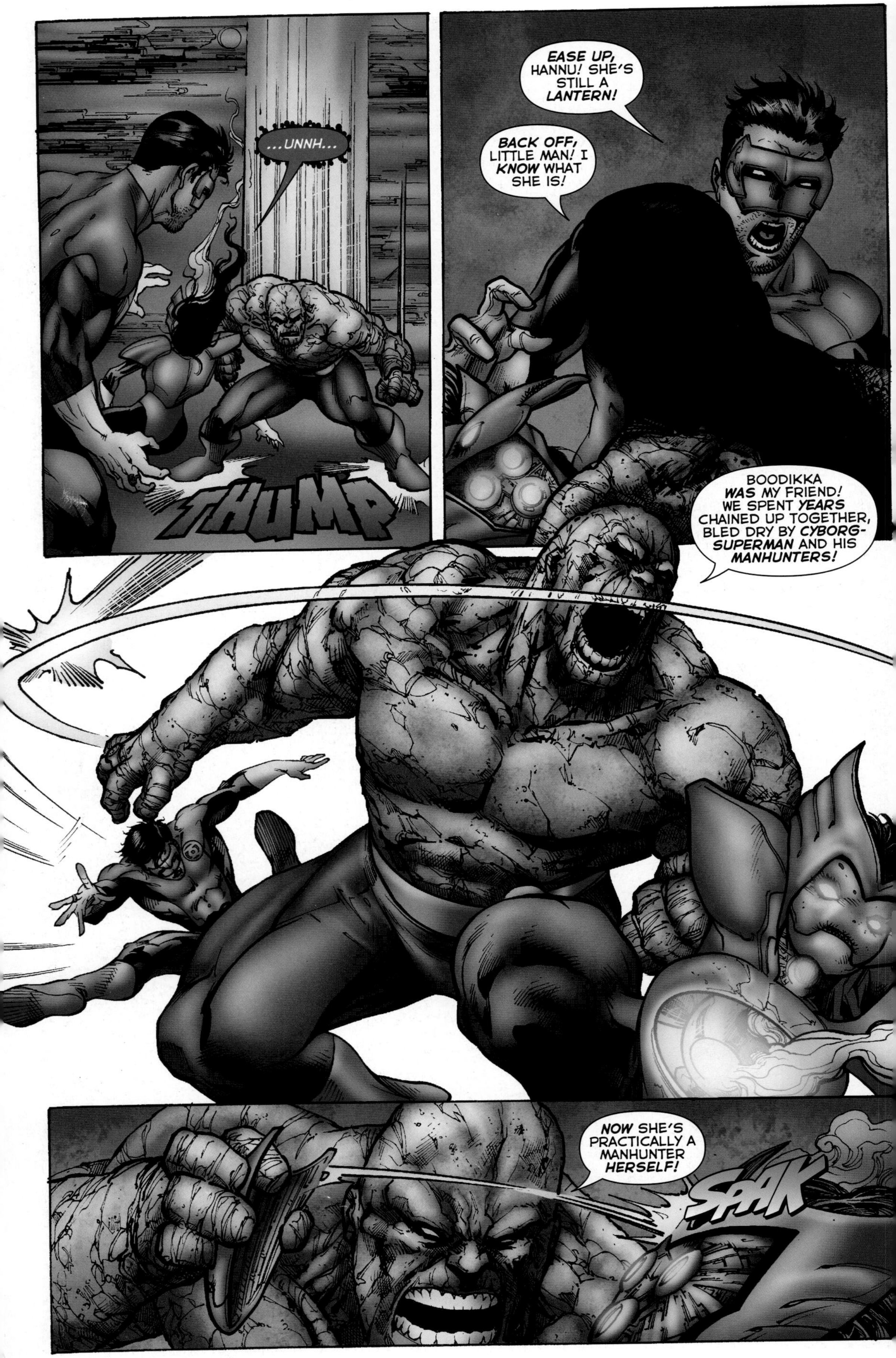
...UNNH...
THUMP
EASE UP, HANNU! SHE'S STILL A LANTERN!
BACK OFF, LITTLE MAN! I KNOW WHAT SHE IS!
BOODIKKA WAS MY FRIEND! WE SPENT YEARS CHAINED UP TOGETHER, BLED DRY BY CYBORG-SUPERMAN AND HIS MANHUNTERS!
NOW SHE'S PRACTICALLY A MANHUNTER HERSELF!
SPAK

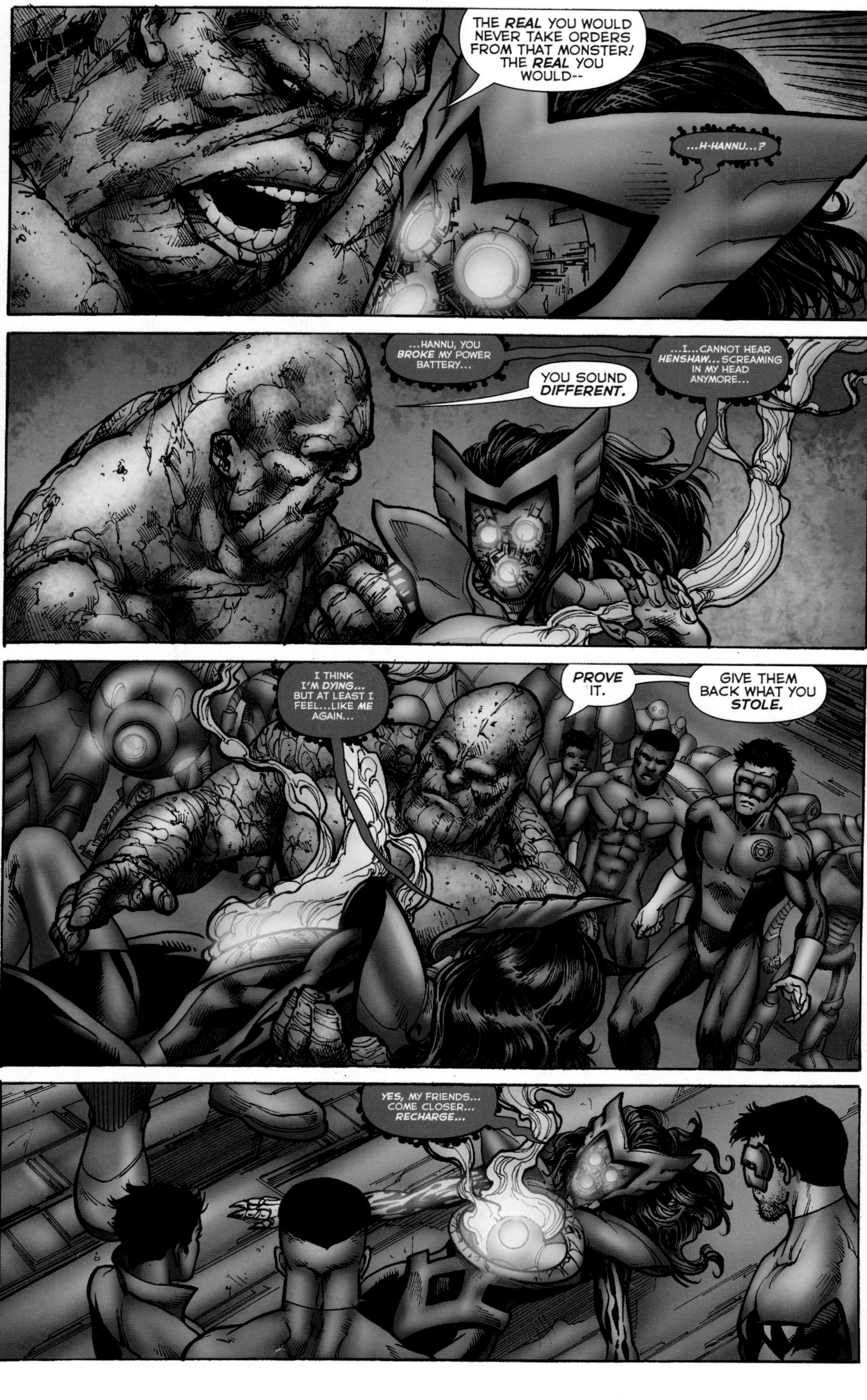
THE REAL YOU WOULD NEVER TAKE ORDERS FROM THAT MONSTER! THE REAL YOU WOULD--
...H-HANNU...?
...HANNU, YOU BROKE MY POWER BATTERY...
YOU SOUND DIFFERENT.
...I...CANNOT HEAR HENSHAW...SCREAMING IN MY HEAD ANYMORE...
I THINK I'M DYING... BUT AT LEAST I FEEL...LIKE ME AGAIN...
PROVE IT.
GIVE THEM BACK WHAT YOU STOLE.
YES, MY FRIENDS... COME CLOSER... RECHARGE...

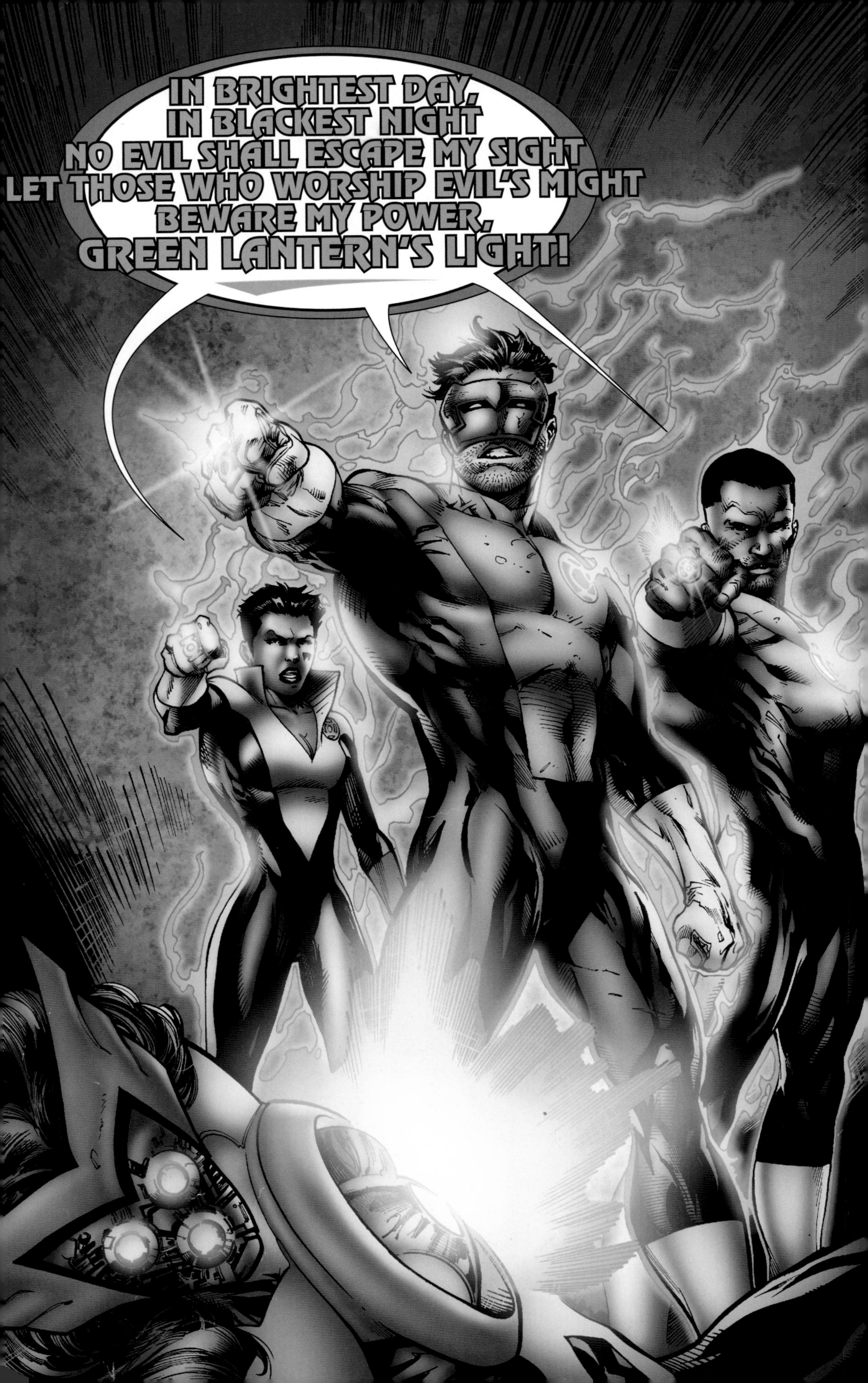
IN BRIGHTEST DAY, IN BLACKEST NIGHT NO EVIL SHALL ESCAPE MY SIGHT LET THOSE WHO WORSHIP EVIL'S MIGHT BEWARE MY POWER, GREEN LANTERN'S LIGHT!

REVOLT OF THE ALPHA-LANTERNS CONCLUSION
Cover by Ardian Syaf, Vicente Cifuentes & Randy Mayor

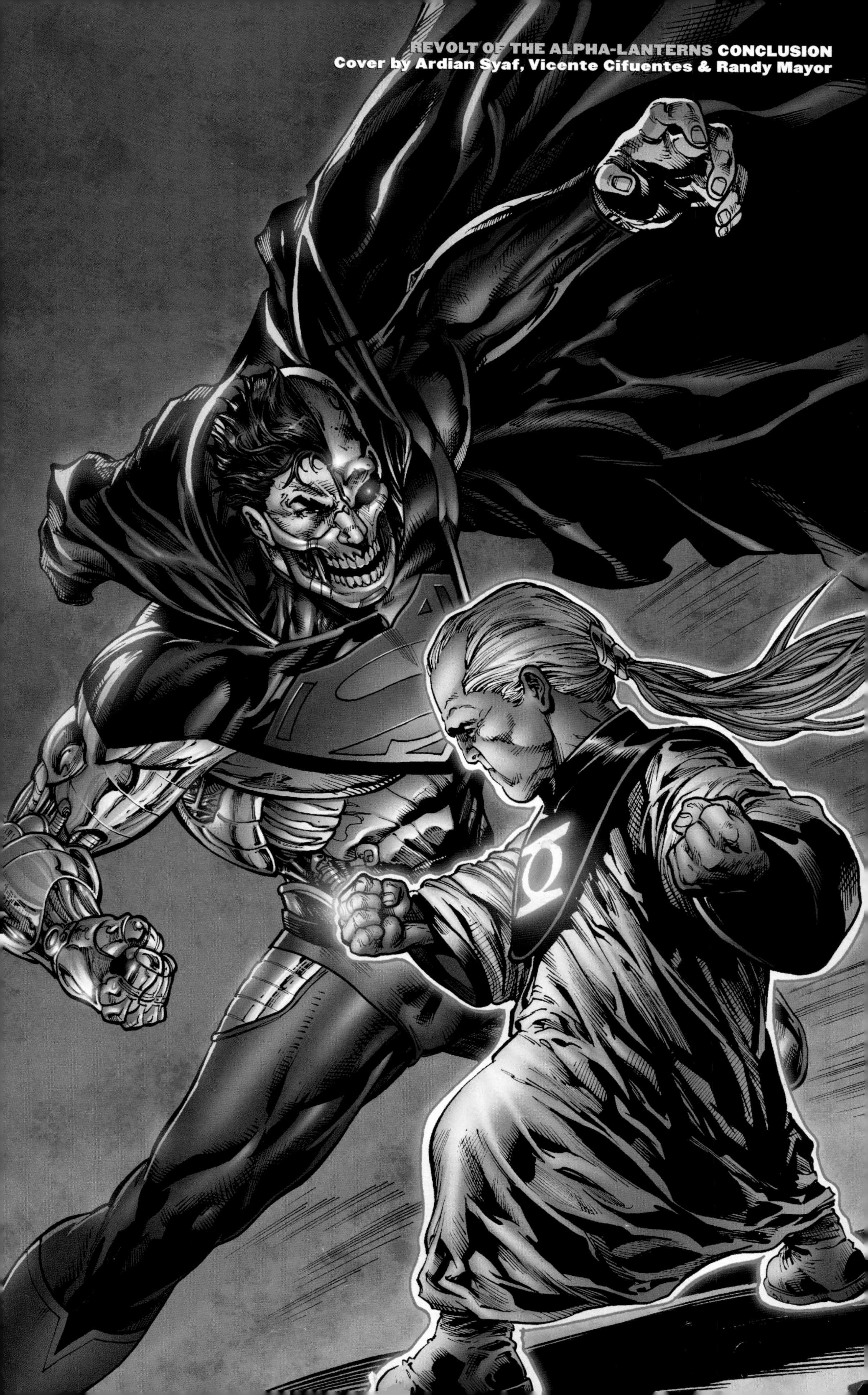

Variant by Patrick Gleason, Mark Irwin & Randy Mayor

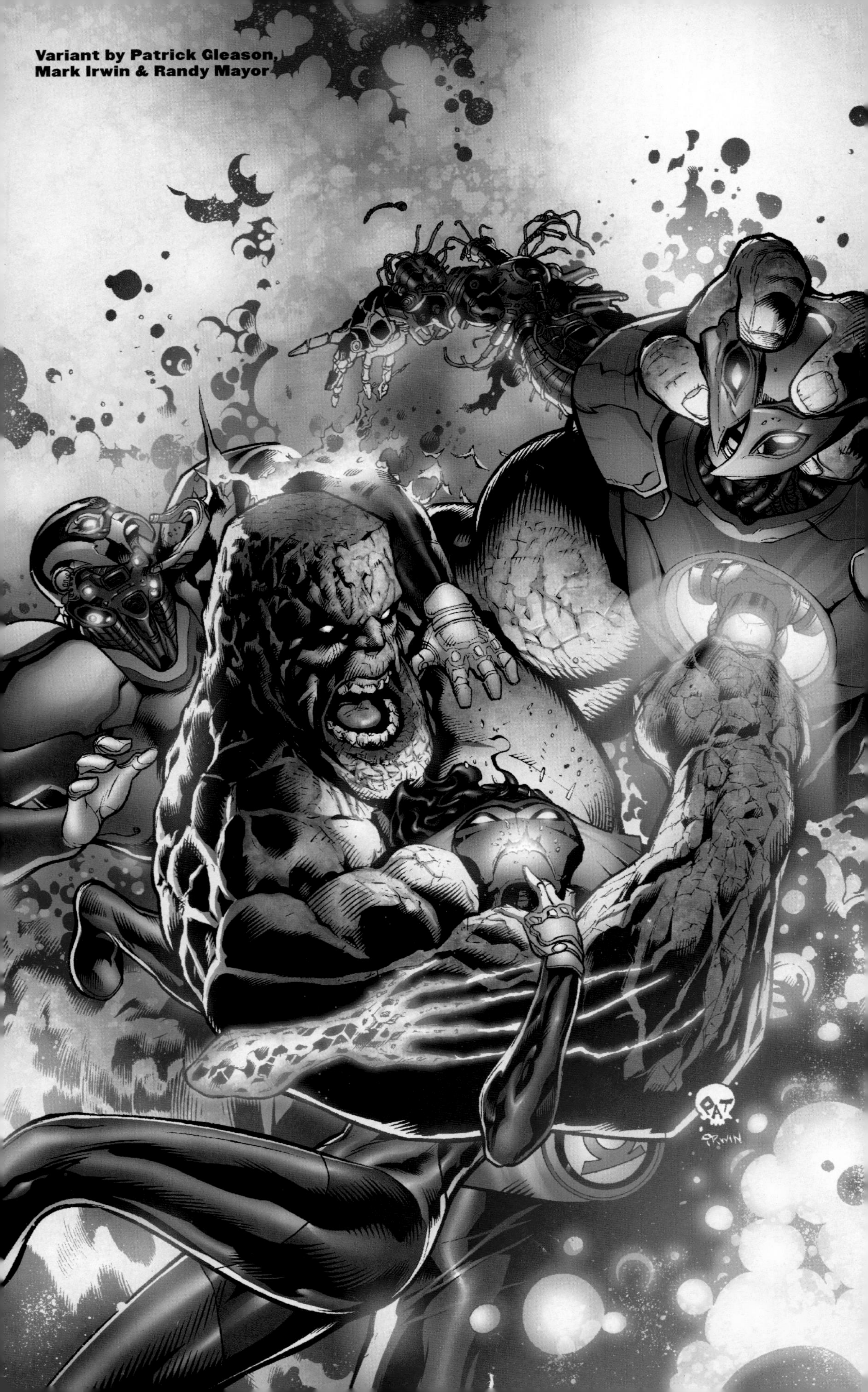

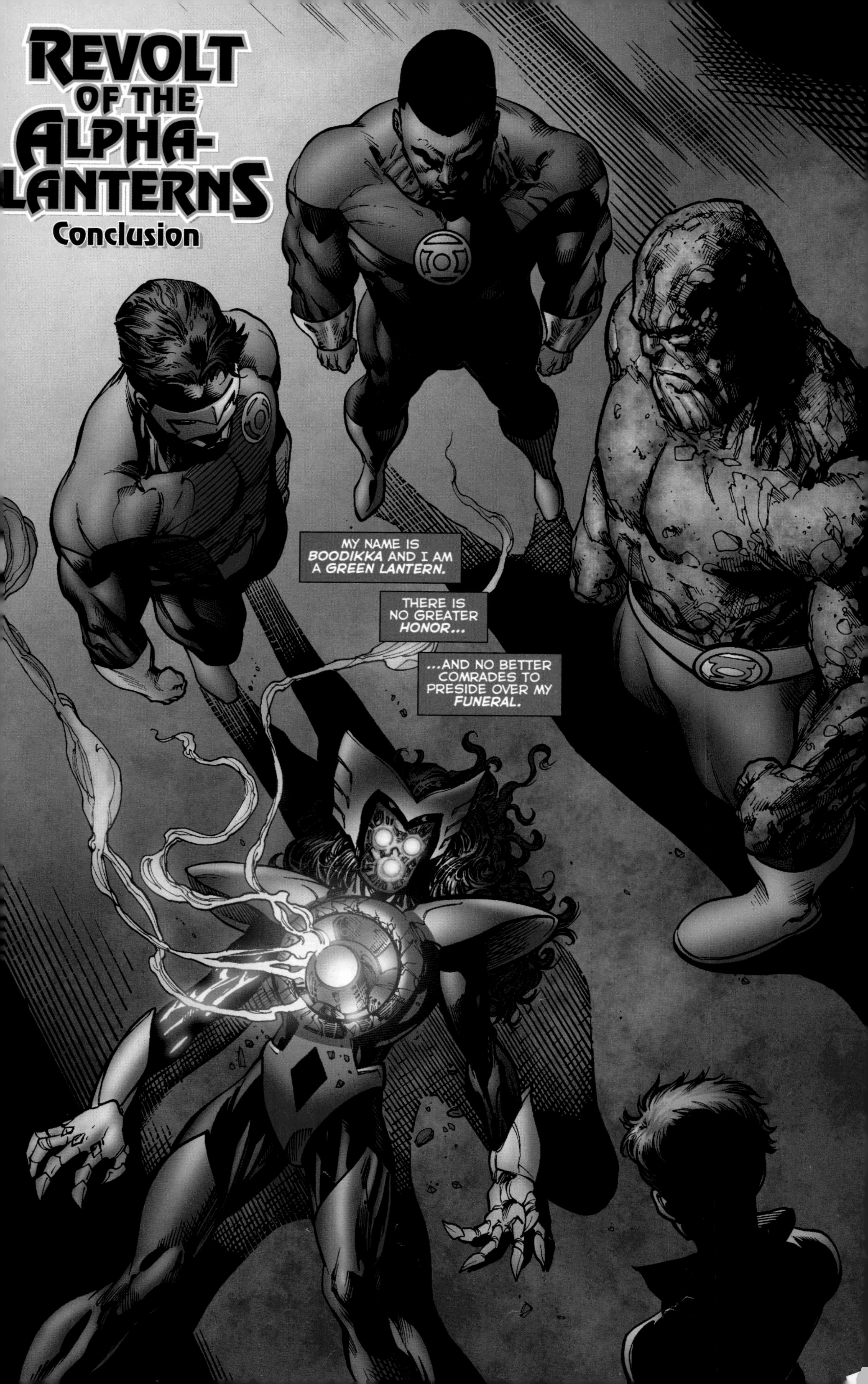
REVOLT OF THE ALPHA-LANTERNS
Conclusion
MY NAME IS BOODIKKA AND I AM A GREEN LANTERN.
THERE IS NO GREATER HONOR...
...AND NO BETTER COMRADES TO PRESIDE OVER MY FUNERAL.

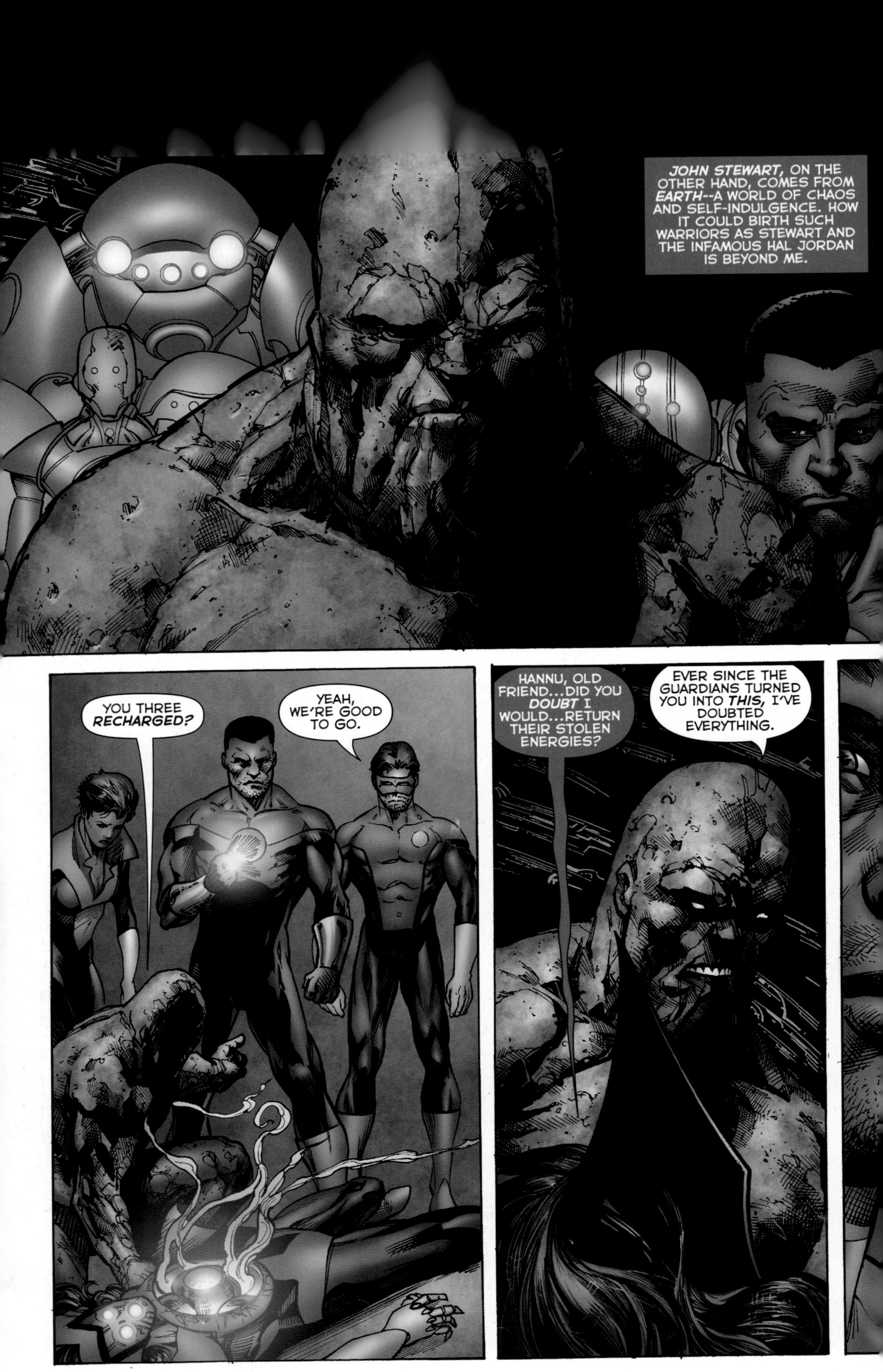
JOHN STEWART, ON THE OTHER HAND, COMES FROM EARTH--A WORLD OF CHAOS AND SELF-INDULGENCE. HOW IT COULD BIRTH SUCH WARRIORS AS STEWART AND THE INFAMOUS HAL JORDAN IS BEYOND ME.
YOU THREE RECHARGED?
YEAH, WE'RE GOOD TO GO.
HANNU, OLD FRIEND...DID YOU DOUBT I WOULD...RETURN THEIR STOLEN ENERGIES?
EVER SINCE THE GUARDIANS TURNED YOU INTO THIS, I'VE DOUBTED EVERYTHING.

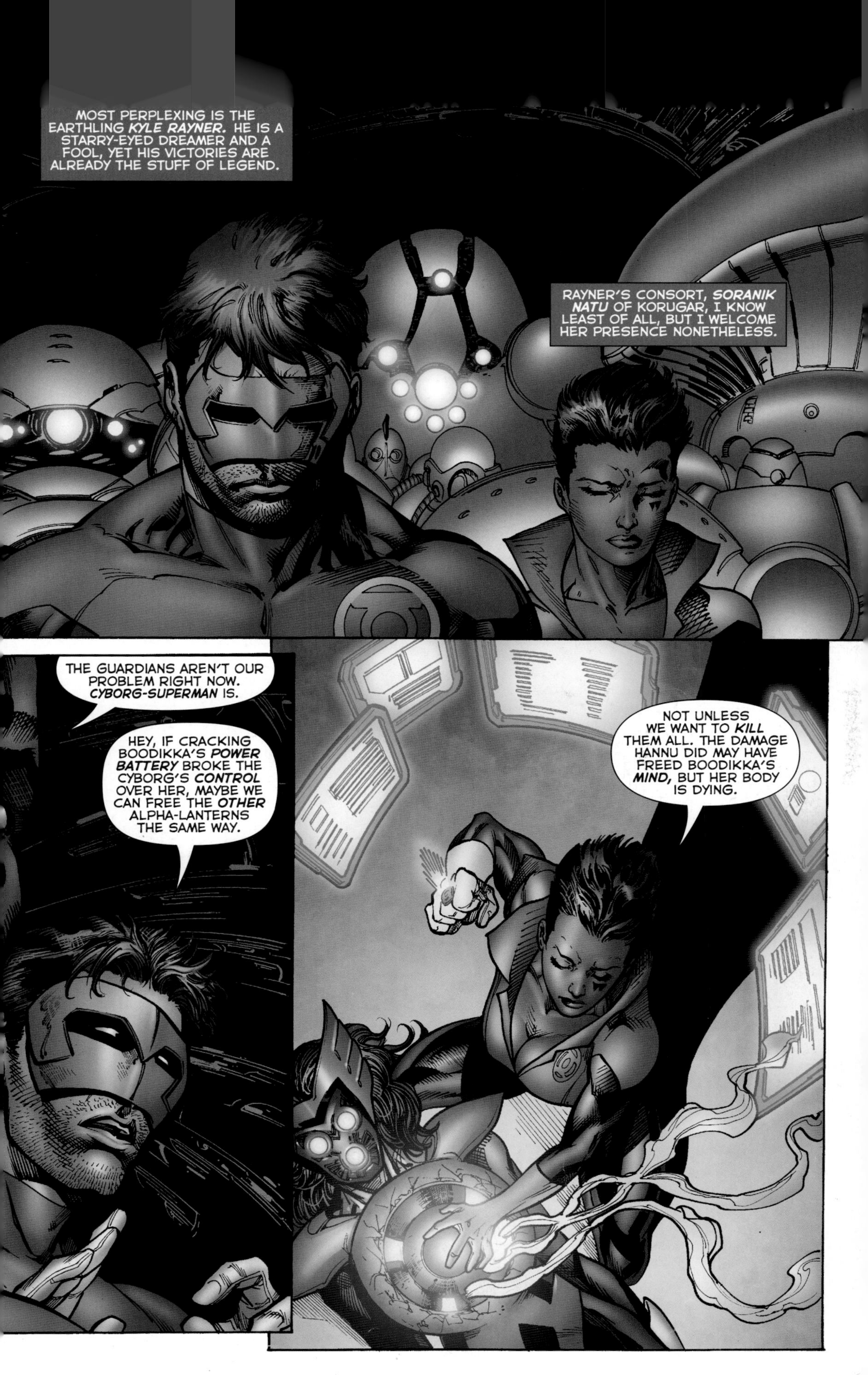
MOST PERPLEXING IS THE EARTHLING KYLE RAYNER. HE IS A STARRY-EYED DREAMER AND A FOOL, YET HIS VICTORIES ARE ALREADY THE STUFF OF LEGEND.
RAYNER'S CONSORT, SORANIK NATU OF KORUGAR, I KNOW LEAST OF ALL, BUT I WELCOME HER PRESENCE NONETHELESS.
THE GUARDIANS AREN'T OUR PROBLEM RIGHT NOW. CYBORG-SUPERMAN IS.
HEY, IF CRACKING BOODIKKA'S POWER BATTERY BROKE THE CYBORG'S CONTROL OVER HER, MAYBE WE CAN FREE THE OTHER ALPHA-LANTERNS THE SAME WAY.
NOT UNLESS WE WANT TO KILL THEM ALL. THE DAMAGE HANNU DID MAY HAVE FREED BOODIKKA'S MIND, BUT HER BODY IS DYING.

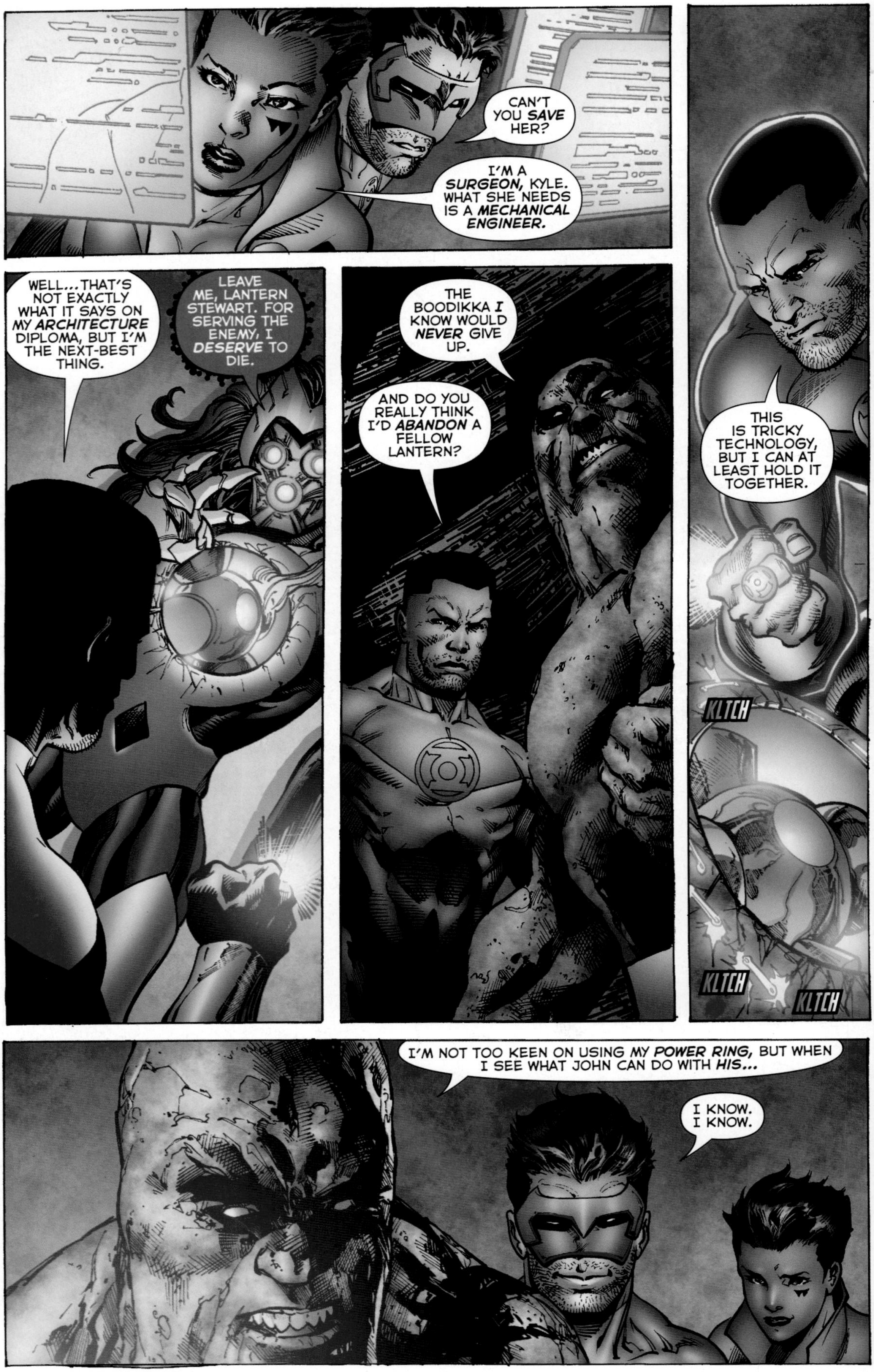
CAN'T YOU SAVE HER?
I'M A SURGEON, KYLE. WHAT SHE NEEDS IS A MECHANICAL ENGINEER.
THIS IS TRICKY TECHNOLOGY, BUT I CAN AT LEAST HOLD IT TOGETHER.
WELL...THAT'S NOT EXACTLY WHAT IT SAYS ON MY ARCHITECTURE DIPLOMA, BUT I'M THE NEXT-BEST THING.
LEAVE ME, LANTERN STEWART. FOR SERVING THE ENEMY, I DESERVE TO DIE.
THE BOODIKKA I KNOW WOULD NEVER GIVE UP.
AND DO YOU REALLY THINK I'D ABANDON A FELLOW LANTERN?
KLTCH
KLTCH
KLTCH
I'M NOT TOO KEEN ON USING MY POWER RING, BUT WHEN I SEE WHAT JOHN CAN DO WITH HIS...
I KNOW. I KNOW.

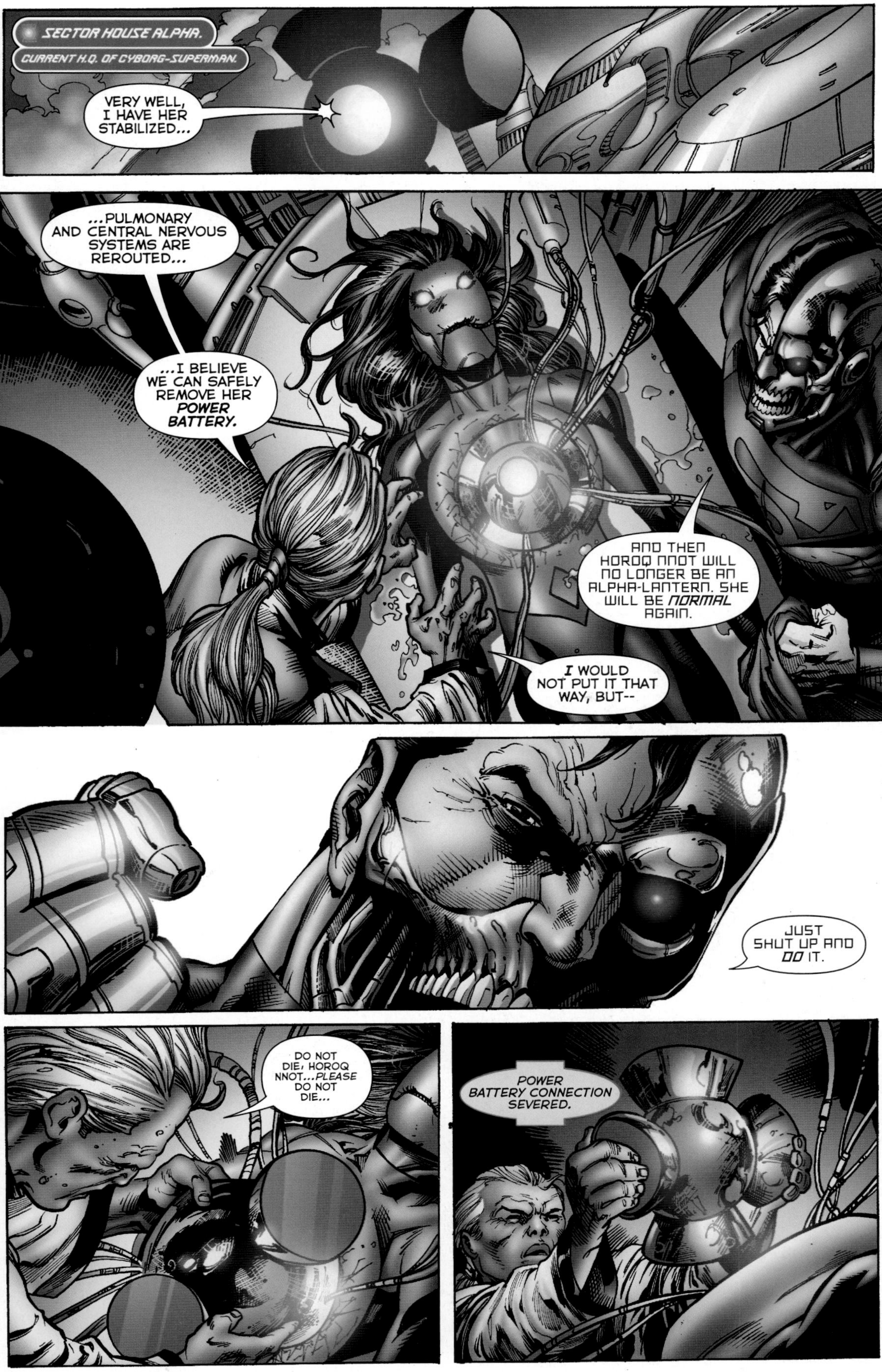
SECTOR HOUSE ALPHA.
CURRENT H.Q. OF CYBORG-SUPERMAN.
VERY WELL, I HAVE HER STABILIZED...
...PULMONARY AND CENTRAL NERVOUS SYSTEMS ARE REROUTED...
...I BELIEVE WE CAN SAFELY REMOVE HER POWER BATTERY.
AND THEN HOROQ NNOT WILL NO LONGER BE AN ALPHA-LANTERN. SHE WILL BE NORMAL AGAIN.
I WOULD NOT PUT IT THAT WAY, BUT--
JUST SHUT UP AND DO IT.
DO NOT DIE, HOROQ NNOT...PLEASE DO NOT DIE...
POWER BATTERY CONNECTION SEVERED.

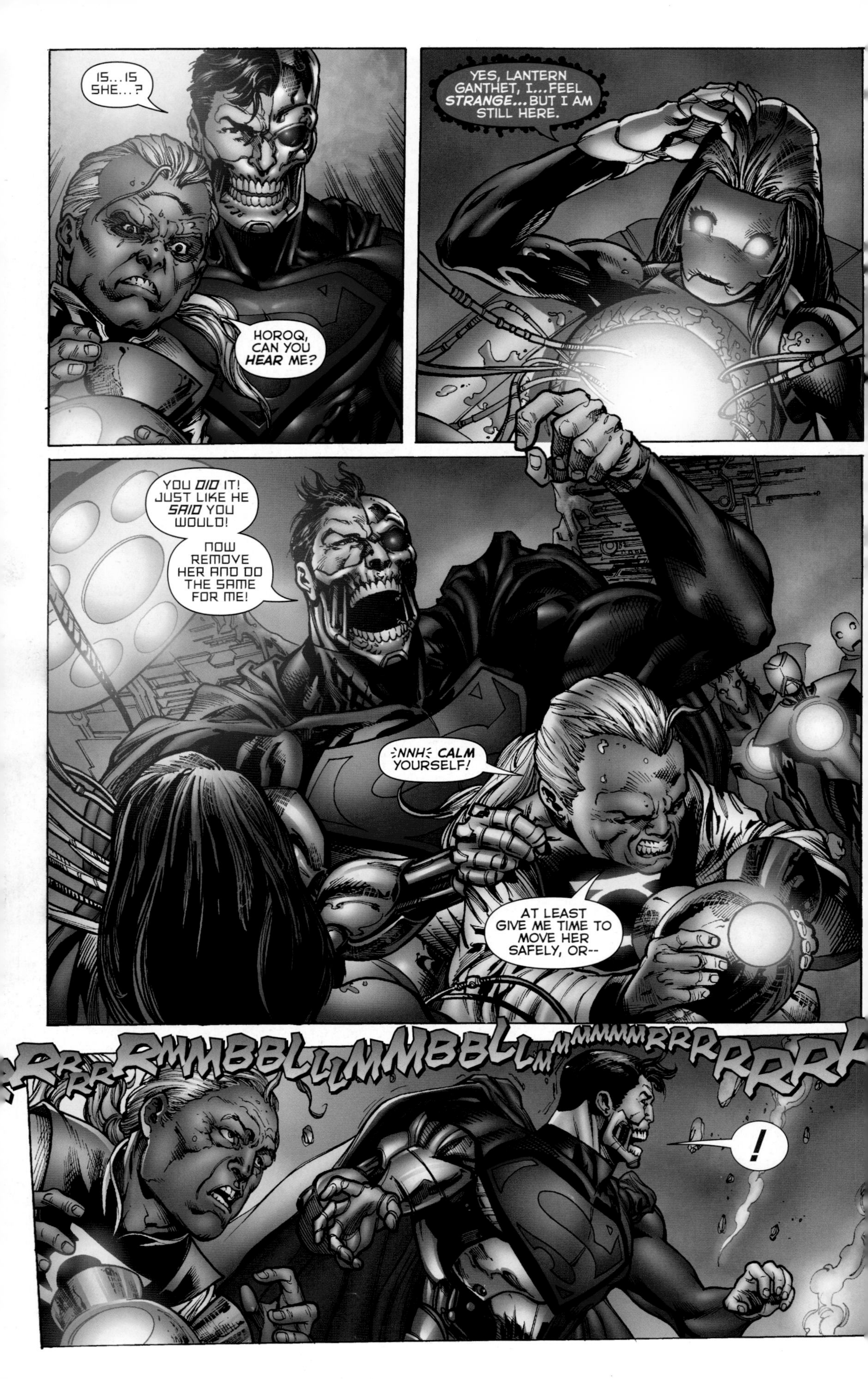
IS...IS SHE...?
HOROQ, CAN YOU HEAR ME?
YES, LANTERN GANTHET, I...FEEL STRANGE...BUT I AM STILL HERE.
YOU DID IT! JUST LIKE HE SAID YOU WOULD!
NOW REMOVE HER AND DO THE SAME FOR ME!
NNH CALM YOURSELF!
AT LEAST GIVE ME TIME TO MOVE HER SAFELY, OR--
RRRRRMMBBLLLMMBBLLMMMMMMRRRRRRRK
!

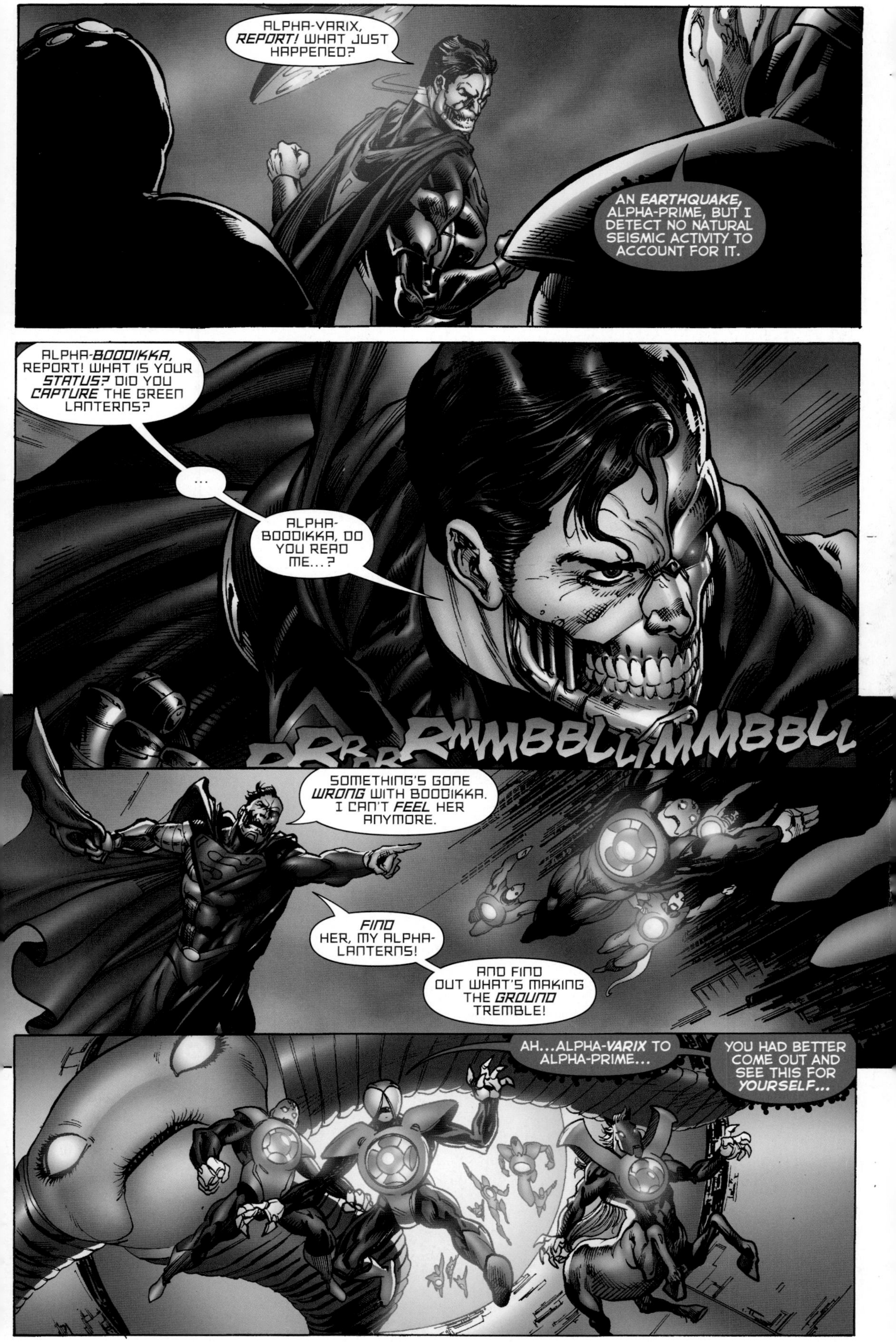
ALPHA-VARIX, REPORT! WHAT JUST HAPPENED?
AN EARTHQUAKE, ALPHA-PRIME, BUT I DETECT NO NATURAL SEISMIC ACTIVITY TO ACCOUNT FOR IT.
ALPHA-BOODIKKA, REPORT! WHAT IS YOUR STATUS? DID YOU CAPTURE THE GREEN LANTERNS?
...
ALPHA-BOODIKKA, DO YOU READ ME...?
RMMBBLLMMBBLL
SOMETHING'S GONE WRONG WITH BOODIKKA. I CAN'T FEEL HER ANYMORE.
FIND HER, MY ALPHA-LANTERNS!
AND FIND OUT WHAT'S MAKING THE GROUND TREMBLE!
AH...ALPHA-VARIX TO ALPHA-PRIME...
YOU HAD BETTER COME OUT AND SEE THIS FOR YOURSELF...

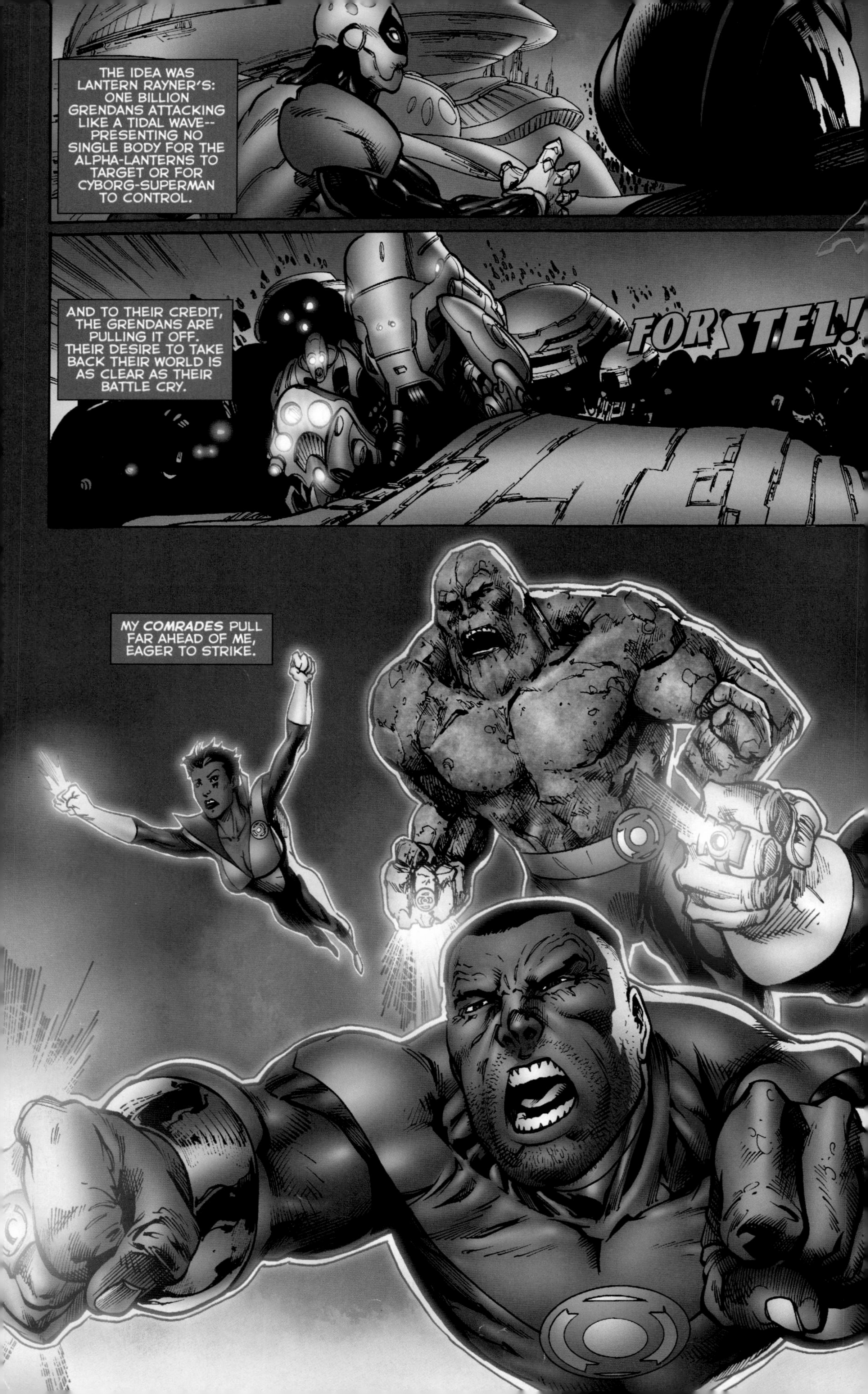
THE IDEA WAS LANTERN RAYNER'S: ONE BILLION GRENDANS ATTACKING LIKE A TIDAL WAVE-- PRESENTING NO SINGLE BODY FOR THE ALPHA-LANTERNS TO TARGET OR FOR CYBORG-SUPERMAN TO CONTROL.
AND TO THEIR CREDIT, THE GRENDANS ARE PULLING IT OFF. THEIR DESIRE TO TAKE BACK THEIR WORLD IS AS CLEAR AS THEIR BATTLE CRY.
FORSTEL!
MY *COMRADES* PULL FAR AHEAD OF ME, EAGER TO STRIKE.

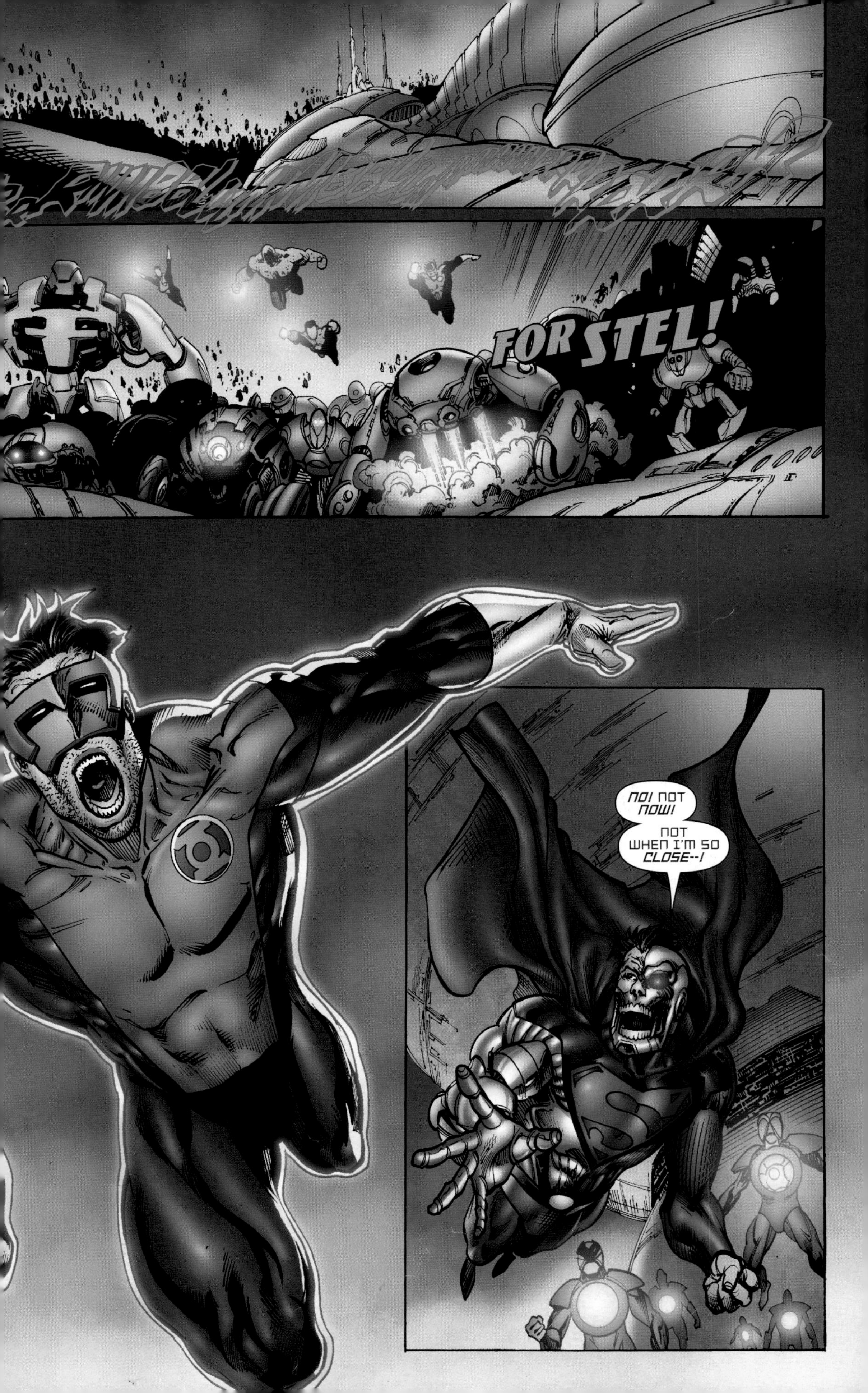
FOR STEL!
NO! NOT NOW!
NOT WHEN I'M SO CLOSE--!

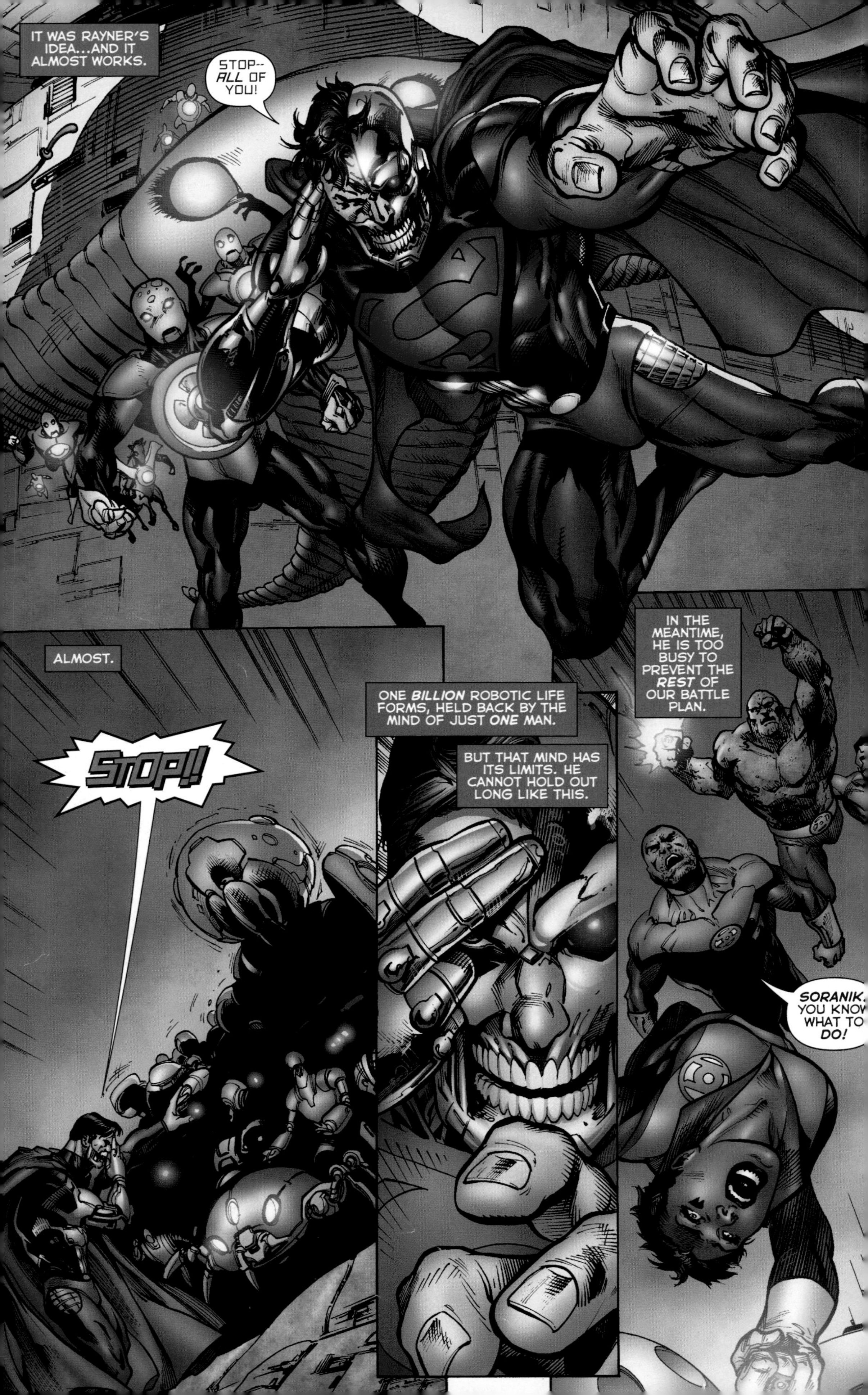
IT WAS RAYNER'S IDEA...AND IT ALMOST WORKS.
STOP-- ALL OF YOU!
ALMOST.
STOP!!
ONE BILLION ROBOTIC LIFE FORMS, HELD BACK BY THE MIND OF JUST ONE MAN.
BUT THAT MIND HAS ITS LIMITS. HE CANNOT HOLD OUT LONG LIKE THIS.
IN THE MEANTIME, HE IS TOO BUSY TO PREVENT THE REST OF OUR BATTLE PLAN.
SORANIK. YOU KNOW WHAT TO DO!

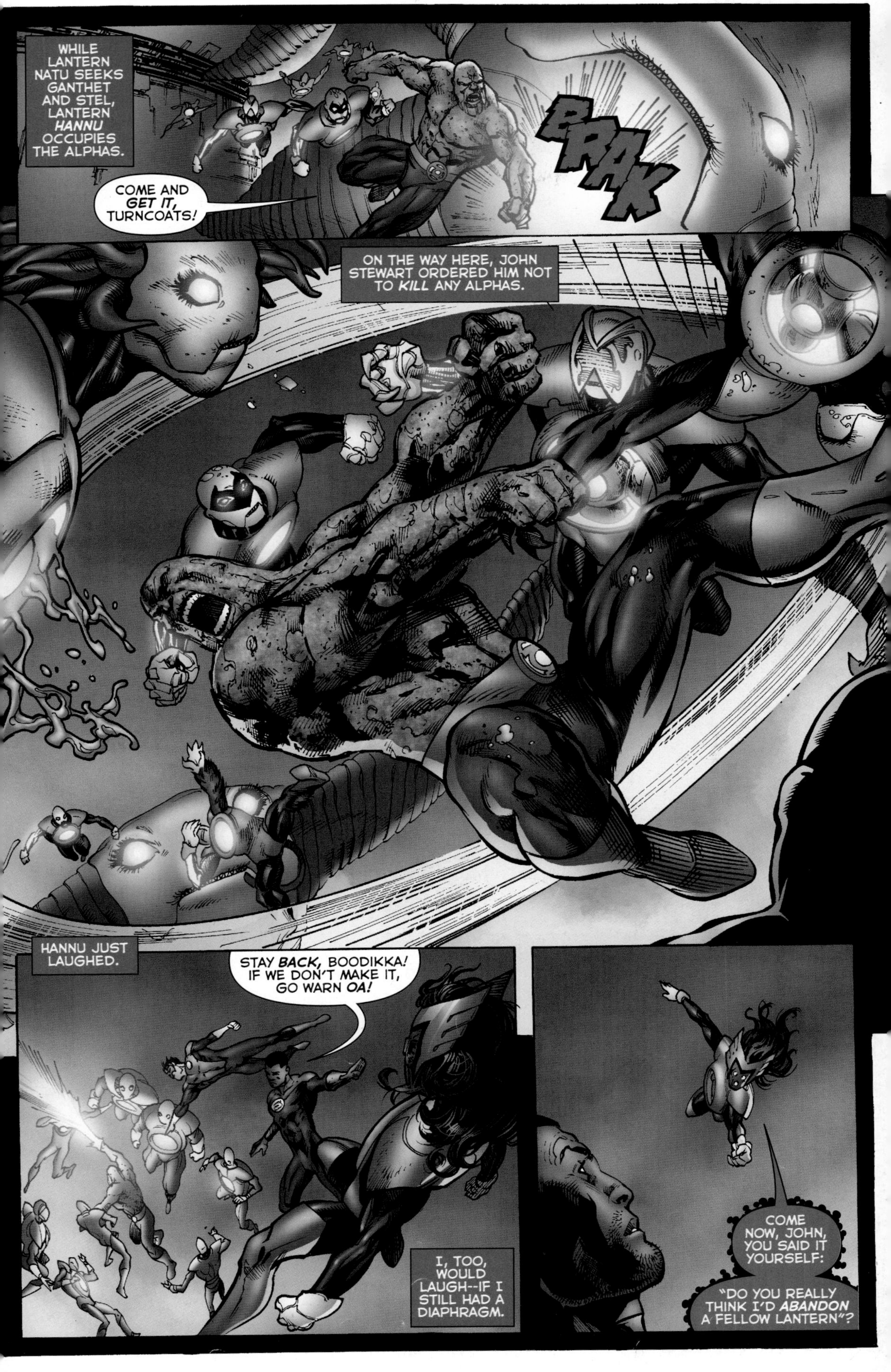
WHILE LANTERN NATU SEEKS GANTHET AND STEL, LANTERN HANNU OCCUPIES THE ALPHAS.
COME AND GET IT, TURNCOATS!
BRAK
ON THE WAY HERE, JOHN STEWART ORDERED HIM NOT TO KILL ANY ALPHAS.
HANNU JUST LAUGHED.
STAY BACK, BOODIKKA! IF WE DON'T MAKE IT, GO WARN OA!
I, TOO, WOULD LAUGH--IF I STILL HAD A DIAPHRAGM.
COME NOW, JOHN, YOU SAID IT YOURSELF:
"DO YOU REALLY THINK I'D ABANDON A FELLOW LANTERN"?

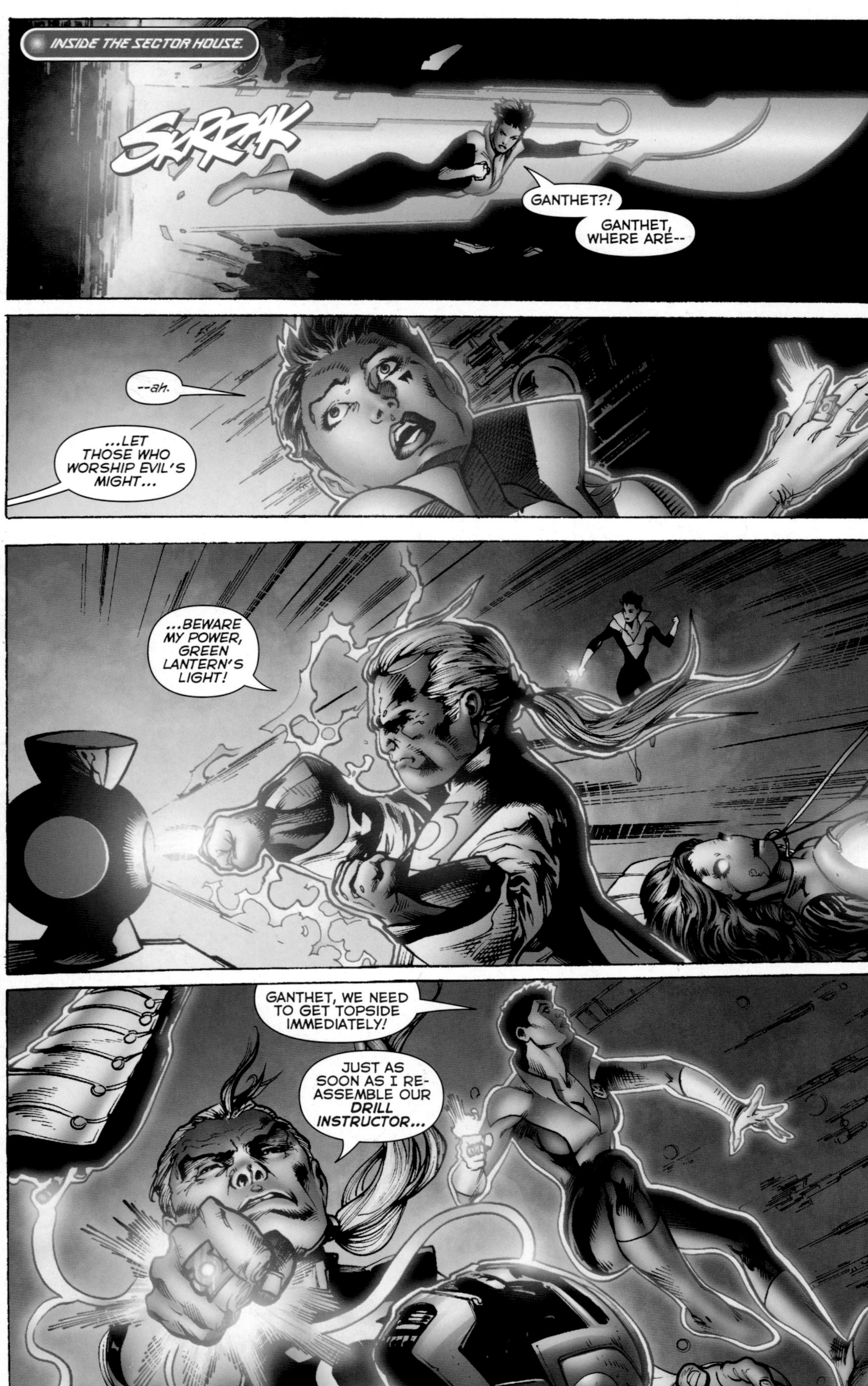
INSIDE THE SECTOR HOUSE.
SKRAK
GANTHET?!
GANTHET, WHERE ARE--
--ah.
...LET THOSE WHO WORSHIP EVIL'S MIGHT...
...BEWARE MY POWER, GREEN LANTERN'S LIGHT!
GANTHET, WE NEED TO GET TOPSIDE IMMEDIATELY!
JUST AS SOON AS I RE-ASSEMBLE OUR DRILL INSTRUCTOR...

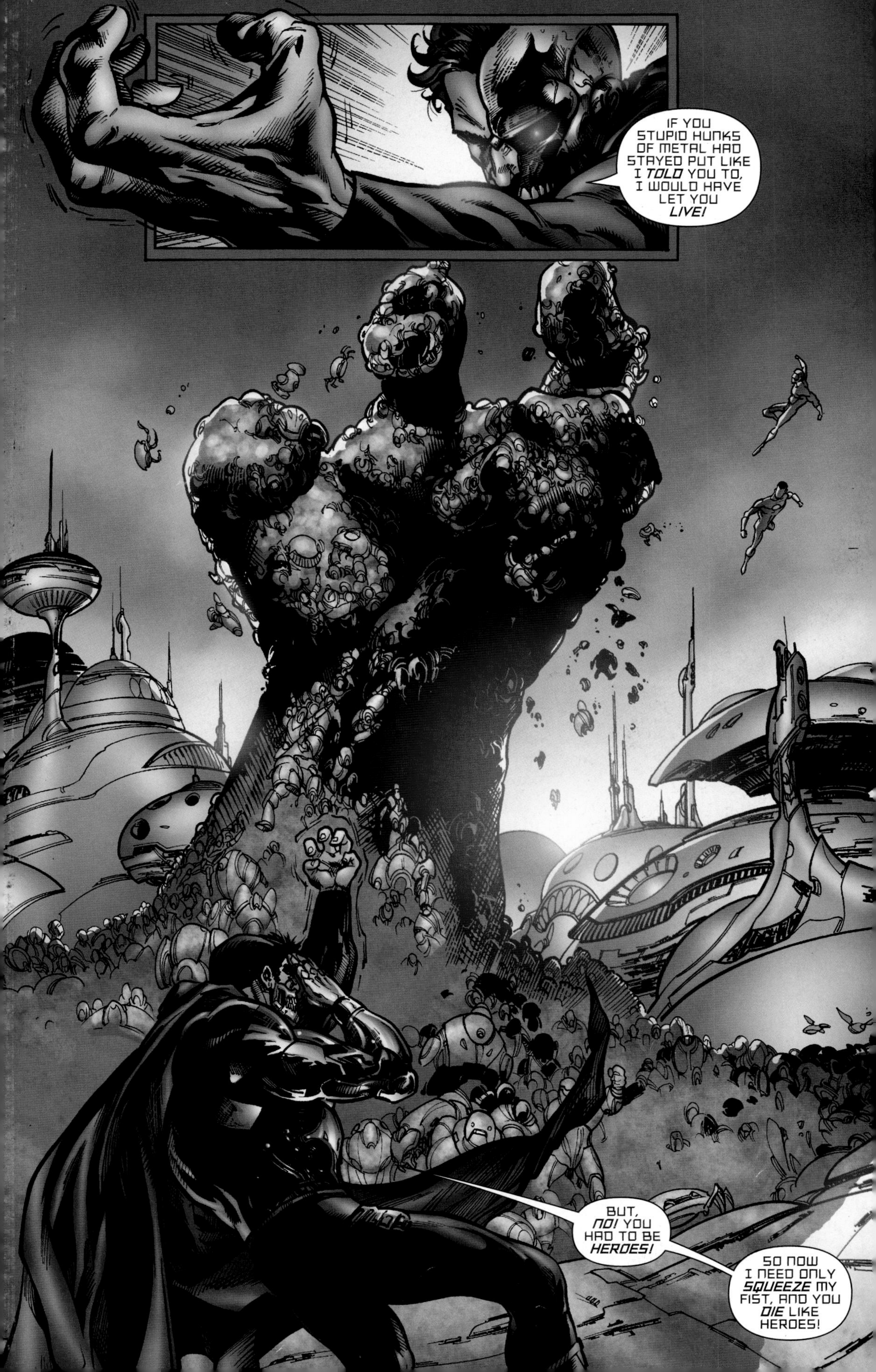
IF YOU STUPID HUNKS OF METAL HAD STAYED PUT LIKE I *TOLD* YOU TO, I WOULD HAVE LET YOU *LIVE!*
BUT, *NO!* YOU HAD TO BE *HEROES!*
SO NOW I NEED ONLY *SQUEEZE* MY FIST, AND YOU *DIE* LIKE HEROES!

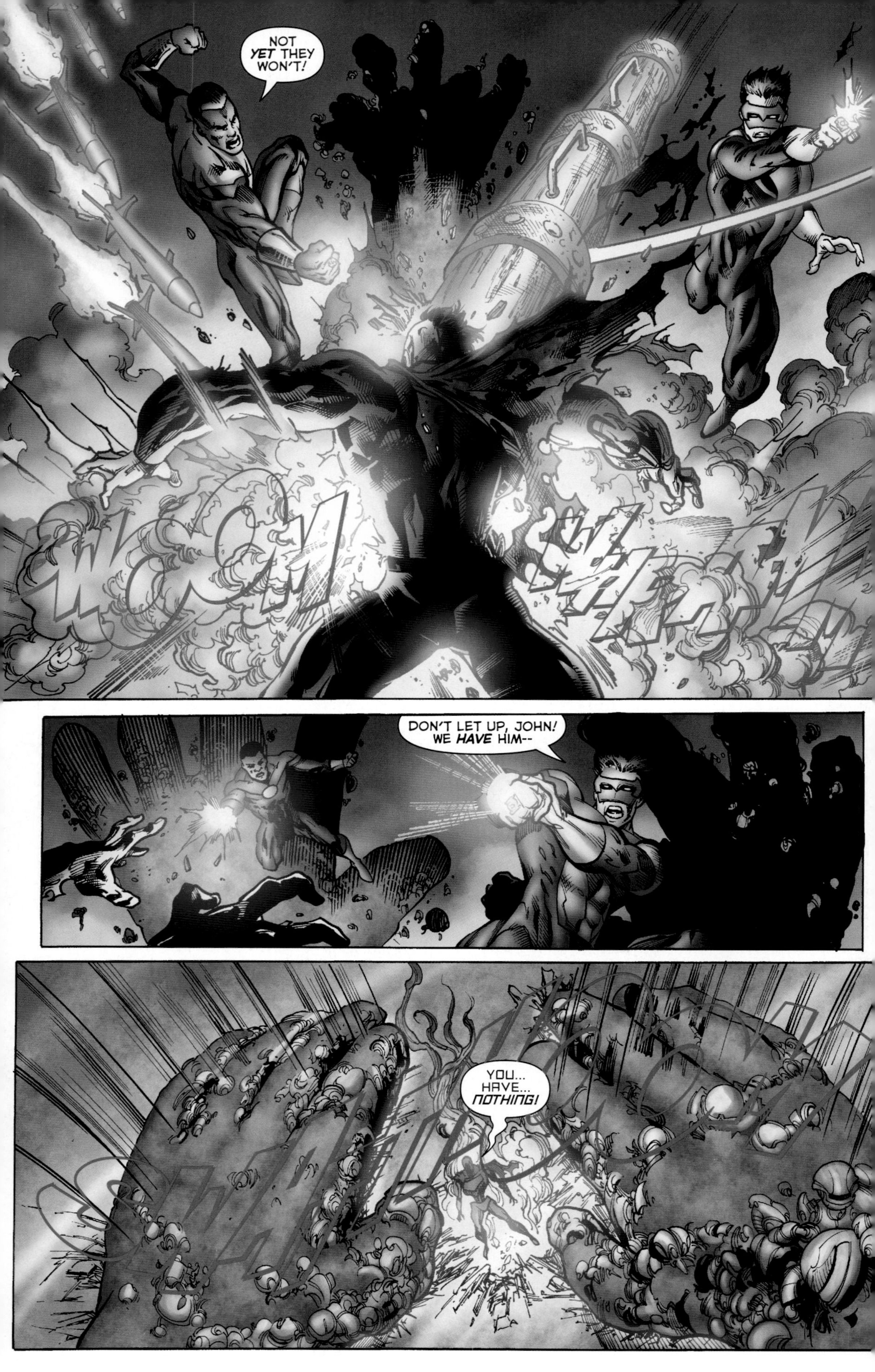
NOT YET THEY WON'T!
DON'T LET UP, JOHN! WE HAVE HIM--
YOU... HAVE... NOTHING!

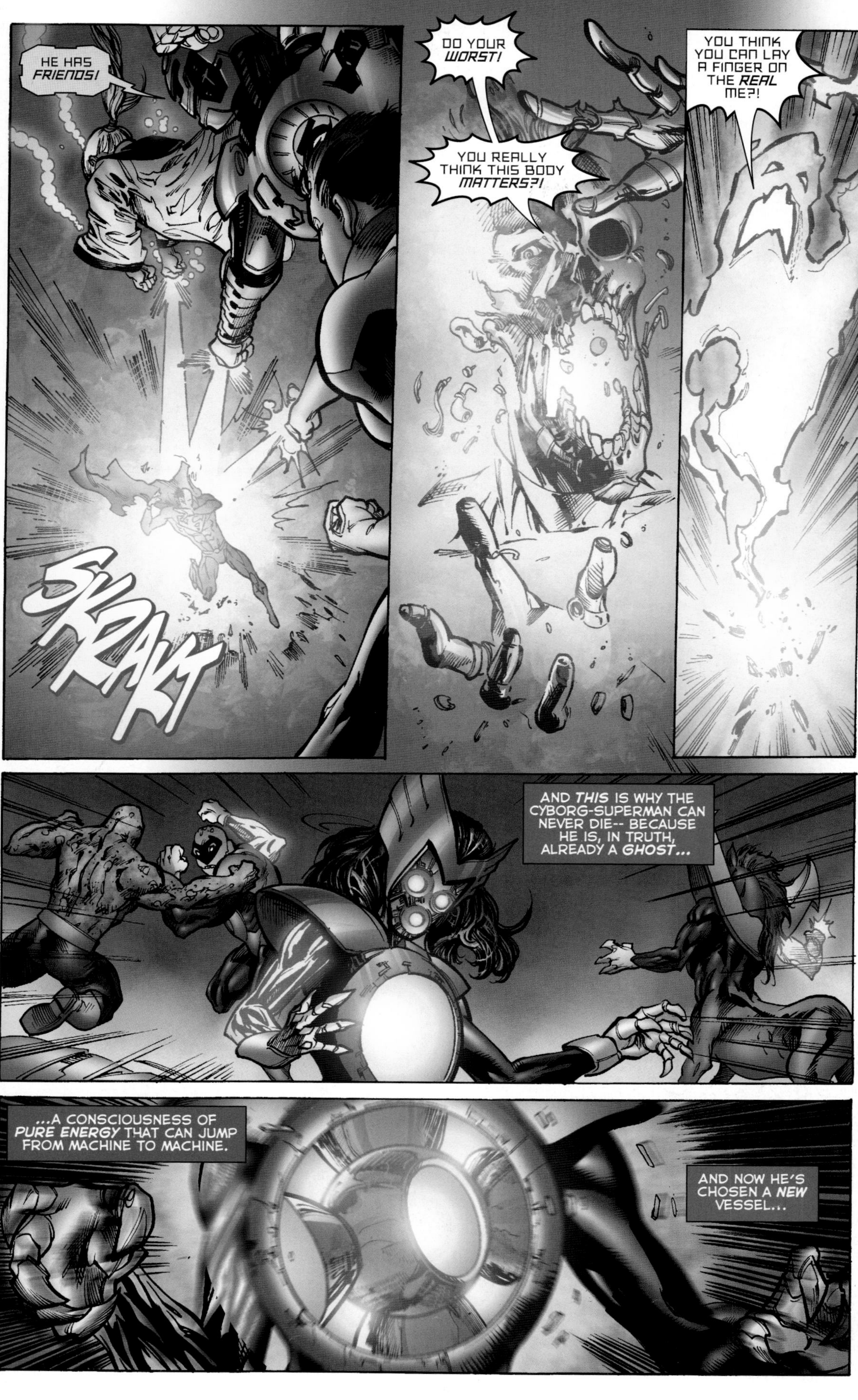
HE HAS FRIENDS!
SKRAKT
DO YOUR WORST!
YOU REALLY THINK THIS BODY MATTERS?!
YOU THINK YOU CAN LAY A FINGER ON THE REAL ME?!
AND THIS IS WHY THE CYBORG-SUPERMAN CAN NEVER DIE-- BECAUSE HE IS, IN TRUTH, ALREADY A GHOST...
...A CONSCIOUSNESS OF PURE ENERGY THAT CAN JUMP FROM MACHINE TO MACHINE.
AND NOW HE'S CHOSEN A NEW VESSEL...

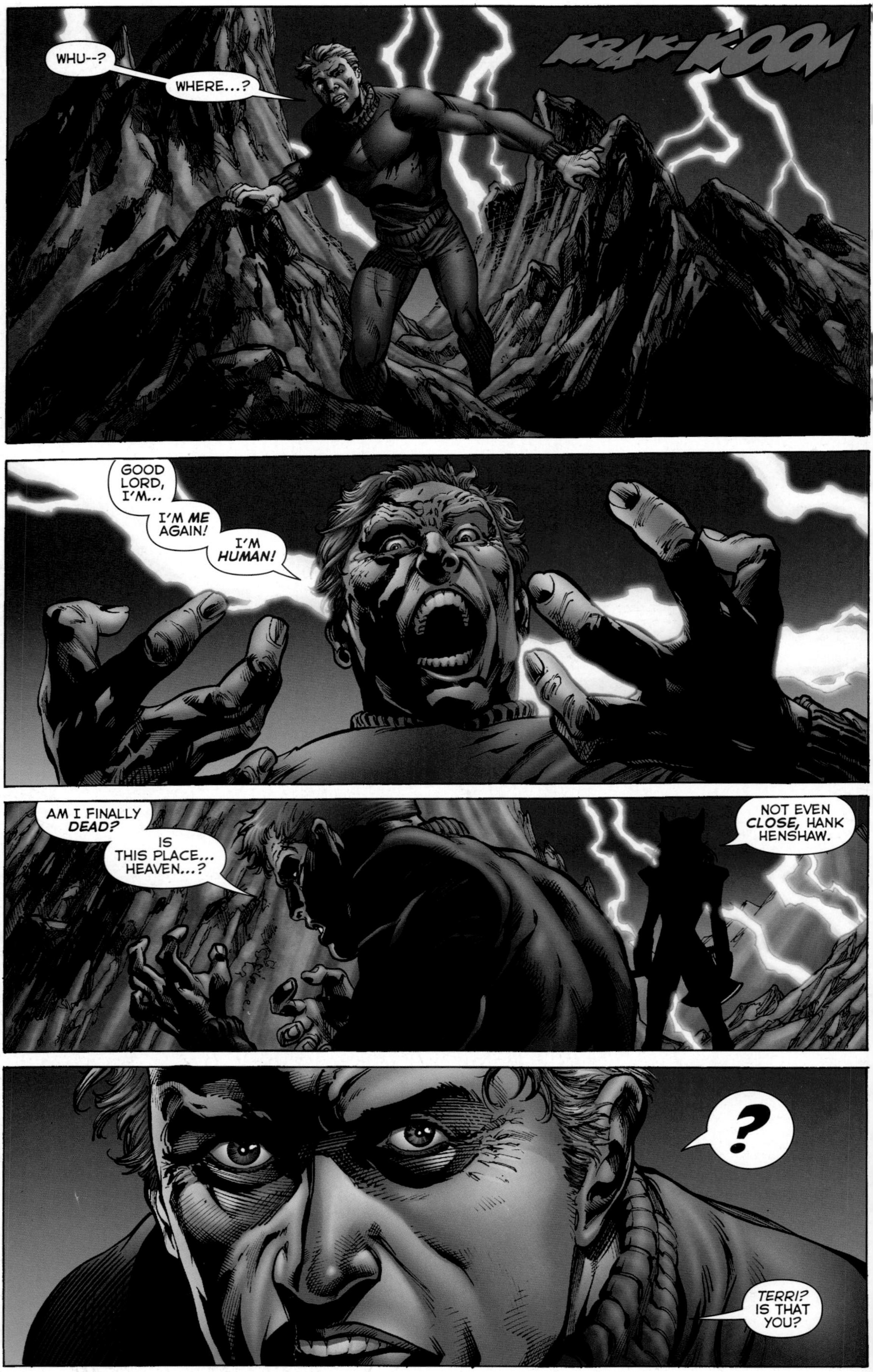
WHU--?
WHERE...?
KRAK-KOOM
GOOD LORD, I'M...
I'M *ME* AGAIN!
I'M *HUMAN!*
AM I FINALLY *DEAD?*
IS THIS PLACE... HEAVEN...?
NOT EVEN *CLOSE,* HANK HENSHAW.
?
TERRI? IS THAT YOU?

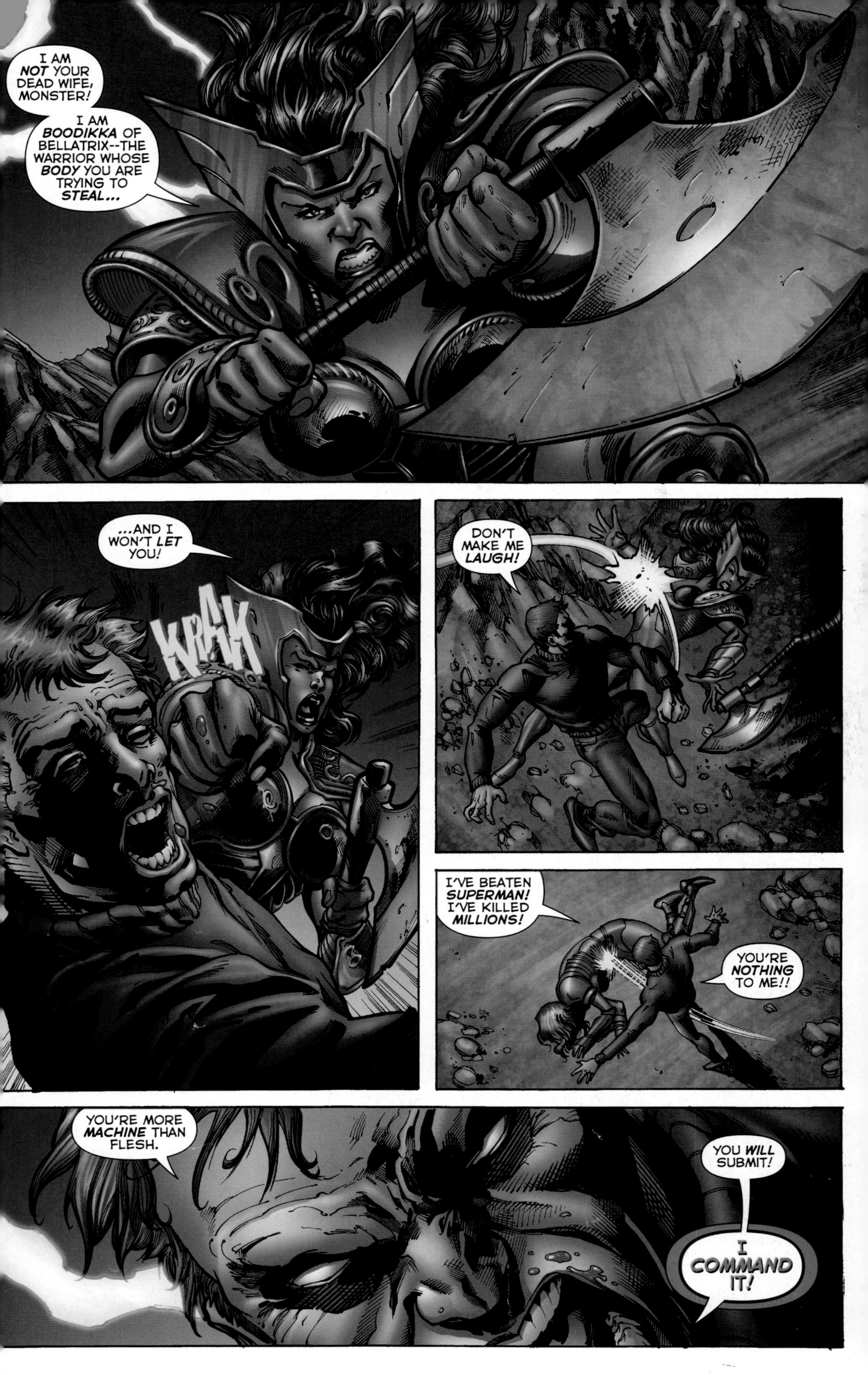
I AM NOT YOUR DEAD WIFE, MONSTER!
I AM BOODIKKA OF BELLATRIX--THE WARRIOR WHOSE BODY YOU ARE TRYING TO STEAL...
...AND I WON'T LET YOU!
KRAK
DON'T MAKE ME LAUGH!
I'VE BEATEN SUPERMAN! I'VE KILLED MILLIONS!
YOU'RE NOTHING TO ME!!
YOU'RE MORE MACHINE THAN FLESH.
YOU WILL SUBMIT!
I COMMAND IT!

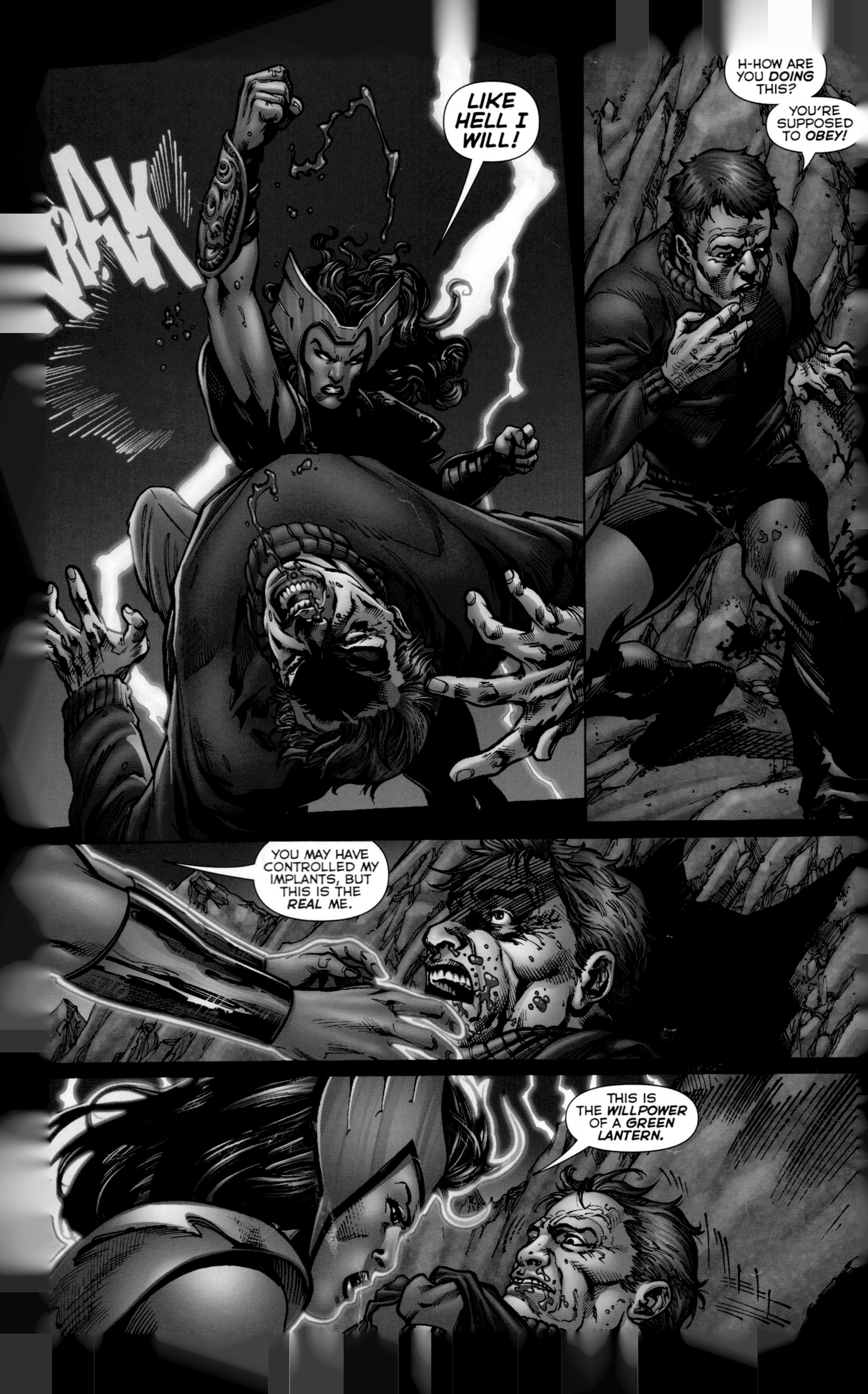
KRAK
LIKE HELL I WILL!
H-HOW ARE YOU DOING THIS?
YOU'RE SUPPOSED TO OBEY!
YOU MAY HAVE CONTROLLED MY IMPLANTS, BUT THIS IS THE REAL ME.
THIS IS THE WILLPOWER OF A GREEN LANTERN.

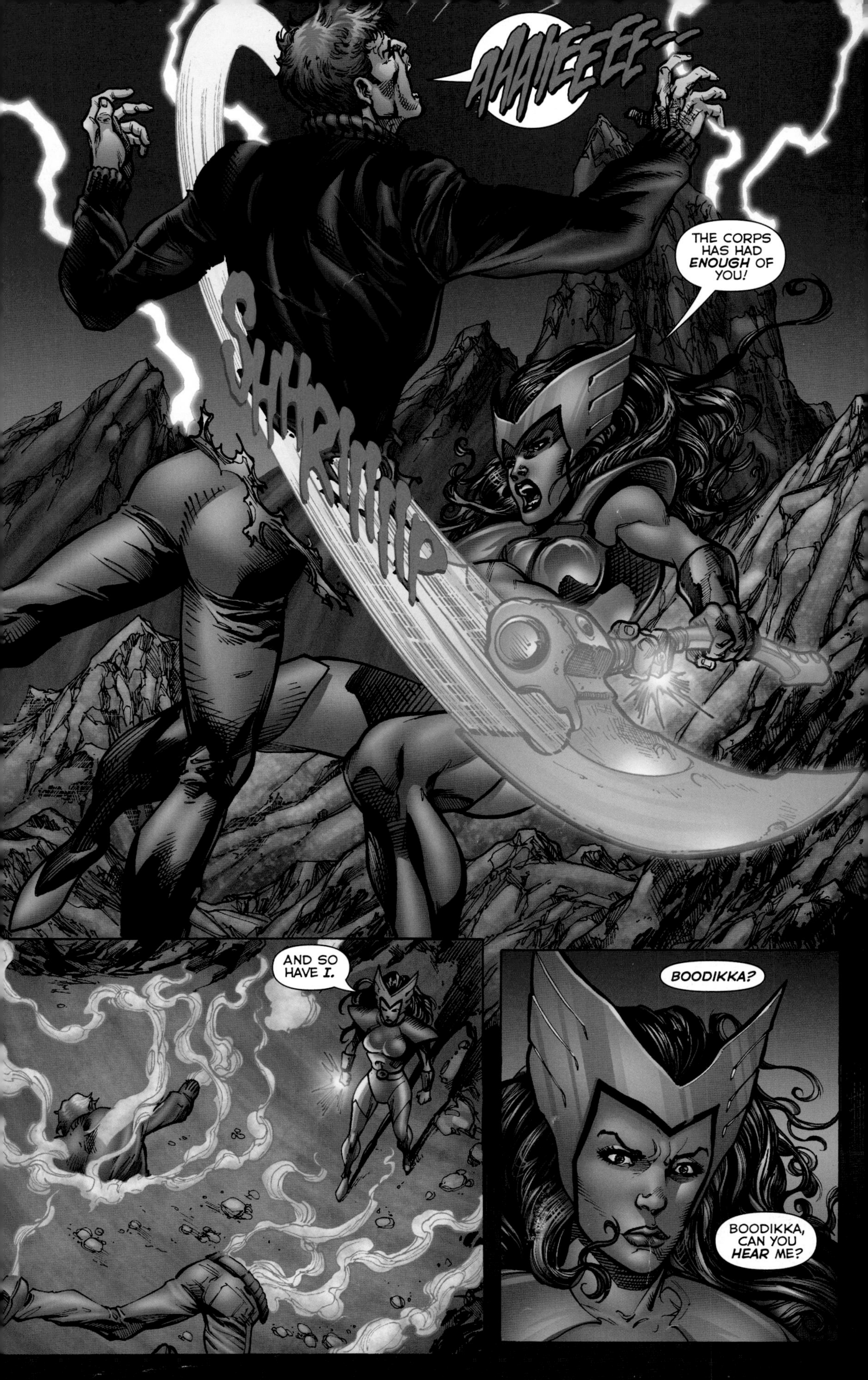
AAAIIEEEEE--
SHHRIIIIP
THE CORPS HAS HAD *ENOUGH* OF YOU!
AND SO HAVE *I.*
BOODIKKA?
BOODIKKA, CAN YOU *HEAR* ME?

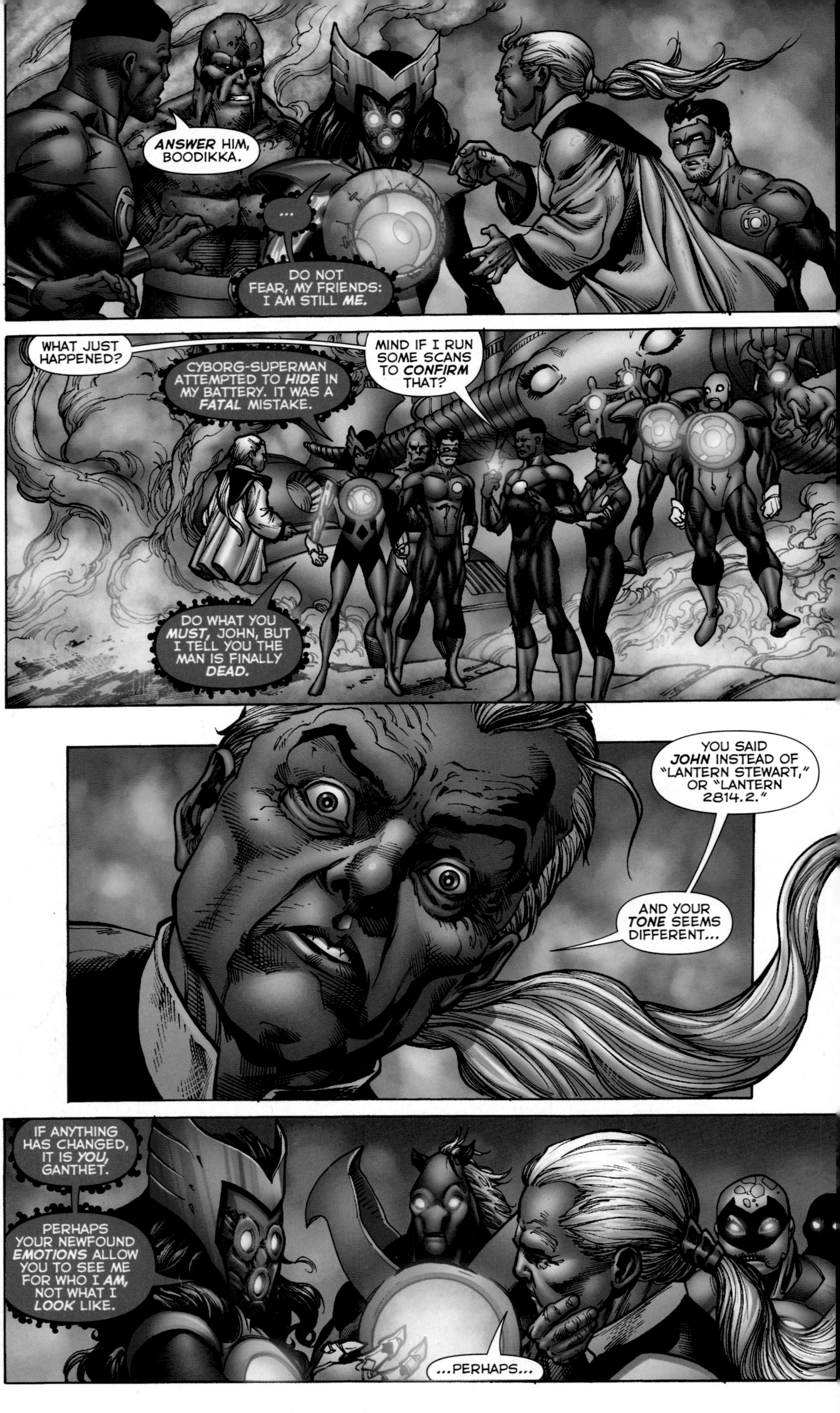
ANSWER HIM, BOODIKKA.
...
DO NOT FEAR, MY FRIENDS: I AM STILL ME.
WHAT JUST HAPPENED?
CYBORG-SUPERMAN ATTEMPTED TO HIDE IN MY BATTERY. IT WAS A FATAL MISTAKE.
MIND IF I RUN SOME SCANS TO CONFIRM THAT?
DO WHAT YOU MUST, JOHN, BUT I TELL YOU THE MAN IS FINALLY DEAD.
YOU SAID JOHN INSTEAD OF "LANTERN STEWART," OR "LANTERN 2814.2."
AND YOUR TONE SEEMS DIFFERENT...
IF ANYTHING HAS CHANGED, IT IS YOU, GANTHET.
PERHAPS YOUR NEWFOUND EMOTIONS ALLOW YOU TO SEE ME FOR WHO I AM, NOT WHAT I LOOK LIKE.
...PERHAPS...

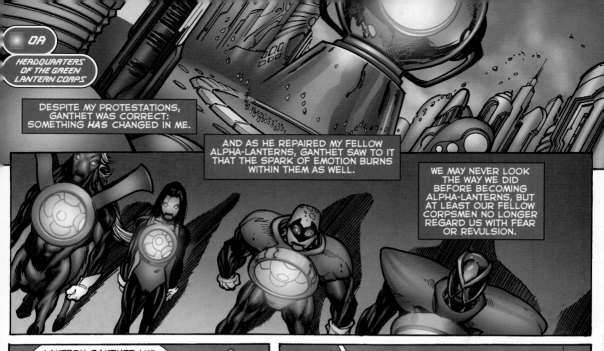

OA
HEADQUARTERS OF THE GREEN LANTERN CORPS
DESPITE MY PROTESTATIONS, GANTHET WAS CORRECT: SOMETHING *HAS* CHANGED IN ME.
AND AS HE REPAIRED MY FELLOW ALPHA-LANTERNS, GANTHET SAW TO IT THAT THE SPARK OF EMOTION BURNS WITHIN THEM AS WELL.
WE MAY NEVER LOOK THE WAY WE DID BEFORE BECOMING ALPHA-LANTERNS, BUT AT LEAST OUR FELLOW CORPSMEN NO LONGER REGARD US WITH FEAR OR REVULSION.
LANTERN *GANTHET* AND ALPHA-LANTERN *BOODIKKA,* YOU HAVE BOTH DISPLAYED GREAT VALOR AGAINST ONE OF OUR MOST TERRIBLE ENEMIES.
TOGETHER WITH LANTERNS STEWART, RAYNER, NATU, HANNU AND STEL, YOU SAVED THE PEOPLE OF GRENDA, EMULATING THE HIGHEST IDEALS OF THE GREEN LANTERN CORPS.
FOR THIS REASON, WE GRANT YOU *HONOR GUARD* STATUS. YOU MAY OPERATE IN ANY SECTOR, SERVING AS AN *INSPIRATION* TO GREEN LANTERNS EVERYWHERE.

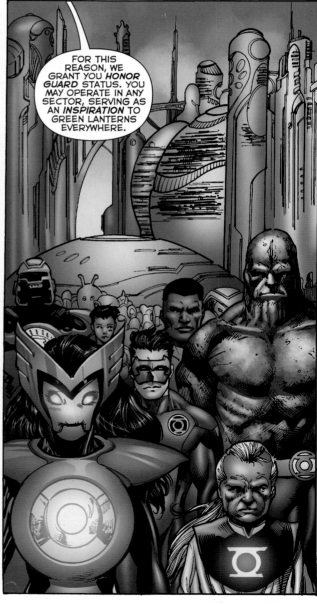

MY NAME IS BOODIKKA AND I AM A GREEN LANTERN.
THERE IS NO GREATER HONOR...
...AND NO BETTER COMRADES TO SHARE IT WITH.

THE CURSE OF THE ALPHA-LANTERN: PART ONE
Cover by Nelson & Guy Major

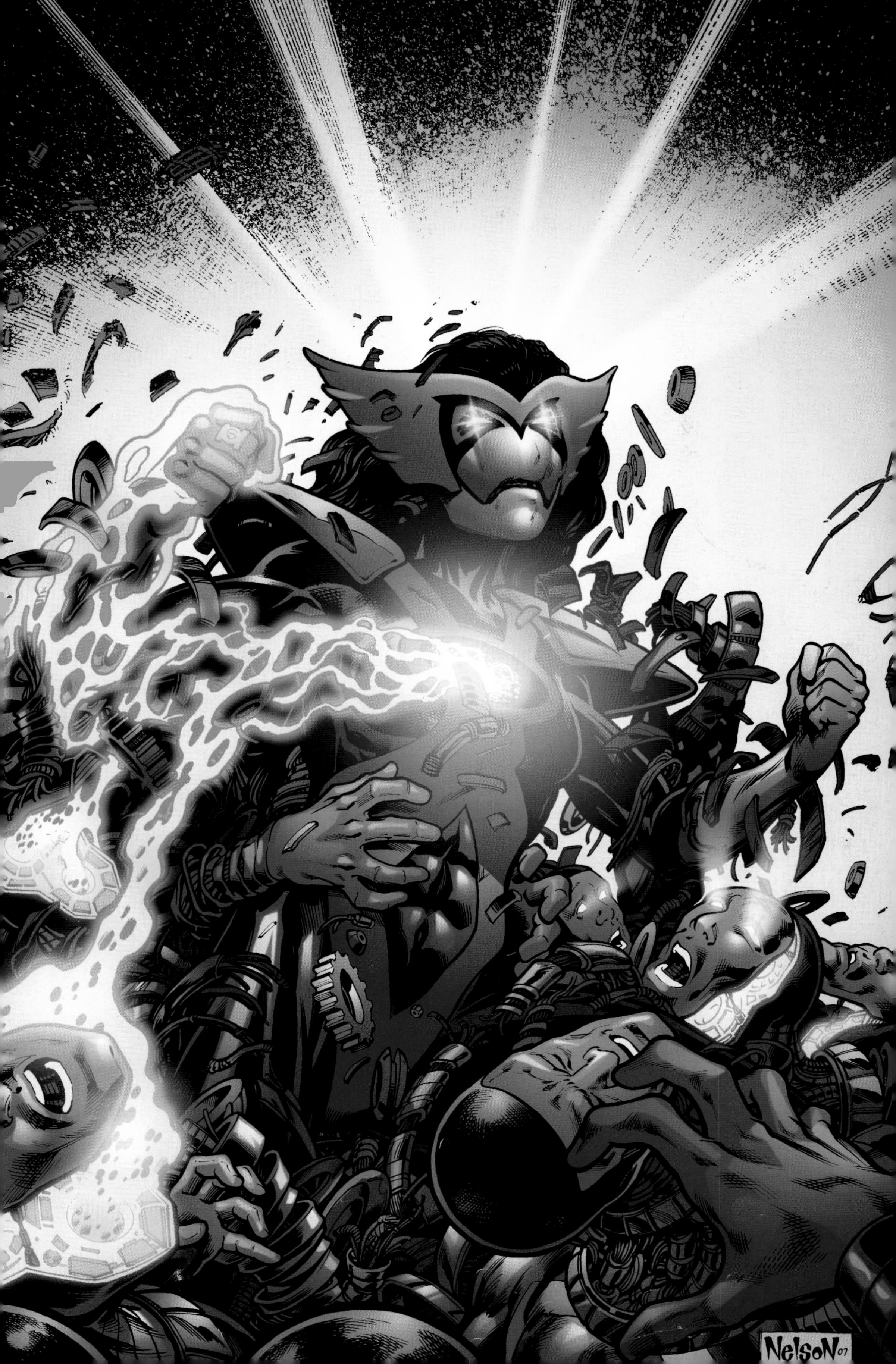
NELSON 07

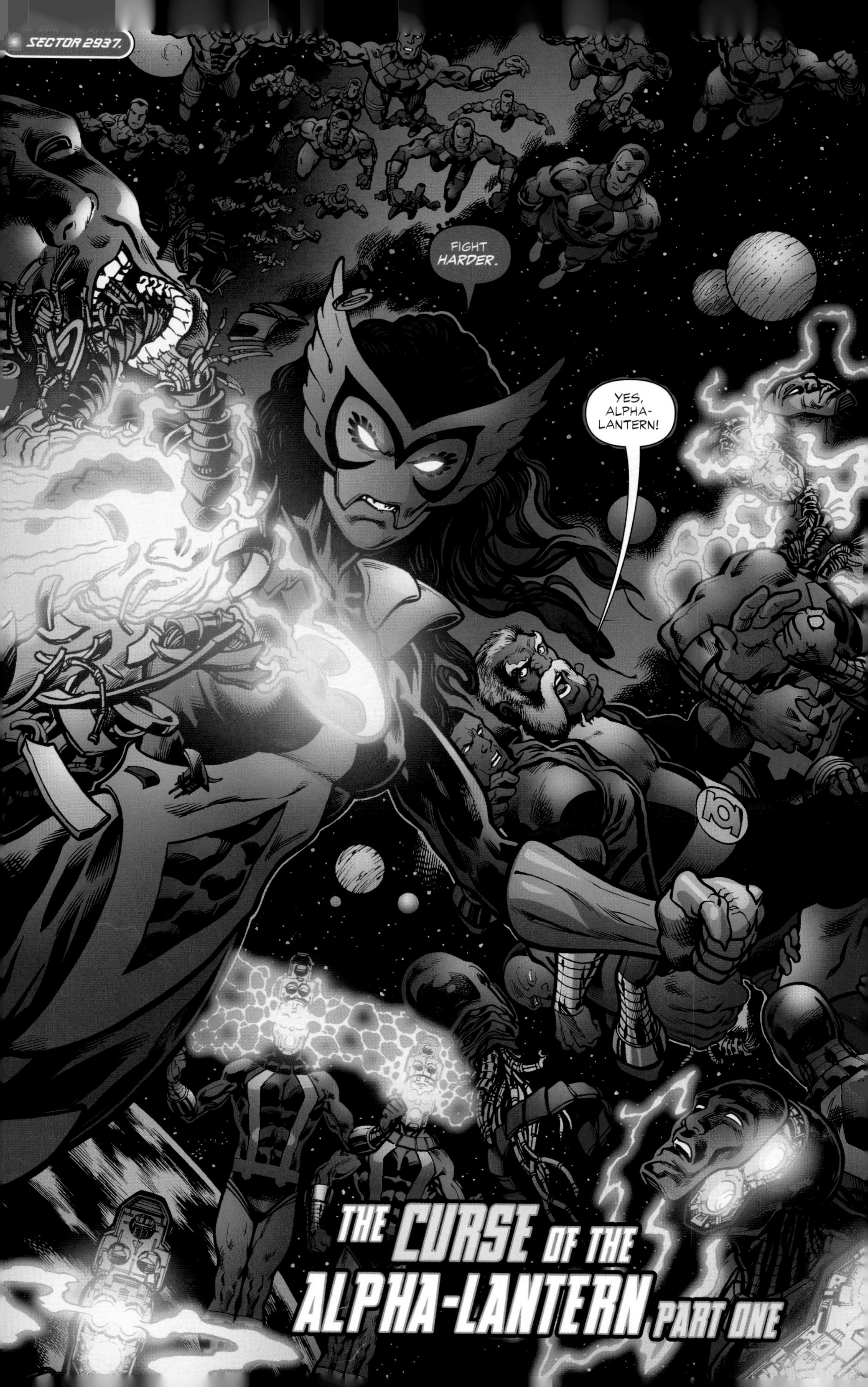
SECTOR 2937.
FIGHT HARDER.
YES, ALPHA-LANTERN!
THE CURSE OF THE ALPHA-LANTERN PART ONE

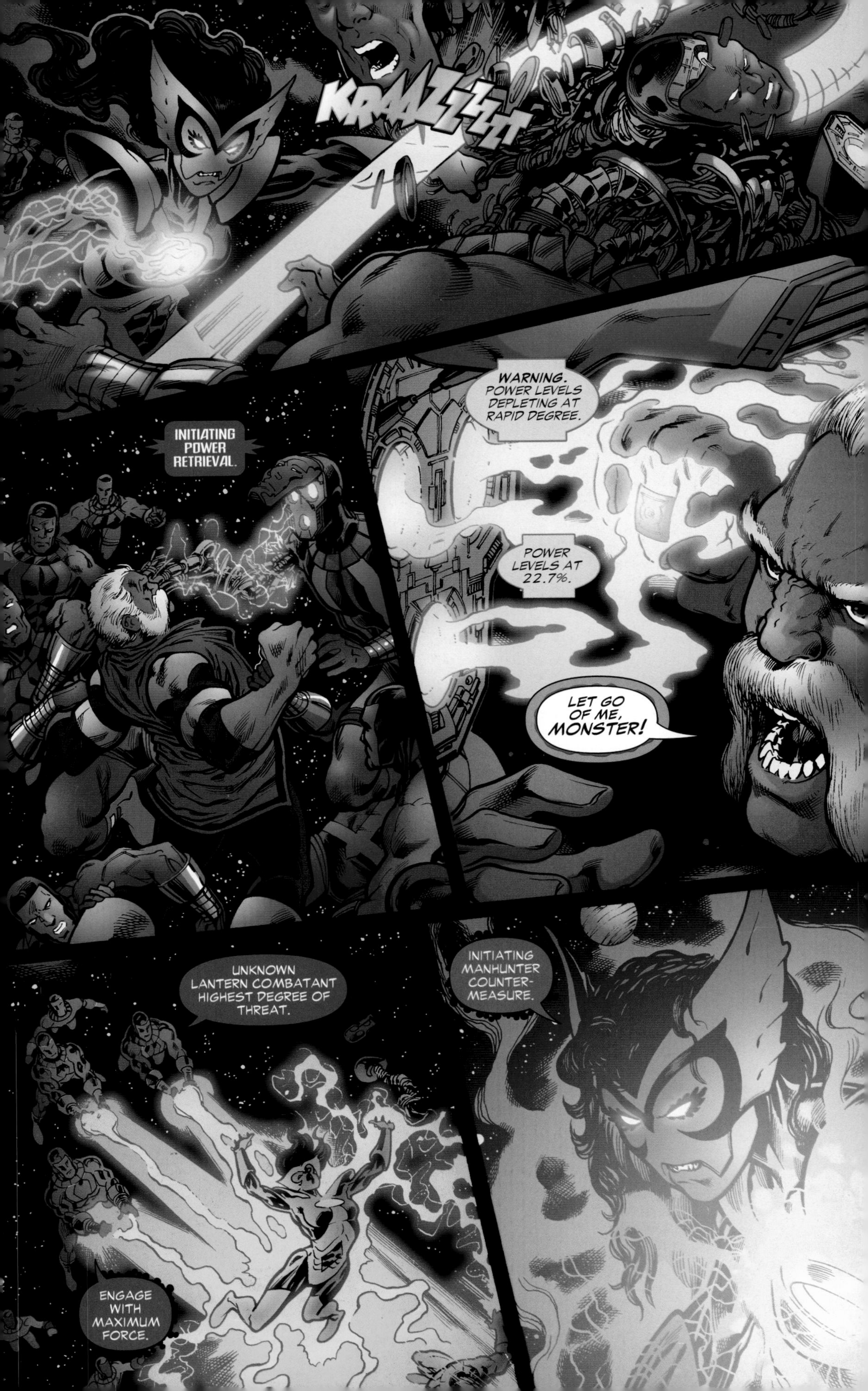
KRAAZZZZT
WARNING. POWER LEVELS DEPLETING AT RAPID DEGREE.
INITIATING POWER RETRIEVAL.
POWER LEVELS AT 22.7%.
LET GO OF ME, MONSTER!
UNKNOWN LANTERN COMBATANT HIGHEST DEGREE OF THREAT.
INITIATING MANHUNTER COUNTER-MEASURE.
ENGAGE WITH MAXIMUM FORCE.

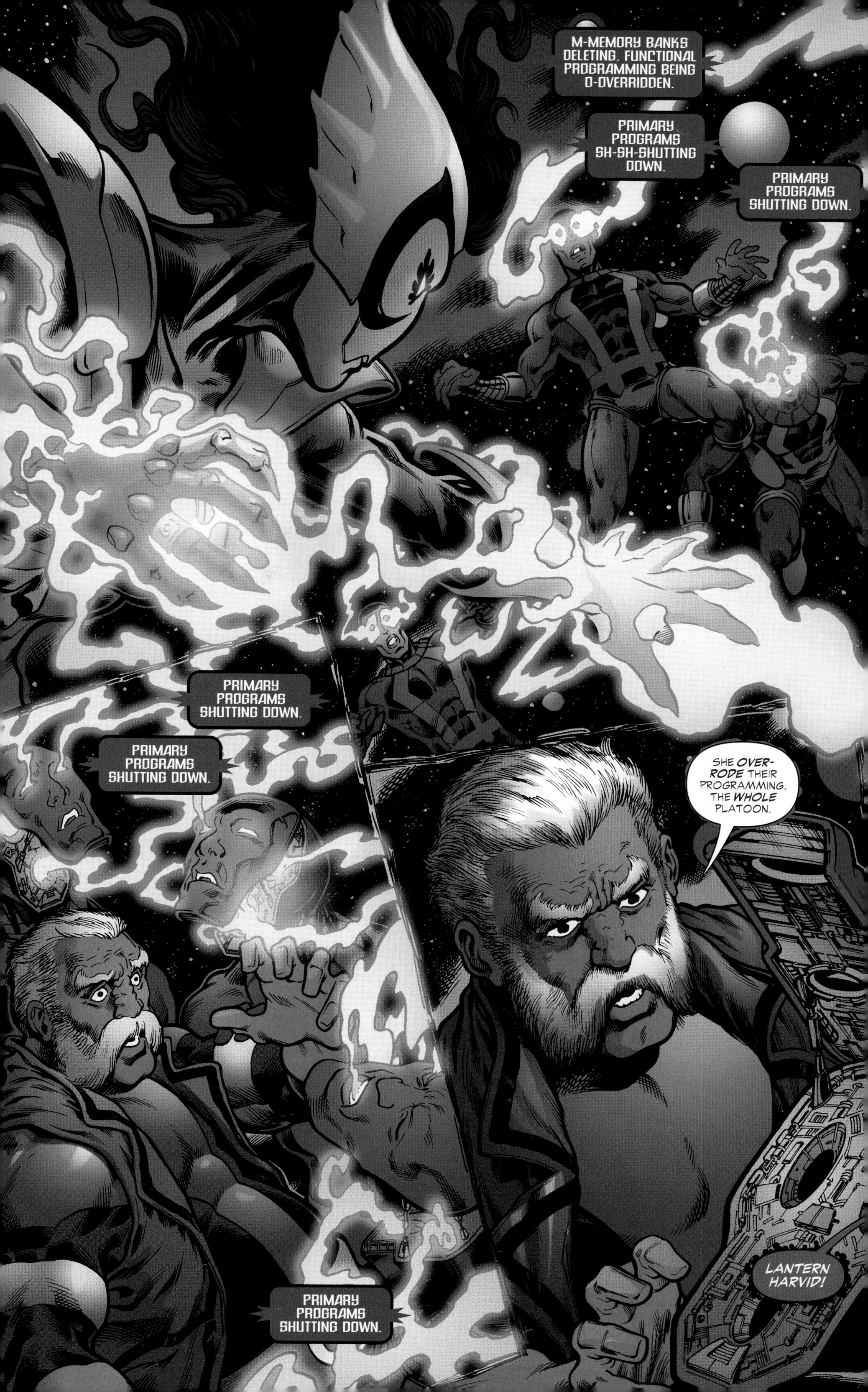
M-MEMORY BANKS DELETING. FUNCTIONAL PROGRAMMING BEING O-OVERRIDDEN.
PRIMARY PROGRAMS SH-SH-SHUTTING DOWN.
PRIMARY PROGRAMS SHUTTING DOWN.
PRIMARY PROGRAMS SHUTTING DOWN.
PRIMARY PROGRAMS SHUTTING DOWN.
SHE OVER-RODE THEIR PROGRAMMING. THE WHOLE PLATOON.
PRIMARY PROGRAMS SHUTTING DOWN.
LANTERN HARVID!

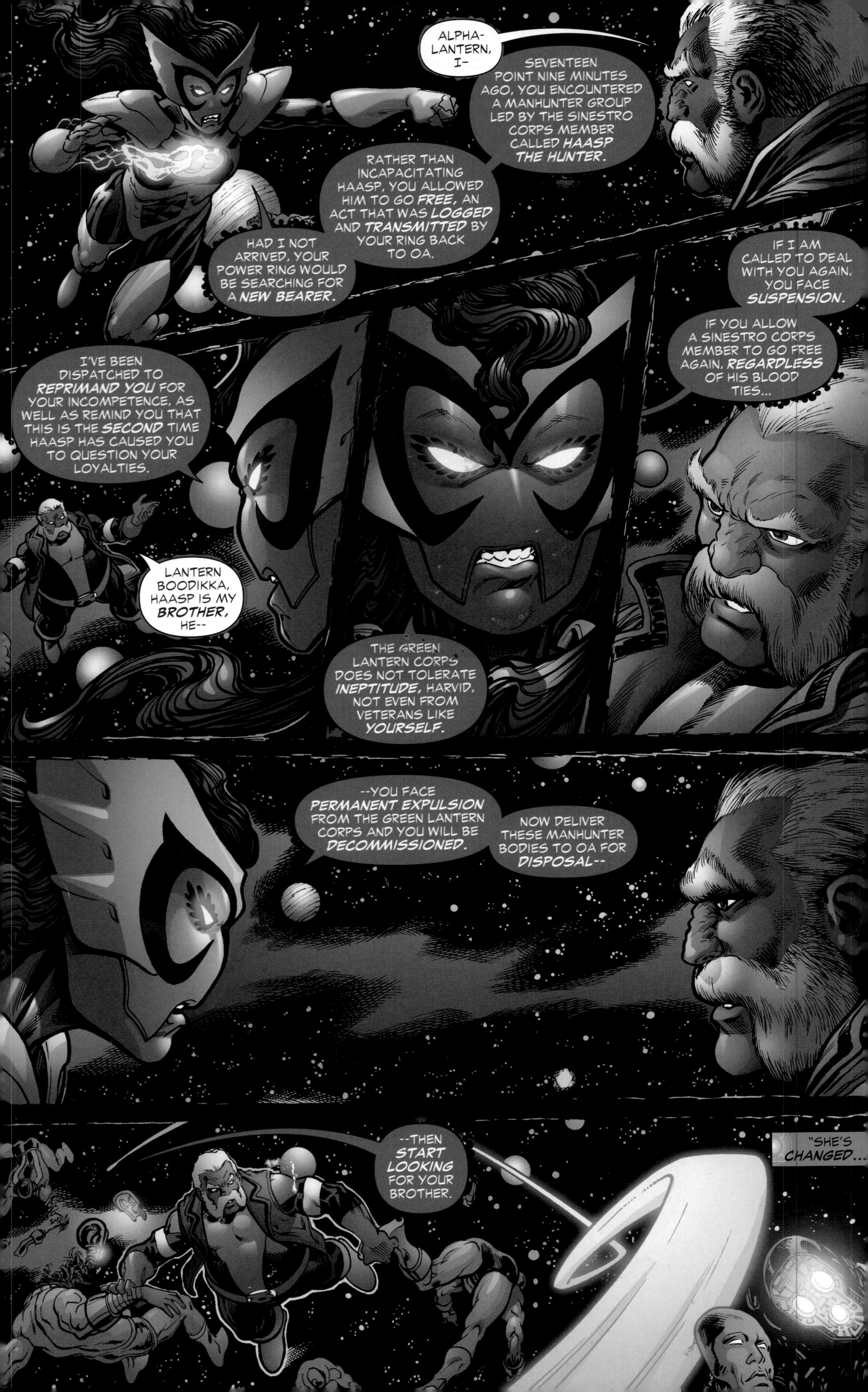

ALPHA-LANTERN, I-
SEVENTEEN POINT NINE MINUTES AGO, YOU ENCOUNTERED A MANHUNTER GROUP LED BY THE SINESTRO CORPS MEMBER CALLED HAASP THE HUNTER.
RATHER THAN INCAPACITATING HAASP, YOU ALLOWED HIM TO GO FREE, AN ACT THAT WAS LOGGED AND TRANSMITTED BY YOUR RING BACK TO OA.
HAD I NOT ARRIVED, YOUR POWER RING WOULD BE SEARCHING FOR A NEW BEARER.
I'VE BEEN DISPATCHED TO REPRIMAND YOU FOR YOUR INCOMPETENCE, AS WELL AS REMIND YOU THAT THIS IS THE SECOND TIME HAASP HAS CAUSED YOU TO QUESTION YOUR LOYALTIES.
LANTERN BOODIKKA, HAASP IS MY BROTHER, HE--
THE GREEN LANTERN CORPS DOES NOT TOLERATE INEPTITUDE, HARVID, NOT EVEN FROM VETERANS LIKE YOURSELF.
IF I AM CALLED TO DEAL WITH YOU AGAIN, YOU FACE SUSPENSION.
IF YOU ALLOW A SINESTRO CORPS MEMBER TO GO FREE AGAIN, REGARDLESS OF HIS BLOOD TIES...
--YOU FACE PERMANENT EXPULSION FROM THE GREEN LANTERN CORPS AND YOU WILL BE DECOMMISSIONED.
NOW DELIVER THESE MANHUNTER BODIES TO OA FOR DISPOSAL--
--THEN START LOOKING FOR YOUR BROTHER.
"SHE'S CHANGED...

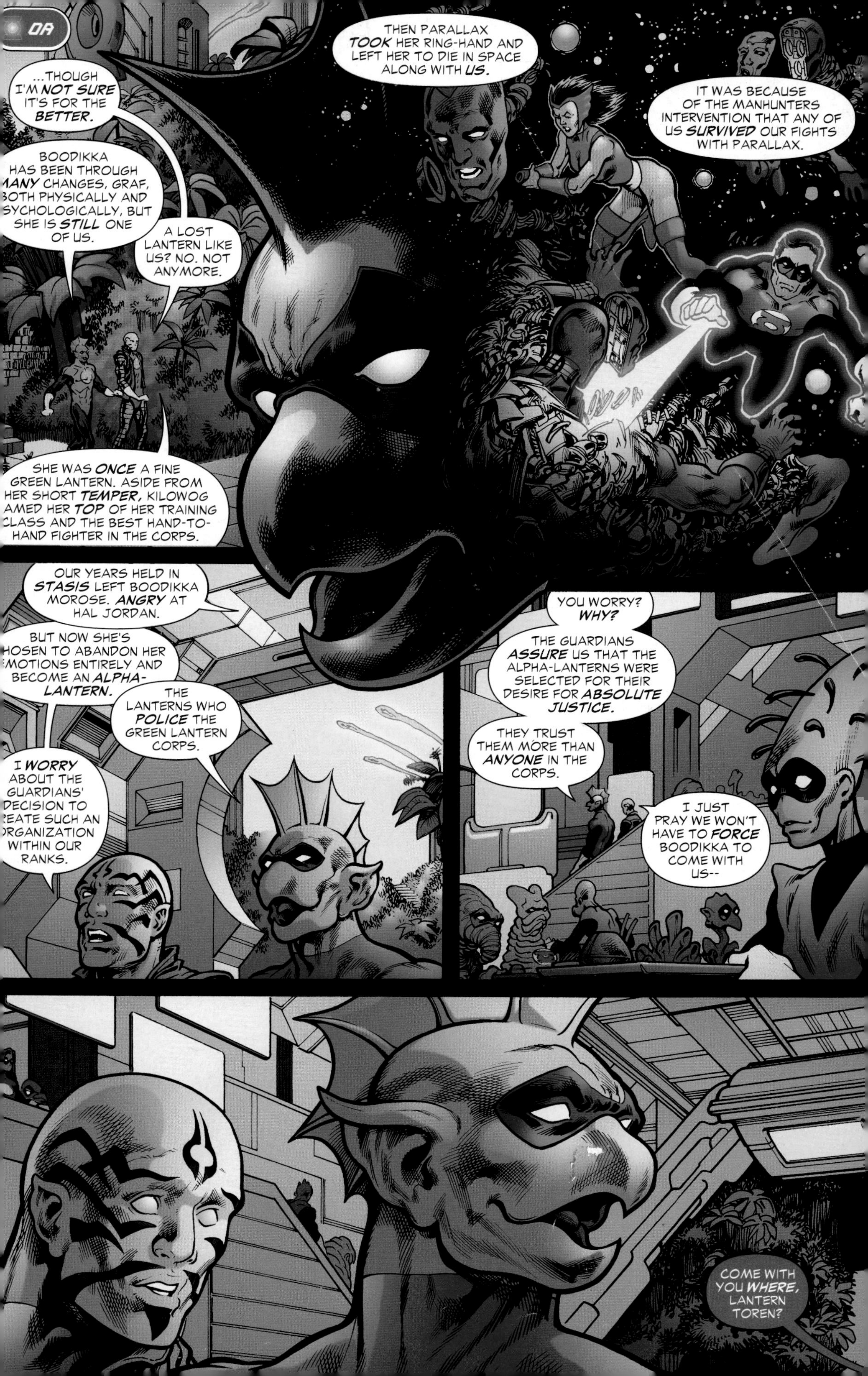
OA
...THOUGH I'M NOT SURE IT'S FOR THE BETTER.
BOODIKKA HAS BEEN THROUGH MANY CHANGES, GRAF, BOTH PHYSICALLY AND PSYCHOLOGICALLY, BUT SHE IS STILL ONE OF US.
A LOST LANTERN LIKE US? NO. NOT ANYMORE.
SHE WAS ONCE A FINE GREEN LANTERN. ASIDE FROM HER SHORT TEMPER, KILOWOG NAMED HER TOP OF HER TRAINING CLASS AND THE BEST HAND-TO-HAND FIGHTER IN THE CORPS.
THEN PARALLAX TOOK HER RING-HAND AND LEFT HER TO DIE IN SPACE ALONG WITH US.
IT WAS BECAUSE OF THE MANHUNTERS INTERVENTION THAT ANY OF US SURVIVED OUR FIGHTS WITH PARALLAX.
OUR YEARS HELD IN STASIS LEFT BOODIKKA MOROSE. ANGRY AT HAL JORDAN.
BUT NOW SHE'S CHOSEN TO ABANDON HER EMOTIONS ENTIRELY AND BECOME AN ALPHA-LANTERN.
THE LANTERNS WHO POLICE THE GREEN LANTERN CORPS.
I WORRY ABOUT THE GUARDIANS' DECISION TO CREATE SUCH AN ORGANIZATION WITHIN OUR RANKS.
YOU WORRY? WHY?
THE GUARDIANS ASSURE US THAT THE ALPHA-LANTERNS WERE SELECTED FOR THEIR DESIRE FOR ABSOLUTE JUSTICE.
THEY TRUST THEM MORE THAN ANYONE IN THE CORPS.
I JUST PRAY WE WON'T HAVE TO FORCE BOODIKKA TO COME WITH US--
COME WITH YOU WHERE, LANTERN TOREN?

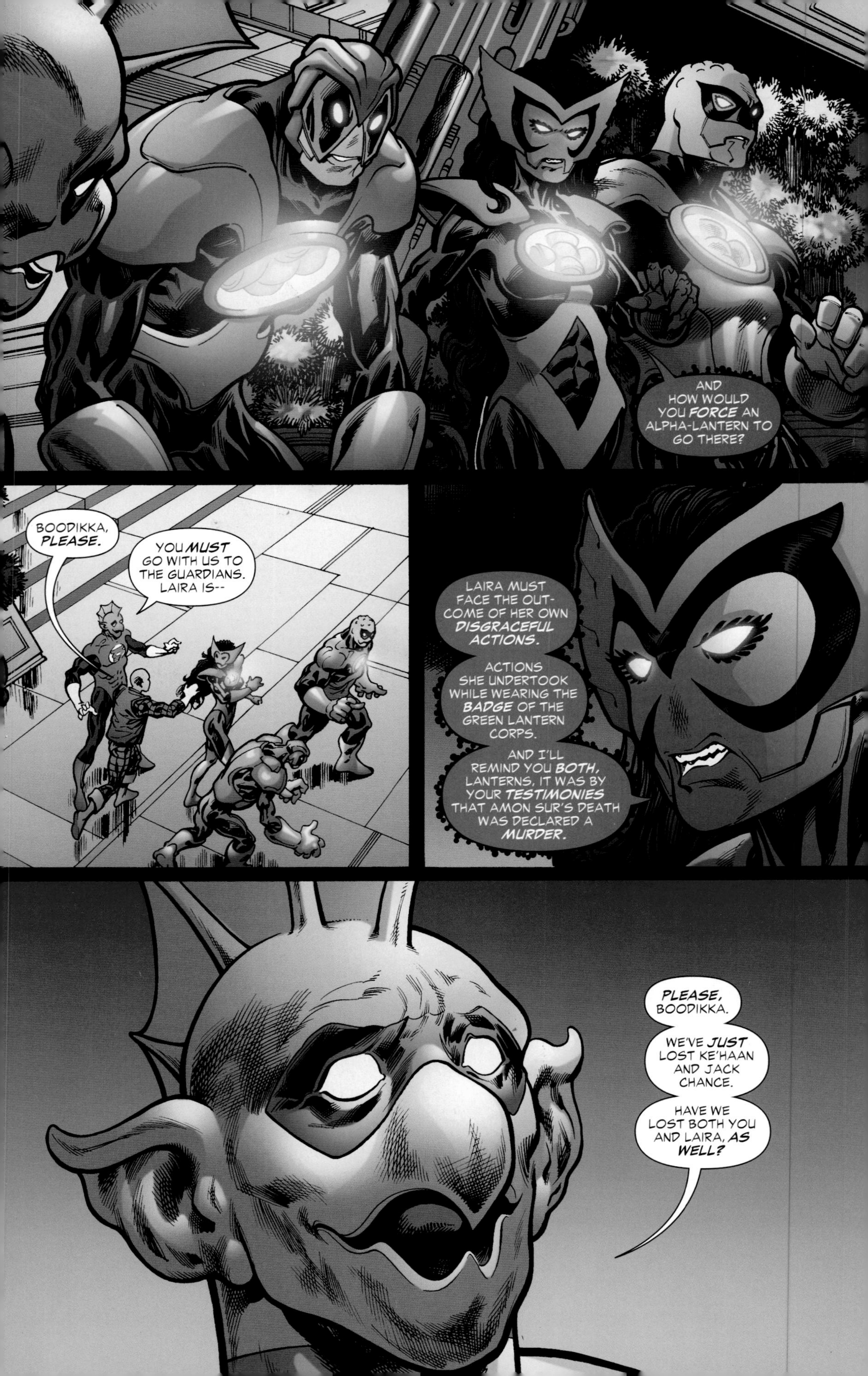
AND HOW WOULD YOU FORCE AN ALPHA-LANTERN TO GO THERE?
BOODIKKA, PLEASE.
YOU MUST GO WITH US TO THE GUARDIANS. LAIRA IS--
LAIRA MUST FACE THE OUT-COME OF HER OWN DISGRACEFUL ACTIONS.
ACTIONS SHE UNDERTOOK WHILE WEARING THE BADGE OF THE GREEN LANTERN CORPS.
AND I'LL REMIND YOU BOTH, LANTERNS, IT WAS BY YOUR TESTIMONIES THAT AMON SUR'S DEATH WAS DECLARED A MURDER.
PLEASE, BOODIKKA.
WE'VE JUST LOST KE'HAAN AND JACK CHANCE.
HAVE WE LOST BOTH YOU AND LAIRA, AS WELL?

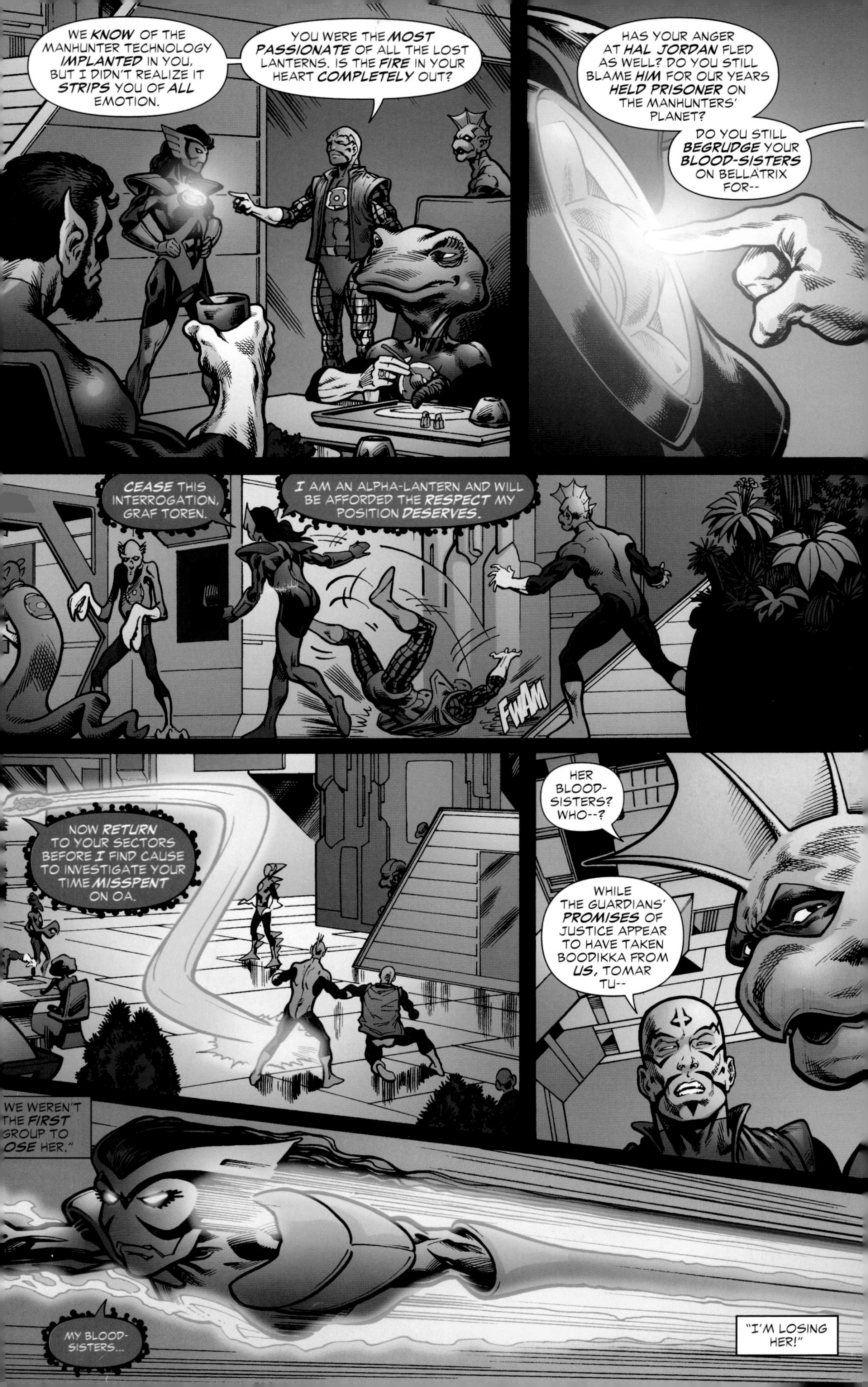
WE KNOW OF THE MANHUNTER TECHNOLOGY IMPLANTED IN YOU, BUT I DIDN'T REALIZE IT STRIPS YOU OF ALL EMOTION.
YOU WERE THE MOST PASSIONATE OF ALL THE LOST LANTERNS. IS THE FIRE IN YOUR HEART COMPLETELY OUT?
HAS YOUR ANGER AT HAL JORDAN FLED AS WELL? DO YOU STILL BLAME HIM FOR OUR YEARS HELD PRISONER ON THE MANHUNTERS' PLANET?
DO YOU STILL BEGRUDGE YOUR BLOOD-SISTERS ON BELLATRIX FOR--
CEASE THIS INTERROGATION, GRAF TOREN.
I AM AN ALPHA-LANTERN AND WILL BE AFFORDED THE RESPECT MY POSITION DESERVES.
FWAM
NOW RETURN TO YOUR SECTORS BEFORE I FIND CAUSE TO INVESTIGATE YOUR TIME MISSPENT ON OA.
HER BLOOD-SISTERS? WHO--?
WHILE THE GUARDIANS' PROMISES OF JUSTICE APPEAR TO HAVE TAKEN BOODIKKA FROM US, TOMAR TU--
WE WEREN'T THE FIRST GROUP TO OSE HER."
MY BLOOD-SISTERS...
"I'M LOSING HER!"

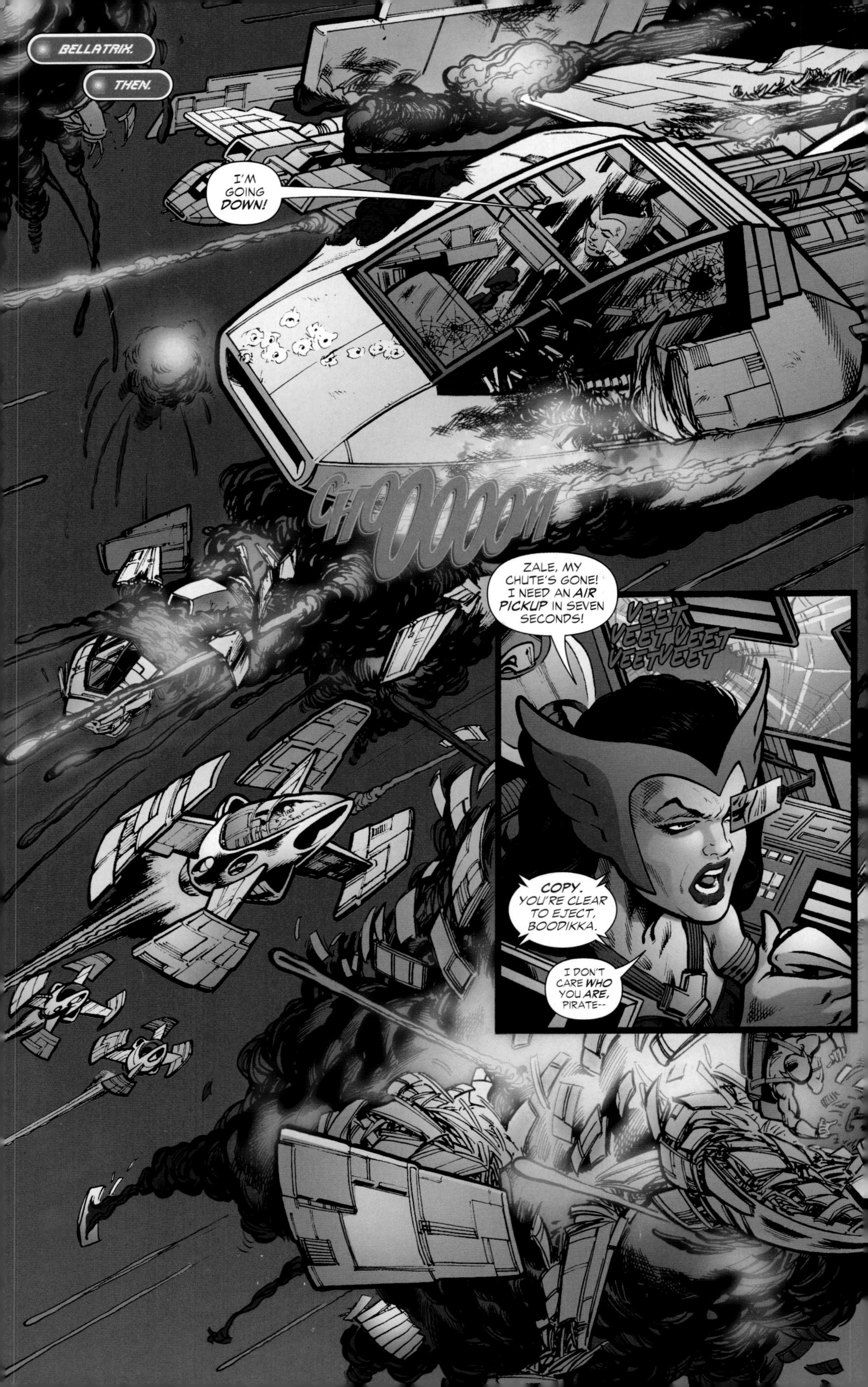
BELLATRIX.
THEN.
I'M GOING DOWN!
CHOOOOOOM
ZALE, MY CHUTE'S GONE! I NEED AN AIR PICKUP IN SEVEN SECONDS!
VEET VEET VEET VEET VEET VEET
COPY. YOU'RE CLEAR TO EJECT, BOODIKKA.
I DON'T CARE WHO YOU ARE, PIRATE--

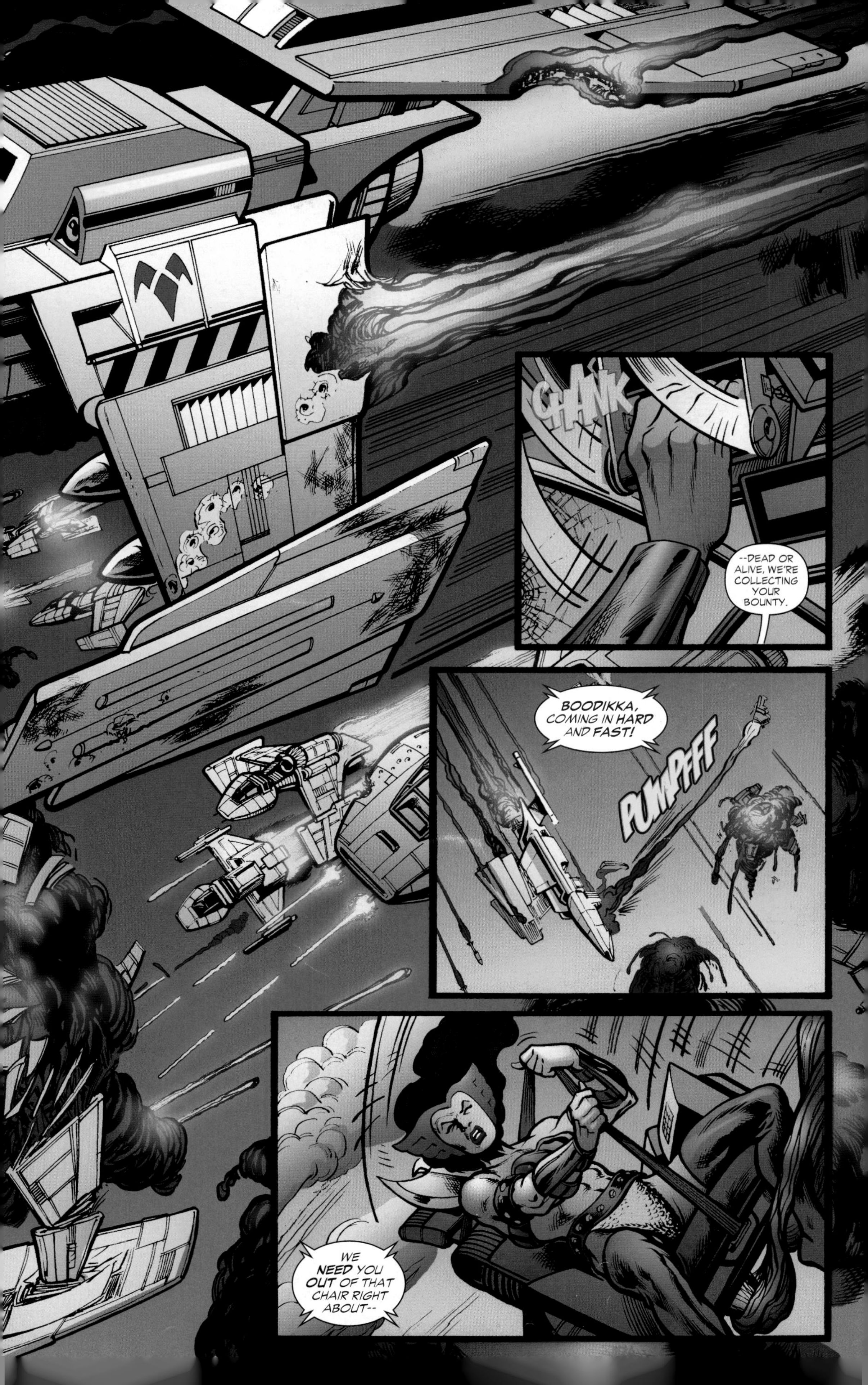
CHANK
--DEAD OR ALIVE, WE'RE COLLECTING YOUR BOUNTY.
BOODIKKA, COMING IN HARD AND FAST!
PUMPFFF
WE NEED YOU OUT OF THAT CHAIR RIGHT ABOUT--

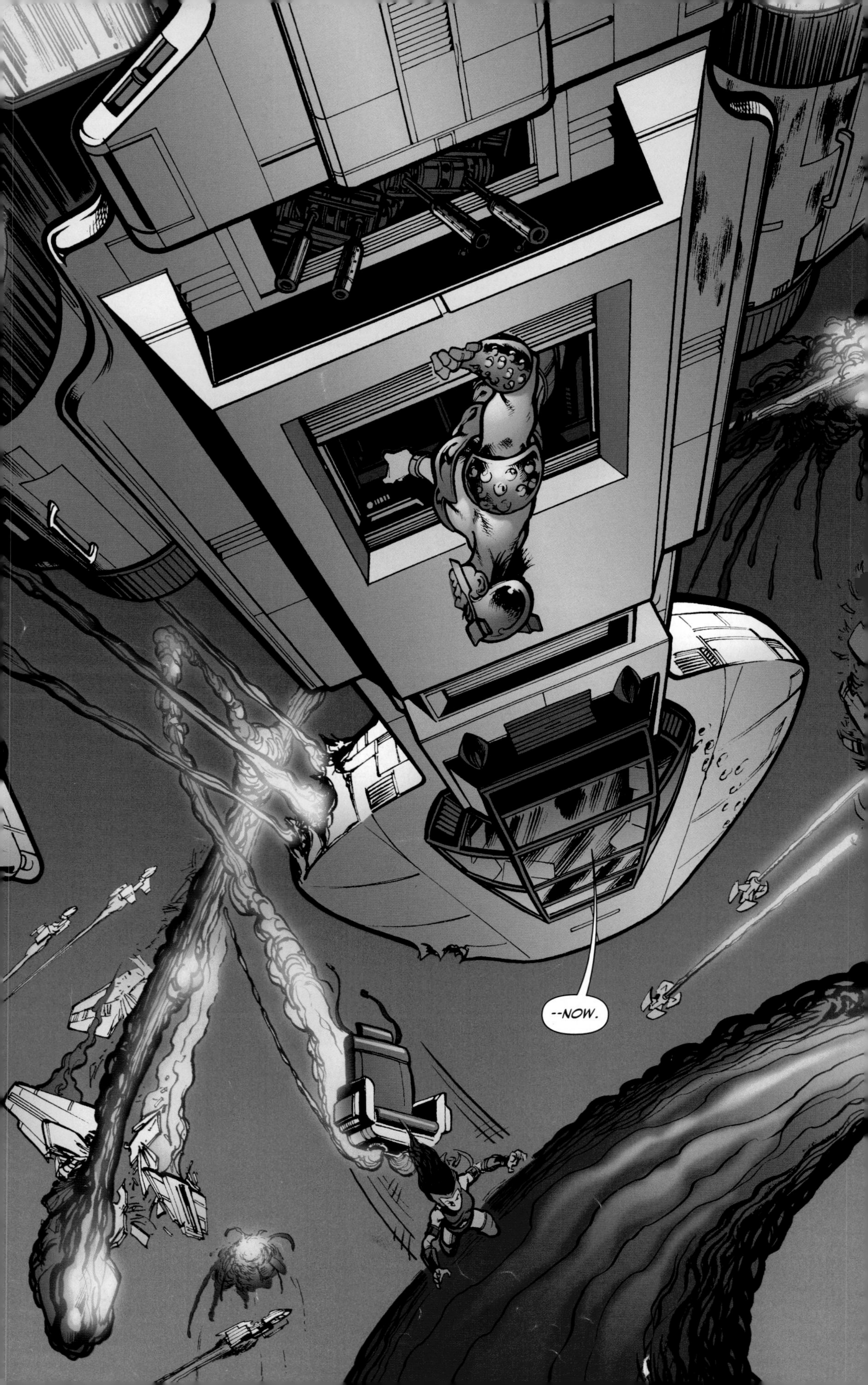
--NOW.

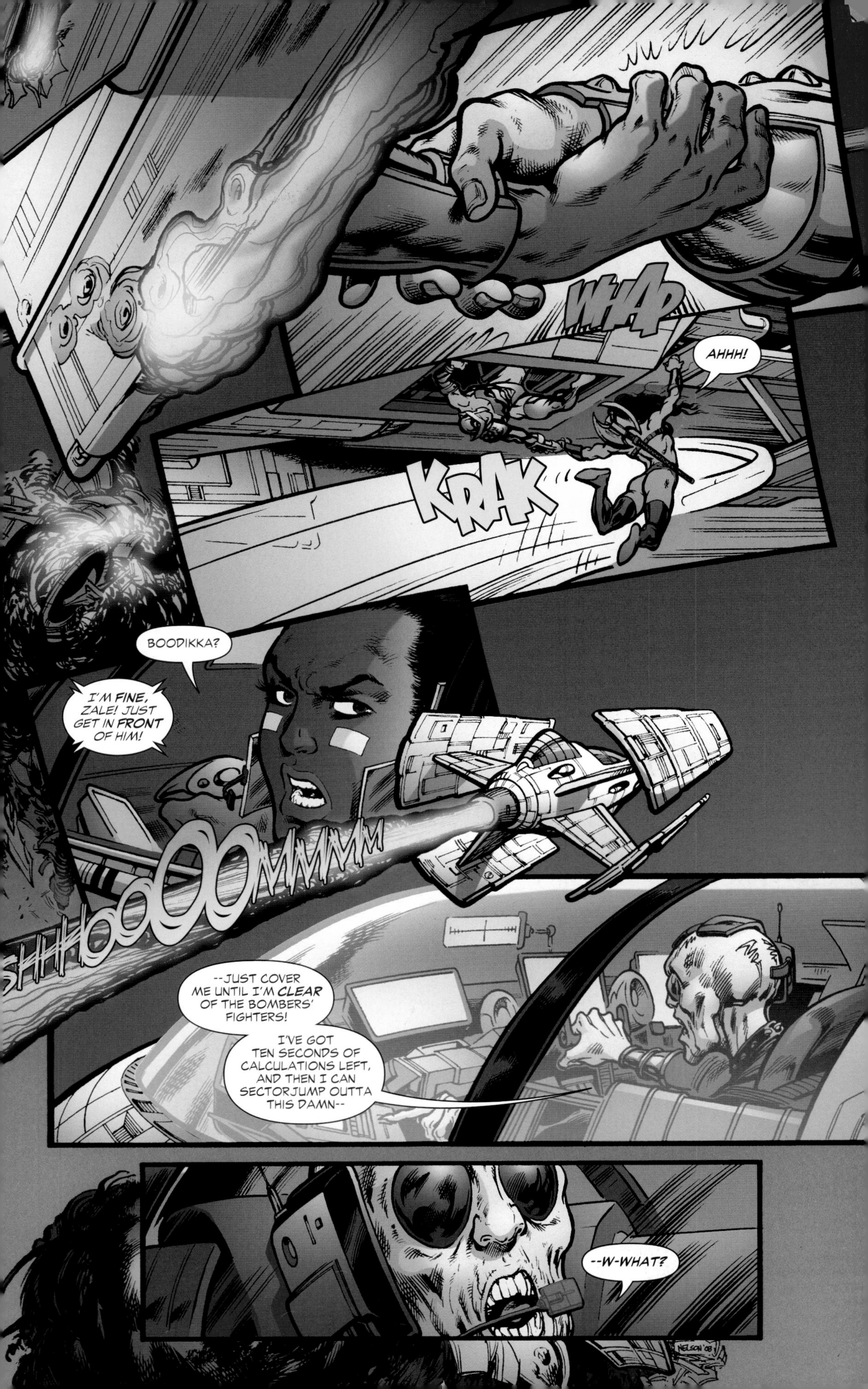

NNNNN
WHAP
AHHH!
KRAK
BOODIKKA?
I'M FINE, ZALE! JUST GET IN FRONT OF HIM!
SHHHooOOMMMM
--JUST COVER ME UNTIL I'M CLEAR OF THE BOMBERS' FIGHTERS!
I'VE GOT TEN SECONDS OF CALCULATIONS LEFT, AND THEN I CAN SECTORJUMP OUTTA THIS DAMN--
--W-WHAT?
NELSON '08

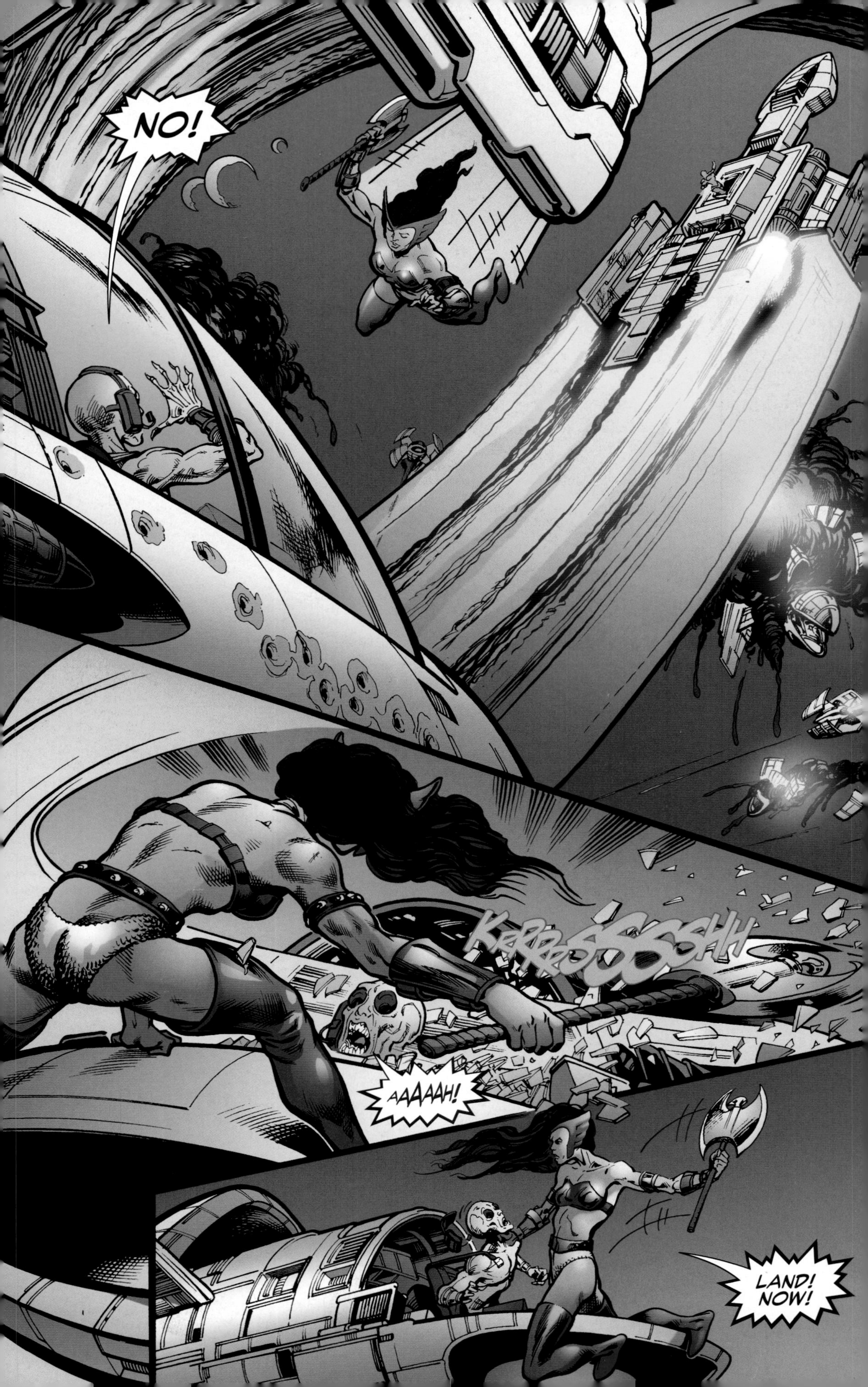
NO!
KRRRSSSSSHH
AAAAAH!
LAND! NOW!

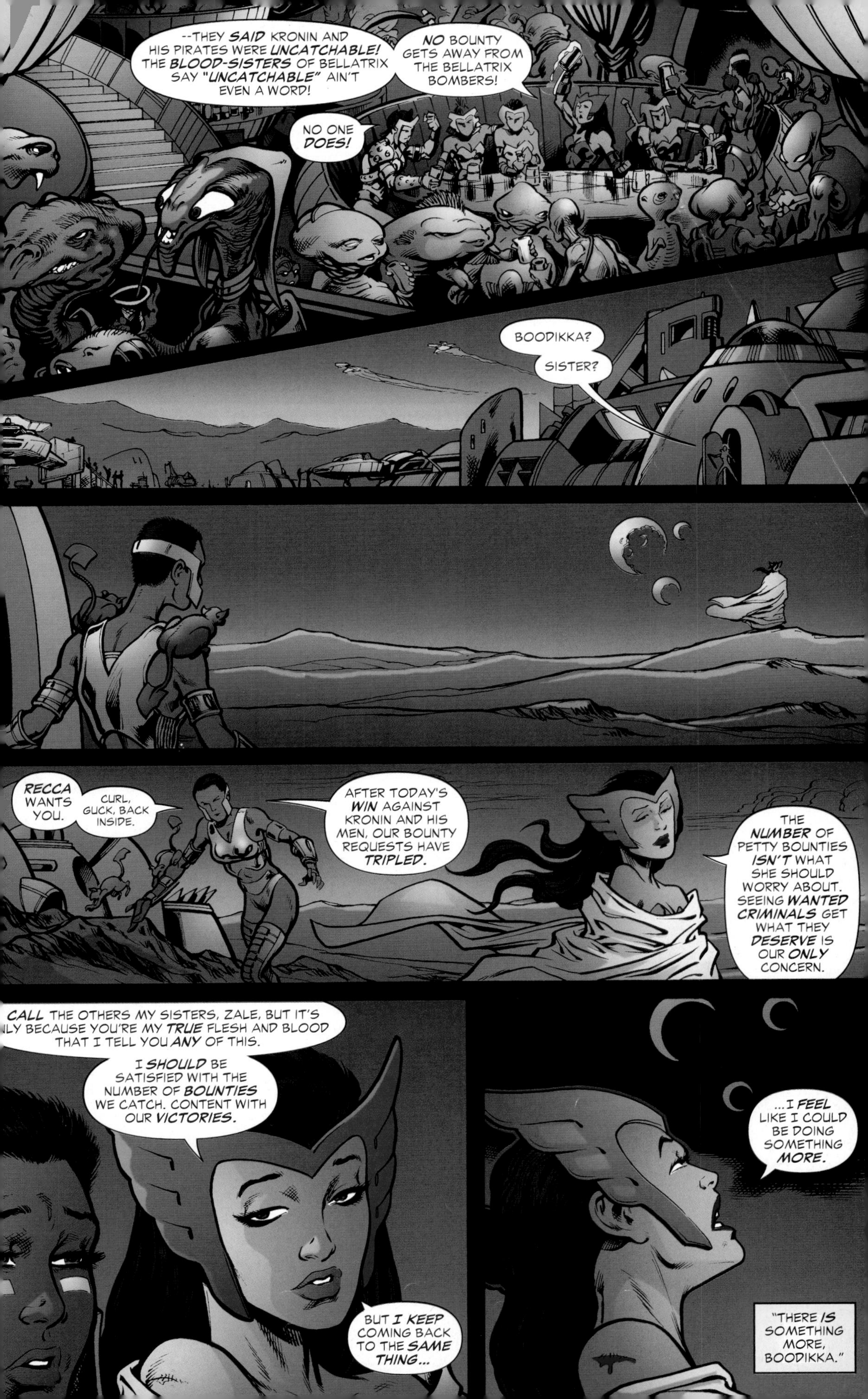
--THEY SAID KRONIN AND HIS PIRATES WERE UNCATCHABLE! THE BLOOD-SISTERS OF BELLATRIX SAY "UNCATCHABLE" AIN'T EVEN A WORD!
NO BOUNTY GETS AWAY FROM THE BELLATRIX BOMBERS!
NO ONE DOES!
BOODIKKA?
SISTER?
RECCA WANTS YOU.
CURL, GUCK, BACK INSIDE.
AFTER TODAY'S WIN AGAINST KRONIN AND HIS MEN, OUR BOUNTY REQUESTS HAVE TRIPLED.
THE NUMBER OF PETTY BOUNTIES ISN'T WHAT SHE SHOULD WORRY ABOUT. SEEING WANTED CRIMINALS GET WHAT THEY DESERVE IS OUR ONLY CONCERN.
CALL THE OTHERS MY SISTERS, ZALE, BUT IT'S NLY BECAUSE YOU'RE MY TRUE FLESH AND BLOOD THAT I TELL YOU ANY OF THIS.
I SHOULD BE SATISFIED WITH THE NUMBER OF BOUNTIES WE CATCH. CONTENT WITH OUR VICTORIES.
BUT I KEEP COMING BACK TO THE SAME THING...
...I FEEL LIKE I COULD BE DOING SOMETHING MORE.
"THERE IS SOMETHING MORE, BOODIKKA."

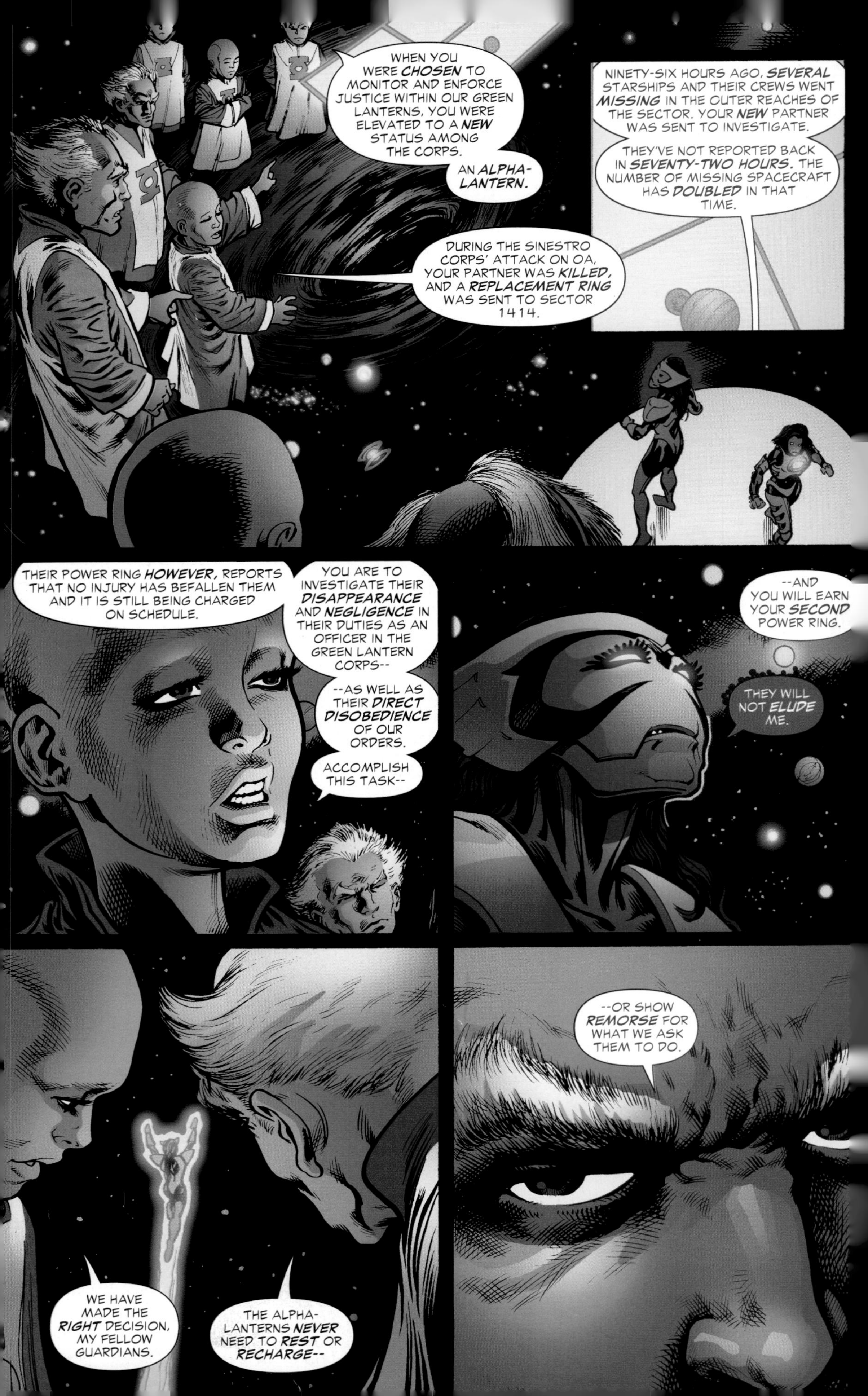
WHEN YOU WERE CHOSEN TO MONITOR AND ENFORCE JUSTICE WITHIN OUR GREEN LANTERNS, YOU WERE ELEVATED TO A NEW STATUS AMONG THE CORPS.
AN ALPHA-LANTERN.
NINETY-SIX HOURS AGO, SEVERAL STARSHIPS AND THEIR CREWS WENT MISSING IN THE OUTER REACHES OF THE SECTOR. YOUR NEW PARTNER WAS SENT TO INVESTIGATE.
THEY'VE NOT REPORTED BACK IN SEVENTY-TWO HOURS. THE NUMBER OF MISSING SPACECRAFT HAS DOUBLED IN THAT TIME.
DURING THE SINESTRO CORPS' ATTACK ON OA, YOUR PARTNER WAS KILLED, AND A REPLACEMENT RING WAS SENT TO SECTOR 1414.
THEIR POWER RING HOWEVER, REPORTS THAT NO INJURY HAS BEFALLEN THEM AND IT IS STILL BEING CHARGED ON SCHEDULE.
YOU ARE TO INVESTIGATE THEIR DISAPPEARANCE AND NEGLIGENCE IN THEIR DUTIES AS AN OFFICER IN THE GREEN LANTERN CORPS--
--AS WELL AS THEIR DIRECT DISOBEDIENCE OF OUR ORDERS.
ACCOMPLISH THIS TASK--
--AND YOU WILL EARN YOUR SECOND POWER RING.
THEY WILL NOT ELUDE ME.
WE HAVE MADE THE RIGHT DECISION, MY FELLOW GUARDIANS.
THE ALPHA-LANTERNS NEVER NEED TO REST OR RECHARGE--
--OR SHOW REMORSE FOR WHAT WE ASK THEM TO DO.

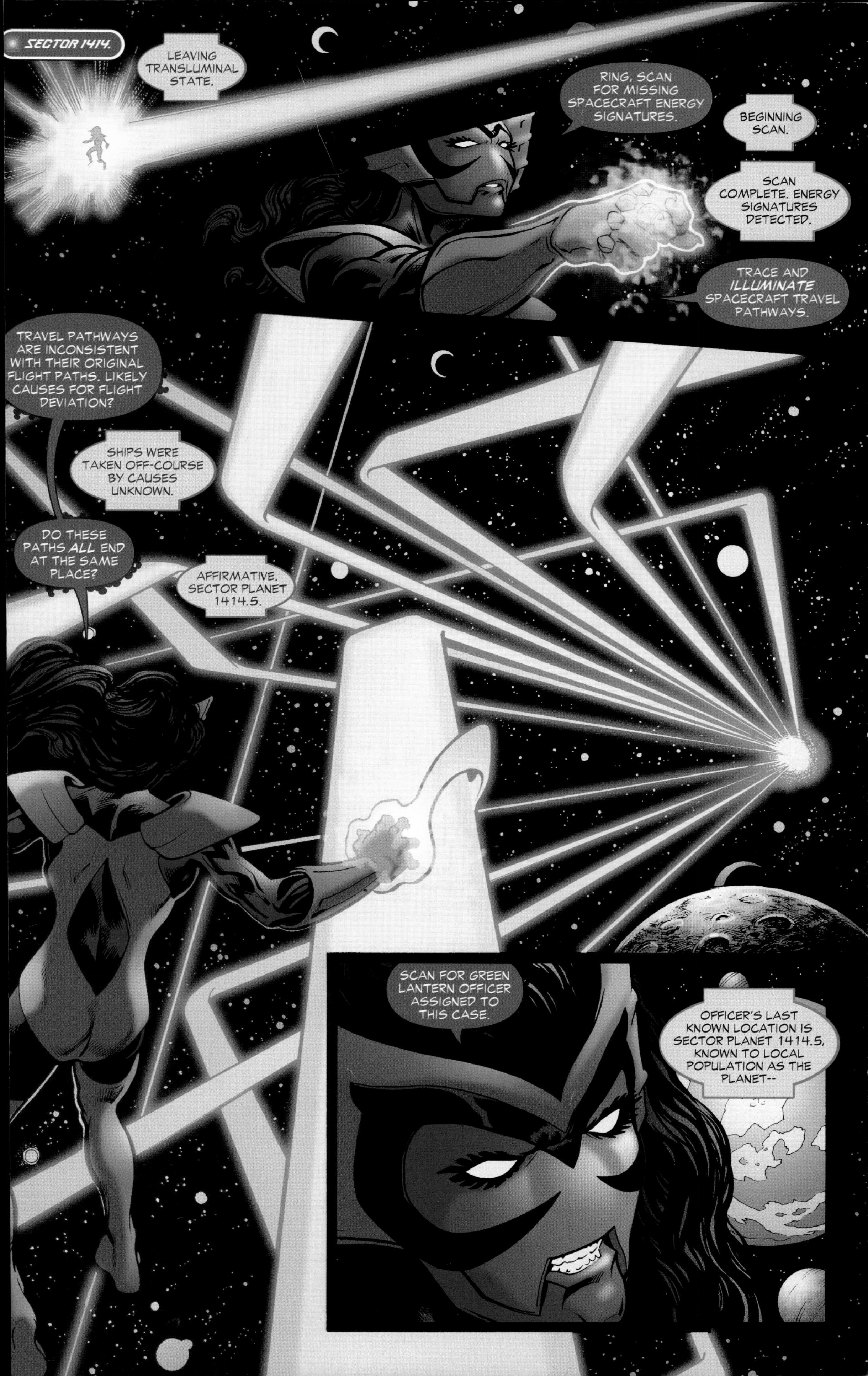
SECTOR 1414.
LEAVING TRANSLUMINAL STATE.
RING, SCAN FOR MISSING SPACECRAFT ENERGY SIGNATURES.
BEGINNING SCAN.
SCAN COMPLETE. ENERGY SIGNATURES DETECTED.
TRACE AND ILLUMINATE SPACECRAFT TRAVEL PATHWAYS.
TRAVEL PATHWAYS ARE INCONSISTENT WITH THEIR ORIGINAL FLIGHT PATHS. LIKELY CAUSES FOR FLIGHT DEVIATION?
SHIPS WERE TAKEN OFF-COURSE BY CAUSES UNKNOWN.
DO THESE PATHS ALL END AT THE SAME PLACE?
AFFIRMATIVE. SECTOR PLANET 1414.5.
SCAN FOR GREEN LANTERN OFFICER ASSIGNED TO THIS CASE.
OFFICER'S LAST KNOWN LOCATION IS SECTOR PLANET 1414.5, KNOWN TO LOCAL POPULATION AS THE PLANET--

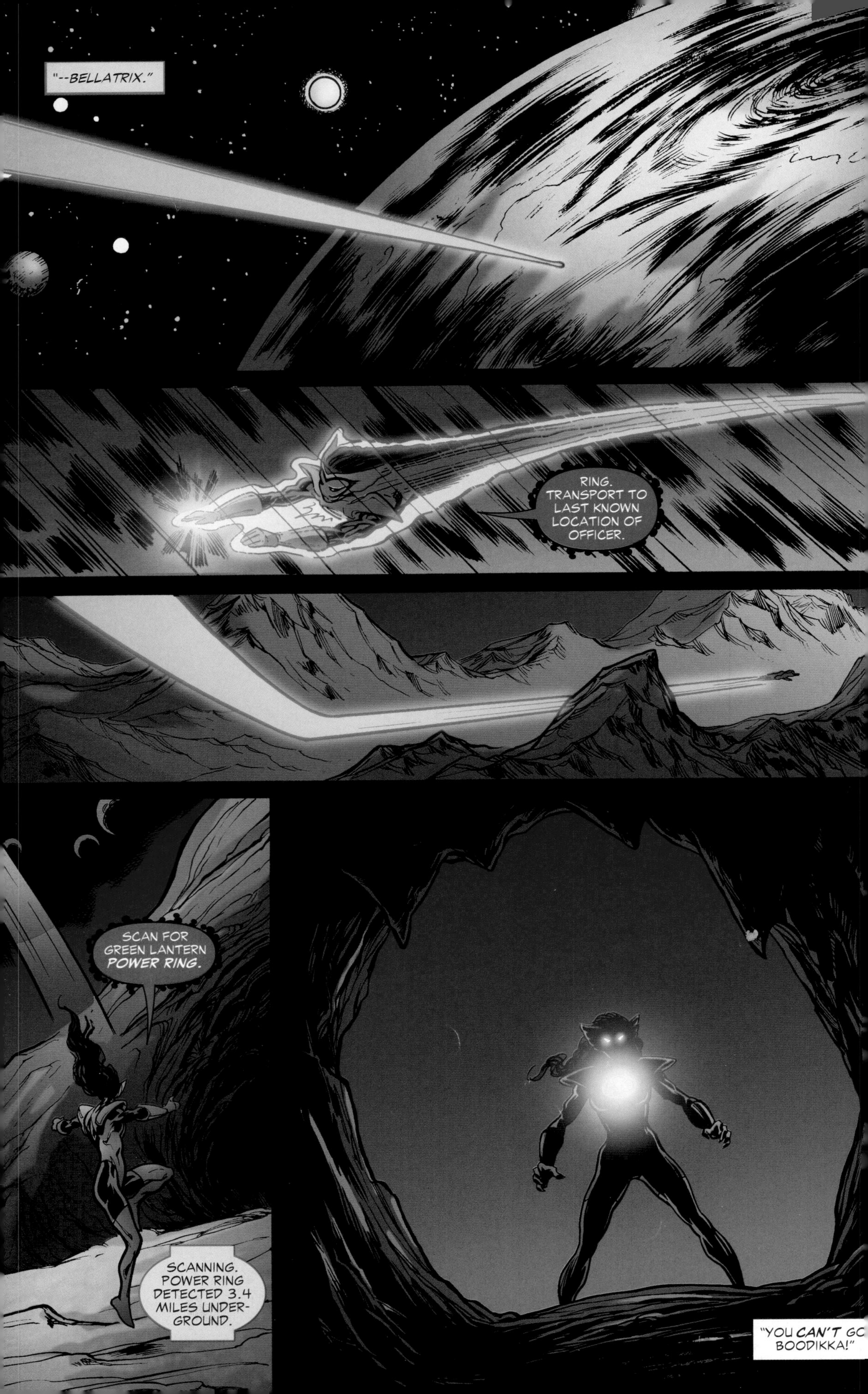
"--BELLATRIX."
RING. TRANSPORT TO LAST KNOWN LOCATION OF OFFICER.
SCAN FOR GREEN LANTERN POWER RING.
SCANNING. POWER RING DETECTED 3.4 MILES UNDER-GROUND.
"YOU CAN'T GO BOODIKKA!"

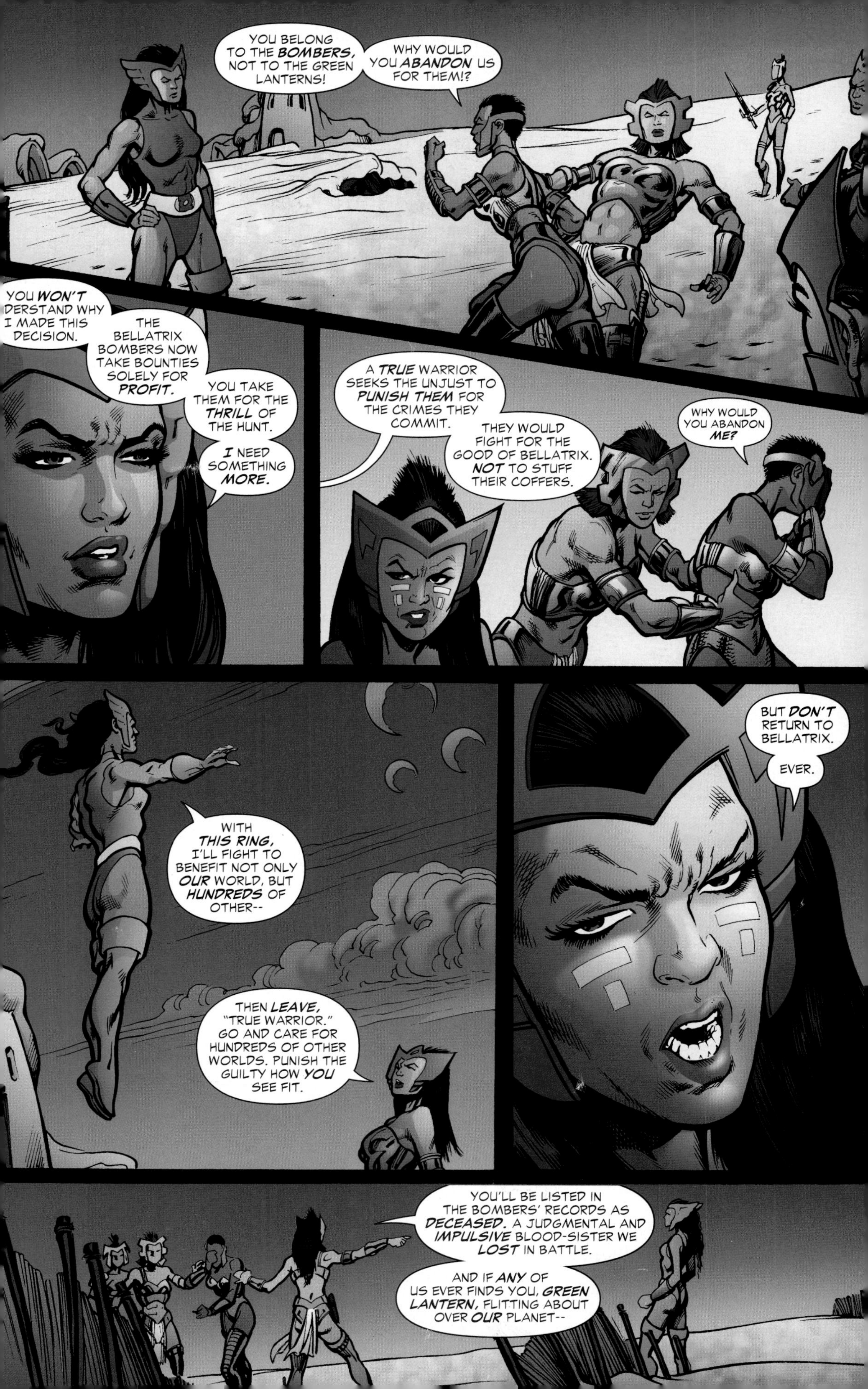
YOU BELONG TO THE **BOMBERS,** NOT TO THE GREEN LANTERNS!
WHY WOULD YOU **ABANDON** US FOR THEM!?
YOU **WON'T** DERSTAND WHY I MADE THIS DECISION.
THE BELLATRIX BOMBERS NOW TAKE BOUNTIES SOLELY FOR **PROFIT.**
YOU TAKE THEM FOR THE **THRILL** OF THE HUNT.
I NEED SOMETHING **MORE.**
A **TRUE** WARRIOR SEEKS THE UNJUST TO **PUNISH THEM** FOR THE CRIMES THEY COMMIT.
THEY WOULD FIGHT FOR THE GOOD OF BELLATRIX. **NOT** TO STUFF THEIR COFFERS.
WHY WOULD YOU ABANDON **ME?**
WITH **THIS RING,** I'LL FIGHT TO BENEFIT NOT ONLY **OUR** WORLD, BUT **HUNDREDS** OF OTHER--
THEN **LEAVE,** "TRUE WARRIOR." GO AND CARE FOR HUNDREDS OF OTHER WORLDS. PUNISH THE GUILTY HOW **YOU** SEE FIT.
BUT **DON'T** RETURN TO BELLATRIX.
EVER.
YOU'LL BE LISTED IN THE BOMBERS' RECORDS AS **DECEASED.** A JUDGMENTAL AND **IMPULSIVE** BLOOD-SISTER WE **LOST** IN BATTLE.
AND IF **ANY** OF US EVER FINDS YOU, **GREEN LANTERN,** FLITTING ABOUT OVER **OUR** PLANET--

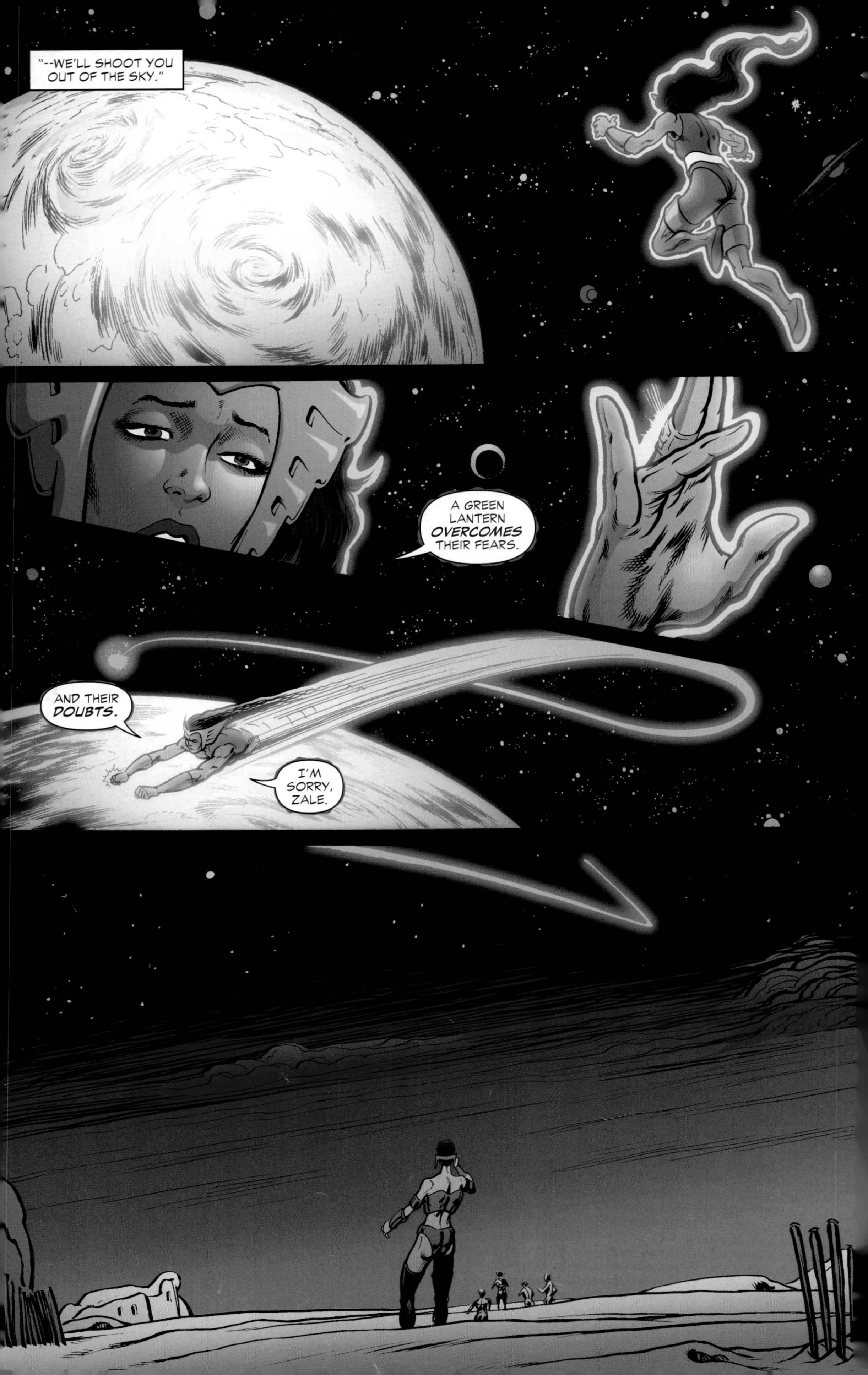
"--WE'LL SHOOT YOU OUT OF THE SKY."
A GREEN LANTERN OVERCOMES THEIR FEARS.
AND THEIR DOUBTS.
I'M SORRY, ZALE.

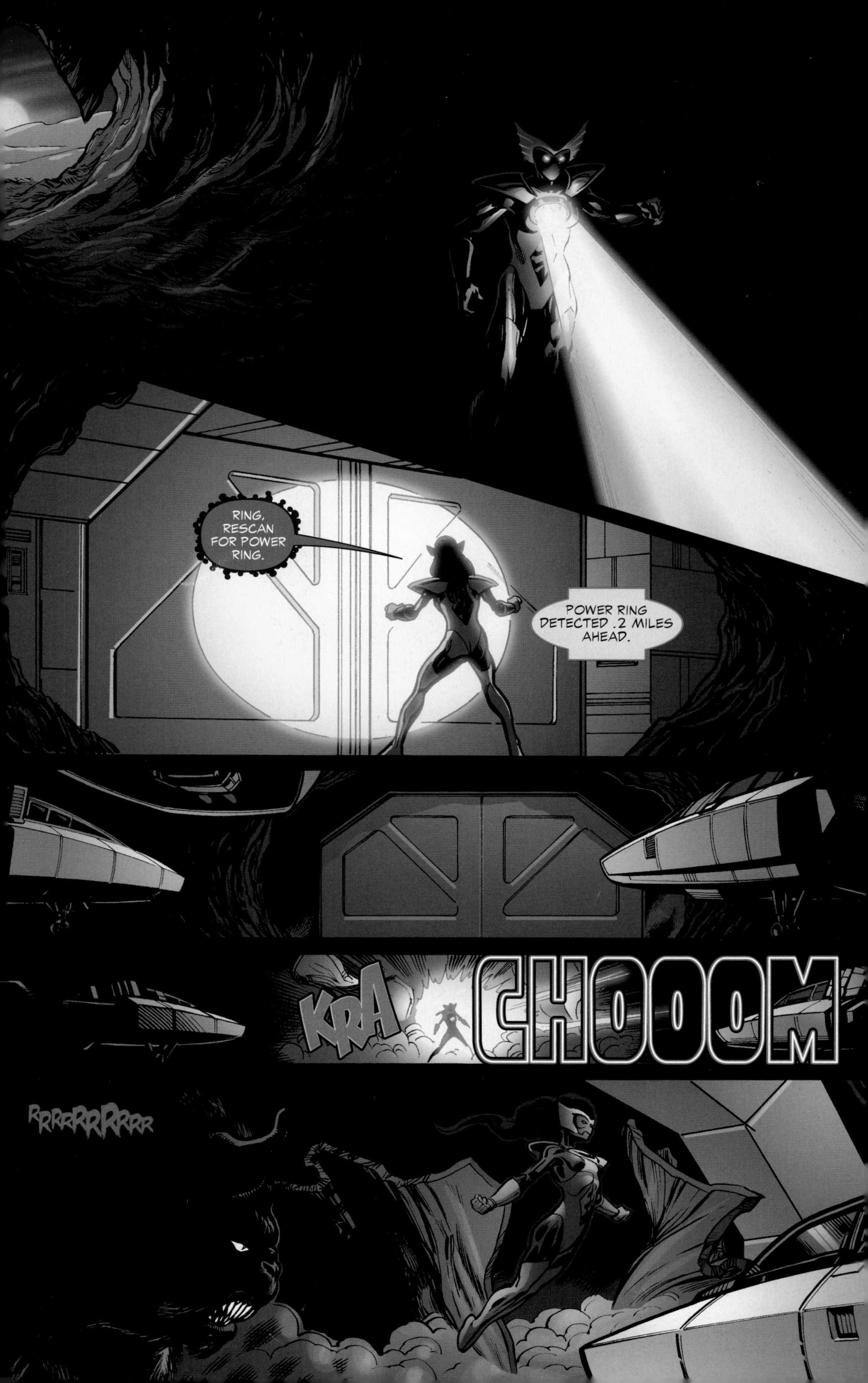
RING, RESCAN FOR POWER RING.
POWER RING DETECTED .2 MILES AHEAD.
KRA
CHOOOM
RRRRRRRRRR

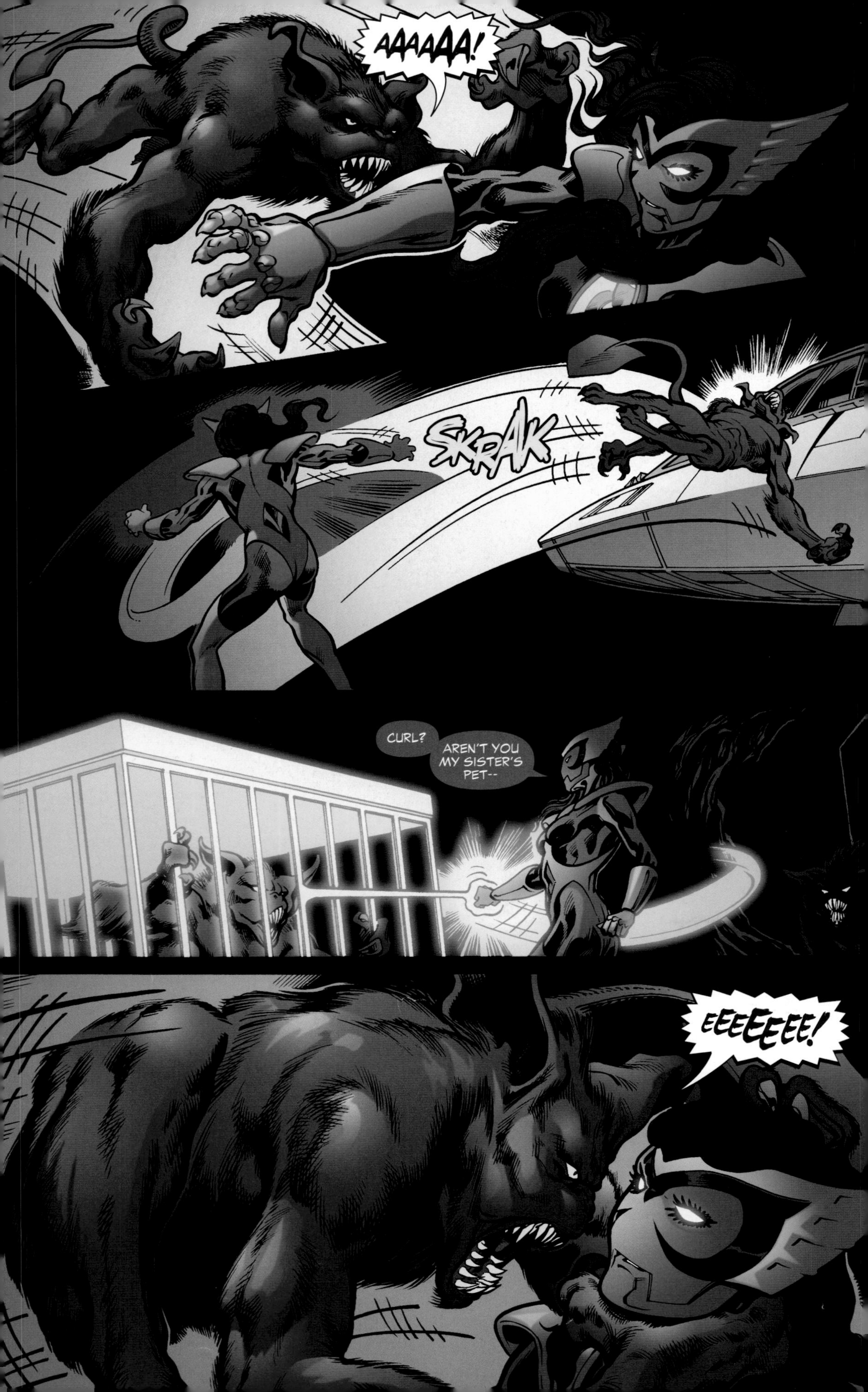
AAAAAA!
SKRAK
CURL?
AREN'T YOU MY SISTER'S PET--
EEEEEEE!

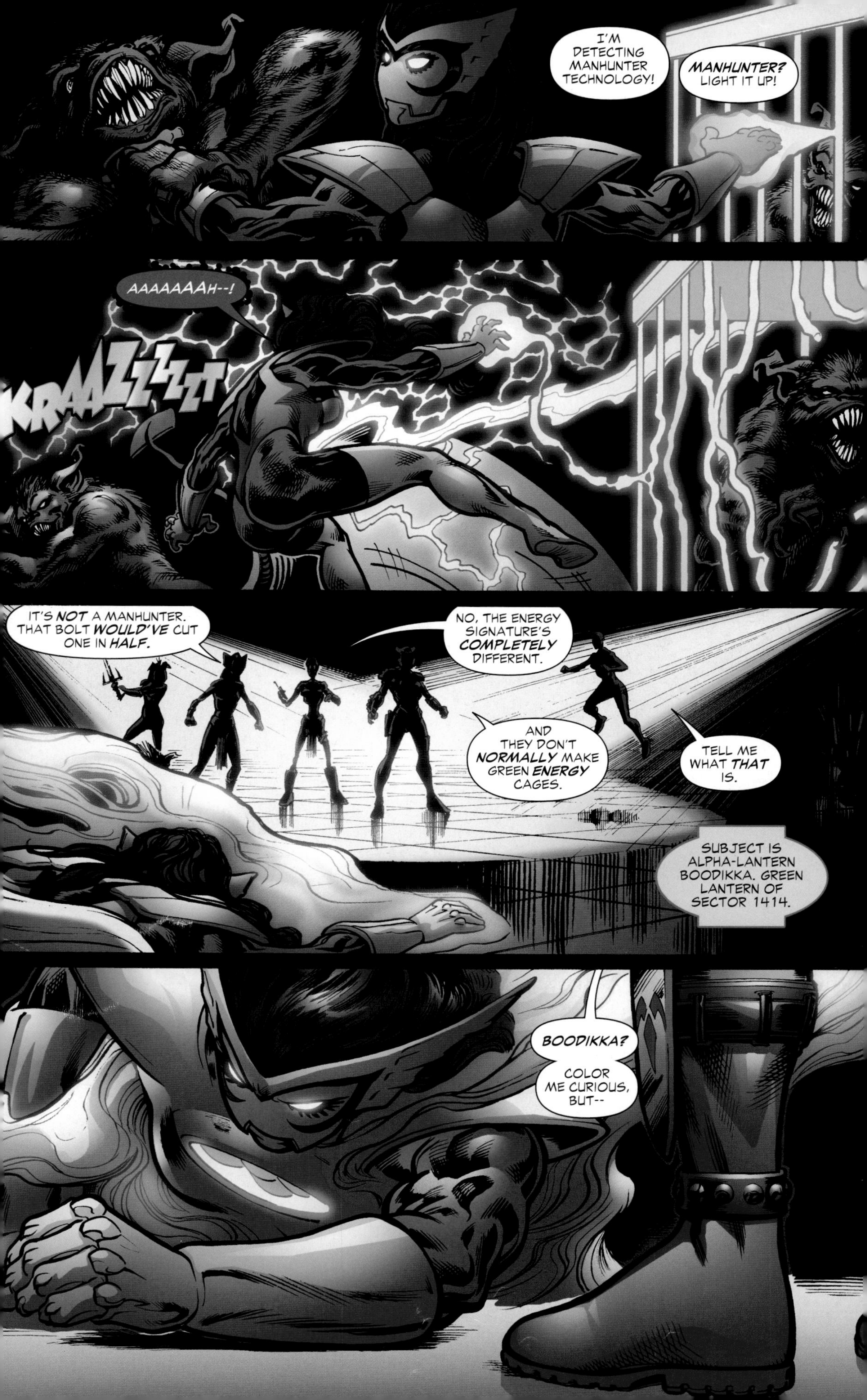
I'M DETECTING MANHUNTER TECHNOLOGY!
MANHUNTER? LIGHT IT UP!
AAAAAAAH--!
KRAAZZZZZT
IT'S NOT A MANHUNTER. THAT BOLT WOULD'VE CUT ONE IN HALF.
NO, THE ENERGY SIGNATURE'S COMPLETELY DIFFERENT.
AND THEY DON'T NORMALLY MAKE GREEN ENERGY CAGES.
TELL ME WHAT THAT IS.
SUBJECT IS ALPHA-LANTERN BOODIKKA. GREEN LANTERN OF SECTOR 1414.
BOODIKKA?
COLOR ME CURIOUS, BUT--

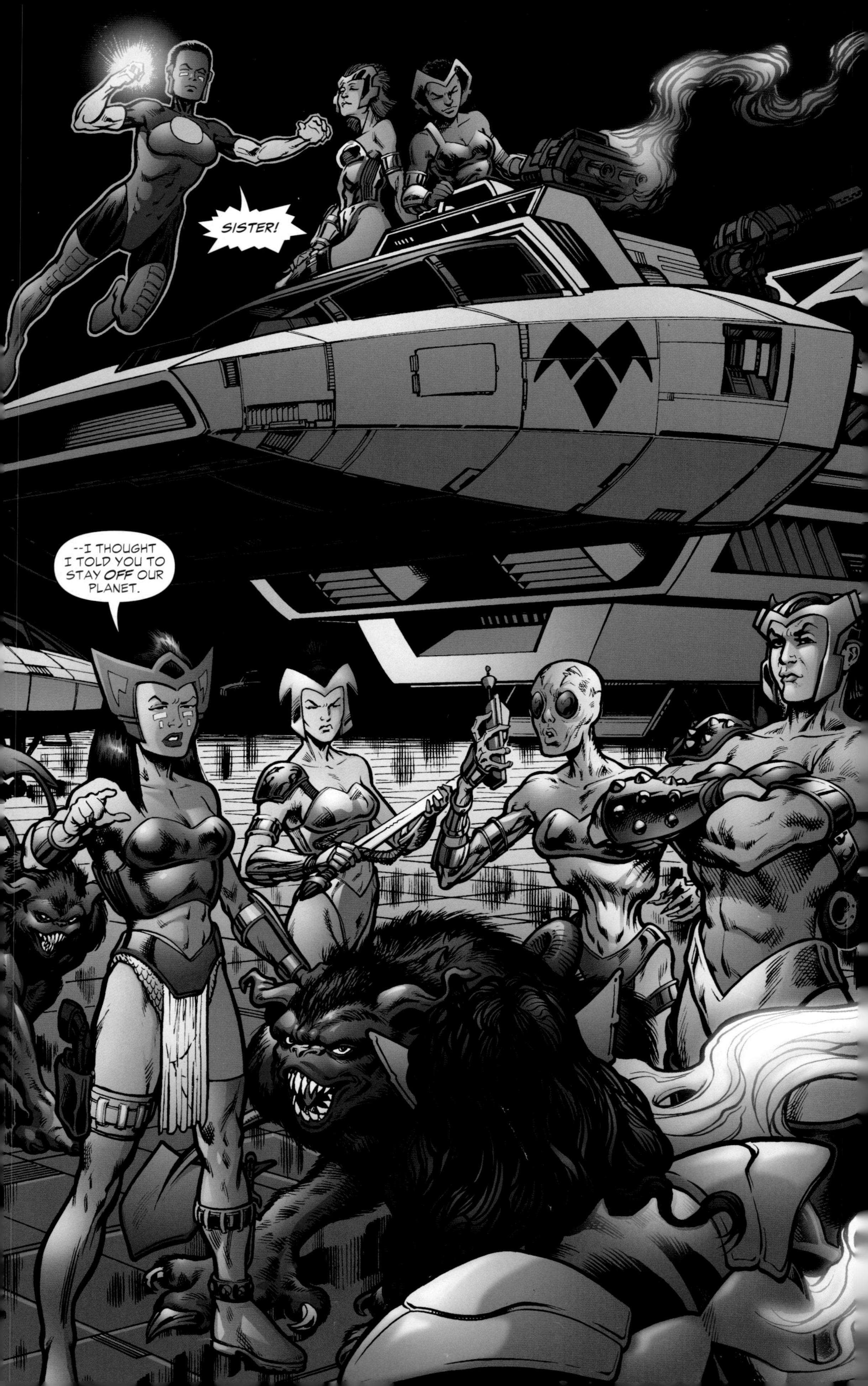
SISTER!
--I THOUGHT I TOLD YOU TO STAY OFF OUR PLANET.

THE CURSE OF THE ALPHA-LANTERN PART TWO
Cover by Rodolfo Migliari

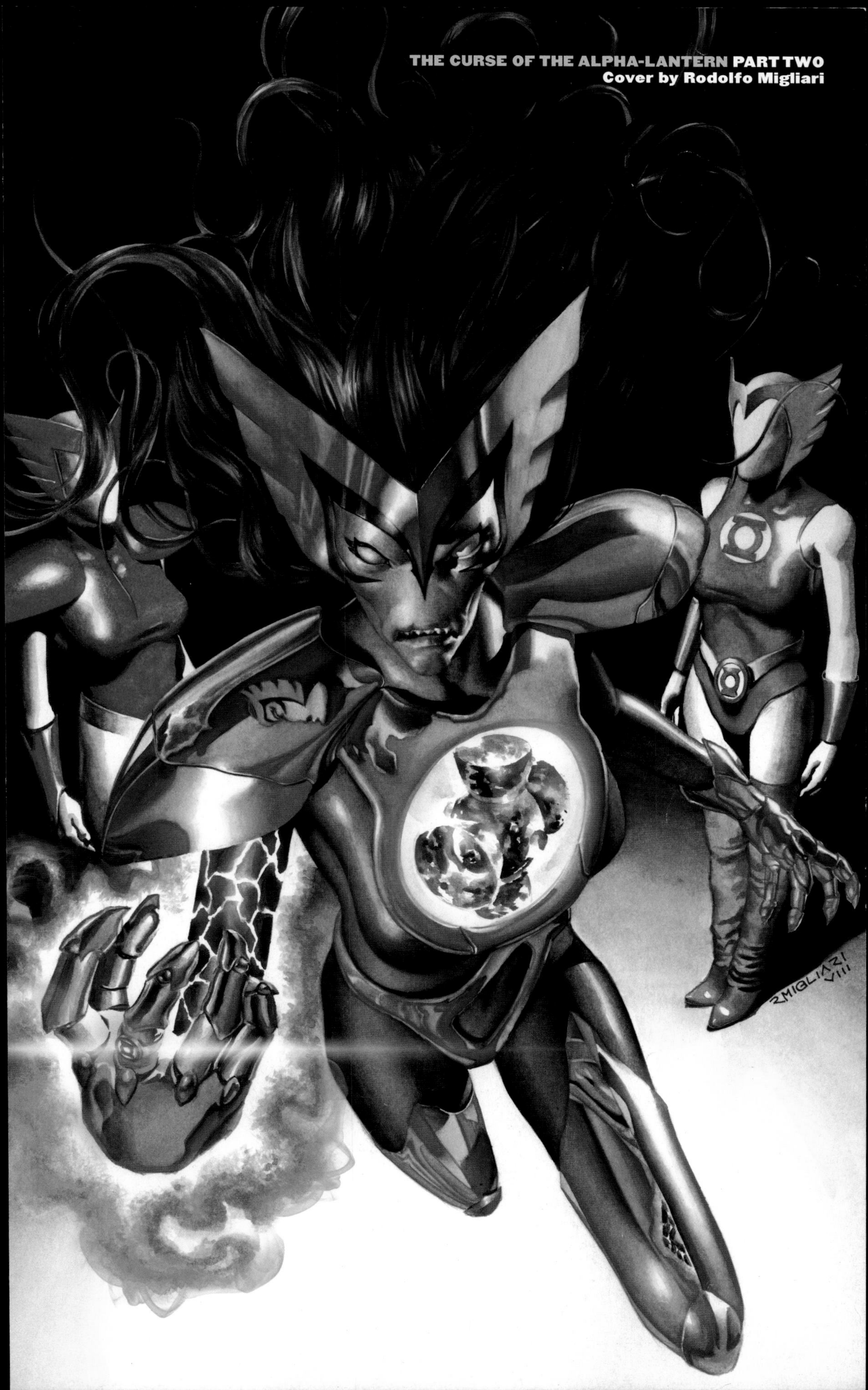
RMIGLIARI
VIII

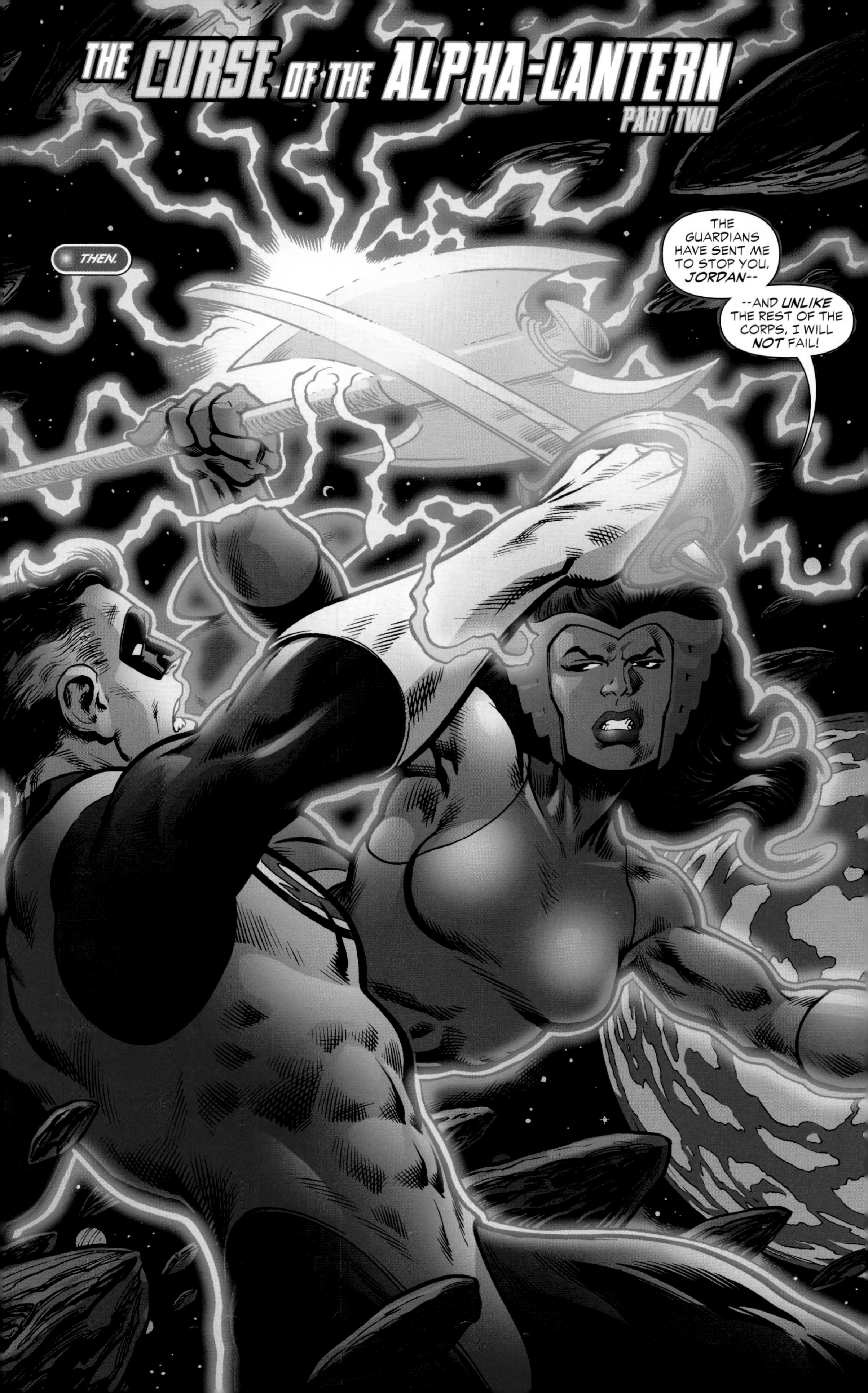
THE CURSE OF THE ALPHA-LANTERN
PART TWO
THEN.
THE GUARDIANS HAVE SENT ME TO STOP YOU, JORDAN--
--AND UNLIKE THE REST OF THE CORPS, I WILL NOT FAIL!

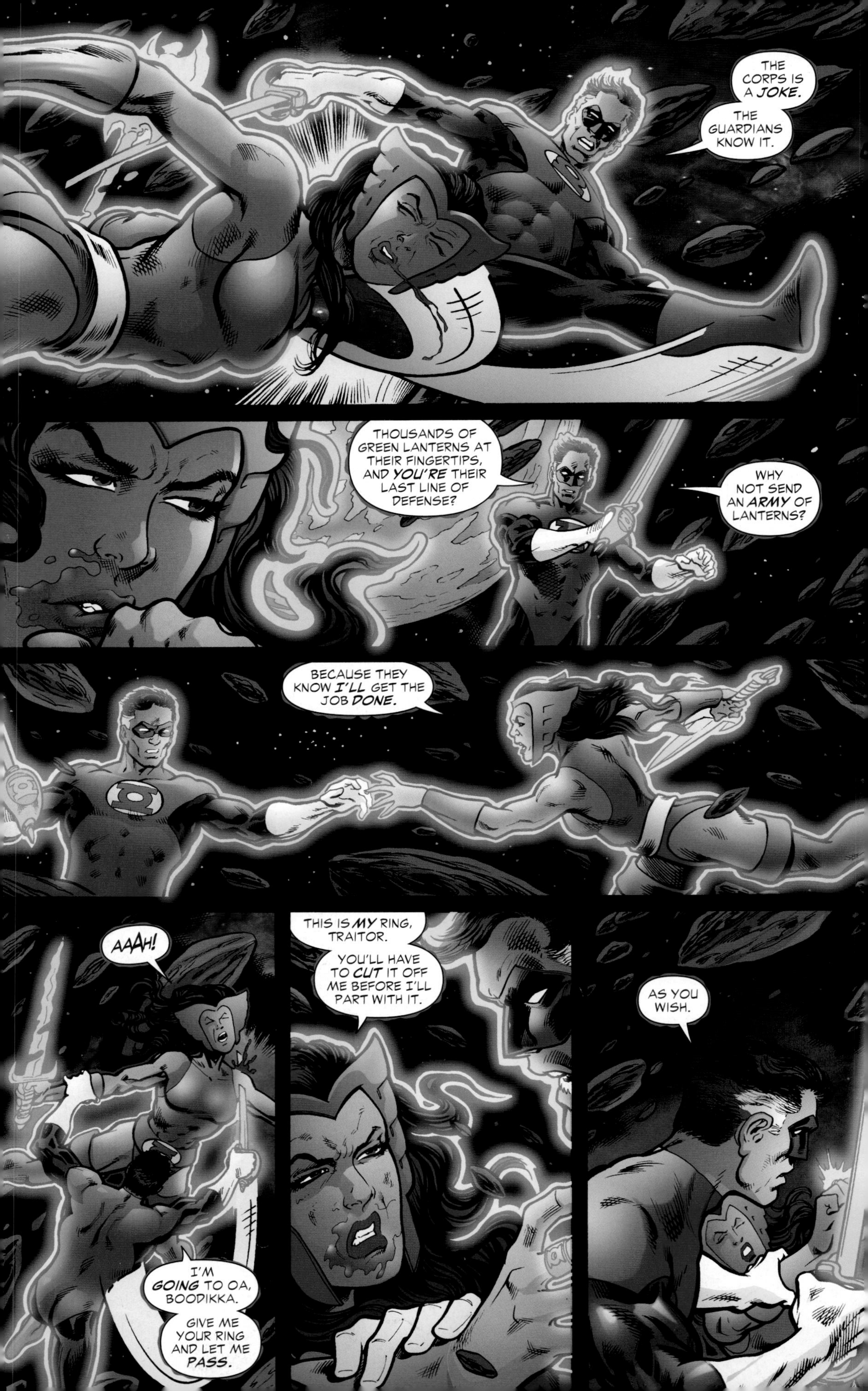
THE CORPS IS A JOKE.
THE GUARDIANS KNOW IT.
THOUSANDS OF GREEN LANTERNS AT THEIR FINGERTIPS, AND YOU'RE THEIR LAST LINE OF DEFENSE?
WHY NOT SEND AN ARMY OF LANTERNS?
BECAUSE THEY KNOW I'LL GET THE JOB DONE.
AAAH!
I'M GOING TO OA, BOODIKKA.
GIVE ME YOUR RING AND LET ME PASS.
THIS IS MY RING, TRAITOR.
YOU'LL HAVE TO CUT IT OFF ME BEFORE I'LL PART WITH IT.
AS YOU WISH.

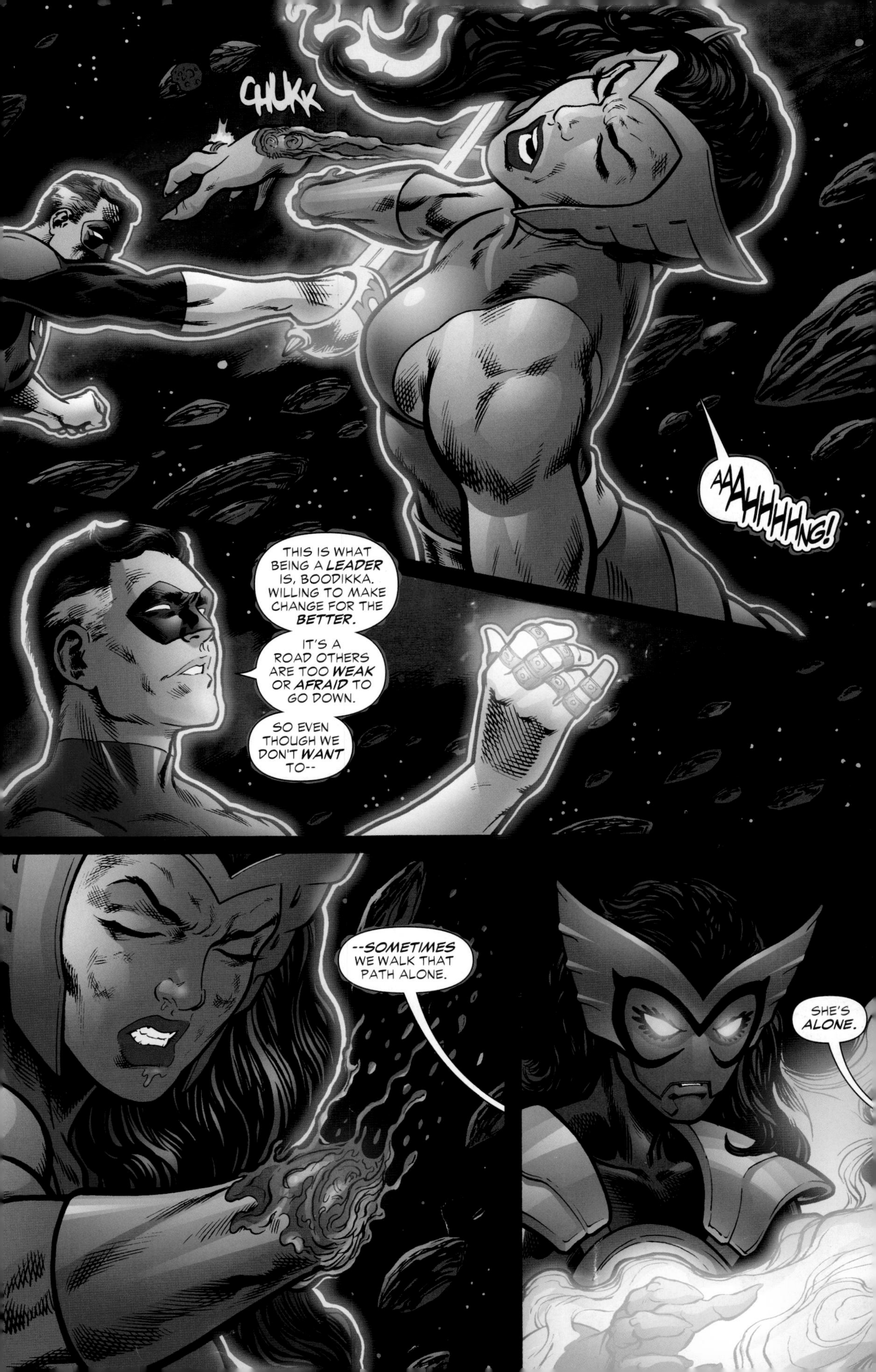

CHUKK
AAAHHHHNG!
THIS IS WHAT BEING A LEADER IS, BOODIKKA. WILLING TO MAKE CHANGE FOR THE BETTER.
IT'S A ROAD OTHERS ARE TOO WEAK OR AFRAID TO GO DOWN.
SO EVEN THOUGH WE DON'T WANT TO--
--SOMETIMES WE WALK THAT PATH ALONE.
SHE'S ALONE.

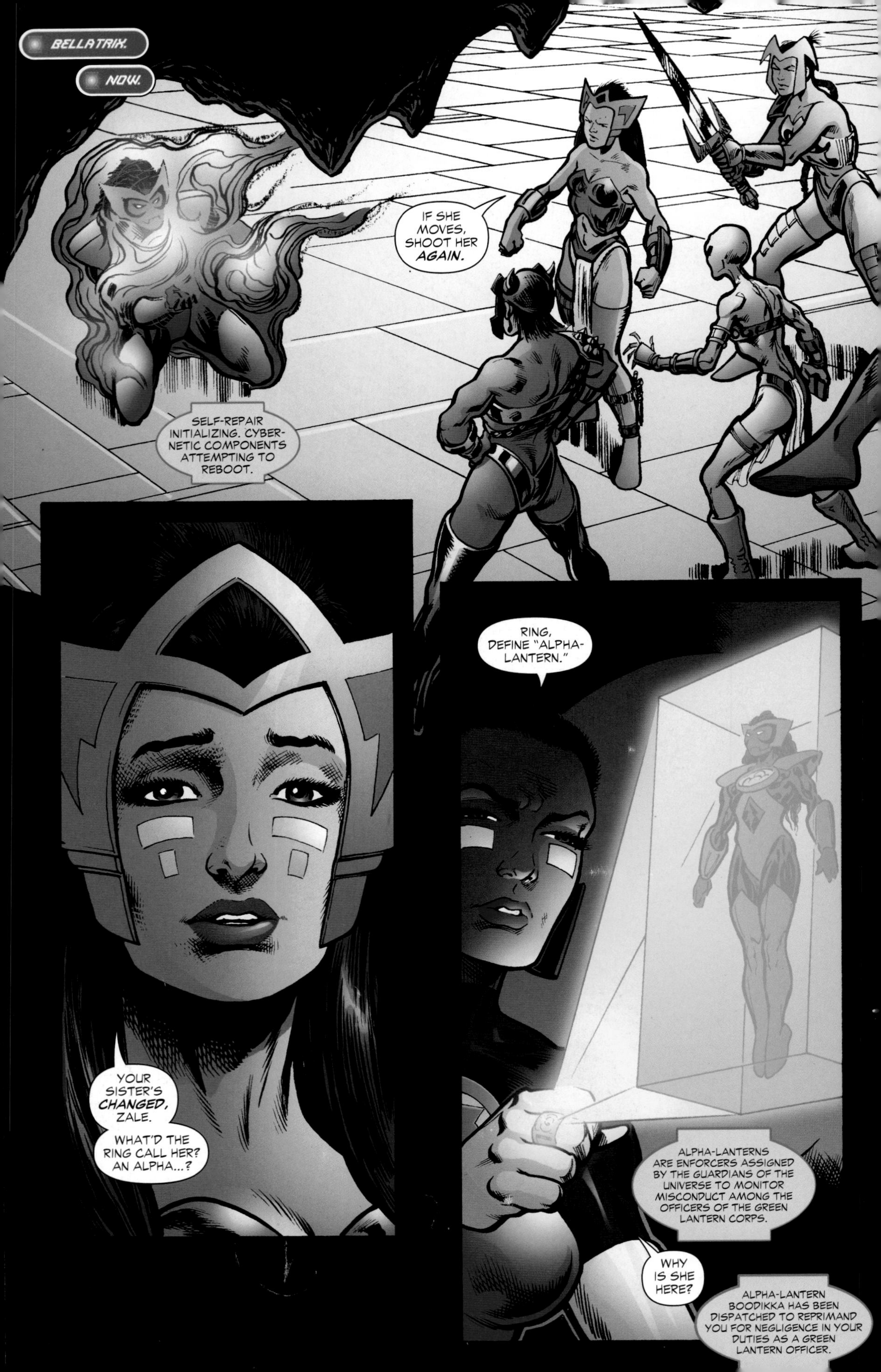
BELLATRIX.
NOW.
IF SHE MOVES, SHOOT HER AGAIN.
SELF-REPAIR INITIALIZING. CYBERNETIC COMPONENTS ATTEMPTING TO REBOOT.
YOUR SISTER'S CHANGED, ZALE.
WHAT'D THE RING CALL HER? AN ALPHA...?
RING, DEFINE "ALPHA-LANTERN."
ALPHA-LANTERNS ARE ENFORCERS ASSIGNED BY THE GUARDIANS OF THE UNIVERSE TO MONITOR MISCONDUCT AMONG THE OFFICERS OF THE GREEN LANTERN CORPS.
WHY IS SHE HERE?
ALPHA-LANTERN BOODIKKA HAS BEEN DISPATCHED TO REPRIMAND YOU FOR NEGLIGENCE IN YOUR DUTIES AS A GREEN LANTERN OFFICER.

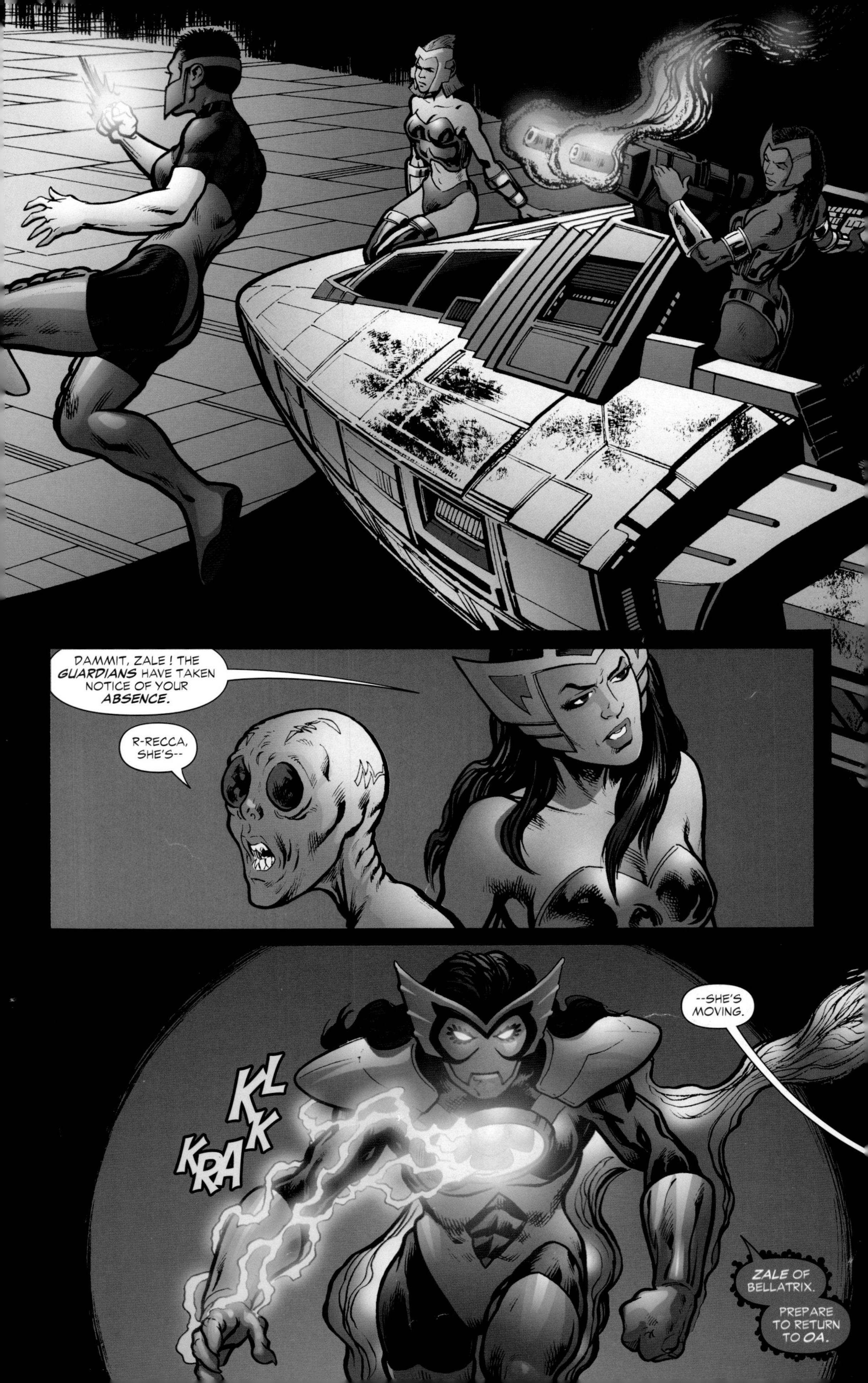
DAMMIT, ZALE ! THE GUARDIANS HAVE TAKEN NOTICE OF YOUR ABSENCE.
R-RECCA, SHE'S--
--SHE'S MOVING.
KLAK
KRAK
ZALE OF BELLATRIX.
PREPARE TO RETURN TO OA.

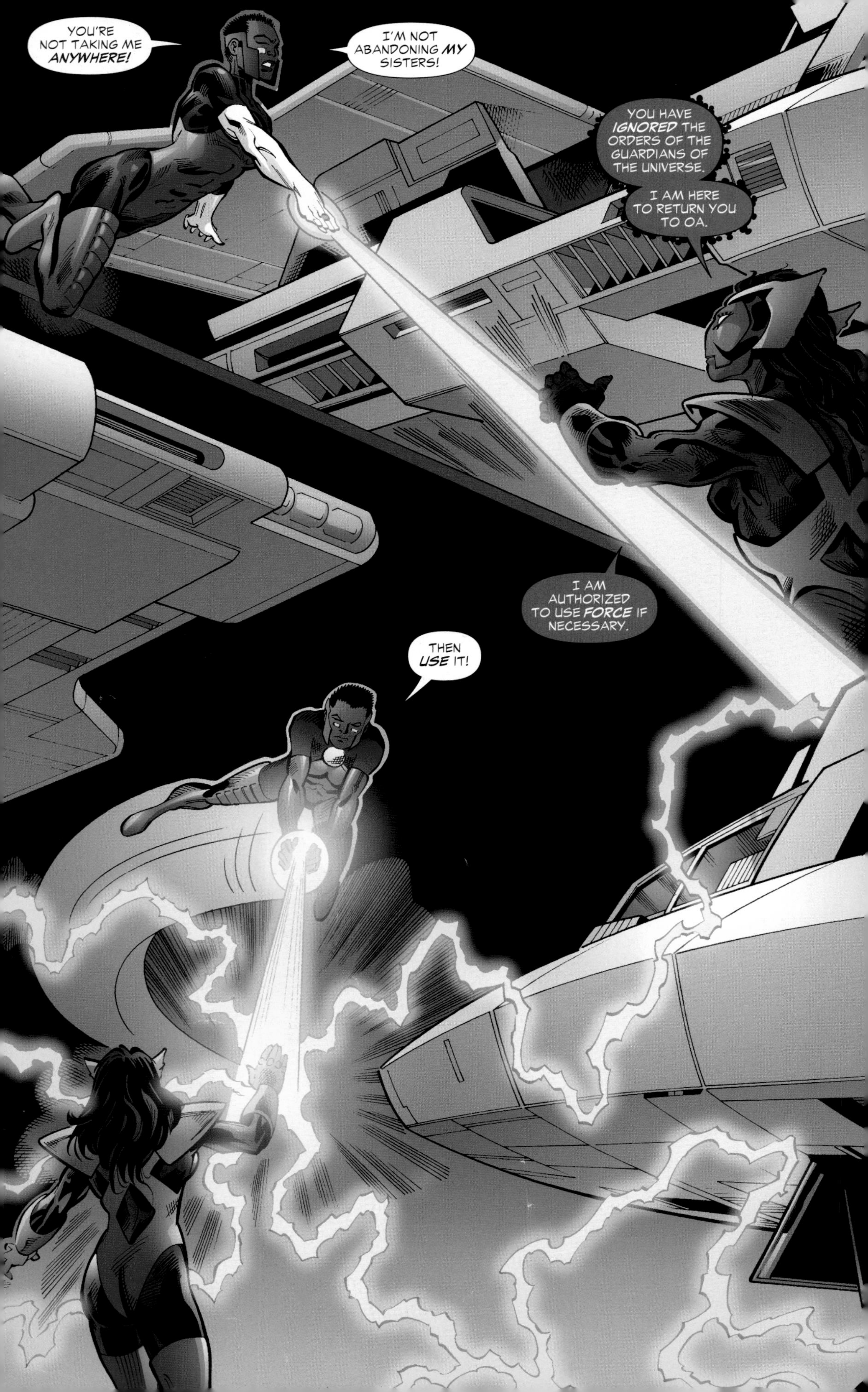
YOU'RE NOT TAKING ME ANYWHERE!
I'M NOT ABANDONING MY SISTERS!
YOU HAVE IGNORED THE ORDERS OF THE GUARDIANS OF THE UNIVERSE.
I AM HERE TO RETURN YOU TO OA.
I AM AUTHORIZED TO USE FORCE IF NECESSARY.
THEN USE IT!

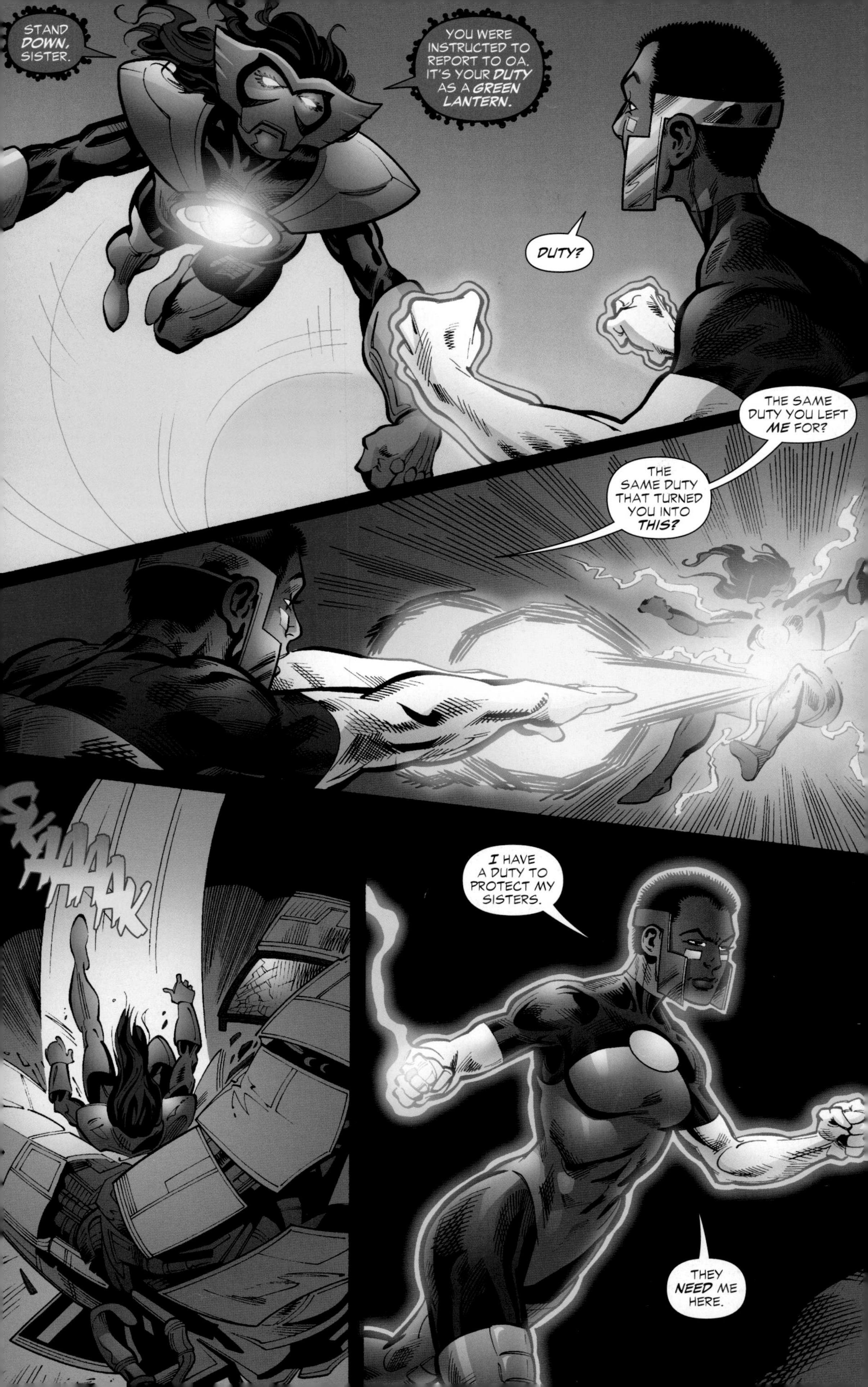
STAND DOWN, SISTER.
YOU WERE INSTRUCTED TO REPORT TO OA. IT'S YOUR DUTY AS A GREEN LANTERN.
DUTY?
THE SAME DUTY YOU LEFT ME FOR?
THE SAME DUTY THAT TURNED YOU INTO THIS?
SKRAAAAK
I HAVE A DUTY TO PROTECT MY SISTERS.
THEY NEED ME HERE.

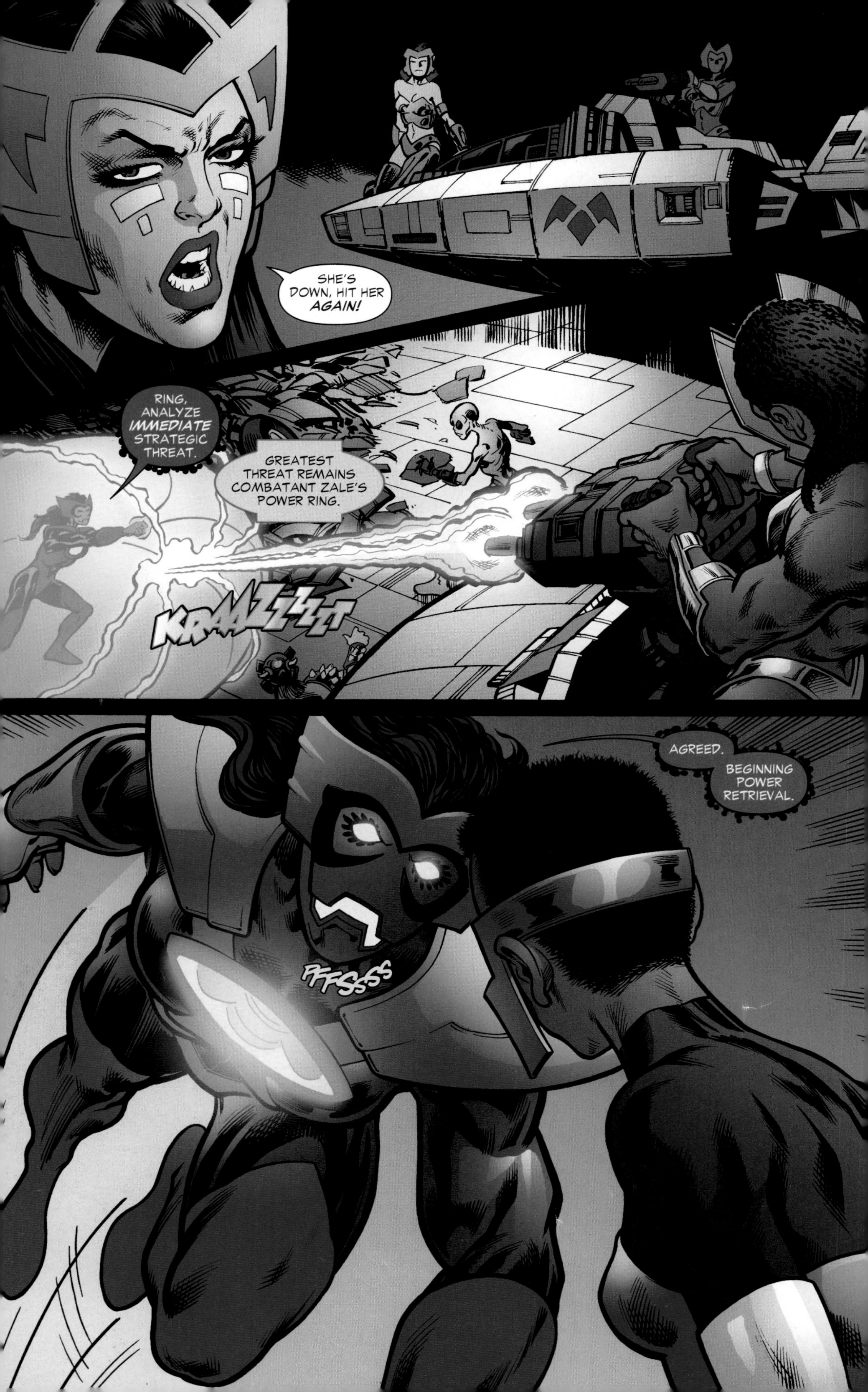
SHE'S DOWN, HIT HER AGAIN!
RING, ANALYZE IMMEDIATE STRATEGIC THREAT.
GREATEST THREAT REMAINS COMBATANT ZALE'S POWER RING.
KRAAZZZZT
AGREED.
BEGINNING POWER RETRIEVAL.
PFFSSSS

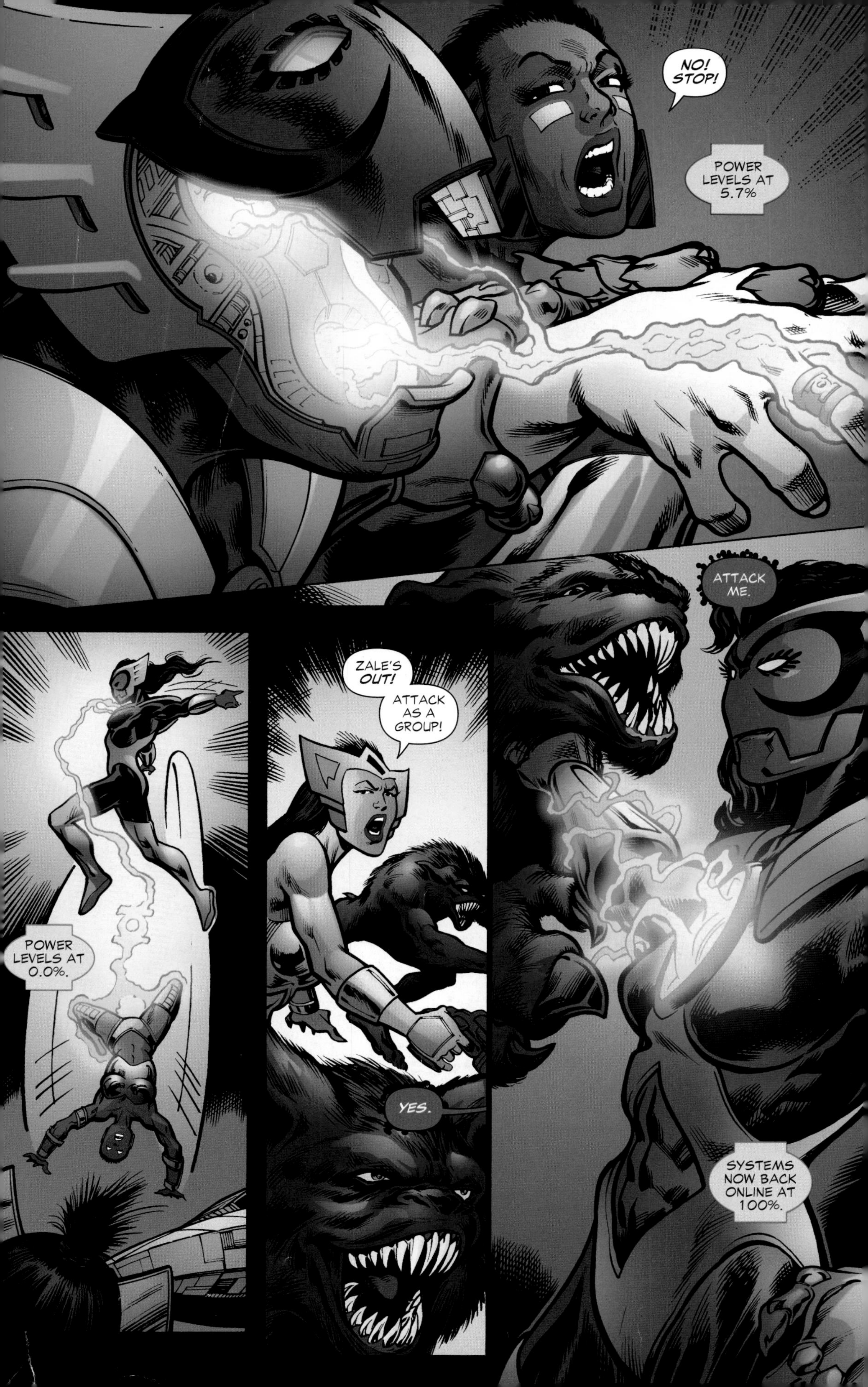
NO! STOP!
POWER LEVELS AT 5.7%
POWER LEVELS AT 0.0%.
ZALE'S OUT!
ATTACK AS A GROUP!
YES.
ATTACK ME.
SYSTEMS NOW BACK ONLINE AT 100%.

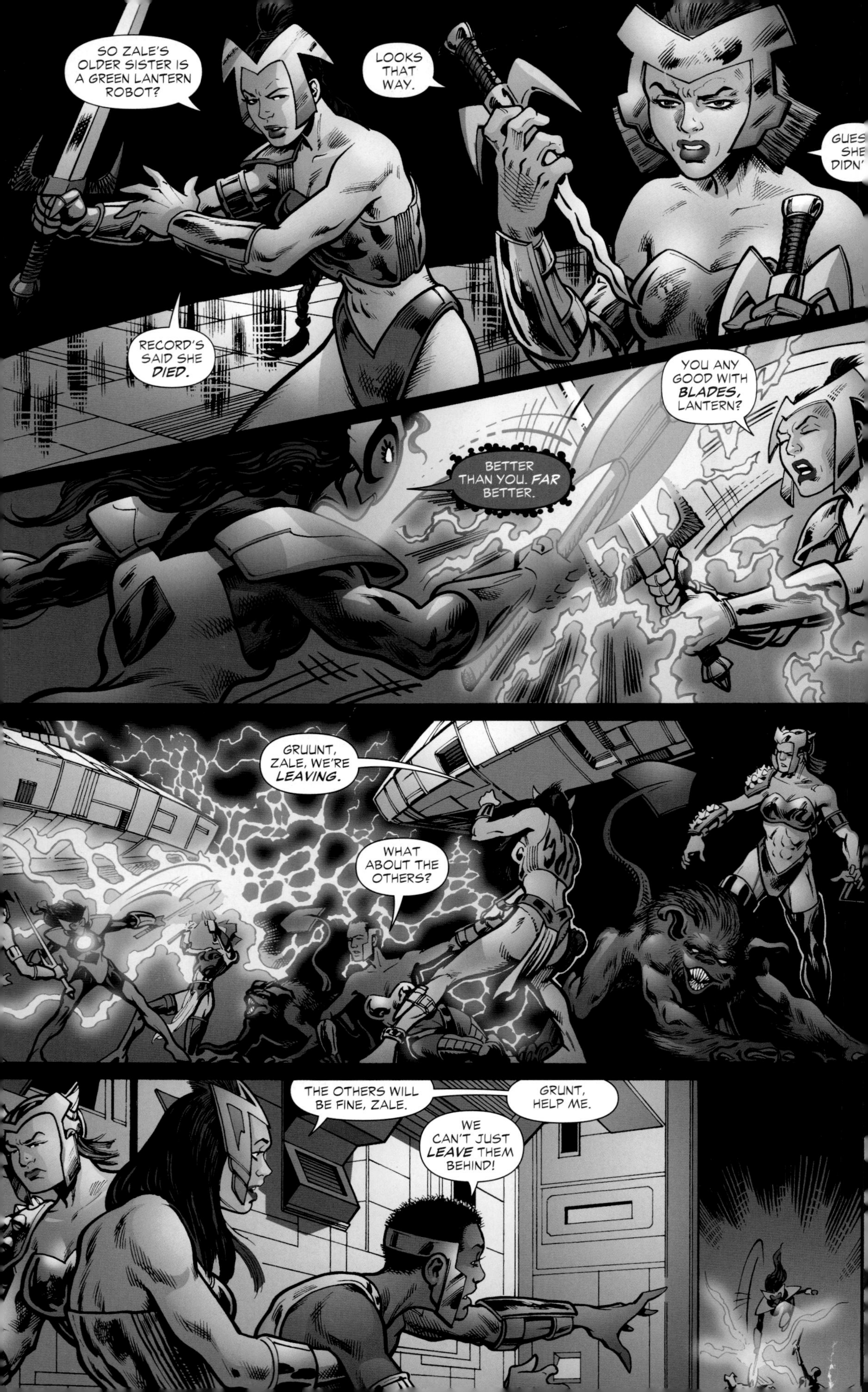
SO ZALE'S OLDER SISTER IS A GREEN LANTERN ROBOT?
LOOKS THAT WAY.
GUES SHE DIDN'
RECORD'S SAID SHE *DIED.*
YOU ANY GOOD WITH *BLADES,* LANTERN?
BETTER THAN YOU. *FAR* BETTER.
GRUUNT, ZALE, WE'RE *LEAVING.*
WHAT ABOUT THE OTHERS?
THE OTHERS WILL BE FINE, ZALE.
GRUNT, HELP ME.
WE CAN'T JUST *LEAVE* THEM BEHIND!

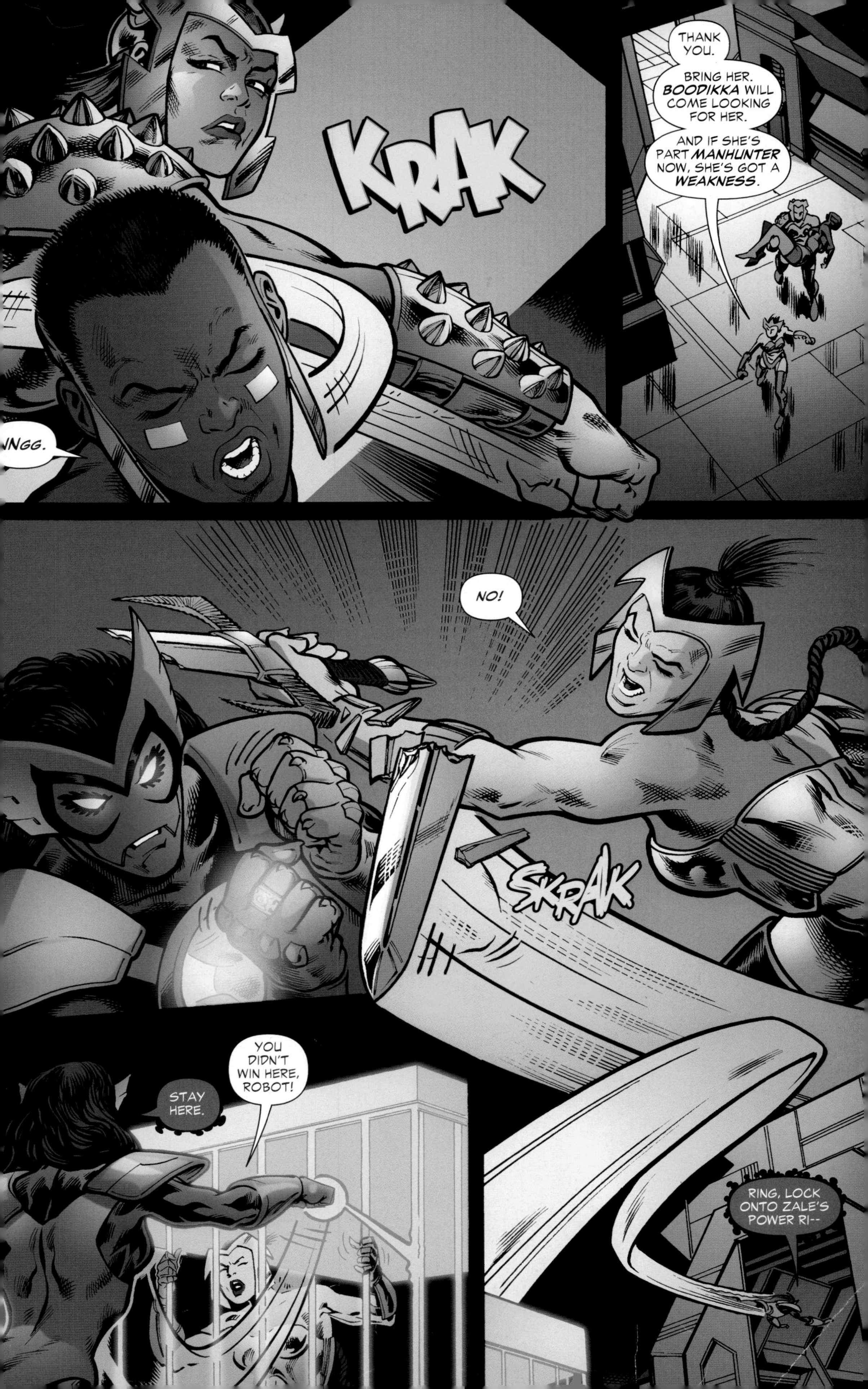
KRAK
NGG.
THANK YOU.
BRING HER. BOODIKKA WILL COME LOOKING FOR HER.
AND IF SHE'S PART MANHUNTER NOW, SHE'S GOT A WEAKNESS.
NO!
SKRAK
STAY HERE.
YOU DIDN'T WIN HERE, ROBOT!
RING, LOCK ONTO ZALE'S POWER RI--

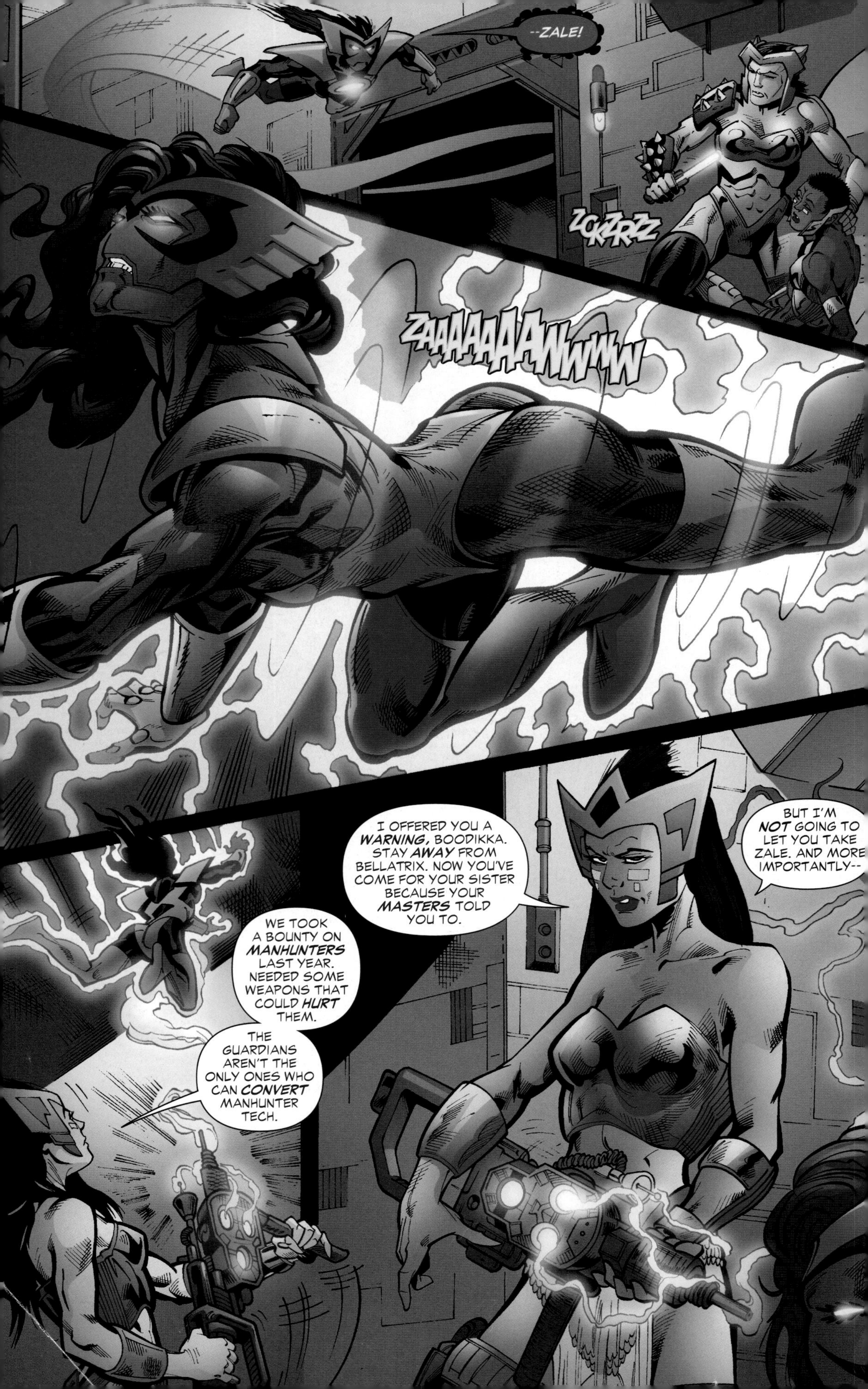
--ZALE!
ZCKZRZZ
ZAAAAAAAWWW
I OFFERED YOU A WARNING, BOODIKKA. STAY AWAY FROM BELLATRIX. NOW YOU'VE COME FOR YOUR SISTER BECAUSE YOUR MASTERS TOLD YOU TO.
BUT I'M NOT GOING TO LET YOU TAKE ZALE. AND MORE IMPORTANTLY--
WE TOOK A BOUNTY ON MANHUNTERS LAST YEAR. NEEDED SOME WEAPONS THAT COULD HURT THEM.
THE GUARDIANS AREN'T THE ONLY ONES WHO CAN CONVERT MANHUNTER TECH.

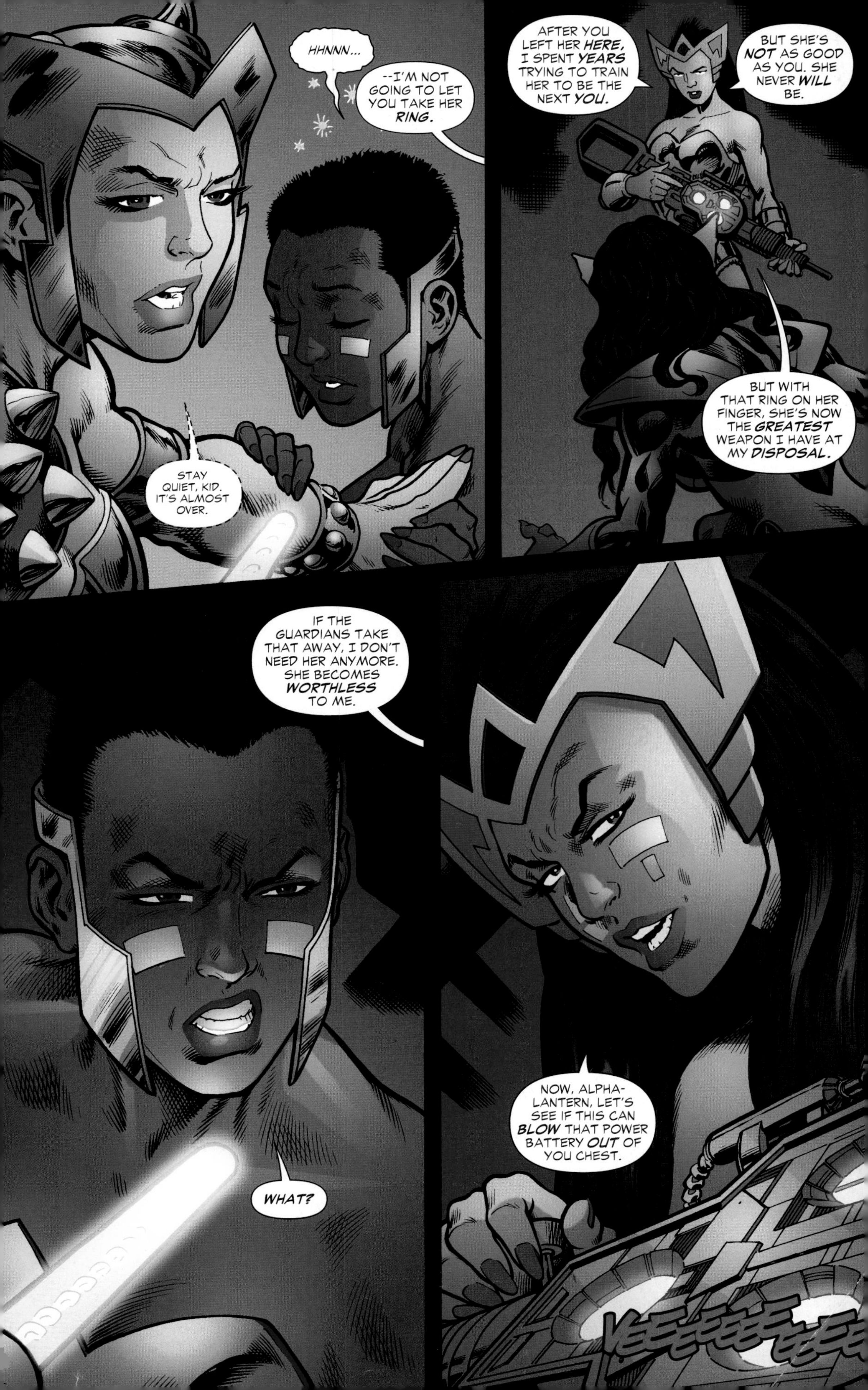
HHNNN...
--I'M NOT GOING TO LET YOU TAKE HER RING.
STAY QUIET, KID. IT'S ALMOST OVER.
AFTER YOU LEFT HER HERE, I SPENT YEARS TRYING TO TRAIN HER TO BE THE NEXT YOU.
BUT SHE'S NOT AS GOOD AS YOU. SHE NEVER WILL BE.
BUT WITH THAT RING ON HER FINGER, SHE'S NOW THE GREATEST WEAPON I HAVE AT MY DISPOSAL.
IF THE GUARDIANS TAKE THAT AWAY, I DON'T NEED HER ANYMORE. SHE BECOMES WORTHLESS TO ME.
WHAT?
NOW, ALPHA-LANTERN, LET'S SEE IF THIS CAN BLOW THAT POWER BATTERY OUT OF YOU CHEST.

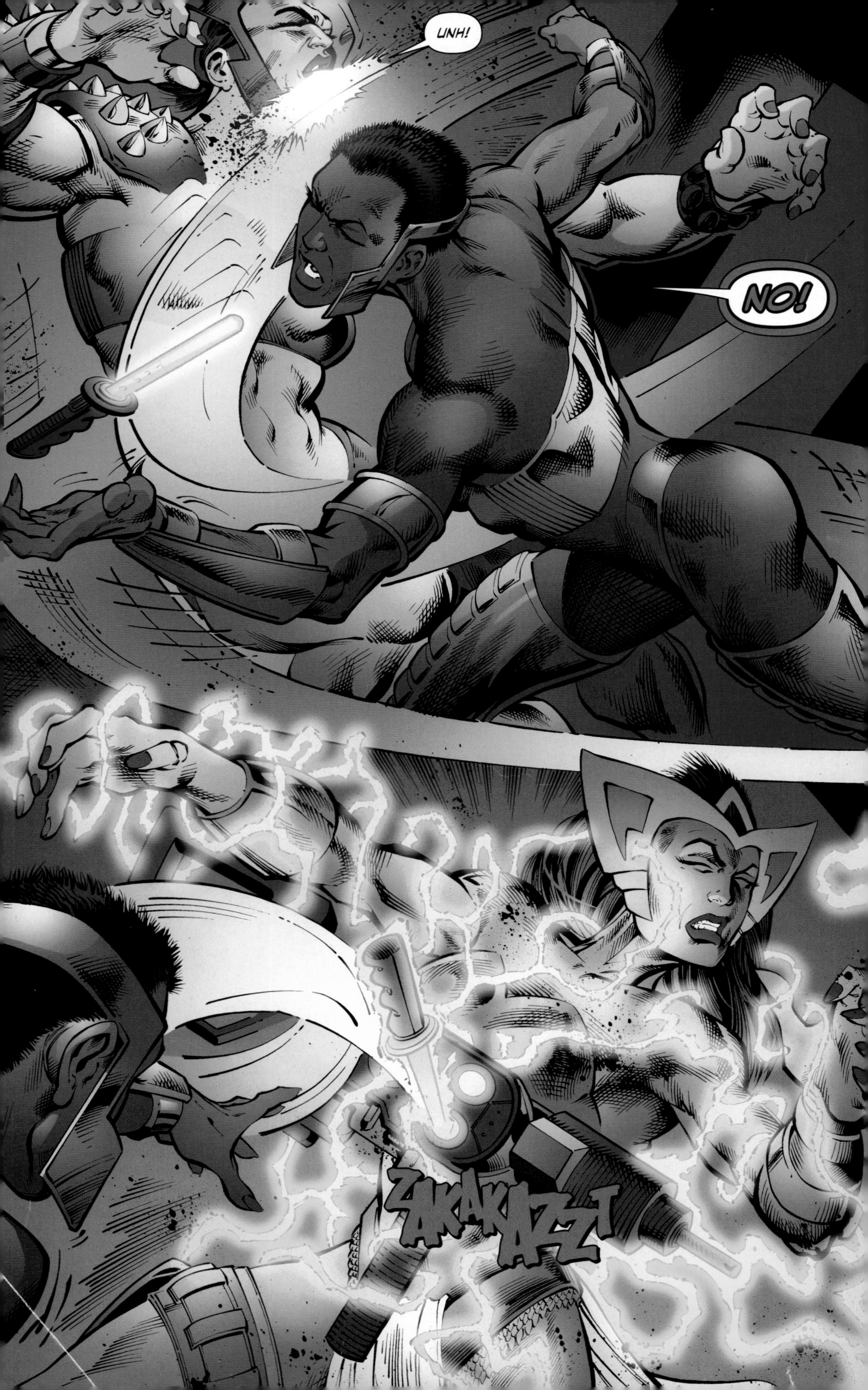
UNH!
NO!
ZAKAKAZZT

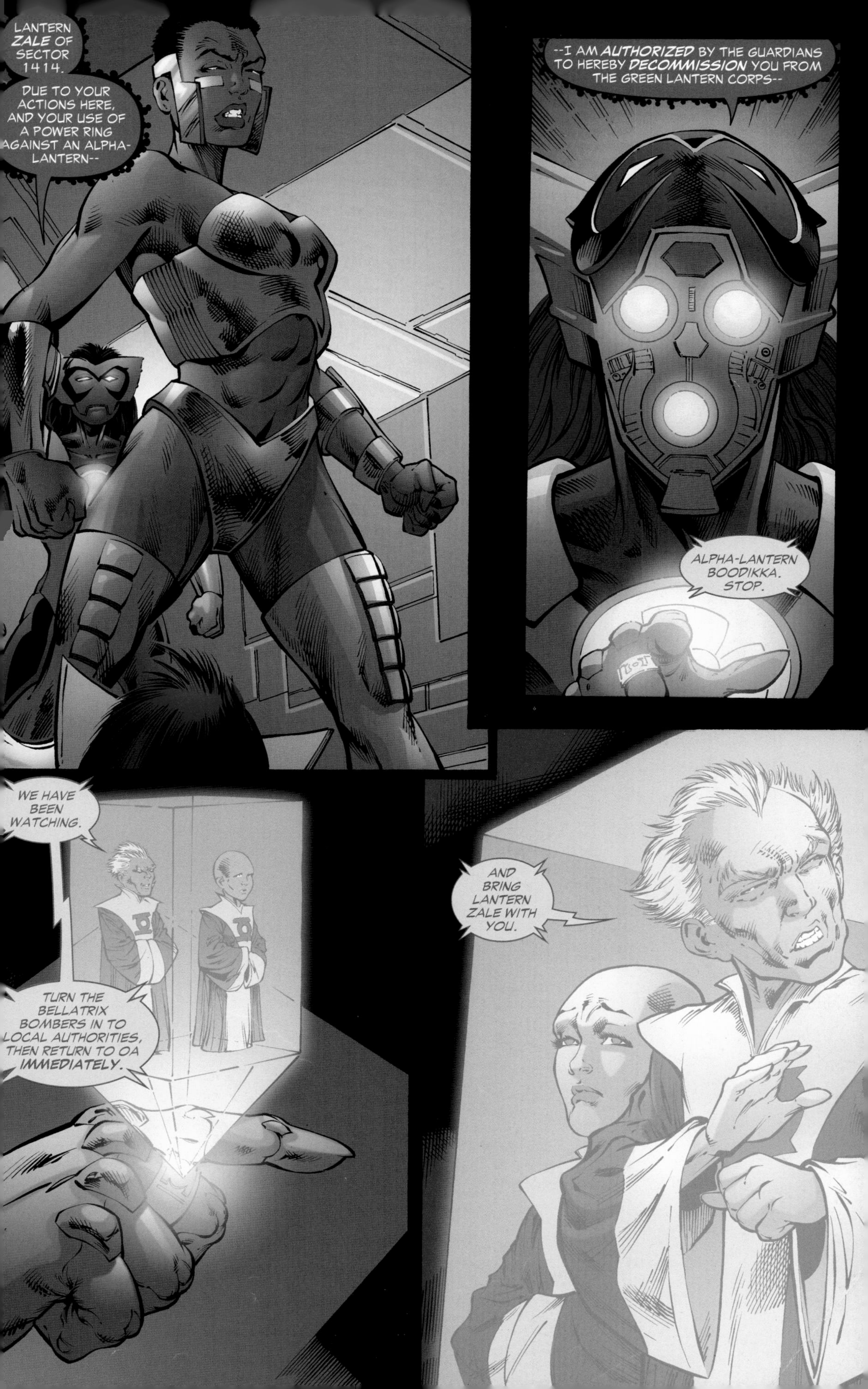
LANTERN ZALE OF SECTOR 1414.
DUE TO YOUR ACTIONS HERE, AND YOUR USE OF A POWER RING AGAINST AN ALPHA-LANTERN--
--I AM AUTHORIZED BY THE GUARDIANS TO HEREBY DECOMMISSION YOU FROM THE GREEN LANTERN CORPS--
ALPHA-LANTERN BOODIKKA. STOP.
WE HAVE BEEN WATCHING.
TURN THE BELLATRIX BOMBERS IN TO LOCAL AUTHORITIES, THEN RETURN TO OA IMMEDIATELY.
AND BRING LANTERN ZALE WITH YOU.

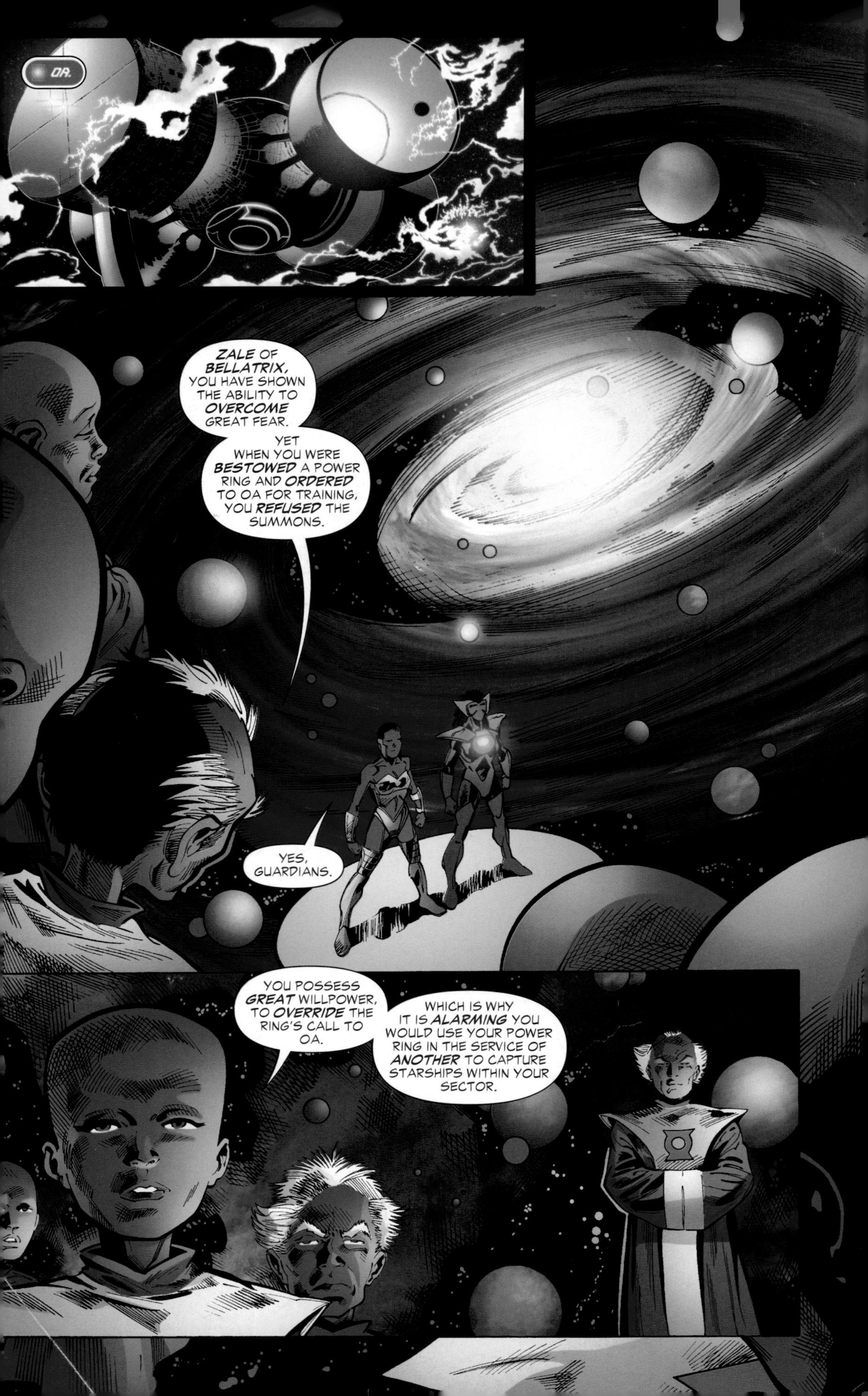
OA.
ZALE OF BELLATRIX, YOU HAVE SHOWN THE ABILITY TO OVERCOME GREAT FEAR.
YET WHEN YOU WERE BESTOWED A POWER RING AND ORDERED TO OA FOR TRAINING, YOU REFUSED THE SUMMONS.
YES, GUARDIANS.
YOU POSSESS GREAT WILLPOWER, TO OVERRIDE THE RING'S CALL TO OA.
WHICH IS WHY IT IS ALARMING YOU WOULD USE YOUR POWER RING IN THE SERVICE OF ANOTHER TO CAPTURE STARSHIPS WITHIN YOUR SECTOR.

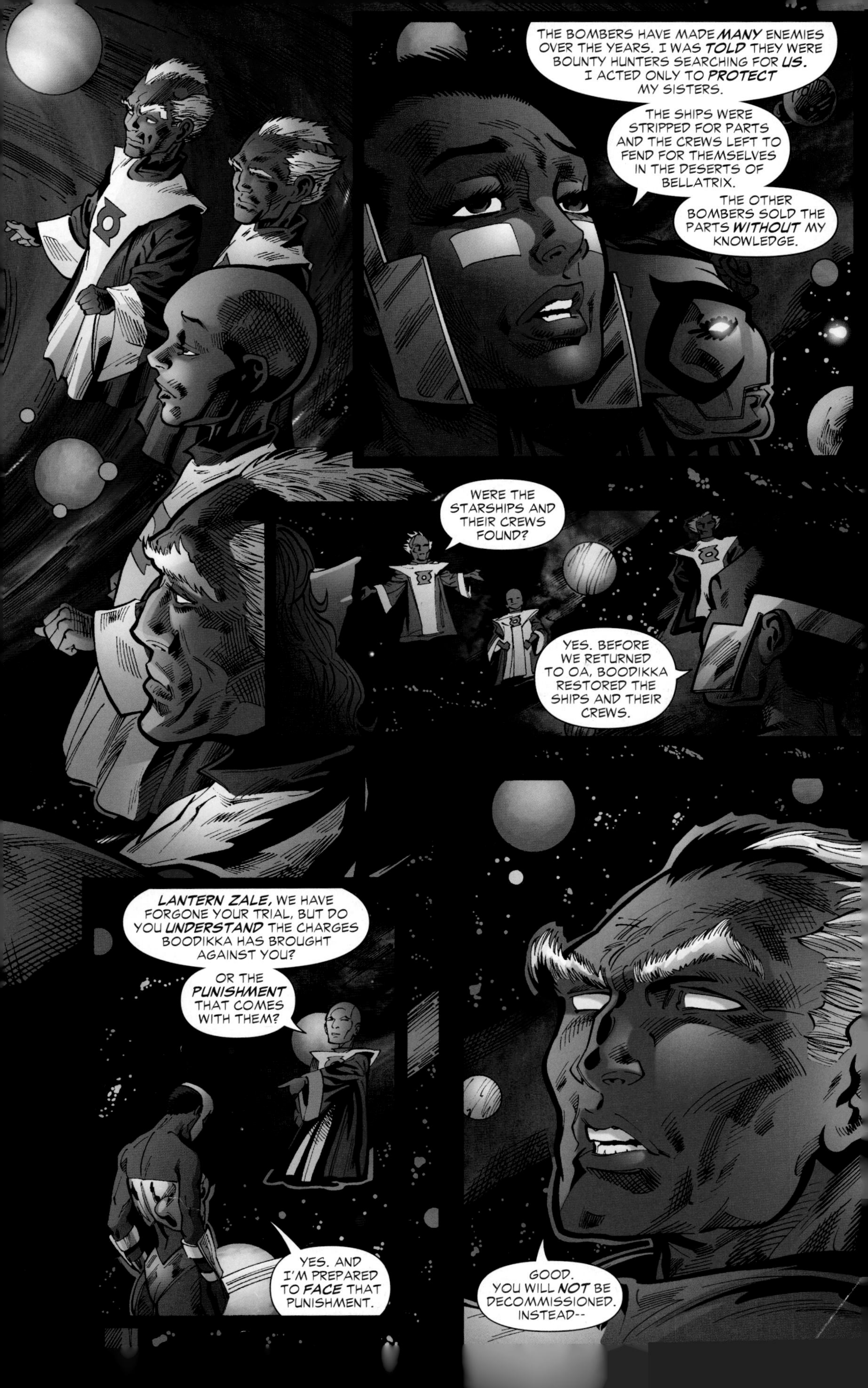
THE BOMBERS HAVE MADE MANY ENEMIES OVER THE YEARS. I WAS TOLD THEY WERE BOUNTY HUNTERS SEARCHING FOR US. I ACTED ONLY TO PROTECT MY SISTERS.
THE SHIPS WERE STRIPPED FOR PARTS AND THE CREWS LEFT TO FEND FOR THEMSELVES IN THE DESERTS OF BELLATRIX.
THE OTHER BOMBERS SOLD THE PARTS WITHOUT MY KNOWLEDGE.
WERE THE STARSHIPS AND THEIR CREWS FOUND?
YES. BEFORE WE RETURNED TO OA, BOODIKKA RESTORED THE SHIPS AND THEIR CREWS.
LANTERN ZALE, WE HAVE FORGONE YOUR TRIAL, BUT DO YOU UNDERSTAND THE CHARGES BOODIKKA HAS BROUGHT AGAINST YOU?
OR THE PUNISHMENT THAT COMES WITH THEM?
YES. AND I'M PREPARED TO FACE THAT PUNISHMENT.
GOOD. YOU WILL NOT BE DECOMMISSIONED. INSTEAD--

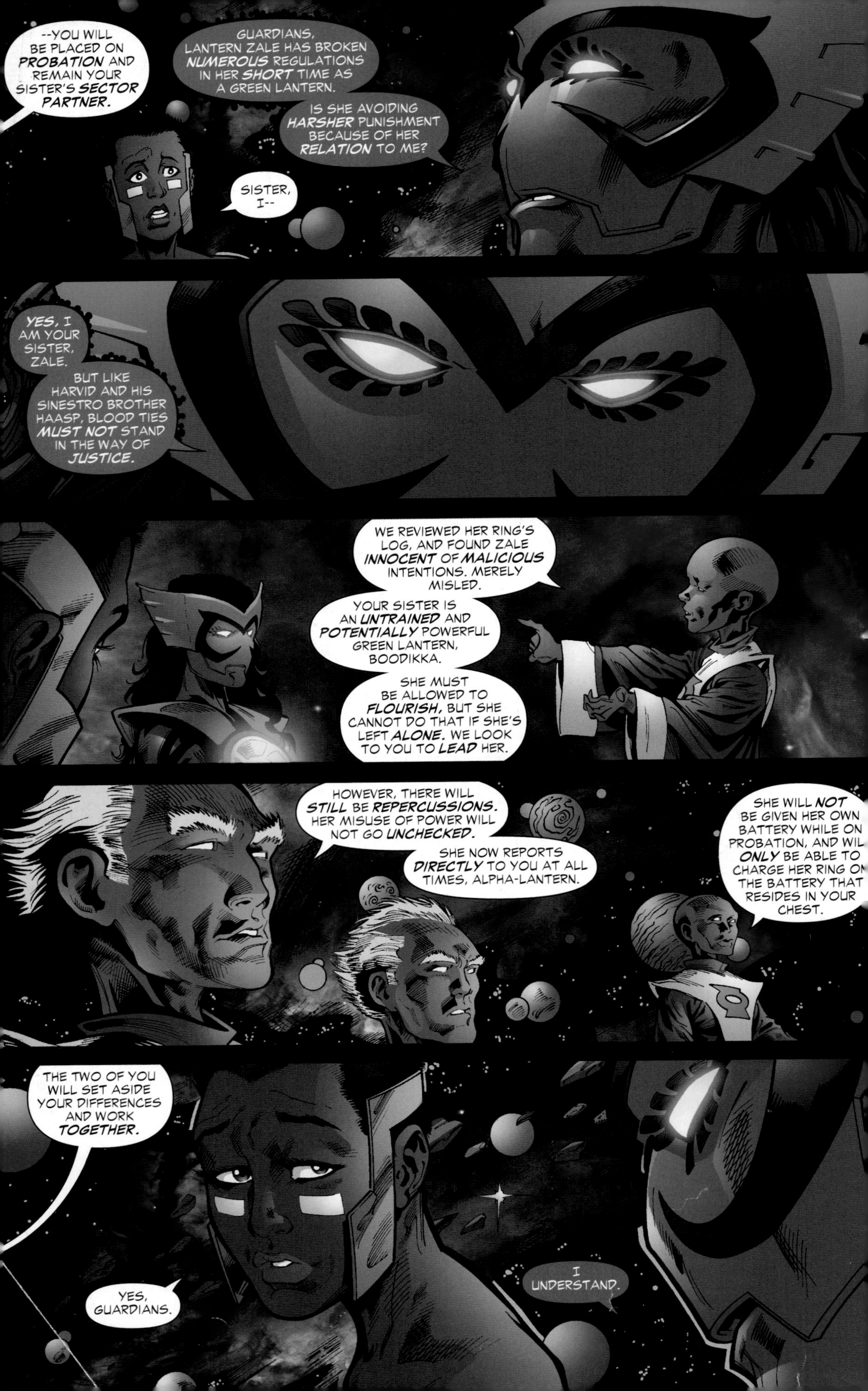
--YOU WILL BE PLACED ON PROBATION AND REMAIN YOUR SISTER'S SECTOR PARTNER.
GUARDIANS, LANTERN ZALE HAS BROKEN NUMEROUS REGULATIONS IN HER SHORT TIME AS A GREEN LANTERN.
IS SHE AVOIDING HARSHER PUNISHMENT BECAUSE OF HER RELATION TO ME?
SISTER, I--
YES, I AM YOUR SISTER, ZALE.
BUT LIKE HARVID AND HIS SINESTRO BROTHER HAASP, BLOOD TIES MUST NOT STAND IN THE WAY OF JUSTICE.
WE REVIEWED HER RING'S LOG, AND FOUND ZALE INNOCENT OF MALICIOUS INTENTIONS. MERELY MISLED.
YOUR SISTER IS AN UNTRAINED AND POTENTIALLY POWERFUL GREEN LANTERN, BOODIKKA.
SHE MUST BE ALLOWED TO FLOURISH, BUT SHE CANNOT DO THAT IF SHE'S LEFT ALONE. WE LOOK TO YOU TO LEAD HER.
HOWEVER, THERE WILL STILL BE REPERCUSSIONS. HER MISUSE OF POWER WILL NOT GO UNCHECKED.
SHE NOW REPORTS DIRECTLY TO YOU AT ALL TIMES, ALPHA-LANTERN.
SHE WILL NOT BE GIVEN HER OWN BATTERY WHILE ON PROBATION, AND WIL ONLY BE ABLE TO CHARGE HER RING O THE BATTERY THAT RESIDES IN YOUR CHEST.
THE TWO OF YOU WILL SET ASIDE YOUR DIFFERENCES AND WORK TOGETHER.
YES, GUARDIANS.
I UNDERSTAND.

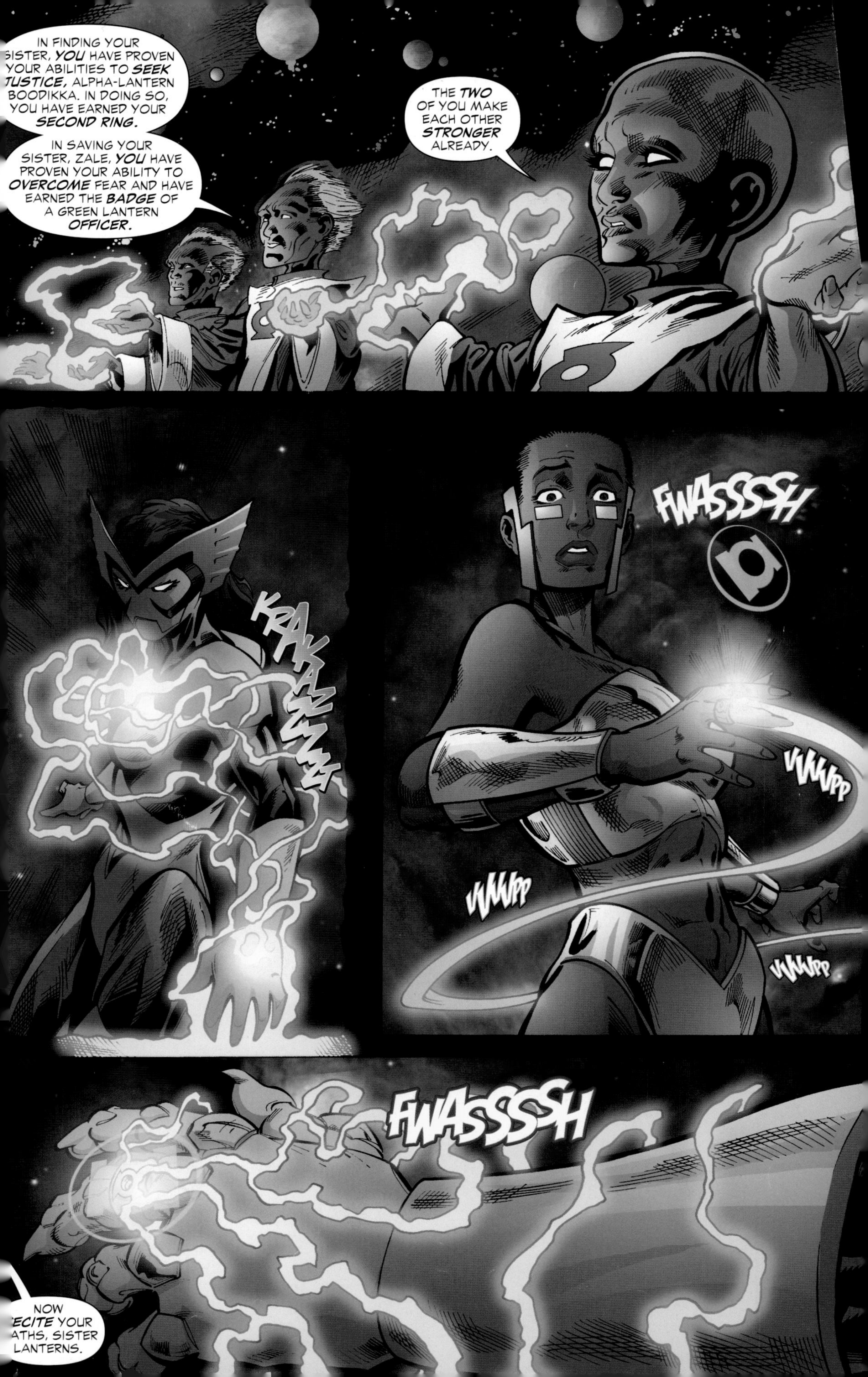
IN FINDING YOUR SISTER, YOU HAVE PROVEN YOUR ABILITIES TO SEEK JUSTICE, ALPHA-LANTERN BOODIKKA. IN DOING SO, YOU HAVE EARNED YOUR SECOND RING.
IN SAVING YOUR SISTER, ZALE, YOU HAVE PROVEN YOUR ABILITY TO OVERCOME FEAR AND HAVE EARNED THE BADGE OF A GREEN LANTERN OFFICER.
THE TWO OF YOU MAKE EACH OTHER STRONGER ALREADY.
KRAKAKZMMM
FWASSSSH
VWWPP
VWWPP
VWWPP
FWASSSSH
NOW ECITE YOUR ATHS, SISTER LANTERNS.

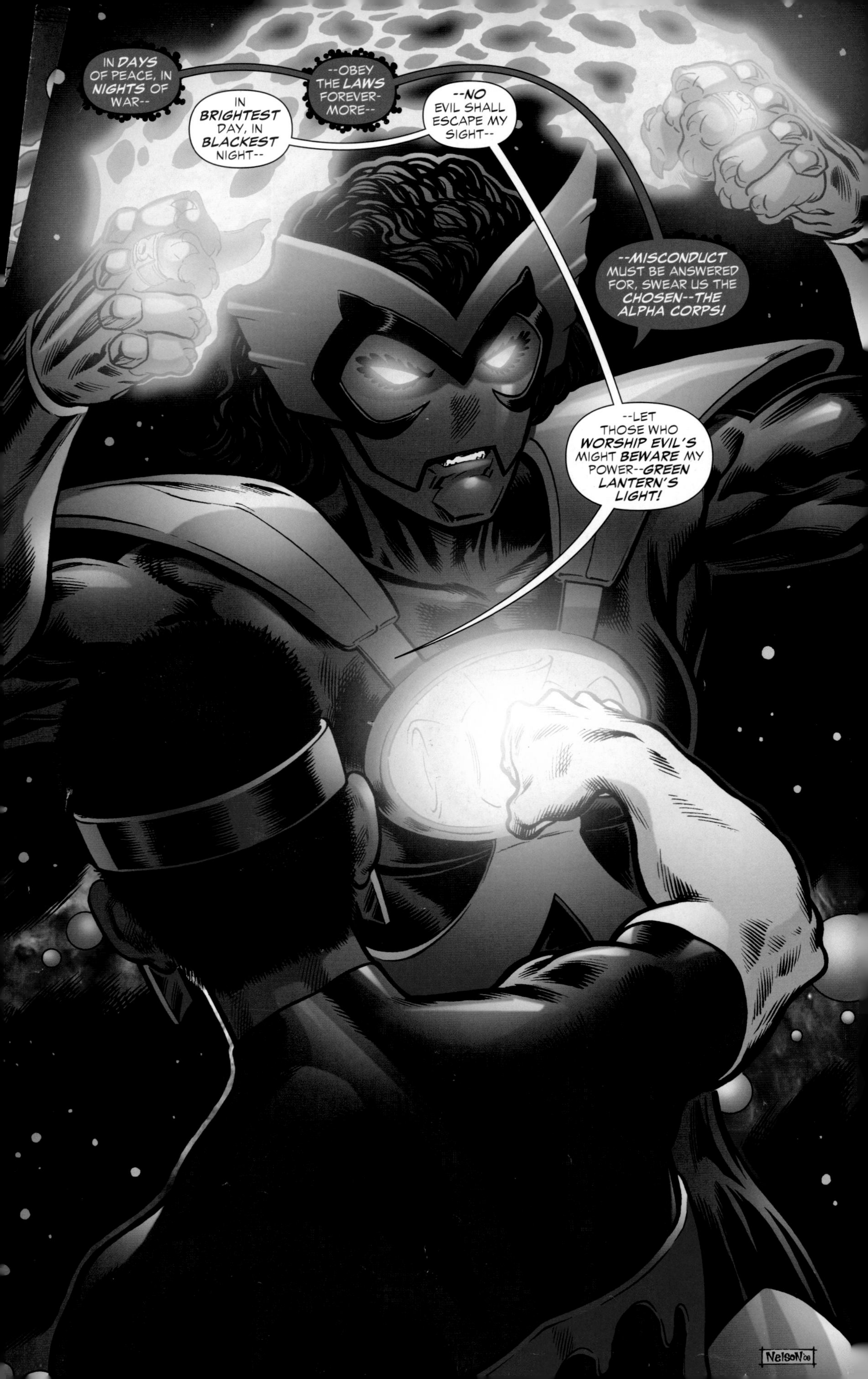
IN DAYS OF PEACE, IN NIGHTS OF WAR--
IN BRIGHTEST DAY, IN BLACKEST NIGHT--
--OBEY THE LAWS FOREVERMORE--
--NO EVIL SHALL ESCAPE MY SIGHT--
--MISCONDUCT MUST BE ANSWERED FOR, SWEAR US THE CHOSEN--THE ALPHA CORPS!
--LET THOSE WHO WORSHIP EVIL'S MIGHT BEWARE MY POWER--GREEN LANTERN'S LIGHT!
NELSON '08

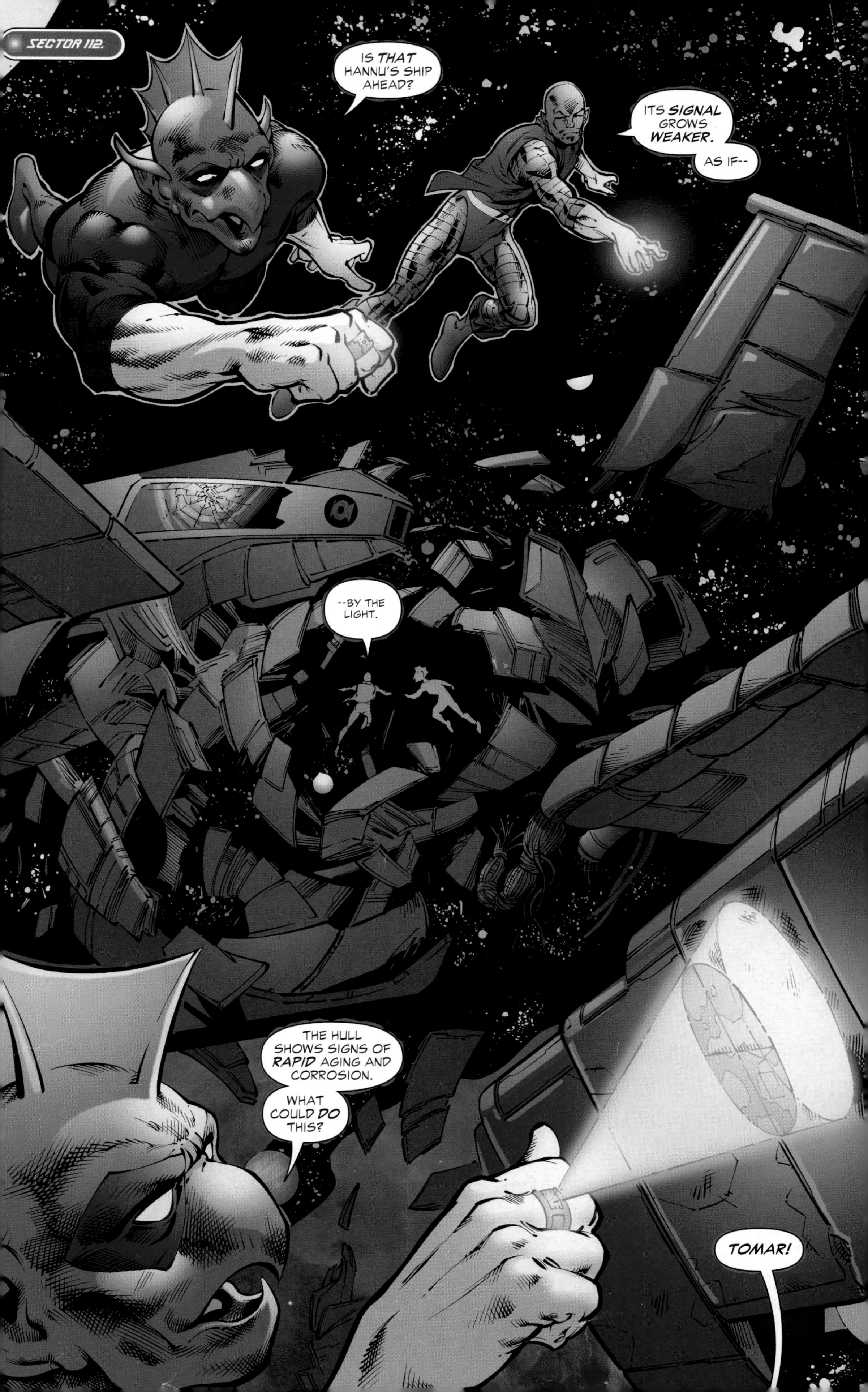
SECTOR 112.
IS THAT HANNU'S SHIP AHEAD?
ITS SIGNAL GROWS WEAKER.
AS IF--
--BY THE LIGHT.
THE HULL SHOWS SIGNS OF RAPID AGING AND CORROSION.
WHAT COULD DO THIS?
TOMAR!

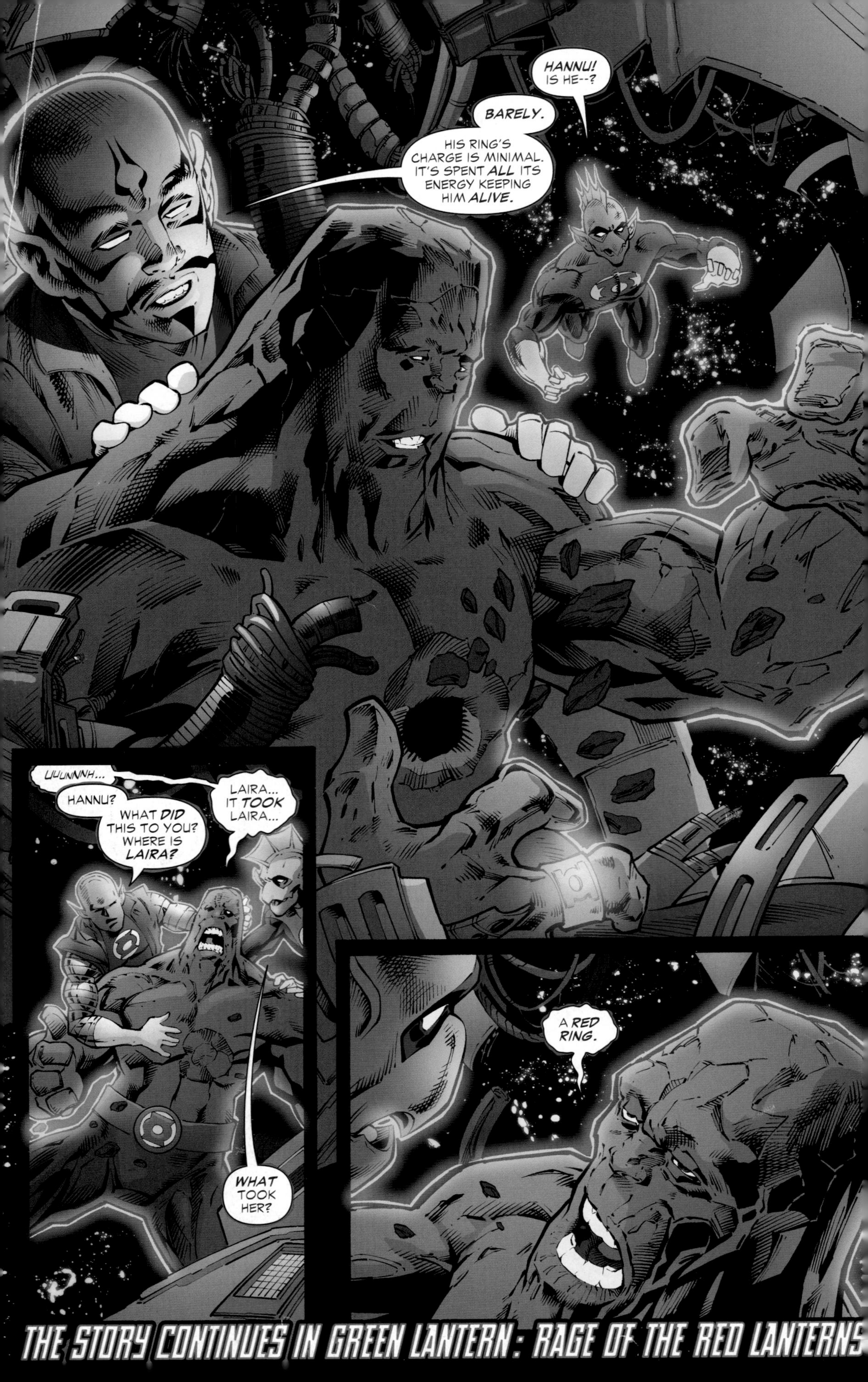
HANNU! IS HE--?
BARELY.
HIS RING'S CHARGE IS MINIMAL. IT'S SPENT ALL ITS ENERGY KEEPING HIM ALIVE.
UUUNNNH...
HANNU?
WHAT DID THIS TO YOU? WHERE IS LAIRA?
LAIRA... IT TOOK LAIRA...
WHAT TOOK HER?
A RED RING.
THE STORY CONTINUES IN GREEN LANTERN: RAGE OF THE RED LANTERNS

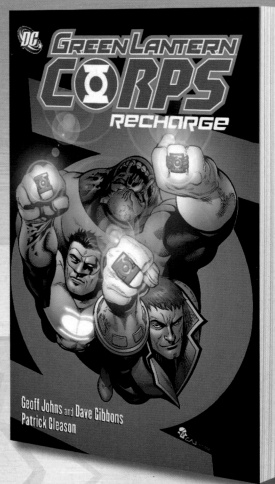

FROM THE WRITER OF THE FLASH AND JSA

GEOFF JOHNS

"Consistently entertaining..."
– NEWSARAMA.COM

"Johns is the master of streamlining the GL mythos and distilling the cool essence of the character."
– BOOKLIST

"Define[s] DC's heroes for a new generation of readers."
– WIZARDUNIVERSE.COM

"Everything Geoff Johns has done with (Green Lantern) has been fantastic."
– SILVERBULLET.COM

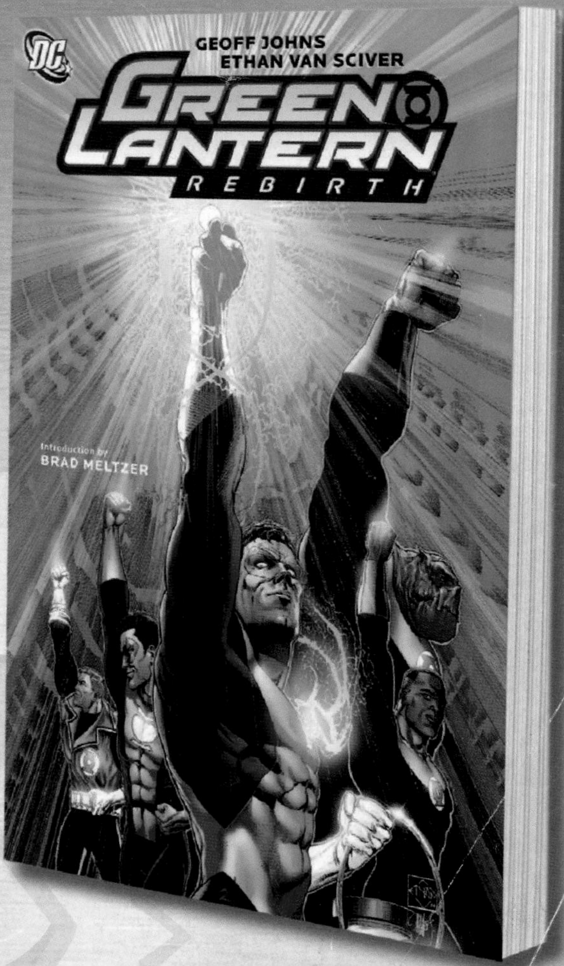
GEOFF JOHNS
ETHAN VAN SCIVER
GREEN LANTERN
REBIRTH
Introduction by
BRAD MELTZER

GREEN LANTERN: NO FEAR

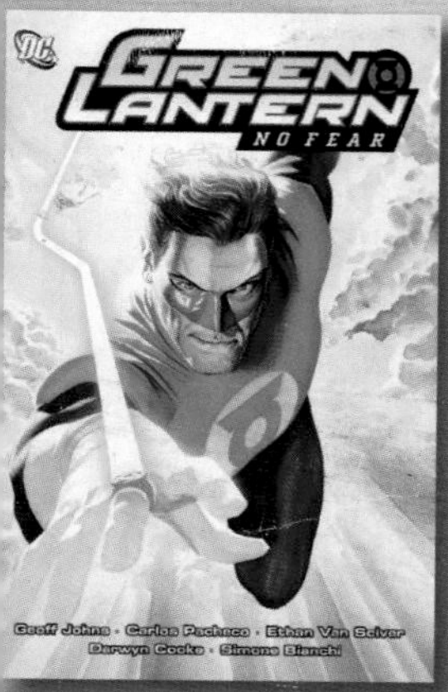
GREEN LANTERN
NO FEAR

with
CARLOS PACHECO & OTHERS

GREEN LANTERN: REVENGE OF THE GREEN LANTERNS

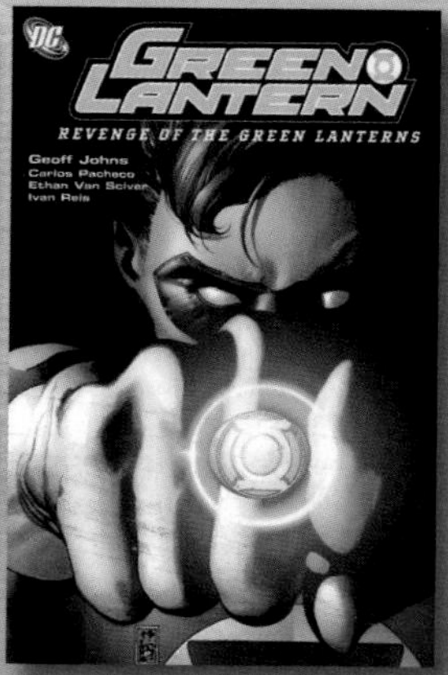
GREEN LANTERN
REVENGE OF THE GREEN LANTERNS
Geoff Johns
Carlos Pacheco
Ethan Van Sciver
Ivan Reis

with
CARLOS PACHECO
ETHAN VAN SCIVER
IVAN REIS

GREEN LANTERN: WANTED – HAL JORDAN

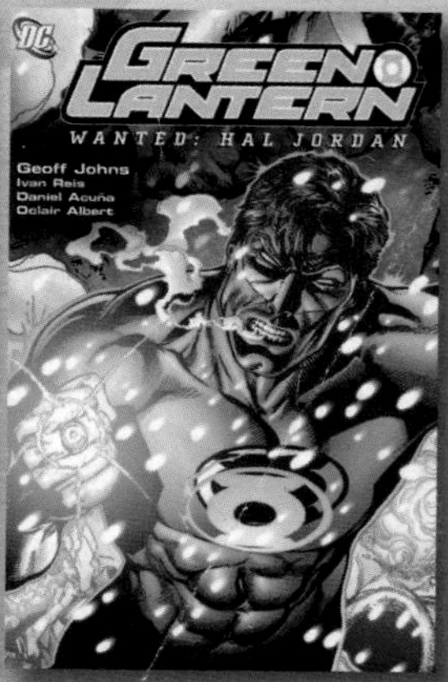
GREEN LANTERN
WANTED: HAL JORDAN
Geoff Johns
Ivan Reis
Daniel Acuña
Oclair Albert

with
IVAN REIS & OTHERS

GREEN LANTERN: THE SINESTRO CORPS WAR VOL. 1

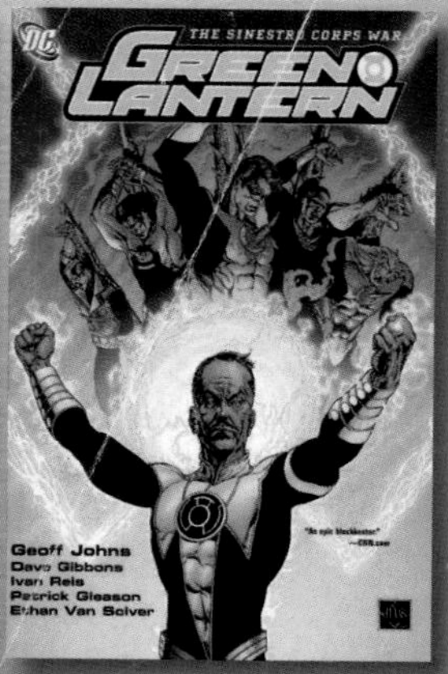
THE SINESTRO CORPS WAR
GREEN LANTERN
Geoff Johns
Dave Gibbons
Ivan Reis
Patrick Gleason
Ethan Van Sciver

with
IVAN REIS
ETHAN VAN SCIVER
& OTHERS

SEARCH THE GRAPHIC NOVELS SECTION OF
DCCOMICS.COM
FOR ART AND INFORMATION ON ALL OF OUR BOOKS!